The
Public Work
of Rhetoric

D1622195

Studies in Rhetoric/Communication
Thomas W. Benson, Series Editor

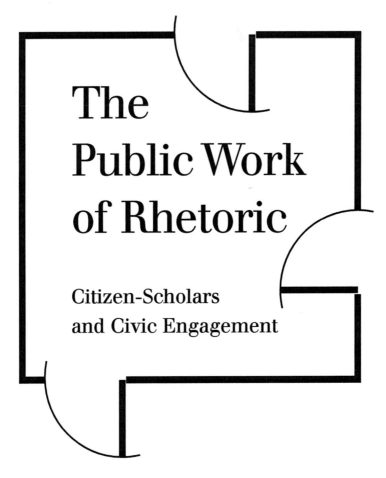

The
Public Work
of Rhetoric

Citizen-Scholars
and Civic Engagement

EDITED BY **John M. Ackerman and David J. Coogan**

FOREWORD BY Gerard A. Hauser

The University of South Carolina Press

Cloth edition published by the University of South Carolina Press, 2010
Paperback edition published by the University of South Carolina Press, 2013
Ebook edition published in Columbia, South Carolina, by the University of
South Carolina Press, 2013

www.sc.edu/uscpress

Manufactured in the United States of America

21 20 19 18 17 16 15 14 13
10 9 8 7 6 5 4 3 2 1

The Library of Congress has cataloged the cloth edition as follows:
The public work of rhetoric : citizen-scholars and civic engagement /
edited by John M. Ackerman and David J. Coogan.
      p. cm. — (Studies in rhetoric/communication)
   Includes bibliographical references and index.
   ISBN 978-1-57003-931-7 (cloth : alk. paper)
   1. Rhetoric—Political aspects. 2. Language and languages—Political
aspects. 3. Political oratory. I. Ackerman, John, 1934– II. Coogan,
David.
   P301.5.P67P83 2010
   320.01'4—dc22

                          2010014494

ISBN: 978-1-61117-303-1 (pbk)
ISBN: 978-1-61117-304-8 (ebook)

Contents

Illustrations

Foreword

GERARD A. HAUSER

This volume on the public work of rhetoric addresses a topic that transcends disciplinary interests. Its essays address the question of how we may bring the study of rhetoric into relationship with the lived practices of our students and ourselves as community members. Through lively and intelligent discussion, it challenges the orthodoxies that stereotype rhetoric and composition offerings as service courses necessary to meet the needs of students to write clear academic arguments. Of course they do that, but these essays point to local communites as places where we as citizen-scholars also encounter and address myriad issues that make life as a citizen and neighbor both challenging and rewarding. For these authors, rhetoric's public work is the constitution of public life as we know it in a democracy.

The content of this collection is timely in light of the mounting concern and sense of urgency that occurred within the U.S. academic community during the George W. Bush administration. Concern arose from the apparent success of a politics of fear; a growing disparity of wealth that resembles that of 1929; attention to cultural issues over those that impact the economic and social well-being of most citizens; prosecution of a war against terror that seems endless and unwinnable because its enemy is a technique; a political agenda geared to protect a base grounded in religious faith; a Supreme Court that is perilously close to an unbreakable conservative majority that may be in place for a decade or more and appears committed to the Bush doctrine of the unitary executive, which invests the president with the right to wage undeclared wars, establish military tribunals, authorize extraordinary renditions, withhold evidence from the accused, conduct domestic surveillance, expand the use of presidential "signing statements" by which the president indicates how he will interpret the law he signs under his authority to interpret the law in question "in a manner consistent with his constitutional authority to supervise the unitary executive branch"; and a growing division of the nation into blue and red states reflected in extremism of elected representatives whose commitments to political orthodoxy have precluded compromises of bipartisanship in favor of ideological victory that often results in gridlock.

The ignition switch for urgency was the evident dire consequences rapidly approaching if these concerns remain untended: climate change that appears to leave less than a decade to reverse current trends in the use of fossil fuels before we pass the point of no return; a doctrine on war that discards the Powell doctrine—before the nation wages war it must have a massive force, a clear objective, and an exit strategy—and replaces it with the Petreus doctrine—political destabilization anywhere constitutes a threat to the United States that must be met with military force, which commits the United States to war anywhere all the time; political polarization bred from fear of the other, which has resulted in the loss of tolerance necessary for political dialogue and branded those who disagree as unpatriotic and thus fair game for "official" witch hunts and misbegotten violence; a financial meltdown that has resulted in losses to every citizen in some way—loss of jobs, homes, retirement; the absence of viable arenas for ordinary citizens to participate in a dialogue about their interests and influence public policy with more than their vote and of rhetorical skills to participate effectively were they available.

The academic community has responded with a call for a new politics that replaces the self-centered brand of "what's in it for me" with one more concerned about "what's best for us." At the level of theory, political scientists have addressed these matters through a growing challenge to the prevailing model of rational choice—a model borrowed from economics based on how to maximize personal gain. This challenge is best reflected in the growing literature on deliberative democracy. It is a voluminous and impressive body of work by some of the most distinguished political theorists of our age. Most of it finds its inspiration in the work of Jürgen Habermas, whose *The Structural Transformation of the Public Sphere* (trans. Fredrick Lawrence, 1962; repr. 1989) advanced a theory of communicative action as the foundation for the normative ideal of a politics based on critical rational consensus. Although most of the deliberative democracy literature takes exception with Habermas's formulation of the bourgeois public sphere as prototypical for contemporary Western democracies, it remains committed to some formulation of rational consensus as the goal of deliberation. Moreover their accounts, for the most part, have remained theoretical explorations that have paid only lip service to democracy as it is lived.

To the credit of feminist scholars, under the inspiration of Nancy Fraser, Habermas's assumptions have been challenged in both theory and praxis (see Fraser's "Rethinking the Public Sphere: A Contribution to the Critique of Actually Existing Democracy," in *Habermas and the Public Sphere*, edited by Craig Calhoun, 1992). Among its more problematic ones are: the exclusionary bias in Habermas's norm of rationality, since it assumed there was but one form; his model of the bourgeois public sphere, since it did not include marginalized voices; and his purely theoretical account of democracy in need of rehabilitation through an account in tune with how it is actually lived, which must include the subaltern spheres of those without access to official spheres of power.

To the credit of rhetoricians, they have both rethought the formulations of Habermas in terms of the realities of lived democracy, which are reflected in and constituted by its rhetoric, and executed specific critical studies that have shown how the realities of democracy have been manifest in politics as it is actually lived. Rhetoricians adhering to the disciplinary vision reflected by the Rhetoric Society of America—a vision that is inclusive of rhetoric's multiple traditions found in communication, English, rhetoric, and composition, and reflected in the work of rhetorically inclined scholars in anthropology, economics, law, mass media, the natural sciences, philosophy, political science, and sociology—have been the leading voices in developing a maturing theory of publics and public spheres as rhetorical all the way down. Rhetoricians have been in the vanguard in theorizing publics and public spheres as constructed rather than given. They have developed the idea and shown through critical studies that publics are multiple and changing, that they are found in rhetorical performances more than opinion polls, and that they include diverse voices, which makes them more than a demographic. Rhetoricians have led the way in exploring the idea that there are a plurality of public spheres, that while some are official, mostly they are constituted rhetorically; that counterpublic spheres are a rich source for studying how marginalized groups constitute arenas of discourse in which they can address issues of identity, establish action agendas, forge group solidarity, and challenge authority; and that public spheres are elastic in what and who they accommodate, that their borders have varying permeability, and their life spans are tied to contingencies of issues, publics, and adaptability to changing circumstances.

This being said, the concerns and urgency that mounted within U.S. academic circles, among others, during the first decade of the twenty-first century found expression among the general citizenry in the presidential election of 2008. Barack Obama's victory expressed a desire for change and a politics of hope based in bipartisan deliberation. The problems of self-interest and pseudo-deliberation that have drawn the attention of academicians to the character of publics and public spheres and the voice of the people in choosing a president espousing a new politics echo the long-noted but not-so-effectively addressed need of capacitating citizens to address present discontents and become effective change agents in their communities. It is a commonplace at least since Dewey in the contemporary American context, although it has been recognized in the Western tradition since the Sophists, that education is critical to the development of a well-functioning polity and that artful, skillful oratory, and later writing, is essential toward that end.

The public problems of facing citizens of democratic states require the participation and collaboration of citizens in making decisions about complex problems that often require technical knowledge. If ordinary citizens are to be included in this process, as a society we require rhetors who can negotiate and translate technical problems to intelligent but less technically trained audiences. This need has received little attention. Public speaking is often absent from secondary school curricula in the United States, and not always required at the collegiate level. Required rhetoric courses in public speaking and writing are often the only exposure most students receive to those skills necessary for them to function as effective change agents. In these required courses, as well as in courses that emphasize writing within the discipline, the main attention usually is on the demands of academic writing over the needs of our communities, which need future civic leaders who are both informed and capable.

The essays in this collection report lively, inventive, intelligent, and engaged responses to the Republic's need for capacitated citizens. They offer impressive studies of how we enter into public problems in our communities, how rhetoric has constituted counterpublics among the underclass, how rhetoric's performative power can serve liberatory ends, how the community can be an invaluable resource for the civic education of our students. It is the place where democracy comes alive in the rhetorical practices of the students and those outside the university whom they engage. The work reported in this volume is noble and important not only for rhetoric studies, not only for rhetoric and composition pedagogy, but as a vision of what higher education might aspire to that goes beyond preparing students to earn a living. They are models of how we might prepare them to make a difference.

Series Editor's Preface

THOMAS W. BENSON

In *The Public Work of Rhetoric: Citizen-Scholars and Civic Engagement*, editors John M. Ackerman and David J. Coogan bring together rhetorical scholars from the fields of English and communication to explore how academic rhetoricians have extended their work into the public realm beyond the university and how they have reshaped their classrooms to bring a sense of public life into the school. The authors offer searching theoretical considerations of what is at stake in the study and practice of rhetoric in public life. These accounts are strongly couched in a discourse of responsibility and enthusiasm for progressive change, and yet they are severely reflective and self-critical—the writers do not let themselves surrender to mere wishful thinking. The currently fashionable term "civic engagement" is itself subjected to a searching rhetorical criticism.

For some of these authors, stepping into the material world outside the university is prompted by high idealism and a search for freedom, inclusion, and equality. Some of the other authors find their rhetorical ideals usefully chastened by the intractability of the public world, in which interests, ideas, and ambitions compete for dominance.

The Public Work of Rhetoric is rich with theoretical and historical considerations of academic rhetoric and the rhetoric of the public realm, and it provides a series of reflexive case studies of rhetorical scholars doing public work in a variety of locations, including the street, the technical and professional world, and the Internet.

Acknowledgments

This book began in conversation at the Alliance for Rhetoric Societies meeting at Northwestern University in 2003, where the authors first met and the idea of a collaborative book on rhetorical engagement as public work took flight. Our subsequent collaboration over the years has extended and deepened that conversation, allowing each of us ample opportunity to talk and listen, to lead and support, to work side by side as equals shouldering the load of building a book with so many moving parts. This book has two authors of equal standing as editors, contributors, and colleagues.

David wishes to thank the Department of English and the College of Humanities and Sciences at Virginia Commonwealth University for funding travel to meetings of the Rhetoric Society of America and the Conference on College Composition and Communication. This was where this manuscript took shape—in panel presentations that grew into essays; in face-to-face meetings about those essays. He would especially like to thank Susan Jarratt for several critical readings of his essay.

John thanks Marlia Banning for her guidance and support throughout this project and for introducing the editors to Candice Rai. He thanks the Department of Communication at the University of Colorado at Boulder for a "Reaping and Sowing" grant. This generous subvention afforded the authors the editorial and critical skills of Katie Cruger, doctoral student par excellence. The department also provided an intranet site to post our drafts. John's writing and editing were inspired by numerous colleagues, most notably Larry Frey and Jerry Hauser, both of whom provided guidance in developing and editing this collection.

John also thanks the Program for Writing and Rhetoric and the Calderwood Family Foundation account for sponsoring David's trip to Boulder and John's trip to Richmond, Virginia, and Linda Nicita for expertly making the arrangements for these visits. The Kent State University (KSU) Research Council provided initial funding for travel and research in fall, 2003. He thanks the city of Kent, Ohio; David Ruller, the Kent city manager; the May 4 Democracy Symposium; and the KSU May 4 Collection for assistance with the research supporting his essay.

Both authors want to thank the series editor for the University of South Carolina Press's Studies in Rhetoric/Communication, Thomas Benson; our acquisitions editor, Jim Denton; and the review board—all for having faith in this book.

Foremost we wish to thank our contributors who have weathered the many cycles of this project. We hope that our readers come to know these people as we do—as friends, as collaborators, as sponsors, as scholars, and as public advocates. And, finally, no book of ours on publics and rhetoric would exist without our many friends and associates in public life who taught us the meaning of *paideia*.

Introduction

The Space to Work in Public Life

DAVID J. COOGAN AND JOHN M. ACKERMAN

This collection illustrates how rhetoric is in the midst of discovering anew its usefulness. We live and work in times of economic confusion and injustice, of geopolitical strife and war, and of global environmental endangerment. We live and work, also, in times of renewed hope with emerging commitments in many quarters to democratic inclusion and to community engagement toward economic renewal. Our new president has asked all citizens to find ways to serve and thus to integrate our academic labor and our occasions for service into the fabric of our universities and communities, which themselves are caught up in moments of innovation and reflection that respond to shifts in regional economics and global uncertainty.[1] The discourse of service and civic engagement is on the rise at our colleges and universities as policies and practices that identify service learning, the scholarship of engagement, community outreach, public consultancy, and public intellectualism as the work before us to do. Yet these locutions as material locations are relatively nascent in our own talk about our home discipline and its place in the world. The premise upon which this book rests is that these locations and practices are vital to rhetoric's ongoing efforts to renew itself and to demonstrate our relevance locally and for a changing world.

As the contributors to this volume illustrate, to study and practice rhetoric "out there" is to embody the role of the rhetor by tapping into new streams of disciplinary life through an embodied practice that is guided by a critical reflexivity and community affiliation. To do rhetoric "out there" requires a shedding of academic adornments, a different professional disposition, new participatory and analytic tools, and a more grounded conception of public need. *The Public Work of Rhetoric*, we argue, is not shaped in our treatises and classrooms alone but in the material and discursive histories of communities outside of academe. These communities can benefit from the increased attention of rhetoricians in pursuit of democratic ideals, but rhetoric can also benefit from community partnerships premised on a negotiated search for the common good—from a collective labor to shape the future through rhetoric in ways that are mutually empowering and socially responsible.

Clearly there is work to be done both in rhetoric as it manifests in communication and in English if we are to rehabilitate the discipline for this civic role. Though "the public" remains a generative launching pad for scholarly studies in communication, for the general public *doing rhetoric* is akin to menacing our fellow citizens with lies and misdirection. In English, where rhetoric and composition are often paired, the public is often imagined as a landing pad for students, a literate place, where they can test what we have taught them with imaginary audiences. What this suggests to us is that our disciplinary achievements have not been earned through everyday contact with publics, but through a hard-earned insularity from them. We have grown strong in academe by becoming answerable to ourselves and to our institutions by putting publics, with their misunderstandings about manipulation and illiteracy, in their place. A closer look at our shared history with publics— those moments that arguably precede a turn toward community engagement —suggests that we have been haunted by the prospect of uselessness. In 1978 Michael Leff described it as a nagging irony of "pure abstraction" in a literature that "keeps insisting that rhetoric is a practical discipline."[2] And in 1997 Dilip Gaonkar noted, in a withering and wicked assessment, that "we place (somewhat frantically these days) things under the sign of rhetoric more to make rhetoric intelligible than the things subsumed under it."[3] Susan Miller questioned if an art form oriented to the great man *speaking* on a great subject was even a suitable tradition to understand technologies of writing and the emergent subjectivity of the student writer.[4] These concerns with too much abstraction, with a globalized Big Rhetoric, or with the seemingly irreconcilable differences between speech and writing, rhetoric and literacy—these are just a few of the twists and turns in our collective story of disciplinary achievement and anxiety, as many have said before us.

The historical trajectory of these differences is well documented, and we do not mean to minimize differences in theoretical orientation, disciplinary history, or pedagogical priorities. Participatory democracy, however, tends not to care. While it remains true that most people, most of the time, in communities near and far, only know rhetoric through its most derogatory inflections, the enactment of rhetoric in public life is nondenominational; all is forgiven when we seek answers to their questions before ours, whenever and wherever scholars of rhetoric "dirty their hands in actual controversy," as Wayne Booth proposed nearly forty years ago.[5]

We offer this introduction as salutation to our readers and as thanks to our contributors. We were inspired by their labors, and in kind we offer a disciplinary context in which this volume can be read. We begin by returning to rhetoric's pursuit of epistemic relevance but turn less inward toward academic expertise and more outward to the *phronesis* of the street, as a physical and figurative placeholder for publicity. The public work of rhetoric, as we imagine and then conduct it in everyday life, brings us closer to the material results of globalization and to opportunities for social change.

RHETORIC'S EPISTEMIC CRISIS

The signals and the steering corrections leading up to this moment can be read in our collective disciplinary history since the 1960s. What we find is a desire to make rhetoric answerable to something beyond itself. Naturally, that desire has manifested differently because composition claims student rhetors as its subject, while communication claims rhetors in a variety of publics. Still, we see more common ground than perhaps has been imagined in the way both fields have struggled to adjust the millennial tradition of rhetoric.

One of the overriding themes at the Wingspread Conference in 1970 was whether and how, under the aegis of a "new rhetoric," that scholarship would become more politically relevant. "At this moment in history, we are compelled to view with great foreboding the character of public communication regarding social and political issues."[6] These words from Douglass Ehninger introduced the committee report on the scope and place of rhetorical study in higher education, and they were consonant with a disciplinary "anxiety" expressed at the conference and through its proceedings. In Edwin Black's retrospective, this was a response to the threat of disciplinary dissolution: the politics of the street in 1970 had reached such a fevered pitch that the discipline was forced to face its complicity in national events—society was falling apart: students were dying on campuses, the Vietnam War was ever raging, cities were burning, communication was failing right and left, and rhetoric had to enlist.

Yet to enlist in public life, to enter into the fray of political unrest and public controversy, comes with a cost, as voiced by Black, who feared the "abrogation of the conventional distinction between the personal, internal life of the individual and the public and political life of that individual." If taken to its logical extreme of "homogeneous consciousness," the discipline would "cease to exist."[7] Then and now, the measure of rhetoric's responsibility to and involvement in public and political life has always been a question of distance. How close do we get to political discourse when it is consumed with violence? How close do we get when solutions to social injustice transcend the limits of scholarly discourse and criticism? How close do we get when the interlocutor is our neighbor, and that neighbor is in trouble?

Not all saw the political and technological changes of the 1960s and 1970s as a challenge to create—or resuscitate—what Lloyd Bitzer, in 1978, described as the "wisdom characterizing a universal public," but there was grave concern in communication for civility, peace, understanding, and reason; for making rhetoric relevant to a generation that appeared to the field to be uncoupling itself from society's center.[8] Communication thus broadened its unit of analysis beyond "the speech"—beyond persuasion and the exalted status of famous orators—and headed into the wilds of political division, media proliferation, and social movements, all the while swimming upstream against the swelling behavioral science of communication studies.

The departure point in 1970 was the assertion that neo-Aristotlean methods, as laid out by Wilchens, valorized persuasion and made exemplary the political speech within the historical context of the state. The scholars at Wingspread endeavored to make sense of that tradition in relation to the cultural and political upheavals of the era. Wallace argued that rhetoricians needed a new set of rules to prepare rhetors in such an environment and a reaffirmation of the liberal arts, which alone could create the copiousness and *phronesis* that young rhetors needed. Samuel Becker sought a much larger definition of the message, a de-centering of attention on the speech, and an interest in rhetorical functions beyond persuasion (ego-defense, knowledge making, values expression).[9]

Both Wallace and Becker struggled to adjust the tradition—and themselves within it. There was in Becker's piece that "pressure cooker" of messages that he sought some sort of purchase on, personified in the figure of "this man" with "his wife telling him to mow the lawn" and "his children . . . pushing him to play" and the media telling him to "use deodorants and to wear a seat belt."[10] Becker then recounts his experience at the Central States Communication Conference in Chicago two days after Martin Luther King Jr. had been shot, where it is not the blur of messages about the subsequent rioting that stands out, but the context in which Becker receives those messages as a scholar on lock-down, wondering "whether it was safe to go out of the hotel for dinner."[11] The disciplinary dilemma framed at Wingspread, of course, is not limited by what Dilip Gaonkar later described in reference to the first passage as Becker's "sympathy for the besieged patriarchy in the fragmented space of late capitalism."[12] What made Becker uneasy—what makes all of us uneasy—were publics that could not be contained by (or easily explained by) the rhetorical tradition, either in substance, style, or medium.

Rhetoricians in composition saw the challenge of the 1960s and 1970s differently: to broaden beyond the old rhetorical treatises with their limited appeal to correctness and form, their authoritative sense of what collects us as a public. Against current-traditional rhetoric and its conduit theories of communication, rhetoricians in English rallied around the neglected canon of invention.[13] Linda Flower and John Hayes's early research into the cognitive process of composing took Lloyd Bitzer's theory of exigency as a point of departure. Writers, like the speakers in Bitzer's work, are seen here responding with discourse to a need in the world. Flower and Hayes employed a tool from psychology—protocol analysis of writers composing-aloud—to theorize the formation of goals, the construction of a rhetorical situation, and the translation to text: "making thought visible."[14] The public tended to function in *writerly* terms here, even when the civic was invoked. Andrea Lunsford and Lisa Ede's influential article, "Audience Addressed, Audience Invoked," constituted student writers in relation to audiences beyond the classroom, at one point, through the effort of one student writer, struggling to conjure like-minded citizens who would not protest the building of a mental health facility in her community.[15] But the primary concern in Flower and Hayes's and Lunsford and Ede's work was not with the formation of publics deliberating about particular social issues but with students learning the heuristic of audience.

What is remarkable is not that English and communication would respond differently in a time of crisis, but that they would soon exhaust themselves in their respective efforts to adjust the rhetorical tradition. The individualism that emerged from the process revolution in English can be read as a turn *away* from the public that scholars in rhetoric and communication wanted to reconceive. But both efforts to generalize "the" public and "the" student writer—the twin forces of common good and agency—did not survive increased scrutiny.

In composition, this second crisis came in the form of questions, which in turn raised the problem of boundaries: Can an education in rhetoric during the first year of college enable rhetorical performance in disciplinary and professional work? If so, how? Kenneth Bruffee elaborated this as a social process of composing; of entering into the "conversation of mankind," which he based on his readings of Richard Rorty and Thomas Kuhn, among others.[16] If thought is internalized language, then writing is internalized language reexternalized. This later move globalized rhetoric, inserting it into the disciplinary, workplace, and professional settings where genres, vocabularies, modes of reasoning, values, and knowledge differed, but where writers' needs and skills could be studied and taught. Though the epistemic turn did not take up publics per se, it arguably reconceived the writer's relation to them through the acquisition of professional status; that public role, say, of an architect. Within the orbit of the social constructivist turn, knowledge claims were contestable, but in Kuhnian fashion, always ameliorating, accelerating toward or within a paradigm. The student's burden was to decode that process.

In communication, the anxiety over the public translated, however indirectly, into the rhetoric of inquiry, the rhetoric of the human sciences—into the "epistemic turn." Instead of descending farther into the embodied realms of the political, it moved swiftly toward questions of epistemological relevance. The latter has coalesced around the writings of Dilip Gaonkar, who begins his oft-quoted and debated article, "Rhetoric and Its Double," with the essay's summation, "rhetoric cannot escape itself."[17] It cannot, as Alan Gross and William Keith restate, because once rhetoric enters through the doorway of literary "supplementation," it has left behind the limits of Aristotelian proof for the uncharted waters of textual "globalization" through rhetoric's "extension to every instance, text, artifact, or communication."[18] Rhetoricity ad infinitum will not completely erase rhetoric from discourse and communication—it joins the class of logocentric, theoretical tropes that include limitless signification, interconnectivity in the heteroglot, and "literariness."[19] In doing so, rhetoric does not cease to exist, but it becomes awfully "thin" because rhetoric must percolate (within its resources) through every discursive utterance and act.

The internment of rhetoric within its own "mereness" is, for Gaonkar, a philosophically necessary and timely corrective to contemporary rhetorical theory and criticism that espouses a rhetorical turn in all disciplines, beginning first with science; and as science goes, the rest will follow. The globalization of rhetoric should result in a form of disciplinary composure and confidence, but, for Gaonkar, rhetoric is condemned to a form of epistemological purgatory because the anxiety that breathes life into rhetorical consciousness is born out of someone else "The emergence of a rhetorical consciousness is directly related to a crisis within a special discourse. . . . The sheer possibility of a rhetorical consciousness, the possibility that rhetoric is a permanent though unrealized opening for man, does not by itself induce a crisis, but it is something always waiting to be exploited when the crisis comes. In short, rhetoric is the medium and not the ground of discursive and cultural crises."[20] For different reasons and from different vantage points, communication and composition took an epistemic turn, inserting rhetoric into the knowledge-making process, raising ethical questions about treating knowledge claims rhetorically.

But with great power comes great responsibility: If rhetoric is the medium and not the grounds of crisis, toward whose ends would rhetoric work? What responsibilities did critics and teachers take on when taking up this tool? As James Berlin argued, rhetoric is not a neutral techne but "a part of social and political structures" that articulate "the nature of the individual within those structures, and the distribution of power in society."[21] Rhetoric, in this context, does not simply help a student arrange an argument but appropriate a place within a contested, discursive framework. That such engagement was itself framed by classrooms and assignments—by the authority of teachers of rhetoric—did not escape Berlin and other proponents of critical pedagogy. Much the same dilemma emerged in communication among proponents of critical rhetoric. John Sloop, for example, argued that "it must be my task, and the task of critics in general, to increase the impact of criticism by finding outlets that increase its prominence as a cultural fragment."[22] But this link between our work as rhetoricians and social change remains vexed, writes J. Elspeth Stuckey, because "schools, like other social institutions, are designed to replicate, or at least not disturb, social division and class privilege," including those privileges that we enjoy (123). Criticism and change remains vexed, as vexed as it is in critical pedagogy. Our universities, J. Elspeth Stuckey explains, are "designed to replicate, or at least not disturb, social division and class privilege," including those privileges that we enjoy as critics and teachers.[23] If we have, in our ethnographic studies of literacy and our rhetorical criticism of publics, tended to propose linguistic solutions to social divisions that are more properly material or economic in nature, it is because we have, in English and communication, tended to see disciplinary prerogatives more easily than others.

One guiding principle that we have shared in compiling *The Public Work of Rhetoric* is that rhetoric should not deny itself: it will never dissolve into itself by entering into the fractious world of political action or by implicating itself in the discourse of others. Our motivations to act are not premised on a particular agenda, a set of social issues, or the settler's itch to unfurl our flag. We are motivated by the embodied practices that we have cultivated in relationship with people in our communities; by a rhetorical labor that we share with others, where the grain size of the discursive act relies upon the authority of individuals in "relevant social groups";[24] acts that are conferred by the cultural economies of actual places. For our purposes, there *is* anxiety in the world, but it is born from much more than discursive and cultural crises. It resides in the communities we frequent and have compassion toward, and therefore cannot be adequately inferred from textual artifacts alone. To discover the coordinates of anxiety in its locally and globally material manifestations, rhetoric will have to reflexively imagine itself outside of fixations on the discursive supplement within the logos-sphere. By doing so, by "going public," rhetoric need not limit its disciplinary identity and social relevance to the degree to which it contributes to science as ur-discipline; nor will rhetoric endanger itself by entering into the political life of the street, not when the streets belong to us, and not when we are the people yelling outside the window. As Carolyn Miller writes in her essay in this collection, "We have said that rhetoric is 'epistemic,' that it affects the conduct of inquiry and the substance of knowledge across the disciplines. . . . Rhetoric's imperialism has reached such a pitch recently that critical alarms have been sounded, urging 'attenuations' of its epistemic claims and challenging its ambitions as a 'universalized,' 'promiscuous,' 'free-floating' 'interpretive meta-discourse.'" Those attenuations include Gaonkar's critique of the rhetorical turn in the human sciences, but they must now include a different calibration of the rhetorical event. Disciplinary reflexivity does not have to result in an infinite epistemological regress when rhetoric accepts its supplementary role within the discursive regime but founds its claims on civic engagement in what Gerard Hauser describes as the "reticulate public sphere."[25] Loïc Wacquant's exegesis of Pierre Bourdieu's theories of reflexive sociology concludes with a similar, recuperative (we would say rhetorical) point of view: "[Reflexivity] is neither egocentric, nor logocentric. . . . It fastens not upon the private person . . . but on the concatenations of acts and operations she effectuates as part of her work and on the collective unconscious inscribed in them. . . . Epistemic reflexivity . . . informs a conception of the craft of research to strengthen its epistemological moorings."[26]

Rhetoric may provide the moment, the acuity, and the discursive terrain for translations of discourses criss-crossing the university and public life, as proposed by Steve Mailloux,[27] but when we hear the call to participate, we are hearing those "concatenations" comprised of participants, events, artifacts, and territories that over time and through practice aggregate (and then disaggregate) as meaningful concordances. If rhetoric occurs routinely in public life, as *work*, it is through routines that establish, in their aggregate, something like a postmodern *paidiea*. We are not all building the same things for the same reasons with the same tools in the same public. And yet we believe this shift toward a common labor with others outside of academe is, in fact, a major shift for rhetoricians who have long claimed to speak for "the public." True, rhetoricians have already worked as policy analysts, critical ethnographers, public teachers, rogue historians, advocates, and community organizers. But rhetoric has not, by and large, positioned these avocations as vocations for disciplinary renewal in English and in communication. As the story goes, throughout the twentieth century rhetoric has been "plagued by feelings of academic and intellectual inferiority and an almost perpetual identity crisis."[28] This collection presents an alternative narrative, a rhetoric of the "lost geographies" of public life that hold within them the political and ethical dimensions of real events and social relations that make our disciplinary identity newly possible.[29]

CITIZEN-SCHOLARS AND COMMUNITY ENGAGEMENT

The "street" that the Wingspread and Pheasant Run conference participants invoked was a geographical marker for the political discourse rattling the windows of the university in 1970 and a figuration of what "shouts, obscenities, sit-ins, and interruptions of lectures" portend for utility of political discourse in society as a whole.[30] As topoi, these material sites were outside of rhetoric, but nonetheless painfully real: public protest had gotten very personal, and it violated the sanctity and common areas of the university, replicating protest in the public streets of major cities.[31] The *street* as a figurative device, from Breton and Baudelaire to more recent scholarship, configures much more than an angry display of political unrest. The street materializes as it represents the prospects of a radically inclusive democracy of human experience. For Henri Lefebvre, it was the location of the "inexorable rhythm" of everyday life[32] and is its "almost total figuration."[33]

And so in Paula Mathieu's aside, "the university and other institutions do not have strategic control over the streets," she too anticipates a scene for public discourse and community engagement in everyday life that is open to the plentitude of rhetorical events and participants and without predetermination of which boundaries matter more than others and of which public actions count as civility.[34] There is no shortage of such rhetorical geographies, no limit to their number or constellation. In this book, they include

City residents facing off over gentrification (Rai)
Public commemoration and planning in the context of tragic
  events (Ackerman)
The reinvention of democracy in post–Cold War Kosova (Cintron)
Geneticists and doctors arguing the value of race in medicine (Condit)
Inner-city teens writing to resist the values of the "street" (Coogan)
High school students with learning disabilities "going public" with
  their labels (Flower)
The Cherokee Nation and the university conjuring a counternarrative
  (Cushman and Green)
Communities organizing to protect public health (Grabill)
Dissident journalists advocating for homeless persons (George
  and Mathieu)
Rural residents using literacy to reverse economic decline (Jolliffe)

The disciplinary "anxiety" of rhetoric within the academy pales in comparison to the anxieties in these scenes from public life, as well as the specific "crises" that would lead us to enter and to engage. The geography of the rhetorical event depends very little on the intellectual home for rhetorical scholarship, and the scenes tend to gather their "social energy," as Ralph Cintron calls it, partly through their close proximity to the wealth and influence of the university and other social and jurisprudential institutions or their comparative lack. Our scenes gather their energy from cultural and economic forces that have worked for decades if not centuries to trouble the bonds of wealth, health, progress, and community. These scenes exist without us; they are rhetorical without our say-so; but we join them in a "third space," a space that is open, hybrid, resistant, and marginal.[35]

Thus the rhetorical exigencies in these public scenes do not gather force solely through the affinity of like-minded audiences, working deliberatively as discourse communities. We find instead a powerful desire for public assembly that gains its legitimacy well beyond the comfortable imaginations and accoutrements of academic life. Though we enter into these scenes as citizen-scholars, and in fact we often use our academic training sometimes as a moral compass and discursive divining rod, in most of our narratives we discover a preexisting conspiracy against the common good in public life that cannot be determined through the intellectual prism of the hermeneutic interpretation. At Pheasant Run in 1970, Lloyd Bitzer proclaimed that our age was a "rhetorical age" because of the pressure of new media upon civic life and new demands on rhetoric to diminish the atrocities of war, hunger, urban decline, and environmental squander. The practical mission for rhetoric is to pursue the "great aspirations of the human community."[36] The scenes that we feature in *The Public Work of Rhetoric,* and the labor that drives our engagement, require in many cases both a return to the street, as the location and figuration of public life, and an awareness of the conspiracies against democracy that coalesce there.

Globalization is fabricating a new category of "the people" as resident and citizen, transcendent of national boundaries and identities, and we are caught up in the drama of how civic life unfolds in these times. For a rhetoric of public works, there can be no safe difference between us and them; as Arjun Appadurai points out, "where the lines between us and them have always, in human history, been blurred at the boundaries and unclear across large spaces and big numbers, globalization exacerbates these uncertainties."[37] One reason to locate rhetorical practice in local communities, and to use these communities as a theoretical frame, is because these "uncertainties" now escape no one. The reason why we present rhetorical practice as "work" in our essays is because, as Ronald Greene has argued, it is fundamentally naive to presume that "rhetorical agency exists outside the domain of capitalist command" and therefore outside the reach of globalization.[38] If the question is genuine as to how rhetoric can best respond to the great aspirations of the human community, then the effects of globalization will be one of our most profound measures of the kinds of labor required to enter into public life for the rhetorical good.

In *Global Dreams,* Richard Barnet and John Cavanagh dispose of the belief that academics as citizens are protected somehow from "a stark reality: A huge and increasing proportion of human beings are not needed and will never be needed to make goods or to provide services because too many people in the world are too poor to buy them."[39] This dire conclusion was drawn nearly fifteen years ago, and it reminds us that there are pressures upon families, communities, and institutions that accumulate faster than books can be written about them. Yet the counterpart to globalization is "the pull of localism in all its forms." As Barnet and Cavanagh continue, "place and rootedness are as important as ever," and the communities where we live and to whom we serve "cannot conceive of living anywhere else, for they are dependent on a piece of ground for their livelihood and on a particular culture and language for their sense of well being."[40]

Thus *The Public Work of Rhetoric* must reject the idea that public life is dead, that it has been stripped of agitation, assembly, and deliberation, and that it is devoid of political discourse beyond shouts of anger. The polis is not "missing" as Andrew King declares, so much as rhetoric, in the intellectual practices it has acquired, reveals a learned hesitation to engage.[41] For King, civic discourse cannot now exist because the city and the nation are in disarray, and he is half right. Numerous authorities on urban life, offering histories of urban sprawl and studies of urban networks, make the same observation—without our extrapolation into public discourse.[42] They offer us a history of the materiality of urban life culminating in newly global distributions of transportation, housing, information, energy, and jurisprudential power. Our neighborhoods are becoming autopoietic, making rhetorical practice all the more relevant in comprehending how this moment came to pass and how the resident best responds.

As Kathryn Hales points out, the circuitry of daily living in a global community may evolve in ways that appear to make it more self-regulating and homogeneous, and require a "a new and startling account of how we know the world." We have a choice to make as critics: we can limit our analyses to the attributes of the circumstance before us, or we can learn from those circumstances how to look at the world differently: "Seeing system and medium together over a period of time, observers draw connections between cause and effect, past and future."[43] Globalization and new distributions of wealth and human communities provide us with rhetorical scenes as civic engagement with the imperative to learn how to comprehend them. This imperative gathers momentum and "expertise" through local communities, and in ways foreign to university life as the twentieth century has known it, although our universities are not idly standing by as the drama of globalization unfolds. In sync with globalization, they are responding to decades of diminished public funding by searching for new revenue streams, some of which translates into incentives for the "scholarship of engagement" as Ackerman explores.

The logic of this translation is known to most academic citizens: civic engagement at the university complements the corporate desire to conflate civic virtue with economic entrepreneurialism; it strengthens the political base of the university and ensures that the university has a key role to play in the redefinition of the polis and city-state. We realize that this raises more than one red flag, and so we begin this book with essays that interrogate the heightened visibility of a discipline notoriously known for cloaking its own artifice (C. Miller); that challenge rhetoric to close the gap between obfuscation and the facts of injustice (Bruner); and that probe the underbelly of topoi like "justice" or "democracy" (Cintron, Rai).

The impetus for this book was the 2003 Alliance of Rhetoric Societies conference at Northwestern University that sought to recalibrate rhetoric's contributions to society by asking: What should be the institutional and social goals for academic rhetoric in the twenty-first century? And how can rhetoric best contribute to the social, political, and cultural environments that extend beyond the university? The citizen-scholars in this collection have contributed as community teachers, ethnographers, Web designers, mediators, consultants, writers, and organizers. But just as important for our sense of *disciplinary* renewal, they have also contributed by reconceiving the classroom. David Fleming does this in his defense of the "artificial" setting of the classroom, as a reflexive space set apart from public life but in no way immune to its influence. Diana George and Paula Mathieu do this by challenging classroom advice about style through a study of exemplary dissident journalists. Ellen Cushman and Erik Green show how traditional classroom routines were upended by a community partnership set up to navigate the new media. And Eric Juergensmeyer and Thomas P. Miller show how university classrooms through conflict resolution can engage the politics of international borders and city identities.

Both in our forays *out there* as rhetors—Celeste Condit resisting the rhetoric of race-based genetics at a forum filled with scientists—and in our classroom forays into the politics of common sense—M. Lane Bruner resisting essentialist identity politics and their role in globalization—we cannot escape what Thomas Farrell calls the "acute discomfort all around the room."[44] We will never achieve the outer limits of our desire in rhetoric. Farrell defines this middling, reflexive space as the "reciprocal middle," as "mediation," as "agonistic," and as proudly and publicly "deliberative." We see it as a stage for what John Lucaites and Celeste Condit call rhetoric's "strategic liberation": "the possibility of improving life within one's community in temporary and incomplete, but nonetheless meaningful, ways."[45] This is the true grit and tumble of public life. This is where we find the space to work.

NOTES

1. Obama, "Call to Service." See also Obama, "New Era of Service," 33.
2. Leff, "In Search," 60.
3. Gaonkar, "Idea of Rhetoric," 34.
4. Miller, *Rescuing the Subject*.
5. Booth, "Scope," 114.
6. Ehninger, "Report of the Committee," 209.
7. Black, "Prospect," 24.
8. Bitzer, "Rhetoric," 91.
9. Wicheins, "The Literary criticism of Oratory," 3–28. Wallace, "The Fundamentals of Rhetoric," 3–20. Becker, "Rhetorical Studies," 23.
10. Ibid., 26.
11. Ibid., 32.
12. Gaonkar, "Idea of Rhetoric," 300.
13. See Young, Becker, and Pike, *Rhetoric*; LeFevre, *Invention*; Lauer, *Invention*.
14. Flower and Hayes, "Cognitive Process."
15. Lunsford and Ede, "Audience Addressed."
16. Bruffee, "Collaborative Learning."
17. Gaonkar, "Rhetoric and Its Double," 194.
18. Gross and Miller, Introduction, 7.
19. Culler, *On Deconstruction*.
20. Gaonkar, "Rhetoric and Its Double," 110.
21. Berlin, *Rhetoric and Reality*, 4.
22. Sloop, *Cultural Prison*, 193.
23. Stuckey, *Violence of Literacy*.
24. Bjiker, *Of Bicycles*, 45+.

25. Hauser, *Vernacular Voices*, 57+.

26. Wacquant, "Structure," 46.

27. Mailloux, "Places in Time."

28. Lucaites, "McGee Unplugged," 8.

29. Smith and Low, Introduction.

30. Baskerville, "Responses," 152.

31. Johnstone, "Some Trends," 80. Samuel Becker in the same volume refers to the Democratic National Convention riots of 1968 and to when he heard of the assassination of Martin Luther King Jr. from a cab driver in Chicago. For Barnet Baskerville in his "Responses, Queries, and a Few Caveats" (151–65), the "streets echo the angry voices of those who would usher in a new order by destroying the old" and thus as an assault on reason. It was noted in *Prospects* that Phillip Tompkins from Kent State University could not participate; the Pheasant Run conference occurred six days after the Kent State shooting on May 4, 1970.

32. Lefebvre, "Seen from the Window," 221.

33. Sheringham, *Everyday Life*, 375. Sheringham quotes from Lefebvre, *Critique*, 309.

34. Mathieu, *Tactics*, xiv.

35. See Soja, *Thirdspace*, 14.

36. Bitzer, "More Reflections," 201–2.

37. Appadurai, *Fear of Small Numbers*, 7.

38. Greene, "Orator Communist," 86.

39. Barnet and Cavanagh, *Global Dreams*, 17.

40. Ibid., 21.

41. King, "Rhetorical Critic," 311.

42. See Hayden, *Building Suburbia;* Graham and Marvin, *Splintering Urbanism.*

43. Hales, *How We Became*, 136–37.

44. Farrell, "Elliptical Postscript," 57.

45. Lucaites and Condit, "Epilogue," 610–11.

Works Cited

Appadurai, Arjun. *Fear of Small Numbers: An Essay on the Geography of Anger.* Durham, N.C.: Duke University Press, 2006.

Barnet, Richard J., and John Cavanagh. *Global Dreams: Imperial Corporations and the New World Order.* New York: Simon and Schuster, 1994.

Baskerville, Barnet. "Responses, Queries, and a Few Caveats." In *The Prospect of Rhetoric: Report of the National Development Project,* edited by Lloyd F. Bitzer and Edwin Black, 151–65. Englewood Cliffs, N.J.: Prentice Hall, 1971.

Becker, Samuel. "Rhetorical Studies for the Contemporary World." In *The Prospect of Rhetoric: Report of the National Development Project,* edited by Lloyd F. Bitzer and Edwin Black, 21–43. Englewood Cliffs, N.J.: Prentice Hall, 1971.

Berlin, James. *Rhetoric and Reality: Writing Instruction in American Colleges, 1900–1985.* Carbondale: Southern Illinois University Press, 1987.

Bitzer, Lloyd. "More Reflections on the Wingspread Conference." In *The Prospect of Rhetoric: Report of the National Development Project,* edited by Lloyd F. Bitzer and Edwin Black, 200–207. Englewood Cliffs, N.J.: Prentice Hall, 1971.

———. "Rhetoric and Public Knowledge." In *Rhetoric, Philosophy and Literature,* edited by Don Burks, 67–93. West Lafayette, Ind.: Purdue University Press, 1978.

Bjiker, Weibe. *Of Bicycles, Bakelites, and Bulbs: Toward a Theory of Sociotechnical Change.* Cambridge, Mass.: MIT Press, 1997.

Black, Edwin. "The Prospect of Rhetoric: Twenty-five Years Later." In *Making and Unmaking the Prospects of Rhetoric*, edited by Theresa Enos and Richard McNabb, 21–128. Mahway, N.J.: Erlbaum Press, 1997.

Blair, Carole. "'We Are All Prisoners Here of Our Own Device': Rhetoric in Speech Communication after Wingspread." In *Making and Unmaking the Prospects for Rhetoric*, edited by Theresa Enos and Richard McNabb, 29–36. Mahway, N.J.: Erlbaum Press, 1997.

Booth, Wayne. "The Scope of Rhetoric Today." In *The Prospect of Rhetoric: Report of the National Development Project*, edited by Lloyd F. Bitzer and Edwin Black, 93–114. Englewood Cliffs, N.J.: Prentice Hall, 1971.

Brint, Steven. "The Rise of the Practical Arts." In *The Future of the City of Intellect: The Changing American University*, edited by Steven Brint, 231–59. Stanford, Calif.: Stanford University Press, 2002.

Bruffee, Ken. "Collaborative Learning and the Conversation of Mankind." In *Cross-talk in Comp Theory: A Reader*, edited by Victor Villanueva, 415–34. Urbana, Ill.: National Council of Teachers of English, 2003.

Culler, Jonathon. *On Deconstruction: Theory and Criticism after Structuralism*. Ithaca, N.Y.: Cornell University Press, 1982.

Cushman, Ellen. "The Rhetorician as an Agent of Social Change." *College Composition and Communication* 47 (1996): 7–28.

de Certeau, Michel. "Walking in the City." In *The Practice of Everyday Life*, 91–114. Berkeley: University of California Press, 1984.

Ehninger, Douglass. "Report of the Committee on the Scope and Place of Rhetorical Studies in Higher Education." In *The Prospect of Rhetoric: Report of the National Development Project*, edited by Lloyd F. Bitzer and Edwin Black, 208–19. Englewood Cliffs, N.J.: Prentice Hall, 1971.

Farrell, Thomas. "An Elliptical Postscript." In *Rhetorical Hermeneutics: Invention and Interpretation in the Age of Science*, edited by Allan G. Gross and William M. Keith, 317–29. Albany: SUNY Press, 1997.

Flower, Linda, and John Hayes. "A Cognitive Process Theory of Writing." In *Cross-talk in Comp Theory: A Reader*, edited by Victor Villanueva, 273–98. Urbana, Ill.: National Council of Teachers of English, 2003.

Gaonkar, Dilip. "The Idea of Rhetoric in the Rhetoric of Science." In *Rhetorical Hermeneutics*, edited by Alan Gross and William Keith, 25–88. Albany: SUNY, 1997.

———. "Rhetoric and Its Double: Reflections on the Rhetorical Turn in the Human Sciences." In *Contemporary Rhetorical Theory: A Reader*, edited by John L. Lucaites, Celeste M. Condit, and Sally Caudill, 194–212. New York: Guilford Press, 1999.

Graham, Stephen, and Simon Marvin. *Splintering Urbanism: Networked Infrastructures, Technological Mobilities, and the Urban Condition*. London: Routledge, 2001.

Greene, Ronald. "Orator Communist." *Philosophy and Rhetoric* 39 (2006): 85–95.

Gross, Alan, and William Keith. Introduction. In *Rhetorical Hermeneutics: Invention and Interpretation in the Age of Science*, edited by Alan Gross and William Keith, 1–24. Albany: SUNY Press, 1997.

Hales, Kathryn. *How We Became Post Human: Virtual Bodies in Cybernetics, Literature, and Informatics*. Chicago: University of Chicago Press, 1999.

Hauser, Gerard. *Vernacular Voices: The Rhetoric of Publics and Public Spheres*. Columbia: University of South Carolina Press, 1999.

Hayden, Dolores. *Building Suburbia: Green Fields and Urban Growth, 1820–2000*. New York: Vintage Books, 2004.

Johnstone, Henry. "Some Trends in Rhetorical Theory." In *The Prospect of Rhetoric: Report of the National Development Project,* edited by Lloyd F. Bitzer and Edwin Black, 78–92. Englewood Cliffs, N.J.: Prentice Hall, 1971.

King, Andrew. "The Rhetorical Critic and the Invisible Polis." In *Rhetorical Hermeneutics: Invention and Interpretation in the Age of Science,* edited by Allan G. Gross and William M. Keith, 299–314. Albany: SUNY Press, 1997.

Lauer, Janice. *Invention in Contemporary Rhetoric: Heuristic Procedures.* Ann Arbor, Mich.: University of Michigan Press, 1967.

Lefebvre, Henri. *Critique of Everyday Life,* Vol. 1. Translated by J. Moore. 1947. Reprint, London: Verso, 1991.

———. "Seen from the Window." In *Writings of Cities,* translated and edited by Eleonore LeFevre, Karen Burke. *Invention as a Social Act.* Carbondale: Southern Illinois University Press, 1987.

Kofman and Elizabeth Lebas, 219–27. Malden, Mass.: Blackwell, 1996.

Leff, Michael. "In Search of Adriadne's Thread." In *Landmark Essays on Contemporary Rhetorical Theory,* edited by Thomas Farrell, 43–63. Mahwah, N.J.: LEA Hergamoras Press, 1998.

Lucaites, John. "McGee Unplugged." In *Rhetoric in Postmodern America: Conversations with Michael Calvin McGee,* edited by Carol Corbin, 3–26. New York: Guilford Press, 1998.

Lucaites, John, and Celeste Condit. "Epilogue: Contributions from Rhetorical Theory." In *Contemporary Rhetorical Theory: A Reader,* edited by John L. Lucaites, Celeste M. Condit, and Sally Caudill, 610–11. New York: Guilford Press, 1999.

Lunsford, Andrea, and Lisa Ede. "Audience Addressed, Audience Invoked." In *Cross-talk in Comp Theory: A Reader,* edited by Victor Villanueva, 77–96. Urbana, Ill.: National Council of Teachers of English, 2003.

Mailloux, Steven. "Places in Time: The Inns and Outhouses of Rhetoric." *Quarterly Journal of Speech* 92 (2006): 53–68.

Mathieu, Paula. *Tactics of Hope: The Public Turn in English Composition.* Portsmouth, N.H.: Boynton/Cook, 2005.

McKerrow, Raymie. "Critical Rhetoric: Theory and Practice." *Communication Monographs* 56 (1989): 441–63.

Miller, Susan. *Rescuing the Subject.* Carbondale: Southern Illinois University Press, 1989.

Obama, Barack. "Barack Obama: A Call to Serve." Time/CNN. September 11, 2008. http://www.time.com/time/magazine/article/0,9171,1840636,00.html (accessed March 23, 2009).

———. "A New Era of Service." *Time,* March 30, 2009, 33.

Pickering, Andrew. "From Science as Knowledge to Science as Practice." In *Science as Practice and Culture,* edited by Andrew Pickering, 1–28. Chicago: University of Chicago Press, 1996.

Sheringham, Michael. *Everyday Life: Theories and Practices from Surrealism to the Present.* New York: Oxford University Press, 2006.

Shor, Ira. *Critical Teaching and Everyday Life.* Chicago: University of Chicago Press, 1987.

Sloop, John. *The Cultural Prison.* Tuscaloosa: University of Alabama Press, 1996.

Smith, Neil, and Setha Low. "Introduction: The Imperative of Public Space." In *The Politics of Public Space,* edited by Setha Low and Neil Smith, 1–16. New York: Routledge, 2006.

Soja, Edward. *Thirdspace: Journeys to Los Angeles and Other Real and Imagined Places.* Malden, Mass.: Wiley-Blackwell, 1996.

Stuckey, J. Elspeth. *The Violence of Literacy*. Portsmouth, N.H.: Boynton/Cook, 1990.

Wacquant, Loïc. "The Structure and Logic of Bourdieu's Sociology." In *An Invitation to Reflexive Sociology*, edited by Pierre Bourdieu and Loïc Wacquant, 2–59. Chicago: University of Chicago Press, 1992.

Wallace, Karl. "The Fundamentals of Rhetoric." In the *Prospect of Rhetoric: Report of National Development Project*, edited by Lloyd F. Blitzer and Edwin Black, 3–20. Englewood Cliffs, N.J. Prentice Hall, 1971.

Wilchens, Herbert A. "The Literary Criticism of Oratory." In *Readings in Rehtorical Criticism*, edited by Carl R. Burgchardt, 3–28. State College, Pa.: Strata Publishing, 2000.

Young, Richard, Alton Becker, and Kenneth Pike. *Rhetoric: Discovery and Change*. New York: Harcourt Brace Jovanovich, 1970.

Zarefsky, David. "Institutional and Social Goals." *Rhetoric Society Quarterly* 34 (2004): 27–38.

[**PART 1**]

Rhetoric Revealed

Should We Name the Tools?

Concealing and Revealing
the Art of Rhetoric

CAROLYN R. MILLER

"Socrates: My accusers . . . told you that you must be careful not to let me deceive you—the implication being that I am a skillful speaker. I thought that it was peculiarly brazen of them to tell you this without a blush, since they must know that they will soon be effectively confuted, when it becomes obvious that I have not the slightest skill as a speaker—unless, of course, by a skillful speaker they mean one who speaks the truth."[1]

Throughout its troubled history, two opposing impulses have persisted within rhetoric, an impulse toward self-aggrandizement and another toward self-denial. Plato's Gorgias announces grandly that rhetoric is "the greatest boon, for it brings freedom to mankind in general and to each man dominion over others."[2] Cicero's Crassus claims that "in every free nation, and most of all in communities which have attained the enjoyment of peace and tranquillity, [eloquence] has always flourished above the rest and ever reigned supreme."[3] This one art, he says, has the ability "to raise up those that are cast down, to bestow security, to set free from peril, to maintain men in their civil rights."[4] And rhetoric is not only powerful, it is ubiquitous; it can speak on any subject: as Plato's Gorgias claims, "rhetoric includes practically all other faculties under her control."[5] Thus rhetoric vaunts itself, both in the academy and in the public sphere.

Such self-aggrandizement is not unfamiliar to contemporary minds, as rhetoric has experienced a disciplinary and intellectual renaissance, with journals and books, curricula and symposia, devoted to its power and ubiquity. We have said that rhetoric is "epistemic," that it affects the conduct of inquiry and the substance of knowledge across the disciplines. We have committed ourselves to using the powers of rhetoric to meet challenges in the public realm, challenges to social justice, democratic process, public responsibility, and civility. Kenneth Burke, in an anaphoric, epanaleptic aphorism we love to quote, told us that "wherever there is persuasion there is rhetoric.

And wherever there is 'meaning' there is 'persuasion.'"[6] Rhetoric's imperialism has reached such a pitch recently that critical alarms have been sounded, urging "attenuations" of its epistemic claims and challenging its ambitions as a "universalized," "promiscuous," "free-floating," "interpretive metadiscourse."[7]

Criticism like this helps to counter rhetoric's grand ambitions, but there is another countervailing force, and that is rhetoric's own enduring impulse toward self-denial. Here, rhetoric seeks not to "flourish" or to "reign," but to disappear, to get out of the way, possibly even to admit to being "mere rhetoric." The motto for this impulse is that the art of rhetoric lies in concealing the art: *ars est artem celare*.[8] Rhetorical treatises, beginning at least with Aristotle, point out the need for rhetorical artifice and strategy to remain hidden: "authors should compose without being noticed and should seem to speak not artificially but naturally. (The latter is persuasive, the former the opposite.)"[9] George Kennedy calls this passage "perhaps the earliest statement in criticism that the greatest art is to disguise art."[10] In *De Inventione*, Cicero noted that brilliance and vivacity of style "can give rise to a suspicion of preparation and excessive ingenuity. As a result of this most of the speech loses conviction and the speaker, authority."[11] Quintilian put the matter plainly: "if an orator does command a certain art . . . , its highest expression will be in the concealment of its existence."[12]

Rhetoric, it seems, must deny itself to succeed. Michael Cahn has called this rule "the very heart of rhetoric," right from its beginning.[13] The principle has become embedded in the tradition, a commonplace passed along and kept alive by writers who include Puttenham, La Rochefoucauld, Butler, Swift, Pope, Burke, Rousseau, and Wilde. The principle is modeled for the Renaissance in Castiglione's concept of *sprezzatura*, glossed by Richard Lanham as a "rehearsed spontaneity" and described by Castiglione himself as a capacity ensuring that "art is hidden and whatever is said and done seems without effort or forethought."[14] *Sprezzatura* is celebrated in the English Renaissance from Herrick to Sidney to Shakespeare.[15] Another Renaissance figure who serves for us as the paragon of dissimulation is Machiavelli, who advises the prince that because it is sometimes necessary to do evil, it is also necessary to dissimulate, to construct what we might now call "plausible deniability," so that "everyone sees what you appear to be, [but] few know what you really are."[16] But the principle of rhetorical concealment is more than the everyday dissimulation of intentions: it is the conviction that the means by which intentions are concealed must also remain undetectable; in other words, we must be convinced that no dissimulation is going on; it is a dissimulation of means as much as of ends. Thus, if "all a rhetorician's rules / Teach nothing but to name his tools," it is best if the tools—and their names—remain under wraps when Sir Hudibras sallies forth.

According to Cahn, rhetoric is the only art with this tradition of self-denial, the one art that "has to live with the requirement of concealing its achievement in order to attain recognition."[17] Indeed, the ancient arts that were often compared with rhetoric, such as medicine, cookery, flute-playing, navigation, and gymnastics, do not seem to have much to hide, and neither do such contemporary arts as engineering or architecture. We can use and appreciate their products or results even if we happen know a great deal about how they are produced, what materials, ingredients, processes, and techniques go into their success. But other arts are different, and these are used by Plato in a series of complex comparisons and classifications that suggest rhetoric's affinity with arts such as cosmetics, seduction, enchantment, hunting, and military strategy.[18] Here the story is different, suggesting that Cahn may not be correct about rhetoric's unique need for concealment. Cosmetics, for example, part of Socrates' elaborate comparison of the sham arts and the true arts in the *Gorgias,* would seem to require concealment.[19] Like theatrical illusion, the effect of the cosmetic art dissipates the more we know about its part in the creation of beauty. We admire the skill involved in exercising the art rather than the appearance of the wearer, the art itself rather than its results.

If dissimulation and concealment are indeed necessary for rhetorical success, we face a number of problems as we contemplate both the public work of rhetoric and the educational role of rhetoric. If rhetoric can be more effective, more useful, more powerful, if it remains concealed, what can it mean for rhetoric to go public? What can its "public work" be? Is there a self-defeating premise built into the educational project? Or an entailment of ever more widespread cynicism? If, through the sustained rhetorical education and public acceptance we seek, rhetoric is indeed revealed as a Gorgianic power available to everyone, will public discourse or our social conditions actually improve? The dilemma that intrigues me is epitomized in a *New Yorker* cartoon, where the public work of rhetoric is unconcealed by naming the tools.

In this essay, I spend some time exploring the principle of concealment in more detail, drawing primarily on the multiple ways that it is expressed in the classical tradition, because the ancients were astute observers of the workings of rhetorical power, particularly in the public realm. I examine these sources for what they can reveal about the justifications for and consequences of concealment. The sources give some clues to the conditions in which rhetoric must work and thus the possibilities for its public role. And I close with some observations about what these conditions mean for the relationship between rhetoric's public work and rhetoric's role in the education of citizens for that work.

The classical sources are suffused with observations and advice about the necessity for concealment.[20] They reveal a series of recurring themes that justify the need to conceal the art of rhetoric. These themes seem to derive from two foundational assumptions that are fully naturalized in our understandings

"That's an excellent prescreened question, but before I give you my stock answer I'd like to try to disarm everyone with a carefully rehearsed joke."

of how humans use language: an adversarial model of human relations and a mimetic model of language.

HUMAN RELATIONS ARE ADVERSARIAL

1. The dominant and most frequent theme is one I call *suspicion.* This theme appears in the passage by Aristotle quoted earlier: artifice is not persuasive, because it makes people suspect "someone plotting against them."[21] We treat the intentions of others as plots against us in a zero-sum game: if you win, I lose. You are likely to be trying to cheat me out of something, to deceive me, so I must be suspicious. Athenian suspicion was embedded into a law against deceiving the democracy, a law justified in Demosthenes' statement to the assembly that "A man can do you no greater injustice than telling lies; for, where the political constitution is based on speeches/words, how can it be safely administered if the words/speeches are false?"[22]

Two examples from the advice about concealment suggest how pervasive the theme of suspicion is in the classical tradition:

> There is an inevitable suspicion attaching to the unconscionable use of figures. It gives a suggestion of treachery, craft, fallacy, especially when your speech is addressed to a judge with absolute authority. . . . So we

find that a figure is always most effective when it conceals the very fact of its being a figure.[23]

Care must be taken to avoid exciting any suspicion in this portion of our speech, and we should therefore give no hint of elaboration in the exordium, since any art that the orator may employ at this point seems to be directed solely at the judge.[24]

2. The second theme, *spontaneity*, identifies the notion that statements we can trust are those that come easily and naturally; conversely, a premeditated statement, one that is obviously crafted and constructed beforehand, deserves our suspicion. For example, the *Rhetorica Ad Herennium* cautions about the use of certain figures involving word-play: "[such figures] are to be used very sparingly when we speak in an actual cause, because their invention seems impossible without labour and pains."[25] The principle of spontaneity presupposes that dissimulation requires more preparation and effort than telling the truth—it requires precisely the effort of concealment. Spontaneity thus serves as a kind of guarantee that no concealment can have occurred and is thus generally understood as a sign of truth or credibility. Here, for example, is Longinus again: "For emotion is always more telling when it seems not to be premeditated by the speaker but to be born of the moment; and this way of questioning and answering one's self counterfeits spontaneous emotion."[26]

But note the "seems" in the quotation and the possibility of counterfeit emotion. Spontaneity itself can be an effect created with no less labor than highly figured speeches, as Cicero makes clear in this passage about the orator Antonius: "His memory was perfect, there was no suggestion of previous rehearsal; he always gave the appearance of coming forward to speak without preparation, but so well prepared was he that when he spoke it was the court rather that often seemed ill prepared to maintain its guard."[27]

In *On the Sophists*, Alcidamas suggests that "the style of extemporaneous speakers" is most effective *and can be imitated*. Quintilian also concedes that spontaneity may be artificial: "Above all it is necessary to conceal the care expended upon it [artistic structure] so that our rhythms may seem to possess a spontaneous flow, not to have been the result of elaborate search or compulsion."[28]

3. Closely related to spontaneity is the theme of sincerity. Spontaneity affects the trustworthiness of statements, and sincerity affects our trust in the speaker; in this way spontaneity *produces* sincerity (or, to be more precise, the impression of spontaneity produces an impression of sincerity).[29] Here is Quintilian, for example: "Who will endure the orator who expresses his anger, his sorrow or his entreaties in neat antitheses, balanced cadences and exact correspondences? Too much care for our words under such circumstances weakens the

impression of emotional sincerity, and wherever the orator displays his art unveiled, the hearer says, 'The truth is not in him.'"[30]

Similarly, the *Rhetorica Ad Herennium* cautions that "we must take care that the Summary should not be carried back to the Introduction or the Statement of Facts. Otherwise the speech will appear to have been fabricated and devised with elaborate pains to as to demonstrate the speaker's skill, advertise his wit, and display his memory."[31]

The sincere speaker says what he or she really believes, which should require no effort, and is more interested in the truth than in persuasive influence. Such a speaker treats communicative relations as cooperative rather than adversarial, or perhaps *as though* they were cooperative rather than adversarial. But cooperation itself may be a disarming strategy, a distraction, a way of concealing adversarial intentions.

The themes of suspicion, spontaneity, and sincerity reinforce each other and together presuppose deeply adversarial communicative relationships, as illustrated in this formulation by Alcidamas: The truth is that speeches that have been laboriously worked out with elaborate diction (compositions more akin to poetry than prose) are deficient in spontaneity and truth, and, since they give the impression of a mechanical artificiality and labored insincerity, they inspire an audience with distrust and ill-will.[32]

Adversarial relationships figure prominently in Plato's classification of the arts, mentioned earlier. He classifies rhetoric with the combative, acquisitive, or conquering arts, such as boxing, wrestling, hunting, and military strategy.[33] The comparison of rhetoric to these arts is endemic to the entire classical tradition. In such competitive endeavors, knowledge of the opponent's art makes it less effective, reducing surprise and enabling countermaneuvers. The hunter and the general both need to conceal the practice of their arts, because the acquisition they seek is—almost by definition—at the expense of others, who will resist. These arts are necessarily adversarial, and thus for them concealment plays an essential strategic role.

The adversarial spirit, and comparisons between verbal and physical contest, permeate the rhetorical tradition. Indeed, the sophistic principle of the *dissoi logoi*, the Aristotelian admonition to argue both sides of the question, and Ciceronian argumentation "*in utramque partem*" all instantiate the adversarial spirit. Aristotle observes that "it would be strange if an inability to defend oneself by means of the body is shameful, while there is no shame in an inability to use speech."[34] Cicero asks, "What . . . is so indispensable as to have always within your grasp weapons wherewith you can defend yourself, or challenge the wicked man, or when provoked take your revenge?"[35] And Quintilian claims, "This gift of arrangement is to oratory what generalship is to war. The skilled commander will know how to distribute his forces for battle, what troops he should keep back to garrison forts or guard cities, to secure supplies, or guard communications, and what dispositions to make by land

and by sea."[36] In perhaps the earliest source, Gorgias made the comparison between persuasion and physical force prominent in his *Encomium of Helen*.

The adversarial arts were taught and practiced in ancient Greece and Rome in a general culture of agonism in which the ground rule is that both sides cannot win. Such agonism is inherent in the forensic encounter, which was the paradigmatic rhetorical situation for much of ancient practice and teaching. Much deliberative rhetoric was also agonistic, with clearly defined adversaries advocating contrary policies. Recent scholarship has explored the way that this agonistic culture influenced rhetoric. Walter Ong's study of the "adversative" spirit in human thought and culture emphasizes the "highly agonistic" sources of rhetoric as a formal art for the world of public debate, and in her study of rhetoric and athletics in ancient Greece, Debra Hawhee notes the multiple ways that the language of athletics (boxing and chariot racing, in particular) became the language of sophistic rhetoric; she claims that an "athletic notion of agonism" informed early Greek rhetorical practice and pedagogy.[37] Noting that Gorgias's epitaph reportedly said that he "armed the soul for contests of excellence," Scott Consigny argues that we can best interpret Gorgias's slim corpus against the widespread agonism of Greek culture.[38] John Poulakos claims that, for Plato, the word for orator (*rhetor*) and the word for contestant (*agonistes*) are "virtual synonyms."[39]

Roman rhetoric was also grounded in agonism.[40] The handbooks, for example, presuppose a hostile or resistant audience in their advice on the *insinuatio*, or indirect introduction, which makes the concealment theme explicit and with it all our worst fears about rhetoric. Cicero's youthful *De Inventione* describes the *insinuatio* as "an address which by dissimulation and indirection unobtrusively steals into the mind of the auditor."[41] The *insinuatio* is to be used in a "difficult" case, in which the auditors are opposed, if not actually hostile, to the proposition to be defended. Cicero says that the audience can be "pacified" or made more "tractable" by strategies that substitute favorable topics for offensive ones, acknowledge the sources of offense and agree with them, work "imperceptibly" to win goodwill away from one's opponents, and "conceal" one's intention to defend the proposition that will offend.[42] The contemporaneous *Rhetorica Ad Herennium* provides similar advice, concluding with the observation that the *insinuatio* seeks to make the audience receptive "covertly, through dissimulation" (*occulte, per dissimulationem*).[43] If we see through these strategies, we immediately suspect that we are being deceived.

The assumption of adversarial relations is not merely a vestige of some earlier time but an important force in contemporary culture. Kenneth Burke, of course, understood well the centrality of adversarial relations in human life, characterizing rhetoric as "*par excellence* the region of the Scramble, of insult and injury, bickering, squabbling, malice and the lie, cloaked malice and the subsidized lie."[44] Lakoff and Johnson have shown how deeply the "argument is war" metaphor is embedded in everyday language.[45] Others suggest that contemporary culture has become too aggressive and polarized. Deborah Tannen, for example, has claimed in *The Argument Culture* that an "adversarial frame of mind" pervades the media, politics, law, and education: "Nearly everything is framed as a battle or game in which winning or losing is the main concern."[46] She finds these adversarial relations to be at least partly responsible for our increasing alienation and loss of community and ultimately to be "damaging to the human spirit."[47] In one of his last books, Wayne Booth described the adversarial version of rhetoric as "win-rhetoric" and, like Tannen, decried its widespread use in politics and the media. He urged us to distinguish between honorable and dishonorable kinds, based on the justice of the cause. Win-rhetoric using deceptive strategies in a cause that the speaker knows to be unjust is what Booth calls "rhetrickery," and he, like Tannen, urges on us a less adversarial approach to communication, which he calls "listening-rhetoric."[48] Our distaste for agonism we owe not so much to the ancients as to our more immediate predecessors, Enlightenment political theorists, who recoiled from the bloody religious wars and divisive nation building of the early modern period with a campaign against rhetoric, as both Stephen Toulmin and Bryan Garsten have shown.[49]

Under the assumption of adversarial relations, rhetoric's problem is plain. Like the general, the orator/advocate must win; for both, the cause must prevail, and for both, the cause justifies any strategic means. For rhetoric, expedience becomes the overriding virtue and dissimulation one of the most effective stratagems in the arsenal. Odysseus models these dubious virtues for the Greeks: he is crafty, flexible, duplicitous; in Sophocles' *Philoctetes* he proclaims, "What I seek in everything is to win."[50] He is, as James Kastely has argued, the "embodiment of rhetoric."[51] At times, notes Don Herzog in his study of cunning, Odysseus seems ingenious and admirable and at times devious and reprehensible.[52] Like rhetoric.

LANGUAGE IS (OR SHOULD BE) MIMETIC

The belief that suspicion on our part, and spontaneity and sincerity on the part of our interlocutors, can protect us against deceptive concealment motivated by adversarial relations rests upon another assumption: that language can be mimetic. If the speaker says what he or she sincerely believes, spontaneously, without premeditation or artifice, then words will reveal the truth unproblematically. The principle of mimesis presupposes that language can (and should) represent nature, or belief, directly, that words and things can (and should) correspond. To the Greek way of thinking, truth itself is a revealing (*a* + *lêtheia*: un-concealment) that removes obscurity or deception. Among the Romans, a fragment from Cato the Elder is often quoted to similar effect: "*rem tene, verba sequentur*" (Fr. 15; grasp the subject, the words will follow). George Campbell maintained that the "most essential" quality of oratory is "perspicuity," which he defined as "transparency, such as may be ascribed to air, glass, water, or any other medium through which material objects are viewed."[53] Rhetorical critics in much of the twentieth century maintained what Gaonkar has referred to as the "transparency thesis," the assumption that oratory is uninterestingly determined by its content, that it is a "mirror" of its object.[54]

When words and things correspond, no rhetoric need be involved; facts, beliefs, and intentions are revealed by the language itself, by a natural mimetic correspondence between language and the world, under a "degree zero of rhetoric."[55] Philosophers have long hoped for such a language: the correspondence theory of truth, in which statements and facts can be matched up together, has its roots in Plato and Aristotle but extends to Bertrand Russell and others in the early twentieth century who sought a theory-neutral observation language.[56] Francis Bacon had advocated purifying the language of the "marketplace" in favor of terms that are close to observation; Thomas Sprat urged scientists to "return back to the primitive purity, and shortness, when men deliver'd so many things, almost in an equal number of words"; and scientists like Linnaeus, Lavoisier, and Whewell spent no little effort attempting to control the vocabulary of science.[57] But ever since Gorgias argued that we cannot put the truth into words, that language is in essence deceptive because words and things are incommensurable, these efforts have been more hopeful than successful.[58]

The mimetic theory persists, however, and the adversarial model helps explain its persistence. Because you *can* use language to lie (that is, to conceal what you believe to be the case or what you believe to be your intentions with respect to making the case to someone), then in order to be believed, you need to draw attention away from the fact that you are using language. One of the ways we do that is to urge on others (and ourselves) the principle of mimesis: suspicion of the possible lie is reduced if language is believed to be determined by whatever is the case, not by the interventions of the speaker. Thus when language is understood to be mimetic, spontaneity and sincerity serve to counteract suspicion. We might conclude, then, that an adversarial model of social relations requires—or at least wants very badly—a mimetic theory of language. A mimetic theory of language allows for the possibility that truth *can* be told, that we *can* hold our adversaries to account for doing so, and that we *can* get closer to the possibly concealed truth by unconcealing our adversary's rhetorical strategies. It is our defense against adversity.

So, although mimesis does not work as a philosophy of language, it works as a strategy.[59] Perversely, it leads directly to the canonical advice about the necessity for concealment, but with a couple of additional twists. First, it emphasizes not just that concealment is necessary but that the fact of concealment must also be concealed. Aristotle notes that "something seems true when the speaker does not conceal what he is doing."[60] So if, in fact, you are concealing something about your intentions, you must conceal the fact that you are doing so. This is a foundational condition of rhetoric. If you want to be believed, to "seem true," you must not conceal what you are doing. Or rather you must *appear* not to conceal; you must conceal your strategies of concealment. This is from Longinus: "This figure [inversion] consists in arranging words and thoughts out of the natural sequence, and bears, so to speak, the genuine stamp of vehement emotion. Just as people who are really angry or frightened or worried or are carried away from time to time by jealousy or any other feeling . . . often put forward one point and then spring off to another with various illogical interpolations . . . so, too, the best prose-writers by the use of inversions imitate nature and achieve the same effect. For art is only perfect when it looks like nature and Nature succeeds only by concealing art about her person."[61]

And here is Dionysius discussing Lysias's sentence structure: "The distinctive nature of its melodious composition seems, as it were, not to be contrived or formed by any conscious art. . . . Yet it is more carefully composed than any work of art. For this artlessness is itself the product of art: the relaxed structure is really under control, and it is in the very illusion of not having been composed with masterly skill that the mastery lies."[62]

What is sought is not mimesis but rather the *appearance* of mimesis. Demosthenes was castigated by Aeschines for this very strategy: "Other deceivers, when they are lying, try to speak in vague and ambiguous terms . . . ; but Demosthenes, when he is cheating you, first adds an oath to his lie, calling down destruction on himself; and secondly, predicting an event that he knows will never happen, he dares to tell the date of it; and he tells the names of men, when he has never so much as seen their faces, deceiving your ears and imitating men who tell the truth. And this is, indeed, another reason why he richly deserves your hatred, that he is not only a scoundrel himself, but destroys your faith even in the signs and symbols of honesty."[63]

The second twist is that in addition to the covert fact of concealment, there is also an overt rhetoric of no-rhetoric.[64] The overt rhetoric assures you that there is nothing to conceal. Shakespeare knew that this was one of the oldest strategies in the book and gave us a paradigmatic statement in Mark Antony's speech over Caesar's body:

> I come not, friends, to steal away your hearts:
> I am no orator as Brutus is;
> But, as you know me all, a plain blunt man. . . .
> For I have neither wit, nor words, nor worth,
> Action, nor utterance, nor the power of speech
> To stir men's blood. I only speak right on.[65]

Socrates' opening in Plato's *Apology* (quoted in the epigraph) is another locus classicus, perhaps the original attempt to disarm listeners by denying rhetoric. As Plutarch cautions, "plain frankness" is to be as much suspected as obvious flattery.[66] Herzog's used-car salesman introduces himself by saying,

"I pride myself on being a straight shooter."[67] The charter document of the scientific plain style, Thomas Sprat's *History of the Royal Society of London,* from 1665, reports the Royal Society's preference for "a close, naked, natural way of speaking; positive expressions; clear senses; a native easiness: bringing all things as near the Mathematical plainness, as they can: and preferring the language of Artizans, Countrymen, and Merchants, before that, of Wits, or Scholars."[68] To invoke the principle of suspicion, the centuries-long occlusion of rhetoric by Enlightenment thought might be seen as a large-scale conceal-ment of rhetoric, a concealment that has aided and abetted the cultural suc-cess of science. The rhetoric of plainness can be understood as the most deeply concealed rhetoric of all.[69]

If, as we saw, the assumption that language is mimetic is sustained by the assumption of adversarial relations, what is the status of the latter assump-tion? Lanham suggests that contest and play, the "engines" of rhetoric, are central human motives, part of our "evolutionary heritage as primates."[70] Burke also sees "division" as our fundamental existential condition: we are "apart from one another," and if we were not "there would be no need for" rhetoric to proclaim unity.[71] Be this ontology as it may, we can also see that this assumption is sustained by the failure of language to be mimetic. Since words do not necessarily correspond to things or facts in any direct way— people can use language to lie, or they can fail to use it effectively, or lan-guage itself may be inadequate—how can we know what to believe? Do we trust, or do we doubt? If the assumption that language can be mimetic is our defense against adversarial relations, the assumption that human relations are adversarial is our defense against the inevitable mimetic failures—the deceptions—of language.

So we can understand the denial of rhetoric, its need for concealment, as the consequence of these two enduring conditions and their interaction. The adversarial relationships and the mystifications of language in which we are entangled make concealment a native dimension of our communication practices—as Herzog puts it, cunning "sprawls across social life." He points out that cunning is necessary not only because some people are dishonest rogues, and not only because we cannot determine reliably which people they are, but also because in some cases "the logic of the social situation" embeds cunning into it. When knowledge is unevenly distributed, when in-terests conflict, as they so often do in greater or smaller ways, cunning, he says, is thrust upon us.[72] In some cases the structure of the situation sets us against each other, as adversaries: but can we reliably know which cases these are? In some cases (at least) language radically fails our meanings: again, how can we know which cases these are?

Perhaps the contest will always be between the skill of the rhetor in con-cealing and the skill of the critic or the immanent suspicion of the audience

in unconcealing. The audience must, it seems, remain the adversary of the rhetor, and vice-versa. As Herzog notes, "the cunning will [always] learn to mimic the virtuous" (this is the dilemma that Aeschines bemoans), and the virtuous are left with no reliable way to signal their honesty and good intentions and may as well join the ranks of the cunning.[73] Another *New Yorker* cartoon represents this hall of mirrors.

For both audience and candidate, whatever else integrity is, it is also an appearance. So recursive and reciprocal are our social relations that the possibility for regress is endless. Art must be concealed, and the concealment must be concealed, and likewise that concealment, and so on. We might conclude that despair is the only recourse—or cynicism.

And this brings us to the problem at hand. What can rhetoric's public role be under these conditions? What can its educational project be? What happens if we teach students to name—and master—the tools? Can rhetoric be useful or powerful if it is revealed—both as a practice and as a discipline? Will public discourse, neighborhoods, civil society, or individual lives fare better with a revealed or a concealed art of rhetoric? Under endemic conditions of suspicion, can rhetoric help build social trust, the essential adhesive of social relations? Should rhetoric go into the streets in disguise? Perhaps this has already happened—we have concealed rhetoric as composition, as cultural studies, as literature, as literacy, as professional communication. The rhetorical arts that have gone public, like advertising, public relations, and political consulting, are often regarded with suspicion, if not disdain, precisely for their emphasis on expedience—on winning. There is an irony here: rhetoric as the unconcealed art of public discourse, as the means for democratic deliberation, has been less successful both academically and culturally than these commercial arts. As taught in departments of speech and speech communication in the twentieth century, in the general college curriculum in much of the nineteenth century, and sometimes in English composition programs, rhetoric was indeed the art of public discourse (or public address, as it was often called). But this effort has not led to either academic status or public respect for the discipline.

Rhetoric does have a long history, as Robert Hariman has pointed out, of marginality, of ranking below a variety of other discourses in status comparisons, notably with philosophy and dialectic and often with poetics. But the margin, as Hariman notes, is essential to the existence of the center; the margin of a society or a psyche "contains what one is but should not be."[74] He also points out that the margin is a "zone of power"—a zone of suppressed potencies.[75] So marginality may be a preferred—or even a necessary—condition for rhetoric, and rhetoric's ability to conceal itself allows it to operate from the margin, to appear natural, centralized, to take form as the real and not the artful, the natural and not the constructed. The margin is also the zone of what cannot be controlled, of the undisciplined, the unsystematizable— and we know that as an art of the *kairos,* rhetoric fits this description as well. But disciplines are ostensibly devoted to unconcealment, to elaboration, to systematization, and they do not survive on the margins—they must promote their own centrality in order to survive. Thus we have rhetoric's "globalization project," as Gaonkar calls it,[76] and thus we have rhetoric's dual identity as the queen of the sciences and the harlot of the arts.

Booth's solution to "reducing rhetorical warfare" and improving the state of our public life is in large part an educational one. We need to teach citizens to listen, to find common ground, to seek good reasons for changing our minds, and to cooperate in progressing beyond our differences, as well as to respond critically to the "rhetrickery" that surrounds us.[77] This solution requires the unconcealment of rhetoric, the naming of the tools. Indeed, rhetorical education, *rhetorica docens* in the scholastic tradition, makes visible our rhetorical practice, *rhetorica utens,* by naming, analysis, imitation. The topics, the genres, the staseis, the parts of the oration, the causes of the emotions, the fallacies, the schemes and tropes—if learning these (or any other rhetorical

canon) is beneficial, this knowledge will make for citizens who can both listen critically and speak and write effectively. But is there not a contradiction
here? Can what is revealed in the classroom remain concealed in the public
forum? *Rhetorica docens* must name the tools, *rhetorica utens* must conceal
them. If citizens become more critical judges of rhetorical practice, they should
also become more cunning practitioners themselves. Yet the strategies of the
cunning practitioner will increasingly be revealed by the increasing critical
acuity of the citizen-audience. We seem to have another endless regress, a
continual escalation of cunning concealment and critical unmasking. Or perhaps an endless circle around which *rhetorica utens* and *rhetorica docens* chase
each other.

As I write this, we are in the 2008 presidential election campaign, in which
each major candidate represents a position under discussion here: one candidate promotes his campaign as the "straight talk express," and the other
candidate's acknowledged eloquence puts him under suspicion. An election
draws public attention to the powers of rhetoric. The editorial pages, political cartoons, television pundits, talk shows, YouTube offerings, and late-night
comedians have been analyzing and satirizing the rhetorical efforts of both
candidates, making visible the strategies and styles of their campaigns, alert-
ing us to the ways we are being manipulated, and in some cases naming the
rhetorical tools explicitly. But as the scholarship makes abundantly clear, the
ancient Athenians were in this same place before us. Jon Hesk characterizes
Athenian oratory as "crucially concerned with its own modes and techniques
of performance in general and deceptive performance in particular."[78] He
shows that the extant speeches employ a number of commonplaces of unconcealment, which unmask the strategies of an opponent and occasionally, in response, justify one's own strategies.[79] Further, as Johan Schloemann suggests,
Athenian audiences had a conscious appreciation of the strategies and styles
of rhetorical performances, an appreciation opposed to their simultaneous
distrust of rhetorical ability: they sustained a dynamic ambivalence about
rhetoric in which they were both eager to be persuaded and at the same time
suspicious of persuasion.[80]

Schloemann goes so far as to propose that the Athenians engaged in "two
different modes of reception": an "entertainment mode" that, we might say,
suspends disbelief, and a "critical mode" that mobilizes disbelief.[81] The dynamic ambivalence created by these two modes echoes Lanham's notion of
the "bi-stable oscillation" between "looking through" and "looking at" a rhetorical performance.[82] In the entertainment mode, when we "look through" a
text the tools and strategies remain concealed and thus can bewitch (or drug
or seduce or deceive) us. In the critical mode, when we "look at" the text we
unconceal its machinery and thus immunize ourselves to its effects. Schloemann insists that the two modes do not represent two segments of the Athenian audience but rather two capabilities of the same audience, and Lanham

claims (by analogy with Gestalt psychology's figure/ground dualism) that we oscillate between these two modes of interpretation but cannot engage them simultaneously. When we suspend our disbelief, submitting to the pleasures of rhetorical engagement, we favor the assumption that language is mimetic, and when we mobilize disbelief, maintaining critical distance, we favor the assumption of adversarial relations. The mutually reinforcing nature of these two assumptions necessitates and help sustains the "ambivalence" about which Schloemann speaks and the "bi-stable oscillation" that Lanham describes. If we favor naive mimesis too strongly, we end in despair, and if we favor the adversarial or critical mode too strongly, we end in permanently disengaged cynicism. Realistically, critical unconcealment can be illuminating about the particular case but does not inoculate us permanently against the next mesmerizing speaker or shrewd marketing campaign.

I do not mean here to dismiss rhetoric as a sham art or to reject it in favor of some other, better description of our communicative dilemmas. I mean, rather, to honor the dangers and powers of rhetoric, which the ancients well understood and which our enthusiasm about the revival of rhetoric may sometimes lead us to forget. We cannot, as Garsten says, avoid the "twin dangers" of pandering and manipulation that arise from the nature of rhetoric itself.[83] Some theorists have encouraged us to reconceive rhetoric as a cooperative rather than an adversarial art, Booth prominent among them. At the same time, he confesses his own failures and inabilities in attempting to practice the cooperative listening-rhetoric he preaches. Booth, Burke, Garsten, and Herzog all conclude that practical affairs, the public realm of *rhetorica utens*, must be dealt with, struggled with, on a case-by-case basis, and that cunning concealment is necessary, dangerous, and morally troubling. I mean as well to urge a realistic attenuation of our hopes for what it is that rhetoric can achieve in public, both in terms of its status as a discipline and in terms of its capabilities to promote the public good. Under endemic conditions of suspicion, we need a rhetoric that helps build social trust. But if the assumptions of agonism and mimesis indeed prevail, such a project cannot be a global or a programmatic one: it must be risked one situation at a time.

NOTES

I am indebted to Judith Ferster for helpful discussion about the relevance of current political discourse, to Richard Graff for both primary and secondary sources, and to the members of a summer writing group at North Carolina State for suggestions on a late draft.

1. Plato, *Collected Dialogues*, 17a–b.
2. Ibid., 452d.
3. Cicero, *De Oratore*, 30.
4. Ibid., 32.
5. Plato, *Collected Dialogues*, 456a; see also Aristotle, *On Rhetoric*, 1.1.1, 1.1.14.
6. Burke, *Rhetoric of Motives*, 172.
7. Cherwitz, "Rhetoric"; Gaonkar, "Idea of Rhetoric," 29, 38, 36.

8. This is a widely attested Latin phrase that seems to have no specific source in this form. See Taylor, "History." For two useful discussions of this theme in classical rhetoric and citations, see Andersen, "Lingua Suspecta"; Cronjé, "Principle of Concealment."

9. Aristotle, *On Rhetoric*, 3.2.4.

10. Ibid., 198, n.18.

11. Cicero, *De Inventione*, 63.26.

12. Quintilian, *Institutio Oratoria*, 1.11.3.

13. Cahn, "Rhetoric of Rhetoric," 79.

14. Lanham, *Electronic Word*, 151.

15. Plett, "Shakespeare."

16. Michelle Zerba argues that the roots of Machiavelli's prescriptions for the prince are in Cicero's *De Oratore*, which she characterizes as "the most fully developed view of the civic leader as one pitched in a heroic battle for preeminence that must rely on the rhetoric of imposture." Zerba, "Frauds of Humanism," 220.

17. Cahn, "Rhetoric of Rhetoric," 79.

18. See Roochnik, *Of Art and Wisdom*, App. 3. Roochnik offers a discussion of Plato's many classifications of techne.

19. Plato, *Collected Dialogues*, 463–65.

20. My collection of about fifty examples of advice about concealing rhetorical art started from these two footnotes: see *Rhetorica Ad Herennium*, IV.vii.10; Cahn, "Rhetoric of Rhetoric," 84, n.45. Caplan concludes that "the idea is widespread in ancient rhetoric." *Rhetorica Ad Herrennium*, 250.

21. Aristotle, *On Rhetoric*, 3.2.4.

22. Hesk, *Deception and Democracy*; Demosthenes, *On the False Embassy*, 19.184.

23. Longinus, *On the Sublime*, 17.1.

24. Quintilian, *Institutio Oratoria*, 4.1.57.

25. *Rhetorica Ad Herennium*, 4.22.32.

26. Longinus, *On the Sublime*, 18.2.

27. Cicero, *Brutus*, 37.139.

28. Http://www.perseus.tufts.edu/hopper/text?doc=Perseus:text:1999.01.0002: speech=3. Quintilian, *Institutio Oratoria*, 9.4.147.

29. The connection between spontaneity and sincerity means that all the advice about concealment is also advice about ethos and helps support Aristotle's contention that ethos is, "almost . . . the most authoritative form of persuasion." Aristotle, *On Rhetoric*, 1.2.4.

30. Quintilian, *Institutio Oratoria*, 9.3.102.

31. *Rhetorica Ad Herennium*, 2.30.47.

32. Alcidamas, *On the Sophists*, 12.

33. See, for example, Plato, *Gorgias*, 452; *Euthydemus*, 290, *Sophist*, 219–25; *Statesman*, 304. I have discussed the use of the hunting analogy at length elsewhere. Miller, "Aristotelian *Topos*."

34. Aristotle, *On Rhetoric*, 1.1.12.

35. Cicero, *De Oratore*, 1.8.32.

36. Quintilian, *Institutio Oratoria*, 7.10.17.

37. Ong, *Fighting for Life*, 26; Hawhee, *Bodily Arts*, 17.

38. Consigny, *Gorgias*, 75.

39. Poulakos, *Sophistical Rhetoric*, 37.

40. Zerba, "Frauds of Humanism."

41. Cicero, *De Inventione*, 1.15.20.

42. Ibid., 1.17.24.

43. *Rhetorica Ad Herennium*, 1.7.11.

44. Burke, *Rhetoric of Motives*, 19.

45. Gorgias, "Encomium of Helen"; Lakoff and Johnson, *Metaphors We Live By*.

46. Tannen, *Argument Culture*, 3, 4.

47. Ibid., 284.

48. Booth, *Rhetoric of Rhetoric*, 43–50.

49. Toulmin, *Cosmopolis;* Garsten, *Saving Persuasion*. Garsten focuses on the political thought of Hobbes, Rousseau, and Kant, whose rhetoric against rhetoric aimed to protect the modern state from the contentiousness of public judgment.

50. Sophocles, *Philoctetes*, 1052.

51. Kastely, *Rethinking the Rhetorical Tradition*, 88.

52. Herzog, *Cunning*, 24–25.

53. Campbell, *Philosophy*, 216, 221.

54. Gaonkar, "Object," 298.

55. Andersen, "Lingua Suspecta," 79. The mimetic principle also operates in the visual arts. In Ovid's *Metamorphoses*, Pygmalion falls in love with the statue of his own creation because the excellence of his art creates a perfect representation of reality, persuading even its creator by its mimetic power. Ovid concludes, "*ars adeo latet arte sua*" (so does his art conceal his art). Ovid, *Metamorphoses*, 10.252.

56. David, "Correspondence Theory."

57. Paradis, "Bacon, Linnaeus, and Lavoisier."

58. See, for example, Ballif, *Seduction;* Consigny, *Gorgias;* Kerferd, *Sophistic Movement*.

59. Closely related to the mimetic principle is what Michael Reddy has called "the conduit metaphor" for communication, the idea that an unproblematic "message" can be neutrally (mimetically) "encoded" and "transmitted" to a "receiver," and he shows how deeply this set of assumptions is embedded in our language about language. Reddy, "Conduit Metaphor."

60. Aristotle, *On Rhetoric*, 3.7.9.

61. Longinus, *On the Sublime*, 22.1.

62. Dionysius, *Critical Essays*, 8.

63. Aeschines, "Against Ctesiphon," 3.99. As Hesk notes, Aeschines' complaint distinguishes two levels or types of deceit: the detectable and the undetectable. Hesk, *Deception and Democracy*, 238.

64. This is different from what Hesk calls "the rhetoric of anti-rhetoric," which consists of explicit attacks on the deceptiveness of speech, or one's opponent's speech, rather than the denial of one's own rhetoric. Hesk, *Deception and Democracy*.

65. *Julius Caesar*, III: ii.

66. Plutarch, *Moralia*, 17.

67. Herzog, *Cunning*, 95.

68. Sprat, *History*, Sect. 20.

69. Consigny has also made this point, noting that such "seemingly neutral discourse" is usually hegemonic. Consigny, "Rhetorical Concealment."

70. Lanham, *Electronic Word*, 110; see also his discussion of the work of zoologist Richard Alexander, who aimed to explain why "hypocrisy evolved as the primary human attribute" (58).

71. Burke, *Rhetoric of Motives*, 22.

72. Herzog, *Cunning*, 121.

73. Ibid., 84, 121.

74. Hariman, "Status," 44.

75. Ibid., 48.

76. Gaonkar, "Idea of Rhetoric"; see also Cahn's discussion of rhetoric's disciplinary status, "Rhetoric of Rhetoric."

77. Booth, *Rhetoric of Rhetoric,* 149.

78. Hesk, *Deception and Democracy,* 203–4.

79. Ibid., 227ff.

80. Schloemann, "Entertainment."

81. Ibid., 144.

82. Lanham, *Electronic Word.*

83. Garsten, *Saving Persuasion,* 2.

WORKS CITED

Aeschines. "Against Ctesiphon." In *Aeschines.* Cambridge, Mass.: Harvard University Press, 1919.

Alcidamas. *On the Sophists.* Translated by Larue Van Hook. *Classical Weekly* 12, no. 12. http://classicpersuasion.org/pw/alcidamas/alcsoph1.htm (accessed July 23, 2008). Translated by Charles Darwin Miller, http://www.perseus.tufts.edu/hopper/text?doc =Perseus:text:1999.01.0002:speech=3.

Andersen, Øivind. "Lingua Suspecta: On Concealing and Displaying the Art of Rhetoric." *Sumbolae Osloenses* 71 (1996): 68–86.

Aristotle. *On Rhetoric: A Theory of Civic Discourse.* Translated by G. A. Kennedy. 2nd ed. New York: Oxford University Press, 2007.

Ballif, Michelle. *Seduction, Sophistry, and the Woman with the Rhetorical Figure, Rhetorical Philosophy and Theory.* Carbondale: Southern Illinois University Press, 2001.

Booth, Wayne C. *The Rhetoric of Rhetoric: The Quest for Effective Communication, Blackwell Manifestos.* Malden, Mass.: Blackwell, 2004.

Burke, Kenneth. *A Rhetoric of Motives.* Berkeley: University of California Press, 1969.

Cahn, Michael. "The Rhetoric of Rhetoric: Six Tropes of Disciplinary Self-Constitution." In *The Recovery of Rhetoric: Persuasive Discourse and Disciplinarity in the Human Sciences,* edited by R. H. Roberts and J. M. M. Good, 61–84. Charlottesville: University of Virginia Press, 1993.

Campbell, George. *The Philosophy of Rhetoric.* 1776. Edited by Lloyd F. Bitzer. Reprint, Carbondale: Southern Illinois University Press. 1963.

Cherwitz, Richard A. "Rhetoric as 'a Way of Knowing': An Attenuation of the Epistemological Claims of the 'New Rhetoric.'" *Southern Speech Communication Journal* 42 (1977): 297–319.

Cicero, Marcus Tullius. *Brutus.* Translated by G. L. Hendrickson. Loeb Classical Library. Cambridge, Mass.: Harvard University Press, 1939.

———. *De Inventione, De Optimo Genere Oratorum, Topica.* Translated by H. M. Hummell. Loeb Classical Library. Cambridge, Mass.: Harvard University Press, 1949.

———. *De Oratore.* Translated by H. Rackham. 2 vols. Loeb Classical Library. Cambridge, Mass.: Harvard University Press, 1942.

Consigny, Scott. *Gorgias: Sophist and Artist.* Edited by T. W. Benson. Studies in Rhetoric and Communication. Columbia: University of South Carolina Press, 2001.

———. "Rhetorical Concealment." Paper read at Theory of Rhetoric: An Interdisciplinary Conference, Minneapolis, Minn., 1979.

Cronjé, J. V. "The Principle of Concealment (to Lathein) in Greek Literary Theory." *Acta Classica* 36 (1993): 55–64.

David, Marian. "Correspondence Theory of Truth." In *Stanford Encyclopedia of Philoso-phy*, edited by E. N. Zalta. Stanford, Calif.: Metaphysics Research Lab, Stanford University, 2005. http://plato.stanford.edu/entries/truth-correspondence/ (accessed June 23, 2008).

Demosthenes. *On the False Embassy*. Cambridge, Mass.: Harvard University Press, 1926. http://www.perseus.tufts.edu/hopper/text.jsp?doc=Perseus:text:1999.01.0072:speech =19 (accessed July 19, 2008).

Dionysius of Halicarnassus. *The Critical Essays*. Translated by S. Usher. 2 vols. Cambridge, Mass.: Harvard University Press, 1974.

Gaonkar, Dilip Parameshwar. "The Idea of Rhetoric in the Rhetoric of Science." In *Rhetorical Hermeneutics: Invention and Interpretation in the Age of Science*, edited by A. G. Gross and W. M. Keith, 25–85. Albany: SUNY Press, 1997.

———. "Object and Method in Rhetorical Criticism: From Wichelns to Leff and McGee." *Western Journal of Speech Communication* 54 (1990): 290–316.

Garsten, Bryan. *Saving Persuasion: A Defense of Rhetoric and Judgment*. Cambridge, Mass.: Harvard University Press, 2006.

Gorgias. "Encomium of Helen." In *Aristotle, on Rhetoric: A Theory of Civic Discourse*, edited by G. A. Kennedy, 283–88. New York: Oxford University Press, 1991.

Hariman, Robert. "Status, Marginality, and Rhetorical Theory." *Quarterly Journal of Speech* 72 (1986): 38–54.

Hawhee, Debra. *Bodily Arts: Rhetoric and Athletics in Ancient Greece*. Austin: University of Texas Press, 2004.

Herzog, Don. *Cunning*. Princeton, N.J.: Princeton University Press, 2006.

Hesk, Jon. *Deception and Democracy in Classical Athens*. Cambridge: Cambridge University Press, 2000.

Kastely, James L. *Rethinking the Rhetorical Tradition: From Plato to Postmodernism*. New Haven, Conn.: Yale University Press, 1997.

Kerferd, G. B. *The Sophistic Movement*. Cambridge: Cambridge University Press, 1981.

Lakoff, George, and Mark Johnson. *Metaphors We Live By*. Chicago: University of Chicago Press, 1980.

Lanham, Richard A. *The Electronic Word: Democracy, Technology, and the Arts*. Chicago: University of Chicago Press, 1993.

Longinus. *On the Sublime*. Translated by J. A. Arieti and J. M. Crossett. Vol. 21, *Texts and Studies in Religion*. New York: Edwin Mellen Press, 1985.

Miller, Carolyn R. "The Aristotelian *Topos*: Hunting for Novelty." In *Rereading Aristotle's Rhetoric*, edited by A. G. Gross and W. Keith, 130–46. Carbondale: Southern Illinois University Press, 2000.

Ong, Walter J. *Fighting for Life: Contest, Sexuality, and Consciousness*. Ithaca, N.Y.: Cornell University Press, 1981.

Paradis, James. "Bacon, Linnaeus, and Lavoisier: Early Language Reform in the Sciences." In *New Essays in Technical and Scientific Communication: Research, Theory, Practice*, edited by P. V. Anderson, R. J. Brockmann, and C. R. Miller, 200–224. Farmingdale, N.Y.: Baywood, 1983.

Plato. *The Collected Dialogues*. Edited by E. Hamilton and H. Cairns. Princeton, N.J.: Princeton University Press, 1961.

Plett, Heinrich F. "Shakespeare and the *Ars Rhetorica*." In *Rhetoric and Pedagogy: Its History, Philosophy, and Practice. Essays in Honor of James J. Murphy*, edited by W. B. Horner and M. Leff, 243–59. Mahway, N.J.: Lawrence Erlbaum, 1995.

Plutarch. *Moralia*. Translated by G. Tullie. Boston: Little, Brown, 1878.

Poulakos, John. *Sophistical Rhetoric in Classical Greece.* Columbia: University of South Carolina Press, 1997.

Quintilian. *Institutio Oratoria.* Translated by H. E. Butler. 4 vols. Loeb Classical Library. Cambridge, Mass.: Harvard University Press, 1920.

Reddy, Michael J. "The Conduit Metaphor—a Case of Frame Conflict in Our Language About Language." In *Metaphor and Thought,* edited by A. Ortony, 164–201. 1979. Reprint, Cambridge: Cambridge University Press, 1993.

Rhetorica Ad Herennium. 1981. Translated by H. Caplan. Loeb Classical Library. Cambridge, Mass.: Harvard University Press, 1981.

Roochnik, David. *Of Art and Wisdom: Plato's Understanding of Techne.* University Park: Pennsylvania State University Press, 1996.

Schloemann, Johan. "Entertainment and Democratic Distrust: The Audiences's Attitudes towards Oral and Written Oratory in Classical Athens." In *Epea and Grammata: Oral and Written Communication in Ancient Greece,* edited by I. Worthington and J. M. Foley, 133–46. Leiden: Brill, 2002.

Sprat, Thomas. *History of the Royal Society of London, for the Improving of Natural Knowledge.* London: J. Martyn at the Bell, 1667.

Tannen, Deborah. *The Argument Culture: Stopping America's War of Words.* New York: Ballentine Books, 1998.

Taylor, Archer. "The History of a Proverbial Pattern." *De Proverbio: An Electronic Journal of International Proverb Studies* 2, no. 1 (1996). http://www.deproverbio.com/DPjournal //DP,2,1,96/PROVERBIAL_PATTERN.html (accessed September 24, 2006).

Toulmin, Stephen. *Cosmopolis: The Hidden Agenda of Modernity.* Chicago: University of Chicago Press, 1990.

Zerba, Michelle. "The Frauds of Humanism: Cicero, Machiavelli, and the Rhetoric of Imposture." *Rhetorica* 22, no. 3 (2004): 215–40.

Power, Publics, and the Rhetorical Uses of Democracy

CANDICE RAI

"The Rhetoric must lead us through the Scramble, the Wrangle of the Market Place, the flurries and flare-ups of the Human Barnyard, the Give and Take, the wavering line of pressure and counter pressure, the Logomachy, the onus of ownership, the Wars of Nerves, the War."[1]

In this essay, I argue that rhetorics, specifically rhetorics of democracy, can be turned on their head, picked up and used to support diametrically opposed agendas. I understand democratic rhetorics as comprised of a tangled discursive web of commonplace myths, symbols, stock tales, and contradictory blueprints for the good life that we collectively associate with democracy. This includes the arsenal of topoi that embody democratic ideals, such as freedom, equality, and liberty. The flexible uses of democratic rhetoric is possible because its topoi function as persuasive rhetorical engines that proliferate meaning and mobilize action by activating discourse already circulating in the social imagination. Kenneth Burke referred to such topoi as "god-terms" because they are capable of "transcending brute objects" and of doing the work of gods by providing the "ground of all possibility; substance . . . truth . . . ideal, plan, purpose."[2] I contend that the "public sphere," one of democracy's core topoi, crystallizes the hopes and ideals, as well as the limits and contradictions, of liberal democracy. The public sphere is predicated on the powerful faith that rational deliberation among private citizens about matters of public concern will produce a more inclusive, empathetic, and just society. The sheer moral force of these promised public goods is capable of obscuring gaps between democratic ideals and material realities, eliding the inherent contradictions within the democratic project, and legitimizing arguments that make use of democratic rhetorics, regardless of content or social consequence.

Whatever it is we imagine democracy to mean, we can be sure that our neighbors will have a very different understanding. That both conflicting claims, mine and my neighbor's, can be theoretically legitimate within a single democratic framework means that determining the content of "democracy" might be more a matter of raw power and rhetorical savvy than about whose argument is more rational, just, or better equipped to secure public goods and increase neighborliness. Since democratic ideals can inspire action toward very different ends, it is dangerous to equate democracy with social justice or to presume that democracy alone can mitigate human suffering and violence, and further, it suggests that democratic politics cannot be comprehended strictly from a god's-eye view.

I situate these arguments, therefore, within fieldwork conducted between 2005 and 2008 in Uptown, a gentrifying Chicago neighborhood, to consider how stakeholders use democratic rhetorics to argue about the future of their neighborhood.[3] I begin by discussing the public sphere, as the conceptual model of democracy, arguing that although the transcendent ideals represented in the model are capable of inspiring conviction and action, the substance of these ideals remains elusive until they are put to use in concrete situations. I then examine the uses of democratic rhetoric in debates over affordable housing in Uptown to consider how democratic rhetorics are used to support very different investments.

One can travel to Uptown's central hub from downtown Chicago by taking the redline train due north for five miles to the Wilson stop. Since its annexation to the city in 1889, Uptown has served as a port of entry for African, Latin American, Asian, and European immigrants and refugees; African American and white Appalachian migrants from the South; and Native Americans displaced by the Relocation Act of 1956.[4] An economically and ethnically diverse population crosses paths while going about their business on Wilson Avenue. The neighborhood's population ranges from the very affluent to the very poor—with people in the upper quintillion of income sharing blocks with people in the lowest. Visitors would immediately face the material evidence of gentrification as they left the train: a new condominium flashes its bronze facade next door to the Wilson Hotel, infamous for housing transient "undesirables."

In the heart of Uptown, there is a five-acre empty lot known simply as Wilson Yard, which stands literally at the crossroads of affluence and decay. There is nothing particularly striking about the lot: it lies sandwiched between the El train and a strip of hodgepodge businesses. The lot made its public debut in 1996 when a fire destroyed a repair shop owned by the Chicago Transit Authority (CTA). The controversial public debates over what to build in this lot have been ongoing since 1997 when the CTA sold the land to the city, prompting Uptown's alderman Helen Shiller to initiate a community-driven, "democratic" planning process to collectively design a project at Wilson Yard.[5] The eventual outcome was to represent the will of the people and stand as a material monument to the ability of inclusive dialogue in the public sphere to create the greatest good for all.

The hotly contested Wilson Yard plan includes a Target, street-level retail, and two ten-story publicly subsidized affordable apartment buildings. One building includes ninety-nine units for low-income seniors, and the other—which lies at the center of this controversy—will house eighty-four units for households making no more than 60 percent of the area median income.[6] Beginning in 1998, dozens of organizations and hundreds of Uptown stakeholders have evoked democratic rhetoric in public discourse and at community meetings to justify and support arguments both for and against affordable housing at Wilson Yard;[7] to both slander and support public officials; and to both legitimate and blast the processes of gentrification. I am interested here in how two such different investments—one claiming that creating affordable housing on behalf of those at risk of being displaced by gentrification is democratic, and the other claiming that such a move is undemocratic because it favors the poor, silences the voices of property owners, and unjustly reappropriates taxes—could both be supported using democratic rhetoric. Many people are invested in Uptown, just not in the same outcomes. To help elucidate these investments, I turn to a description of the contention at Wilson Yard, and to a consideration of how competing publics in Uptown illustrate the theoretical and practical contradictions within the democratic project.

DEMOCRATIC THEORY, POWER, AND THE LIMITS OF THE PUBLIC SPHERE TROPE

By analyzing Uptown's emergent public in action, one bears witness to what Chantal Mouffe calls the "paradox of democracy." Mouffe articulates this "paradox" as the incompatibility between political liberalism (which foregrounds a politics of liberty and individual rights) and democracy (which foregrounds a politics of equality). Arguing that this paradox is an inherent and valuable feature of democracy, she advocates "agonistic pluralism," a politics that secures contestation as a permanent and foundational condition of democracy. In rejecting the possibility of "establishing a consensus without exclusion," agonistic pluralism calls for the maintenance of democratic institutions and processes that keep "democratic contestations alive."[8] Compelling in theory, "agonistic pluralism" presents serious limitations in the material world where concrete, timely, and compromised decisions must finally be made. In Uptown, something must be developed at Wilson Yard despite what could be an infinite debate over what should be built. There is much to be learned from the stalemate of competing rhetorics in Uptown, in that eventually, public policy must *act*, and often act in ways that some part of the constituency may deem "undemocratic."

Alderman Shiller has publicly referred to Wilson Yard, which still awaits construction in 2009, as a "virtual basket" because its design emerged from ostensibly democratic, community-driven planning processes. Rather than something like a public park, which would certainly be easier to claim as a universal public good, the development is a pastiche that represents a bit of everyone's interest while simultaneously fulfilling no one's. With a Target, a large parking structure, and two mid-rise affordable apartment buildings jammed into a five-acre lot, one can see how Wilson Yard earned the name "Franken-development" from an Uptown dissenter. In the following ethnographic scene, which recounts the public unveiling of Wilson Yard on September 8, 2004, Mouffe's "democratic paradox" can be empirically observed not only in the tension between stakeholders but also in the competing interests that are captured in the literal design of space. A six-year "democratic" process preceded this meeting in which multiple spaces where these and other adversarial positions about the future of the neighborhood were vetted.

Over 600 Uptown stakeholders crowded into Truman College's cafeteria to hear about the Wilson Yard plan. The room was electric with tension. The sound of buzzing chatter and metal chair legs scraping on waxed linoleum punctuated the palpable anticipation of the homeowners, renters, community organizers, urban planners, city officials, business owners, religious leaders, and journalists who gathered. It was apparent on which side of the affordable housing controversy people stood. Those who opposed it were primarily members of the Uptown Neighborhood Council, which was formed explicitly to oppose low-income housing at Wilson Yard. These activists wore bright orange T-shirts that read "Unite Uptown" on the front, and "Build a Better Community through the Arts" on the back. The "Orange Shirts," as they are known, argued that if affordable housing must be built, and they would prefer that it was not, that it should be reserved as an artists' residence. Those who favored affordable housing at Wilson Yard wore green stickers that read "Uptown Supports Affordable Housing." This contingency represented a variety of political agendas that converged around the support of affordable housing as a means of counteracting gentrification, and included longtime Uptown residents and members of a diverse array of neighborhood organizations such as Jesus People, Queer to the Left, Organization of the North East, and Coalition of Uptown Residents for Affordability and Justice (COURAJ). Shouts and countershouts were blurted throughout the meeting in an effort to discredit speakers. Those in orange shouted things like: "This development will concentrate poverty. We have enough subsidized housing in Uptown!" "We don't want our tax money to be spent on this." "This isn't democracy. I didn't want this." Those in green shouted: "This represents all of our interests. We need affordable housing. Uptown needs to take care of all of its citizens!" After the formal presentation, things became so raucous that, at one point, the president of Truman College came to the microphone with great exasperation to tell the crowd to calm down or she would have to end the meeting.

The rather unruly "public" that emerged on this evening is a far cry from idealized images of citizens engaged in empathetic, rational deliberation about the common welfare. This public appears nothing like John Rawls's ideal liberal model where stakeholders bracket their private interests behind a "veil of ignorance" in order to derive universal principles of justice that ensure the greatest good for the greatest number. On the contrary, Uptown stakeholders nakedly display their investments with visual flair—agendas literally emblazoned on brightly colored stickers and T-shirts. Splintered by competing investments, this is a public incapable of deriving consensus.

And further, the trump card in the Wilson Yard debates is often "democracy" itself. Below, affordable housing advocates and members of Queer to the Left discuss the tactical uses of democratic discourse in Uptown. Marie reflects on the Wilson Yard planning charrettes that took place between 1998 and 2000, and the others on statements made at the public unveiling described above:

MARIE: Everyone was invited [to the charrettes]. They were held at Truman College. I mean what is not democratic . . .

GENE: One of the people who spoke at the last Wilson Yard meeting [in 2004] said that this process is not legitimate because this process has taken so long. They said, "You are basing the project on principles that were laid out in 1999–2000, but we are all different now, and we were left out and we should have a say in what gets built. Now, we want a voice. We're new and we were left out."

DIANE: You know there are problems with democracy because I can imagine us on that side. This example makes that clear. I can image us organizing around this argument. "Well . . . but . . . now *we* are here and *we* want to be consulted." . . . There is something about the whole thing that is fraught with indeterminacy.

This scene crystallizes some of the logomachy that underscores the uses of democracy in Uptown and exemplifies Julia Paley's argument that the "use of the word 'democracy' occurs neither alone, nor steadily, nor completely; it is, rather, ethnographically emergent. Therefore we must ask: Whose term is it? What does its usage in any particular case signify? Where does the term arise and where not?"[9] Democracy is "ethnographically emergent" because the indeterminate meanings of democratic topoi can only be understood within the concrete contexts within which they are evoked.

By insisting that the solution to the problems of democracy does not reside in a more participatory or better-executed democracy, Barbara Cruikshank calls into question the large body of public sphere theory dedicated to conceptualizing an ever-more robust, inclusive, and just civil society. Rather than accepting democracy as an a priori virtuous good, she understands democratic government, like all government, as "relations of power" that are "continually recreated."[10] It is not that we need a more accurate model of the public sphere, therefore, but a way to theorize how democratic politics produce subjectivities and sentiments that are reinforced and activated through "relations of power" in particular circumstances that make certain beliefs and actions seem more reasonable (and more "democratic").

In the unveiling of Wilson Yard, the core tensions within democratic subjectivity manifest through two pulls. In the first, democracy is framed as individual liberty, which appears in the Orange Shirts' claim that the plan is undemocratic because their private interests are not being served (*This isn't democracy. I didn't want this.*), and that taxpayers should have control over how their money is spent (*We don't want our tax money to be spent on this.*). The second pull frames democracy in terms of social equality, which appears in the mobilization of affordable housing as a "public good" (*We need affordable housing. Uptown needs to take care of all of its citizens!*). My concern here is not to determine which sentiment is morally superior to the other, but to highlight that both pulls are always legitimately at play in liberal democracies. Rather than representing two distinct conceptions of democracy, these pulls signal contradictory tensions within a single theoretical framework. The democratic subject circumscribes the desire for both liberty and equality, for both individual and social rights, and thus encompasses the paradoxical stalemates to which these competing transcendent ideals point.

Before returning to a discussion on the uses of democratic rhetoric in Uptown, I turn to a consideration of how we might regard the "public sphere" in light of these stalemates. Jürgen Habermas's model of the public sphere catalyzed a body of criticism on the possibilities and limitations of democracy as a deliberative, nonviolent means of deriving principles to guide a demos that is both inclusive and radically diverse. Theorists—including Nancy Fraser, David Fleming, and Gerard Hauser—have critiqued the Habermasian model as idealized, each driven by a similar impetus to conceive a public that better accounts for the political complexities that confound democratic deliberation.

Hauser rightly moves away from Habermas's idealism, offering what he calls the reticulate public sphere, which he defines as "a discursive space in which individuals and groups associate to discuss matters of mutual interest and, where possible, to reach a common judgment about them."[11] Hauser's insistence that "publics do not exist as entities but as processes" is predicated on the idea that "collective reasoning is not defined by abstract reflection but by practical judgment," and therefore, a public's "awareness of issues is not philosophical but eventful."[12] To say that a public is "eventful" is to say that it manifests, kairotically, in response to exigencies in concrete material space. While Hauser notes that "rhetorically salient meanings are unstable," he also hopes that the physical proximity of agents in local publics might make contestation less volatile and more prone to the "formation of shared judgments."[13] Similarly, Fleming pursues a public sphere—rooted in embodied experiences, vernacular tactics, and local exigencies—that remains "open to hybridity, pluralism, and mobility." He seeks a "commonplace" that is both material and conceptual "where we can disclose our differences to one another but also solve our shared problems, where we can encounter conflict and opposition but still feel that we belong and matter."[14] He considers urban neighborhoods as ideal sites where such publics might emerge as a "space between community and society" that offers a "setting which is true to human diversity but still allows for 'commonality' and 'solidarity.'"[15] While Fleming and Hauser have contributed much to our understanding of the rhetoricality of actually existing publics, I understand their projects—given their desire to accommodate social plurality without exclusion or violence—as reinvesting Habermas's idealism into miniaturized, competing, vernacular public spheres that may be more qualitatively grounded, but no less idealistic.

However, tensions within democratic society are not a matter of scale, but rather cut down to the very core, to the most local, to the most finite detail of social interaction and knowledge production: down to the production of the democratic subject itself. The irresolvable conflicts in Uptown emerge not from a lack of rhetorical competency, a dearth of material spaces for debate, or a disconnect from official channels of power. Democratic publics do not fail simply because of misunderstanding, procedural distortion, or failure to achieve rhetorical stasis. In Uptown, we see a radically diverse public actively engaged in deliberation, but completely unable to agree on a collective vision of their neighborhood's future. Democratic participation abounds around the Wilson Yard development—in city hall, in neighborhood meeting rooms, in community organizations, on the streets, in public discourse, and in public oratorical performances. The impasse reached by this public has not resulted from procedural malfunction. The commitment to solving the problems of democracy by practicing "better" democracy requires one to hold on to a transcendent conception of democracy that does not exist. There is no available Platonic truth that Uptown stakeholders might discover through more refined dialectical practice.

Rather than understanding democratic politics as occurring "out there, in the public sphere," Cruikshank insists that we are better served by understanding how democracy works at the "very soul of subjectivity."[16] Cruikshank is particularly interested in how what Foucault called "biopower" "operates to invest the citizen with a set of goals and self-understandings."[17] Biopower complicates the image of the democratic subject defined as free and autonomous. As Cruikshank argues, the "citizen and subjects are not opposites," rather "citizens are made and therefore subject to power even as they become citizens," and "although democratic citizens are formally free, their freedom is a condition of the operationalization of power."[18] In light of Cruikshank's rendering of democratic subjectivity, the question of how to better facilitate solidarity among autonomous, free citizens in the public sphere shifts to a concern with how "democracy" (its practices and rhetorics) leverages power unevenly through the active participation of citizens who are collectively engaged in defining contested urban space. The preoccupation in public sphere theories with how to produce more effective persuasion is undermined by the limit written into the impossibility of rational deliberation to produce consensus, a shared sense of justice, or material force. Moreover, the tendency in public sphere theory to cast rhetoric in the role of superhero is sorely challenged by this case study, which reveals the shakiness of democracy's moral foundation, in lieu of which sheer power typically bowls over rhetorical competency.

IN THE FIELD: Uptown's "Public" and the Rhetorical Uses of Democracy

In a gentrifying neighborhood, housing is a good lens through which to see the core tensions in democratic society because its accessibility literally determines who can afford to remain part of the "demos." The frenzied Chicago real estate market that began gathering momentum in the mid-1990s started showing signs of distress in 2006.[19] Beneath this boom loomed an affordable housing crisis characterized by gentrifying inner-city neighborhoods, an aging housing stock overconcentrated in poverty-stricken areas, a net loss of 11,000 public housing units under Chicago's Plan for Transformation, and dwindling federal and state dollars for housing. In 2006 approximately 30 percent of Chicago's households were rent-burdened (paying more than 30 percent of their income on rent), and of those households, 72 percent were classified as "extremely low-income" (earning $20,350 or less for a family of four).[20]

Uptown was particularly affected by this housing boom, given its access to Lake Michigan and downtown, abundance of public transportation, and ample stock of historic brownstones. Between 1990 and 2000, Uptown's median rent increased 38 percent, and the median home value nearly doubled, increasing 94 percent from $139,000 to $270,000.[21] Although Uptown became less "affordable," it is critical to note that at the end of the 1990s, 18.2 percent of Uptown's housing stock was publicly subsidized through various city, state, and federal agencies,[22] and in 2000, 25 percent of Uptown's population lived at or below the poverty line.[23] Although Wilson Yard is not public housing, the images of "stockpiling" the poor (which evoke the horrific conditions of Chicago's public housing complexes built during urban renewal) are commonplace. The fear that the housing will become gang- and drug-invested "towers of desperation" that breed poverty and social dysfunction runs rampant in public discourse.[24] The general concern over the further concentration of poverty is not without cause, as Uptown has a large homeless population and visible street drug culture. Further, the Wilson Yard Tax Increment Financing (TIF) district encompasses two census tracts where 44.2 percent and 35.1 of the respective population is already living at or below the poverty line.[25] The concentration of poverty and subsidized affordable housing in Uptown has been the basis for some to reasonably argue that the neighborhood is already saturated beyond the tipping point.

Advocates of affordable housing tend to rest their arguments on the ideal of social equality, arguing that all citizens should have a right to decent, affordable housing. Chicago's Housing Affordability Research Consortium, a coalition of housing advocates, asserts that "one of the main obstacles to increasing public support for development of affordable housing is the perception that the free market will ultimately provide sufficient housing if left to do so."[26] The belief that affordable housing needs will be met through market demand, however, is untenable, in part because the very idea of affordable housing necessitates selling or renting below the market rate, which runs counter to market logic and requires government intervention to achieve.

The Chicago Rehab Network, a coalition of community organizations that advocates balanced development, frames affordable housing as a basic human right: "We believe we are better off with all people being better off—and having basic rights of food, clothing, and shelter. We believe it is in valuing affordability that we return to a core principle of democratic practice for our neighborhoods and city."[27] Here the "core principle of democratic practice" is construed as guaranteed equal rights to basic public goods for all citizens. By positing "housing" as one of these guaranteed rights, the argument carries a weighty, moral force. Counterarguments waged against affordable housing are most forceful when they respond with universal appeals for public goods that carry equal moral heft, such as public safety. The jockeying for moral high ground, abetted through inventive deployments of democratic rhetoric, underscores the arguments for and against housing at Wilson Yard that I discuss below.

In the following sections I analyze how democratic topoi are used flexibly in Uptown affordable housing debates to structure responses, mobilize action, establish ethos, and both support and blast competing understandings of what it means to live and act within democratic society. The two interconnected topoi I examine (democracy as an inclusive, deliberative process and democracy as justice) are by no means exhaustive.

TOPOS ONE: Democracy as an Inclusive Deliberative Process

Attacking the credibility of a democratic process is one effective rhetorical strategy for discrediting the outcome of that process, and Uptown residents who oppose affordable housing commonly resort to this tactic. When asked to comment on the legitimacy of the Wilson Yard planning process, one dissenter said, "Ha! And, how good was that study . . . if we can even call it a survey? Number one, I believe the charrettes were done in the middle of the day, and most people . . . have full time jobs and couldn't attend. Number two, it was far and away not a scientific survey. . . . I mean how many people actually did the survey, 400?" That this is factually incorrect (1,762 completed the survey, and charrettes were held on Saturday mornings) is beside the point. The "truth" of the matter is less important than the way this speaker discredits the ethos of the democratic process itself, thereby discrediting the resulting plan.[28] It is important to note that Chicago aldermen, as democratically elected representatives, are generally under no obligation to gather extensive community input on development projects.[29]

In contrast, proponents of affordable housing stress the inclusiveness of the community process as evidence that the outcome of Wilson Yard is democratic. The following Uptown renter since 1998, who organized for affordable housing, describes such a take: "The TIF did open a process for involvement. Our alderman opened the process for us. It helped to have a progressive alderman. I think in the Wilson Yard project, we all felt that there was a possibility of having a voice in the process." This resident establishes a moral ethos for both the process and its outcome by framing them as a consideration of people who "belonged here" and "who had the right to be here." This sentiment can easily be turned on its head, however. As mentioned earlier, the Wilson Yard process is sometimes discredited by claiming that because the demographics of the neighborhood have changed in the ten years that have elapsed since the process began, the plan no longer can be said to represent the demos. The perceived fairness and transparency of the democratic process continue to be debated; kairotic discursive jabs around the virtue or corruption of the process have been endemic in public discourse.

TOPOS TWO: Democracy as Justice

One might argue that the substance of "justice" within a liberal-democratic framework becomes clearer as one moves closer to concrete interaction on the ground, but this is not the case in Uptown. In some instances, justice is predicated on the fairness of the "democratic" process, and in other cases, justice is defined as development that represents all interests. Sometimes justice is perceived as the satisfaction of individual preference, and at others times, as social and economic equality for all. For some, "consensus" signals justice, and for others, it is a form of violence that evacuates politics from public debate, which, in Mouffe's words, becomes the "very condition" for the "elimination of pluralism from the public sphere."[30]

The simplest, but most consistent, reason used to argue against the affordable buildings at Wilson Yard is straightforwardly because "I don't want them." As an argument for public policy, this statement stands on a perception of democracy as a system that protects private interests and that legitimates planning decisions as "just" only if they appear to represent everyone's interests and seem to favor no one's. Alderman Shiller supports affordable housing at Wilson Yard as a project that self-consciously intervenes in the housing market to correct a material inequality, an arguably democratic impetus; however, she is often accused of being undemocratic in her favoring the poor and for supporting a project that divides the community. For example, one Uptown resident expressed this latter perception: "I think that [Shiller] is a divisive figure. . . . A good leader would be someone who could bring people together. I would suggest that if you wanted to have no trash on the streets and a more functional El station, then you [should not be seen as being] against the poor, hating them and wanting to kick them out. . . . That is inflammatory and divisive language. That's not the kind of language that fosters common ground."

Another argument, which attacks the claim that low-income individuals should have formally protected rights to remain in a gentrifying neighborhood, is offered by an Uptown homeowner since 2003: "There are no indigenous people in a neighborhood. It is a complete fallacy. Neighborhoods change and if they don't, they die. By that standard . . . Uptown used to be a playground for the wealthy and socialite in the 20s. Are those the indigenous people?!? . . . I don't agree with this idea that you have the right to live in any neighborhood that you want to live in. I don't have that right. You don't have that right. If I want to live in the Gold Coast [an affluent Chicago neighborhood], do I have that right? Does the government or someone have the obligation to subsidize my desire to live in the Gold Coast?"

This Uptowner aims to undercut the "rights"-based social-justice arguments in favor of affordable housing by suggesting that no one has the right to demand that the government fund his or her preference to stay in a particular neighborhood, and discredits housing at Wilson Yard by attacking the moral foundation that subsidized housing rests upon: namely, that people have a right to not be displaced by uneven market forces, that everyone has a right to decent housing, and that the government has an obligation to provide universal public goods. Further underscoring this argument is a perception of neighborhood change as natural, inevitable, and "good."

Although many Uptown Neighborhood Council members (that is, the Orange Shirts) were not living in Uptown during the Wilson Yard planning process, they nevertheless feel shut out of the process, arguing that the process was not democratic because it excluded them. One member says: "We were not part of the process. So, what this comes down to is that the community has been disrespected by those who are using our tax dollars to fund their development."

This comment implies, furthermore, that because property owners invest in a neighborhood by paying taxes, they should have a say in what is built. This argument is strengthened by the fact that the affordable housing is funded through TIF. Property owners who live within the Wilson Yard TIF district and oppose affordable housing will nevertheless pay over 30 percent of the project's projected cost of $151 million through property taxes. The construction of the housing is commonly framed by dissenters as an unjust means of reappropriating private money to fund public goods that are unwanted by taxpayers.[31]

An affordable housing activist responds to the argument that taxpayers should have more say than others in Wilson Yard's outcome: "You know its interesting this thing about hearing people saying they don't want their tax dollars spent on this project. . . . I mean we all sort of bemoan the fact that our tax dollars go to Iraq or whatever. It is more of a consumer ideal of citizenship; that I want to be able to direct my money wherever I think it will benefit me the most."

Here, the "consumer ideal of citizenship" is defined through a conflation of individual preference with the right to demand of the social contract exactly what one wants. Within this model, anything that is funded with my tax dollars that I do not want is perceived as unjust. Some homeowners believe they are paying for something that is not only harmful to their investment and the general public, but is celebrated as a democratically derived decision, for which they had no opportunity to intervene. Unlike other commodities, housing is not mobile—it is a socially relational investment. Housing creates a social and economic bond between neighbors because the return on investment is intertwined in the "success" and "quality" of one's neighbors and neighborhood. Such economic bounds between neighbors certainly come to head in gentrifying neighborhoods.

Discussing the rights of property owners in the neighborhood, one resident who moved to Uptown in 2001 adds: "I don't think that my rights as a property owner are any different than someone who rents. . . . I think I have equivalent rights. But that's the problem, I feel like people try to diminish my voice . . . to assert . . . that the condo owners are bad and only interested in increasing our property values. I don't think of my property values. I think of where I could walk with my daughter and not expose her to bad things."

This defense of condo owners is important. The dynamics in Uptown no doubt place individuals in contradictory positions; for example, a left-leaning middle-class homeowner who believes in equal access to decent, affordable housing must come to terms with the reality that such housing might conflict with his or her desire for better schools, higher property values, quality shopping, and safer streets. Interestingly, the resident quoted above is concerned about being silenced; yet he is, at least economically speaking, quite privileged in relation to citizens who would benefit from the right to affordable housing. Nevertheless, this claim of being silenced fits squarely into the democratic mythos, which claims, on the one hand, to protect private interests, and, on the other, to secure public goods. In attempting to protect the interests of those disenfranchised by gentrification, it would seem that Alderman Shiller and her supporters may have excluded the interests of those who do not support affordable housing. However, the inequities of redistribution within capitalism that systematically disenfranchise along class lines open the question of what responsibilities democratic citizens, leaders, and institutions have to "correct" such inequities.

Conclusion

The city is commonly theorized as a model of the democratic public sphere—a catalyst and depository for our collective and contradictory democratic hopes. Iris Marion Young described the city, which she considered an ideal model for liberal democracy, as the "being together of strangers." She understood "city life" as "a vision of social relations affirming group difference" that "instantiates social relations of difference without exclusion."[32] This compelling vision of the city as a space for greater tolerance, radical diversity without exclusion, dynamism, creativity, and openness has fueled wave after wave of urban planning schemes and community-based efforts designed to bring forth the "ideal city," which always seems just beyond reach. An Uptown renter since 1995 characterized the Wilson Yard controversy as a debate over what a city is and who has the right to live in one: "Some of this fight," she said, is "about what it means to live in the city. And how people imagine the city. . . . I think a lot of this has to do with the vision of what a city should be and what a city should function as."

Despite its shortcomings, the public sphere remains a very powerful topos. Rather than a means to a transcendent end, the model might be better understood as a process that can be used to make claims for rights that accommodate wide-ranging ideologies; a heuristic for locating the foundational questions, contradictions, limitations, and possibilities of democratic life; and as a conceptual and material site for rhetorical invention, where arguments that inspire and justify a range of "democratic" actions and sentiments can be discovered and effectively mobilized in this or that fleeting moment of persuasion.

Democratic rhetorics have, historically, inspired some of the most courageous (and fraught) extensions of rights. Concern over whether something is or is not democratic obscures the more important question of whether various social investments do or do not produce desirable and just social consequences. However, it is precisely the question of what constitutes the content of desirable and just action that democratic rhetorics cannot finally determine. Despite the deep contradictions within the public sphere, it is, ironically, the promised ideals reflected within the model that provide many with the courage and power, along with the rhetorical toolkit, to continually dream up and work toward new worlds that are more just and less cruel—worlds that we hope might finally transcend the horrors, contradictions, and suffering found within our material circumstances. And yet here again we hit the absolute limit, the endgame: for democracy alone cannot ensure peace, dignified actions, material stability, or shared conceptions of justice.

More than twelve years after a fire destroyed the old Wilson train yard in 1996, all that remains is an empty lot. The reasons for continual construction delays remain publicly murky but, in part, involve finances. In 2006 the movie theater company slated for construction in the original plan declared its investment as cost prohibitive and backed out of the project, leaving a gaping hole. In 2008 the Orange Shirts formed a nonprofit group called Fix Wilson Yard, which had raised over $60,000 for a legal injunction waged against Alderman Shiller, the city of Chicago, and the Department of Planning to stop the project in the name of "democracy." Their core claim was that TIF is being used illegally to fund a project that is detrimental to the community and antithetical to the will of the citizens.[33] Fix Wilson Yard phrases their mission as a collective, citizen-led movement to correct the "failures and abuses of the current Wilson Yard TIF and Redevelopment Plan while protecting the rights and interests of Chicago's taxpayers."[34] Meanwhile, affordable housing activists push to secure 183 units of affordable housing ten years (and counting) in the making from going up in smoke. The prevailing emptiness of Wilson Yard signifies the ultimate limits of democracy; unravels the conception of democracy as a morally virtuous, noncomplicit social project; and points to the demise of the democratic hope to secure a radically inclusive future that avoids exclusion.

NOTES

1. Burke, *Rhetoric of Motives*, 23.
2. Ibid., 276, 298–301.
3. The fieldwork presented in this essay is part of an ongoing ethnographic project that explores the democratic processes occurring in Uptown. All of the names of private individuals have been changed to protect their identity.
4. In the 2000 census Uptown's population of 63,000 was 42 percent non-Hispanic White, 21 percent African American, 20 percent Latino, 13 percent Asian, and 4 percent "other." Uptown's median income rose from 75 percent of the Chicago median in 1990 to 84 percent in 2000. See Haas et al., *Uptown Housing*, 12.
5. In 1998 the Wilson Yard Redevelopment Taskforce conducted a survey in six languages to gather community input. There were 1,762 respondents. Survey results were initially presented at two community meetings in October 1998. In June 1998 and again in June 2000 the public was invited to participate in a charrette-type planning session to discuss their reactions to the survey, brainstorm for new ideas, and voice dissent. The current proposal is based on the results of the survey and the input gathered at these charrettes.
6. In Chicago, 60 percent was $45,240 for a family of four in 2008. See City of Chicago, "Maximum Household Income." Further, in this latter building 23 percent of the units are restricted to "extremely low income" earners (households making up to 30 percent of the Chicago Area Median Income [AMI], which was $0–$22,600 for a family of four in 2006); 56 percent for "very low income" (households making 30–50 percent of the AMI at $22,600–$37,700; and 21 percent for "low income" (households making 50–80 percent of the AMI at $37,700–$59,600). See U.S. Department of Housing and Urban Development, "Median Income."
7. When I refer to stakeholders, I refer to the broadest definition: Uptown's renters, homeowners, business owners, workers, organizers, politicians, activists, homeless individuals, and so on.
8. Mouffe, *Democratic Paradox*, 105.

9. Paley, "Towards an Anthropology," 486.

10. Cruikshank, *Will to Empower,* 18.

11. Hauser, *Vernacular Voices,* 61.

12. Ibid., 64.

13. Ibid., 63.

14. Fleming, *City of Rhetoric,* 34

15. Ibid., 52.

16. Cruikshank, *Will to Empower,* 124.

17. Ibid., 41.

18. Ibid., 20, 22.

19. The sale of single-family homes dropped 15 percent between June 2005 and June 2006. Umberger, "Chicago Feels Housing Chill."

20. *Affordable Housing Conditions,* 2–4.

21. Ibid., 34.

22. Haas et al., *Uptown Housing,* 18–19. These agencies include: the city of Chicago's Department of Housing, the Illinois Development Agency, the Chicago Housing Authority, the U.S. Department of Housing and Urban Development, and the Housing Choice Voucher program (Section 8 program).

23. Chicago Metropolitan Agency for Planning, "Greater Chicago Housing."

24. This fear should be read within the context of CHA's Plan for Transformation, a ten-year, $1.5 billion overhaul of public housing that called for the demolition of approximately 22,000 of CHA's 39,000 units, the construction of 8,000 units, and the rehabilitation of the remaining 17,000 units. In its final phases in 2006, the plan called for a massive relocation of tens of thousands of public housing residents into mixed-income housing and onto the private rental market through the Housing Choice Voucher program. That Wilson Yard will be solely populated by voucher holders, thus functioning informally as public housing, is a real possibility.

25. Chicago Metropolitan Agency for Planning, "Greater Chicago Housing."

26. Nyden, Lewis, and Williams, *Affordable Housing,* 2.

27. *Affordable Chicago,* 2.

28. Other critiques of the process include that there were no trained facilitators present at the charrettes; that the decks were stacked for affordable housing at planning tables by Uptown community organizers and activists; and that the survey was unscientific and biased. The survey yielded more community input than is typical, but in terms of the survey's credibility, although "low cost housing" was ranked second behind "movie theater" in response to the question about desired development, "retail" yielded a much higher number of votes overall. Critics argue that this fact was obscured by the survey design, which asked people to check off very specific types of stores, such as Starbucks, Target, and so on, as opposed to one general box for a corporate retail chain.

29. Wilson Yard is partially funded through TIF, which captures incremental property tax growth over twenty-three years, redirecting it toward development projects within a given geographic area. While TIF law requires public hearings for all TIF proposals and a formal municipal approval process, "state law does not require the City to respond to those comments or act on public input regarding TIF districts." See Neighborhood Capital Budget Group, "TIF Process." Alderman Shiller, therefore, was not legally required to initiate the extensive community-based process that she did to determine what to build at Wilson Yard.

30. Mouffe, *Democratic Paradox,* 49.

31. The criticism that TIF may not promote economic development, and that it might negatively affect property values, is fairly novel in the sense that TIFs are typically criticized for prompting economic development without taking into account the social repercussions of gentrification. In this case, the TIF, often considered a neoliberal development policy, is being used both for prompting economic development and for counteracting the social consequences of development by constructing affordable units.

32. Young, *City Life and Difference*, 227.

33. In 2008 members of the Uptown Neighborhood Council started the Fix Wilson Yard Organization, which, as its Web site claims, "evolved as a grass-roots effort by dedicated volunteers in the Uptown community" to stop the project through legal injunction. The organizers wrote in August 2008: "Despite years of trying to work with the public officials to develop a responsible use of taxpayer dollars, they were not willing to listen. This summer, without announcement, they began pre-construction preparation, leaving us no choice but to start the legal battle." See Fix Wilson Yard, "What Is Wilson."

34. Fix Wilson Yard, "What Is Wilson."

WORKS CITED

Affordable Chicago: The Next Five Year Housing Plan, 2004–2008. Chicago: Chicago Rehab Network, June 2003.

Affordable Housing Conditions and Outlook in Chicago: An Early Warning for Intervention. Nathalle P. Voorhees Center for Neighborhood and Community Improvement. Chicago: University of Illinois at Chicago, March 2006.

Burke, Kenneth. *A Rhetoric of Motives*. Berkeley: University of California Press, 1969.

Chicago Metropolitan Agency for Planning. "Greater Chicago Housing and Community Development Website." Chicago Metropolitan Agency for Planning, July 20, 2008. http://www.chicagoareahousing.org/List_CCA.asp. Path: Uptown.

City of Chicago, "Maximum Household Income Area Median Chart." City of Chicago, July 15, 2008. http://www.aldermanshiller.com/content/view/450/169/. Path: 60% of the Area Median Income.

Cruikshank, Barbara. *The Will to Empower: Democratic Citizens and Other Subjects*. Ithaca, N.Y.: Cornell University Press, 1999.

Fix Wilson Yard, "What Is Wilson Yard?," Fix Wilson Yard, August 18, 2008. http://www.fixwilsonyard.org/index.html#Update.

Fleming, David. *City of Rhetoric: Revitalizing the Public Sphere in Metropolitan America*. Albany: SUNY Press, 2008.

Haas, Peter, Philip Nyden, Thomas Walsh, Nathan Benefield, and Christopher Giangreco. *The Uptown Housing and Land Use Study*. Chicago: Center for Urban Research and Learning, December 2002.

Habermas, Jürgen. *The Structural Transformation of the Public Sphere: An Inquiry into a Category of Bourgeois Society*. Translated by Thomas Burger with Frederick Lawrence. Cambridge, Mass.: MIT Press, 1989.

Hauser, Gerard A. *Vernacular Voices: The Rhetoric of Publics and Public Spheres*. Columbia: University of South Carolina Press, 1999.

Mouffe, Chantal. *The Democratic Paradox*. New York: Verso, 2000.

Neighborhood Capital Budget Group. "The TIF Process: Understanding the Process Step-by-Step." Neighborhood Capital Budget Group. 2005. August 8, 2006. http://www.ncbg.org/tifs/tif_process.htm.

Nyden, Phil, James Lewis, and Kale Williams, eds. *Affordable Housing in the Chicago Region: Perspectives and Strategies*. Housing Affordability Research Consortium, Chicago 2003.

Paley, Julia. "Towards an Anthropology of Democracy." *Annual Review of Anthropology* 31 (2002): 469–96.

Rawls, John. *A Theory of Justice*. Cambridge, Mass.: Harvard University Press, 1999.

Umberger, Mary. "Chicago Feels Housing Chill." *Chicago Tribune,* July 26, 2006. News-Bank Inc. University of Illinois at Chicago, Daley Lib. August 10, 2006. http://www .uic.edu/depts/lib/.

U.S. Department of Housing and Urban Development, "Median Income and Income Limits for Section 8 Program." U.S. Department of Housing and Urban Development, April 5 and September 9, 2006. http://www.huduser.org/datasets/il/ilo6/ index .html. Path: Illinois; Open the PDF file; Chicago-Naperville-Joliet.

Young, Iris Marion. *Justice and the Politics of Difference*. Princeton, N.J.: Princeton University Press, 1990.

The Public Work
of Critical Political
Communication

M. LANE BRUNER *[handwritten: The gap between symbolic vs. Real]*

Using the term "critical" political communication, I have worked over the last several years to complement mainstream approaches to political communication in a variety of ways: by applying critical philosophy to theories of the public, by considering the relationship between public discourse and public memory, by bringing together identity studies and critical rhetorical theory, and by otherwise seeking to characterize the healthy state. In pursuing this task, the following types of questions have emerged: What are the interrelationships among our real and imagined worlds? How does the construction of public memory impact the health of the state? What constitutes political corruption, and what constitutes effective resistance to corruption? What, in sum, is the relationship between identity construction and the healthy state? Working to answer such questions, I argue, is one way of doing the public work of rhetoric.

Few statements are as open to attack, however, as the claim to study the interrelationship between our real and imagined worlds. Critical philosophers since Kant have worked to reveal the *ineradicable* distance between subject and object, the sensory and linguistic limits of our knowledge, and the political consequences of those limits.[1] More recent poststructural and psychoanalytic philosophers have persuasively argued that humans cannot possibly have complete access to the real, and this is fully in line with Kantian epistemology.[2] Poststructuralist philosophy, based on the insights of semiotics, provides devastating critiques of objectivity.[3] Some psychoanalytic theorists suggest that the real constitutes that which cannot be represented; therefore, there is a fundamental and ultimately unbridgeable distance between the natural world and our symbolic and imaginary ways of experiencing that world.[4] Since the material/real ultimately escapes signification, and since no system of representation captures materiality in all its impossible detail, we are always negotiating our distance from the real in "fictional," "tropological," "imaginary," yet politically consequential, ways.[5]

If overly emphasized, however, accounts of the unbridgeable distance between our material existence and our discourses threaten political critique itself. If the real is ultimately unknowable, save through certain politically consequential fictions, then how are we to engage in ideological criticism? How is the enlightenment project of working to constantly test and improve discursive limits to proceed? If no one can stand outside of language or, worse yet, outside of some fictional fantasy (based on repression no less), then on what grounds can we responsibly critique discursive practice? What would constitute an improved human condition and an improved subjective practice? How can we even think about characterizing the relationship between the real and the discursive if the discursive *necessarily* distorts the real?

To my mind, much of critical philosophy, while rationally based upon the apparent laws of language in use, takes us too far away from the practical communication work being done by people seeking to improve the human condition. Yes, we should keep in mind Michel Foucault's warnings about disciplinary discourses, and how even the best-intentioned people can engage in all kinds of repressive measures, but he never gave up on the power of speaking truth to power.[6] Still, some poststructural and psychoanalytic approaches to human subjectivity direct our attention away from "commonsense" confrontations with human suffering, which is very *real*, and yet which all too often is caused by "sick" discourses.[7] The question is how to critique "sick" discourses, and upon what normative standard.

One normative standard for assessing and judging the distance between the material and discursive economies can be based, perhaps paradoxically enough, on the insights of critical philosophy, particularly as they relate to the political dimensions of our discursive negotiation with the real. Rather than focusing on the ineradicable gap between subject and object, however, the focus should be on the nature and consequences of that ever-changing gap. Perhaps we will learn that sometimes the gap between our material realities and the way we imagine them is ultimately progressive and helpful, while sometimes the gap leads directly to disaster. Critical political communication, therefore, can be usefully conceptualized as an ongoing investigation into the relationships among disciplinary discourses, identity construction, and the healthy state.[8] The critical analysis of communication is a political project related to the public work of rhetoric based on a clear set of guiding maxims taken from critical philosophy. For example, to engage in essentialism, or to fail to recognize that subjects change as discursive conditions change, is to ignore the rational dimensions of language in use; therefore, individual beliefs and collective identities based on intractable essentialist assumptions are by definition unreasonable.[9] Also, since all forms of consensus necessarily

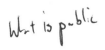
What is public

marginalize some set of discourses, constant vigilance toward the limits of consensus, and the necessary promotion of responsible transgression at those limits, is essential for political justice to prevail over time.

Based upon these and other normative assumptions, based in turn upon the insights of critical philosophy, I shall proceed, then, to offer a translation of the basic tenets of critical political communication, to provide a theoretical defense for what I think is a helpful critical conception of the public, and then to provide three increasingly complex examples of identity criticism that illustrate the public work of rhetoric described here. I begin by briefly characterizing how my own work attempts to move through critical philosophy to return to a more theoretically informed conception of the interrelationship between discourse and materiality.

THEORIZING CRITICAL POLITICAL COMMUNICATION

It does not take great philosophical insight to determine when your car runs out of gas, how many in a community are homeless, where people are starving, or whose daughter was killed in a war. It takes considerably more insight, however, to discern the primary political, economic, and discursive reasons why cars are so fuel inefficient, or why communities fail to provide housing for their more vulnerable members, or why much-needed food is thrown away instead of shipped where it is needed, or what idiocies start wars. We could quibble, of course, over definitions, or over the fact that we can really never fully understand how discursive political economies work, or over the impossibility of completely grasping all of the factors involved in war. Such quibbling would be meaningless, however, to those without energy, shelter, food, health, peace, or opportunity.

Because it is obvious that people have radically uneven access to the conditions for a happy subjectivity, it does take philosophical insight to understand why we as a species have proven ourselves utterly incapable of constructing widespread patterns of identification, and political systems based on those patterns, capable of radically ameliorating human misery. Our world is populated by billions who are poor, unhealthy, underfed, inadequately housed or educated, or at war. Even relatively happy communities are not as happy as they might be, and solutions to the basic problems of subjectivity and community continue to elude us. Why is this so? What can be done?

It is patently true that, on the whole, humankind is still very far from being enlightened about the nature of language in use and its necessary dangers, and this unnecessarily compounds human misery. Patterns of collective identity construction that were useful before capitalism (for example, tribal, religious, patriarchal), and at an earlier age of capitalism (the feudal monarchical state, the totalitarian state, the liberal nation-state), now stand in the way of more enlightened communicative practices, locally and globally. Today what passes for global political reason, at least in the "advanced" parts of the world, is a combination of neoliberal capitalism, cultural hybridization, and competitive self-interest. While "market democracy" works to dissolve the religious, ethnic, and cultural prejudices that not so long ago were the engines for world war, who can deny that our political world still teeters on the edge of catastrophe because of various "patriotisms" and essentialist reactions to the present process of cultural and economic globalization? It is crucial, therefore, to provide a convincing case for post-neoliberal, postnationalist, and postessentialist political visions, and doing the public work of rhetoric can help with this task.

If one is to investigate the relationship between identity and politics, or the relationships among public memory, national identity construction, and statecraft, grappling with critical philosophy is only the beginning. In addition to studying how language works, and how language inevitably leads to politically consequential patterns of identification,[10] it also helps to study the history of political theory (including constitutional theory) and the history of republican politics, since history suggests that the healthiest states tend to be republics of a certain type.[11] Close attention to the rhetorical arts and the history of rhetorical theory, with special attention to critical rhetorical theory, is also important, since one cannot responsibly critique the political except in light of rhetorical practice. This is not to say that the political can be *reduced* to rhetoric, for it also has material consequences, but to say instead that matters related to economic and state power can always be traced back to the ways we imagine our world, and the ways we are imagined by others.

Situated by such studies to consider the public work of rhetoric, in my own research I have reasoned as follows. Just because what individuals and groups believe to be true is always some distance from what is actually true, this does not entail that all beliefs are equally distant from the true. It is manifestly obvious that some people are more taken in by violent collective fantasies (for example, of racial superiority, fundamentalist dogmas) than others, that entire populations live in discursive worlds that produce highly destructive collective fantasies, and that other populations manage to live in a relatively healthy, happy, and peaceful prosperity. This is not to say there is "a perfect fantasy," or "a discourse that precisely mirrors the real," or any such thing, but to claim that the more we come to collectively understand the relationship between the ways we speak and the kinds of worlds we live in, the more enlightened as a species we become.

I have maintained in my work, therefore, that the public work of rhetoric is to critique the distance between our ideational and material economies *as best we can*.[12] What, I have asked, are the qualities of the ideational economy, or the economy of ideas in specific political communities? What constitutes healthy interrelationships between what people believe and the trajectory of policies and institutions? What can be done to remedy the political sickness that oftentimes follows when people's beliefs about their political situation seem to be radically at odds with their actual situation, and when those beliefs make material conditions worse not only for themselves but for others? How can we trace the difference between beliefs and conditions, and agency and structure, given the limits of language and subjectivity?

In an attempt to do this kind of work, I have critiqued, for example, the rhetorical dimensions of national identity construction, where I studied "strategic memory," ideological narratives of belonging, and discourses that challenged those narratives.[13] I have studied the process of economic globalization, the rhetoric of free trade that sustains it, and how that process and rhetoric impacts world politics.[14] I have analyzed and critiqued political protests in different states, as well as transnational norm revolutions.[15] I have also studied the global collapse of Communism, the newly hegemonic discourse of neoliberalism, and the political, economic, and discursive consequences of that transformation.[16] Together, this work has attempted to determine what political communication means from a critical theoretical stance and in so doing to engage in the public work of rhetoric at the level of collective identity construction.

THEORIZING THE PUBLIC WORK OF RHETORIC

But why does the critique of "political communication" constitute doing the public work of rhetoric? Characterizing precisely what "the public" is, and what the "public work" of rhetoric might be, is not so simple. The term "public" is a complicated concept with a long and interesting history. Just to name three of the many conceptions of the public that hardly overlap, there are feminist, neoliberal, and classical republican theories of the public.[17] Some feminist theories conceptualize the private sphere as the home and the public sphere as everywhere outside of the home; neoliberals tend to conceptualize the private sphere as the market and the public sphere as the state; and classical republican theories conceptualize the public sphere as a realm of critical citizenship outside of both the market and the state. My own theoretical approach at present is based in part on John Dewey's notion that "the public" is a term referring to concerns that issue indirectly from conjoint action; therefore, the most just political state is composed of institutions artfully constructed to address those ever-emerging concerns.[18] It is also based in part on the work of Ernesto Laclau, who argues that states and dominant cultures can usefully be conceived as "hegemonic" publics, or particular collections of factions or interests within a community who claim to represent the people.[19] In so doing, such "publics" always, according to a political logic based on the language philosophy of Laclau, necessarily create a field of unmet demands.[20] When isolated, those demands can be repressed, ignored, or integrated into the hegemonic system. When those unmet demands come together, however, they can form a "populist" movement, or "counterpublic," with sufficient force to transform the hegemonic public.[21] This new hegemonic public, however, in turn creates yet another set of unmet demands, and the process continues ad infinitum.[22] Every "people," every "public," every "hegemony," and every "counterpublic" is based on identifiable discourses, and one can trace the outlines of these discourses and determine what they exclude and why via rhetorical critique.[23] By engaging is such a critique, it becomes clear that some discourses, some counterpublics, some hegemonic publics, and some states do a better job of addressing the indirect consequences of conjoint action, and of improving the material conditions of human life, than others.

Based on the rule of law tempered by a reflexive appreciation for the violence of the law, consensus, and so on, healthy publics, and, therefore, healthy states, institutionally guarantee thick public spheres, and in so doing they maximally anticipate the indirect consequences of conjoint action by encouraging the proliferation of "counterpublics" with sufficient force to ensure the constant critique of laws, institutions, and disciplinary measures. Sick publics, and, therefore, sick states, conversely, suppress critical thought in a wide variety of ways, both intentionally and unintentionally, that cause them to fail to address the problems created by the indirect consequences of conjoint action.[24] Following such reasoning, the public work of rhetoric, conceived as critical political communication, is to better understand the relationship between discourse and the political in order to use the arts, educational systems, scholarly and civic activism, social movements, and revolutionary activity, when necessary, to productively transform sick publics and states into healthy publics and states.

The violence of human history, from the perspective of critical political communication offered here, is primarily the result of both intentional and unintentional forms of miscommunication (cynical and self-interested manipulation and ideological blindness); therefore, there is a direct relationship between the quality of human communication and the good state. When the hegemonic public's perception of history dramatically diverges from their actual history, or their actual condition and its causes, political illness is usually the result.

However, and as we know, political illness is all too obviously the norm.

One main reason for the persistence of political illness, and, therefore, an equally important reason for engaging in the public work of rhetoric, is the innumerable intentional "communicative" forces deployed precisely to keep people from realizing historical/material truths (Richard Nixon's "I am not a crook," William Clinton's "I did not have sex with that woman," George W. Bush's "They hate us because of our liberty," and so forth).[25] There are public relations agencies, marketers, spin doctors, brand managers, White House press agents, propaganda ministers, and similar forces all designed precisely to keep people informed in a particular way at the expense of other, perhaps more truthful, ways. These agents of self-interest are directly responsible for what Guy Debord defined as the "society of the spectacle," and when coupled with the "natural" dangers of identification (for example, being raised in idea-tional economies where religious fundamentalism, racism, jingoism, sexism flourish), we can plainly see some of the challenges facing those who would do the public work of rhetoric: revealing how these discourses contribute to the human condition so we can more responsibly reflect on them in order to construct the healthiest possible publics and the healthiest possible states.[26]

Three examples—one from the realm of fiction, one from recent world his-tory, and one more concrete and extended example taken from my work on West German national identity construction just prior to the reunification of Germany—will hopefully elaborate my main point that there is indeed a nec-essary distance between what people think and their material conditions, but that some distances are greater than others, that some politically consequen-tial fictions are more healthy than others, and that the public work of rheto-ric is to map and diagnose those distances as accurately as possible in order to help promote the healthy and beautiful state.

MAPPING THE UNSPEAKABLE AND DIAGNOSING IDENTITY

A first and clear example of the distance between what people think is true and what is actually true, and the terrible consequences of that distance, is taken from the experience of Paul Bäumer in Erich Remarque's *All Quiet on the Western Front*, a fictional account of a German soldier's experience of the First World War. As a young and impressionable student, Paul listens to his teacher Kantorek, who convinces him and his fellow students to join the "glorious" war effort. When Paul experiences war firsthand, however, he quickly sees the distance between the illusion of the "glory" of war and its grim reality. Returning home on leave, after seeing most of his comrades killed and with little hope of surviving the horrors of the front upon his return, Paul tries to reason publicly with the jingoistic men from his small hometown. He tells them of the horrors of the war, and of the excellent chance that nothing they desire will be accomplished by it. They angrily and summarily denounce his negative, though firsthand, characterization of the war, however, exclaiming that Paul knows "nothing about it!"[27] The narcotic of jingoistic patriotism has blinded them. In truth (albeit it a fictional truth in this case) it is of course the townspeople who know "nothing about it," save for their tragic and dis-torted way of imagining the war, its causes and it consequences.

But who will deny there was a *real* First World War that included hostili-ties between two political entities that were imagined (really) in politically consequential ways as "Germany" and "France"? Who will deny that careful historical work could, with relatively high precision, inform us about the ideational, economic, and material causes of the war?[28] Remarque provides a fictional example of how public perceptions of the First World War and its actual causes and effects were almost totally unrelated. In reality, however, we know the deadly results of those perceptions for millions of people consumed by their imaginary interpretation of the material situations in which they found themselves.

A more difficult but productive way to pursue the kind of mapping that I am calling for here is through a study of the attacks against the United States on September 11, 2001. The attacks, of course, were *very real,* and *very real* people died and suffered. So much is uncontroversial. But if we attempt to understand the historical causes of those attacks, and the ideational and material forces that were at work, things become much more complicated. We are once again dealing with a deep distance between what most people imagined was true and what was actually true, but we are now seeing an example of the very real *violence* of collective identity construction and public memory at work, as well as the forces of anti-enlightenment.

According to former president George W. Bush, the reason for the attacks was simple: the terrorists hated U.S. citizens because of their democracy and freedom. According to Bush, in his speech to a joint session of Congress in the immediate aftermath of the attacks: "They [the terrorists] hate what they see here in this chamber: a democratically elected government. Their leaders are self-appointed. They hate our freedoms: our freedom of religion, our freedom of speech, our freedom to vote and assemble and disagree with each other."[29]

Whether or not the causes of the "war on terror" are so simple, and they patently are not, this was the way the executive branch of the U.S. government characterized the attacks to the U.S. Congress and U.S. citizens, who collectively were far from able to think about other key historical factors: the history of U.S. imperialism, particularly in the Middle East; the relationship between the Central Intelligence Agency and the training of Osama bin Laden; the relationship between the Bush family and other executive branch officials and the Bin Laden family through their investments in the Carlyle Group; the former role of the United States in helping to establish and maintain a puppet regime in Iran; the use of Saddam Hussein in "managing" the so-called Kurdish problem; the influence of the oil industry on U.S. policy; not to mention long-term planning by the Pentagon for "managing" the Middle East, and so on. We are talking here about historical facts that are radically at odds with the characterization provided by the Bush administration.

Those who dared to question Bush's account, or to raise these *real* historical factors, were demonized.[30] Those who dared to mention such factors were *unwelcome,* not just by the Bush administration but by average U.S. citizens. One can hardly wonder about such historical repression, given the present nature of most political power, coupled with the global educational economy. Still, it is arguably the case that a more contextual and open public discussion, on a mass scale, about U.S. political history could help citizens to have a more accurate understanding of the historical, economic, and ideational factors involved in the attacks, and thus a better stance from which to judge executive branch policy (and to better understand the radical reactions to it).

One cannot help but wonder, however, if one wants to engage in the public work of rhetoric from a critical political perspective, about the forces that keep such fantasies alive and such historical realities at bay, and about the costs of the distances we see between fantasy and reality.

And who will deny that much of our lives today are passed in a similar way, and that the distance between the fictional experiences of Paul Bäumer and our own mediated experiences are not similar in historically and politically important ways, with a vast gulf existing between the material conditions of our world and our feeble understanding of those conditions? Surely Slavoj Žižek's argument in his *Welcome to the Desert of the Real* suggests that these distances are costly, connecting as he does the penchant in recent U.S. films for suggesting, á la *The Matrix* and *The Truman Show*, that citizens of the United States sense somehow deep down inside that they *really* do not have a clear sense about the world they inhabit, but that instead they inhabit a world that is somehow *staged* for them.[31]

But this is all the more reason to tackle more complicated (if less controversial) examples of the distance between the ideational and material economies. In this final example, the distance between public memory and historical fact is easy to trace. It is more difficult, however, to judge the consequences of that distance. Here we also see a collective identity that was "staged," in the sense that it was based on the willful erasure of certain historical facts, but it also was an identity that arguably "worked" to help construct a healthier state. National identity construction in West Germany, then, raises a number of issues, perhaps the most important of which is this: just because there is a distance between imagined identity and reality that can be mapped (through the analysis of "transgressive" speech), how can we tell a "good" imagined identity from a "bad" one?

As one can well imagine, among the hardest things to remember in Germany are the Holocaust in particular and World War II in general. So how, precisely, was the Holocaust and the Second World War remembered in Germany in the years leading up to reunification? What can this retracing of public memory tell us about the public work of rhetoric? I was initially drawn to this topic after viewing Holocaust denial programs on cable television when studying for my doctorate, and I was horrified by the "scientific" tactics used to "prove" their point. This led me to study Holocaust remembrance in Germany, and this led on to the study of public memory and national identity construction in East and West Germany.

It must be difficult, I thought, to have "pride" in one's "nation" when it was the "home" of National Socialism, whose adherents were the architects of the Holocaust. How, I wondered, could this history possibly be remembered in Germany?[32] To answer this question, I turned to a critical rhetorical method I have referred to elsewhere as a critical-materialist-genealogical approach (or "limit work").[33] It is an approach to analyzing discourse based in part on Foucault's notion of genealogy, or the diachronic transformation of "disciplinary" language over time. Limit work is *genealogical* because it traces the transformation of "disciplinary" discourses over time. It also draws in part upon the work of Ernesto Laclau, Chantal Mouffe, and other political theorists who in turn draw heavily upon contemporary theories of discourse.[34] It is *materialist* inasmuch as it assumes that there is indeed an empirically determinable material reality out there that is somehow distinct from the way it is apprehended through language, that the distribution of resources is part and parcel of the relationship between experienced reality and its transformation via language, and that that relationship is thoroughly political. It is rhetorical *criticism* inasmuch as it is a procedure by which one analyzes and diagnoses unhealthy differences between the real (for all intents and purposes) and the represented.

Following Foucault's and Laclau's notion that the limits of a hegemonic discourse are only revealed by transgressions, or antagonisms, I looked for dramatically rejected public discourses about the character of the German nation. I found my object of study when Philip Jenninger, the parliamentary president of West Germany, gave a speech memorializing the fiftieth "anniversary" of the *Kristallnacht,* or the night that Nazi intimidation of the Jews in Germany turned violent in November 1938. In his speech, Jenninger attempted to explain why the German people were initially drawn toward National Socialism, and he stressed Germany's responsibility for the crimes against the Jews, as well as the necessity of directly confronting Germany's Nazi past. Just moments into the speech he began to be heckled mercilessly, and eventually over fifty parliamentarians walked out as he spoke. Newspapers across West Germany claimed that Jenninger had "distorted German history" and attempted to "justify" Hitler. Within days, Jenninger was forced to resign.

What could Jenninger have possibly said that was so offensive? What "hegemonic limits" did he transgress, and what can that tell us about German national identity and its function in the late 1980s? To answer this question required doing some historical work, ensuring that multiple sources from a variety of ideological perspectives based on thorough scholarship converged on the same facts. There were two types of historical facts to determine: what actually happened materially, economically, and institutionally in Germany, and what actually was *said* about what happened. These are two radically different types of *archaeological* work—uncovering the historical conditions in a given period of time and uncovering the dominant and alternative discourses circulating in that same period of time. This, in short, is the materialist part of the project: determining through thorough historical research the *actual* material conditions and the *actual* discursive conditions in the period and situation under review. The next step is genealogical: how did relevant discourses and conditions change over time?

Here is what I discovered. First, the division of Germany at the end of World War II had a profound impact on public memory, and if one were to even risk discussing the Holocaust and National Socialism in either East or West Germany, one had to be very careful indeed. One needed to proceed carefully because the defenders of the National Socialist state, the perpetrators of that state's crimes, and most of the lingering consequences of that state and its crimes had been erased from public memory. Jenninger problematically dared to claim publicly that "the German people" had been perpetrators, making a clear distinction between "we, the German people" and "the victims," which was *completely* unacceptable ideologically. Here is why. After the war, Communists in East Germany could hardly be called the perpetrators of National Socialism, since it was the Communists themselves who had helped to defeat the Nazis. It was those West German capitalists, under the disguise of democracy, who were the real perpetrators! But how could one blame the West Germans for National Socialism? After all, they were now clearly on the side of the democratic and capitalist West. It was those East Germans who were still totalitarians! Of course the truth was that the *real* perpetrators were still living out their old age in both East and West Germany, but they had been conveniently erased from public recognition.

Interestingly enough, a few years earlier Germany's president Richard von Weizsäcker had delivered a speech that was universally praised for "properly" memorializing the fortieth anniversary of the end of World War II. Perhaps it should come as no surprise that in his speech he also spoke of the victims of National Socialism, including the Jews, but the ultimate victims in his speech were the German people themselves, who had been "tricked" by Hitler and a handful of his henchmen, and who had "suffered" the division of themselves (politically and spiritually, as a people). Summing up his commemoration by observing that the Germans had suffered long enough, he then made a plea to the international community to reunite the divided German state.

As we all know, Weizsäcker's plea was heard. East and West Germany were reunited not long after Jenninger's departure, and soon a new memorial was built to publicly commemorate the Holocaust in the center of Berlin.[35]

We know that the U.S. government actively promoted the image of West Germany as an ally against Communism, and that President Ronald Reagan visited West Germany just before reunification, claiming in advance that "none of [the West German people] who were adults and participated in any way" in World War II were still alive, and "very few . . . even remembered the war."[36] Why would Reagan fictionally erase Germans his own age? And he did more. Reagan also visited a cemetery in Bitburg, where a few SS soldiers were buried, giving a short speech standing beside German chancellor Helmut Kohl. When challenged by reporters in advance of his visit, Reagan replied, "there's nothing wrong with visiting that cemetery where those young [SS] men are victims of Nazism also. . . . They were victims, just as surely as the victims in the concentration camps."[37] How are we to judge these erasures and equivocations?

We should not deceive ourselves into thinking that all of those who were sympathetic to National Socialism *really* disappeared; instead, their "disappearance" was put to use. According to Steven Brockmann, the U.S. executive branch wanted to "construct a history that would be useful to Cold War Ideology."[38] Kathryn M. Olson notes that Reagan "seemed motivated by gratitude to Kohl for being the European point player in favor of deploying Pershing 2 and cruise missiles," and he was also seeking support for his space-based missile defense plan and for involvement in Nicaragua.[39] "According to Allied decree in 1945," notes Brockmann, "the German Reich had ceased to exist, and as it was decreed so it came to pass. Suddenly there was no more German Reich, and there were no more Nazis, and the United States began to use the services of those who had ceased to be Nazis in the continued fight against communism, the new Nazism."[40] No doubt the Soviet Union had its "back story" as well.

But perhaps it is just "as well." After all is said and done, the German state continues to pay reparations, it is diplomatically deferential to Israel, and from all accounts the Germans have become one of the most "democratic" peoples in the West. Not only have most traces of National Socialism been suppressed in that state, but the country is now a leading member of the New World Order of market democracies. The country is actively participating in the ongoing construction of the European Union (though perhaps from too neoliberal a bias), which is helping to temper the forces of ethnic and cultural nationalism with constitutional patriotism (though neoliberal influences continue to stand in the way of a reasonable European constitution). The outcome on the whole, however, has hardly been negative for world politics, given that a peaceful, social democracy based on republican principles and the rule of law has come to replace two authoritarian regimes.

But what of the costs of these erasures, and of equating the German people with the victims of National Socialism? Who, today, is publicly discussing the historical roots of National Socialism and the potential relationship between Fascism and capitalism? What are the requisite conditions for Fascism to reemerge? What would those conditions look like, and how might we anticipate them? How might we protect ourselves from another outbreak of ethnic nationalism in Europe? What, in sum, does it mean for the human political community to have the causes and perpetrators of National Socialism "off limits" for public discussion, save for in a highly mythologized way?

These are questions for the future, perhaps, but the political consequences of collective identity construction are continuously emerging around the world. Even as I write, "Georgia" and "Russia" are fighting viciously over "Ossetia." What does "Ossetian," "Georgian," and "Russian" identity mean in the conflict, and how are those identities being "mobilized"? Collective identity construction can disrupt even normally peaceful and prosperous states, like Canada. Just over a decade ago, an ethnic-nationalist separatist movement erupted in Quebec that almost tore the state in two, though the movement ideologically claimed it was multicultural.[41] Why should Quebec secede from Canada? How do those who identify themselves as "Québécois" imagine their historical relationship with Great Britain? Why would an ethnic-nationalist movement insist on its multicultural status?

And just where does the logic of sovereignty stop? In the wake of the collapse of the Soviet Union, there was a "parade of sovereignties," as "peoples" rose up to claim their independence. Not only large territories known as Lithuania, Armenia, Ukraine, and Georgia, but even many of the territorial units within the Russian Federation declared their sovereignty. Even some *cities* declared their sovereignty![42] Since national identity construction is still going strong all across the world, and wars between "sovereign" states seem to erupt on a monthly basis, one way we can do the public work of rhetoric is by mapping the distance between history and memory, understanding how far those imaginaries are from historical fact, and with what consequence.

CONCLUDING THOUGHTS

The previous three examples of the public work of rhetoric as critical political communication are not meant to delimit the objects of such study, or to claim that this is the only way to responsibly engage in "public work." Language works to create identities in all sorts of ways: in ways that increase and decrease human suffering. There are numbers of suitable subjects for such work, from the intrapersonal to the transnational, and we need not limit our focus to broad collective identities such as race, gender, ethnicity, class, or nationality. All discourses, or all embodied ways of interpreting the world, are "disciplinary." No matter what the discourse, some statements are simply unacceptable, others are unwelcome. How might we map these "unspeakable" zones in order to determine their effects?

What of the pressing questions of our own day? Is the skyrocketing federal debt a problem or not? Is global warming a real threat? What is the world's oil supply today, really, and what does that suggest for our long-term economic and political future? Do the "evildoers" have weapons of mass destruction, and who, really, are the evildoers? Why is it "OK" for Pakistan to possess nuclear weapons, but not Iran? Do Iran, Iraq, and North Korea truly constitute an "axis of evil"? What should be done about illegal immigration? Should we have built the prisons in Guantanamo Bay and in other secret locations? Are our state or local school boards corrupt, and what, after all, constitutes responsible education in an age that would become postessentialist? There are so many questions about our world that there is really no time, or will, to learn the answers. So what to do? Must so-called elites manage information for us? How can we trust that they themselves are not misguided or misinformed, or, worse yet, self-interested and deceptive? Can we reform our educational system to reinforce the average citizen's ability to weigh public argument?[43]

What role can communication scholars play in alleviating this world-historical problem of the persistent distance between fact and opinion, between knowledge and belief, and between the unfolding of history and its complex causes and the way that history is characterized and interpreted? If rhetorical critics could even begin to unravel the mysteries that are these distances, what realistic chance do they have of actually impacting the trajectory of political events?[44]

It seems prudent, therefore, to consider how we might transform our pedagogical and research practices in order to make a world-historical impact on the process of identity construction. Recognizing the seemingly innumerable anti-enlightenment forces that stand in our way—from metaphysically comforting essentialisms to cynical and unenlightened self-interest—there is much to be done. As Carolyn Miller notes elsewhere in this volume, it may well be that "dissimulation and concealment are indeed necessary for rhetorical success." That said, however, different types of "concealment" lead to different types of consequences. While we may indeed need to mask our arts of critique in order to make them more effective, let us hope Miller is incorrect when she claims that "such a project cannot be a global or a programmatic one." If that is the case, then the un-enlightened forces of identity construction will undoubtedly defeat the forces of enlightenment.

NOTES

1. Critical philosophy differs from analytic philosophy. See Todd May, *Gilles Deleuze: An Introduction* (New York: Cambridge University Press, 2005), 1–25. Ernesto Laclau and Slavoj Žižek recently engaged in an interesting debate on the nature of the real and the political. See Slavoj Žižek, "Against the Populist Temptation," *Critical Inquiry* 32 (Spring 2006): 551–74; Ernesto Laclau, "Why Constructing a People Is the Main Task of Radical Politics," *Critical Inquiry* 32 (Summer 2006): 646–80; and Slavoj Žižek, "Schagend, aber nicht Treffend!" *Critical Inquiry* 33 (Autumn 2006): 185–211. See also Kant, *Political Writings;* Mouffe, *Democratic Paradox;* and Laclau, *On Populist Reason,* for a sampling of critical political theory.

2. Arthur Schopenhauer neatly characterized Kant's fundamental argument: "Kant's greatest merit is the distinction of the phenomenon from the thing-in-itself, based on the proof that between things and us there always stands the intellect, and that on this account they cannot be known according to what they may be in themselves. . . . The complete diversity of the ideal from the real, is the fundamental characteristic of Kantian philosophy" (*World as Will,* 417–18). If Kant is correct, this means that the public work of rhetoric must deal directly with the nature of this "intellect," or the discursive ways in which we come to negotiate and understand our world.

3. Semiotic theory can be traced to the rather different work of Ferdinand de Saussure and Charles S. Peirce. The main difference between their two semiotic theories is that Saussure, a linguist, did not feature the referent (or the material object), as did Peirce, with, in my opinion, serious consequences for *practical* thinking about the relationship between systems of signification and the material world. For a succinct discussion of

these two theorists and their impact on studies of subjectivity, see Silverman, *Subject of Semiotics.*

4. For a representative interpretation of Jacques Lacan's theory of the Real, see Žižek, "Schagend, aber nicht Treffend," 195–97.

5. For an introduction to the political dimensions of Lacan, see Stavrakakis, *Lacan.* See also McConnell and Gillett, "Lacan"; Biesecker, "Rhetorical Studies."

6. On how the discursive construction of madness has itself been historically mad, see Foucault, *History of Madness;* see also Foucault, *Fearless Speech.*

7. The term "common sense" is fraught with conceptual complications that cannot be explored adequately here. For those interested in the range of such complications, see Schaeffer, *Sensus Communis;* Holton, "Bourdieu"; Lyotard, "Sensus Communis"; Bormann, "Some 'Common Sense.'"

8. One lives within a personal state (both a material state and a "state of mind"), a web of interpersonal and professional "states" (and states of mind), and within a web of collective states (political, religious, racial, gendered, and so forth) with their material and imagined dimensions. All of these states are interwoven with the ultimately unknowable and ever-emerging reality of nature. The public work of rhetoric, conceptualized as the construction of the healthy state, therefore, has multiple dimensions and can take place at many levels. My focus here will only be on the rhetorical construction of collective (national) identities.

9. Once one is aware of the discursive dimensions of subjectivity, however, one still may engage in "strategic essentialism" when combating essentialist problems. See Martin, "Methodological Essentialism." See Sandoval, *Methodology of the Oppressed,* for other types of "differential consciousness."

10. The literature on identity and politics is vast and ranges from the political dimensions of personal identity, to debates in aesthetics, to collective identity construction. For a mere sampling, see Goffman, *Presentation of Self;* Morgan, *Inventing the People;* Anderson, *Imagined Communities;* Bourdieu, *Language and Symbolic Power;* Sennett, *Fall of Public Man;* Rajchman, *Identity in Question.* Such texts, obviously, only scratch the surface of what is available on the broad topic of language and identity.

11. I defend this claim in detail in my most recent book, *Democracy's Debt.*

12. One well-known attempt to explain the logic of the relationship between the material and ideational economy was made by Karl Marx. Marx, *German Ideology.* For a critique of the essentialist assumptions in Marxism, see Laclau and Mouffe, *Hegemony and Socialist Strategy.*

13. See Bruner, *Strategies of Remembrance;* Bruner, "Rhetorics of the State.

14. Bruner, *Democracy's Debt,* esp. chapter 2; Bruner, "Taming 'Wild' Capitalism"; Bruner, "Global Constitutionalism"; Bruner, "Global Governance."

15. Bruner, "Carnivalesque Protest"; Bruner, "Norm Revolutions"; Bruner and Marin, "'Democracies' in Transition."

16. Bruner and Morozov, *Market Democracy.*

17. Weintraub, "Theory and Politics."

18. See Dewey, *Public and Its Problems.*

19. For histories and theories related to the construction of "peoples," see Morgan, *Inventing the People;* Bruner, "Rhetorical Theory"; McGee, "In Search of 'the People.'"

20. For Laclau's theory of the public, see *On Populist Reason.*

21. On the notions of subaltern and counterpublics, see Fraser, "Rethinking the Public Sphere"; Asen and Brouwer, *Counterpublics and the State;* Warner, *Publics and Counterpublics.*

22. No hegemonic system—and, therefore, no state—can fully meet the demands of everyone, and thus there is always a certain "violence" associated with such systems/states. Derrida grappled with the violence of justice and its relationship to the limits of rationality and reason in several of his later essays. See Derrida, *Rogues*. For a much earlier essay dealing with similar issues, see Benjamin, "Critique of Violence."

23. See Bruner, "Rhetorical Criticism."

24. Deconstructionists are right to point out that "fields of vision" are enabled by a "blind spot," or a necessary and organizing absence. This, then, is the radical gap within subjectivities themselves, and it is not the same as the gap between subjectivity and materiality.

25. For an enlightening look at deceptive public memory and history education in the United States, see Loewen, *Lies My Teacher Told Me*. For a look at how corporate communication impacts "public" spaces, see Klein, *No Logo*; Mayhew, *New Public*.

26. Debord, *Society of the Spectacle*; Debord, *Comments on the Society*.

27. Remarque, *All Quiet on the Western Front*, 165–67.

28. This is hardly a controversial claim, for the Second World War can be traced in no small part to debt relations between the United States, Britain, and France, and the ultimate impact of U.S. debt policy on German war reparations (though there were many other important reasons, not the least of which was the political/economic history of nationalism). On the role of debt in the world wars, see Hudson, *Super Imperialism*, 58–161.

29. For a complete transcript of Bush's address, titled "Freedom at War with Fear," see http://www.whitehouse.gov/news/releases/2001/09/20010920-8.html (accessed May 24, 2006). Frighteningly enough, Joseph Goebbels's "New Year's Speech" on December 31, 1939, has an eerily familiar ring: "[Our enemies] hate our people because [they are] decent, brave, industrious, hardworking and intelligent. They hate our views, our social policies, and our accomplishments. They hate us as a Reich and as a community. They have forced us into a struggle for life and death. We will defend ourselves accordingly." For a transcript of the speech, see http://www.calvin.edu/academic/cas/gpa/goeb21.htm (accessed May 26, 2006).

My point in drawing this comparison is not to equate the Bush administration and National Socialism (although his family's financial dealings are quite "interesting"), but simply to provide examples of how official state discourse tends to create grand and abstract explanations for very real and specific historical causes, and since the general public's understanding of historical facts is so thin, these abstract explanations become the basis for their own understanding, oftentimes with dire consequences. For accounts of Prescott Bush's "interesting" financial activities, see Aris and Campbell, "How Bush's Grandfather"; Phillips, *American Dynasty*.

30. Bill Mahr and the Dixie Chicks are two of the more well known examples, though content analyses of actual media coverage leading up to the war reveals the almost complete absence of voices providing anything in the way of historical or political context. See, for example, Hudson Mohawk Independent Media Center, "Independent Media in a Time of War," http://video.google.com/videoplay?docid=-6546453033984487696 (accessed June 8, 2008). Cynics might argue that any account of political context would necessarily be biased, and some psychoanalysts might argue that of course the hegemonic public is incapable of dealing more directly with the terrible Thing (ultimately unknowable Nature), but this, I maintain, is to categorically confuse the necessary distance between language and materiality and the relative distance between accounts of materiality and that which actually occurred.

31. Žižek, *Welcome to the Desert*. See also Baudrillard, *Simulacra and Simulation*, 29–40. According to the theoretical perspective presented here, the "stage" is set in both intentional and unintentional ways.

32. For a sampling of the literature on public memory, memorialization, and the politics of memory, especially in Germany, Russia, and Canada, see Bruner, *Strategies of Remembrance*, 125–35.

33. Bruner, "Rhetorical Criticism."

34. See Laclau, *On Populist Reason*. However, Laclau completely ignores the important work on collective identity construction done by rhetoricians in the United States.

35. The memorial stirred considerable controversy. For a thorough critique of Holocaust memorials as an exemplary instance of the public work of rhetoric, see Carrier, *Holocaust Monuments*.

36. Hartmann, *Bitburg in Moral*, xii.

37. Ibid., xiv. Kathryn M. Olson also discusses how Reagan attempted to redefine the notion of "victims" prior to and during his Bitburg visit. See Olson, "Controversy."

38. Brockmann, "Bitburg Deconstruction."

39. Olson, "Controversy."

40. Brockmann, "Bitburg Deconstruction," 163.

41. Bruner, *Strategies of Remembrance*, 68–88; Charland, "Constitutive Rhetoric."

42. On the parade of sovereignties, see Bruner, *Strategies of Remembrance*, 40–41.

43. The debate between those supporting elite management of public opinion and those supporting public education is nicely traced in the work of Walter Lippmann and John Dewey. See Lippmann, *Public Opinion*; Dewey, *Public*.

44. Rhetorical critics, who tend to publish their work in obscure academic journals, are, as would be expected, generally ignored when it comes to their political warnings. For example, in 1939 Kenneth Burke penned a critical essay on Hitler's rhetoric, warning that Hitler's dark "magic" was likely to spell doom for Europe. Nobody listened. See Burke, "Rhetoric of Hitler's Battle."

WORKS CITED

Althusser, Louis. "Ideology and Ideological State Apparatuses." In *Lenin and Philosophy*, 127–86. Translated by Ben Brewster. London: New Left Books, 1977.

Anderson, Benedict. *Imagined Communities*. New York: Verso, 1991.

Aris, Ben, and Duncan Campbell. "How Bush's Grandfather Helped Hitler's Rise to Power." *Guardian*, September 25, 2004.

Asen, Robert, and Daniel C. Brouwer. *Counterpublics and the State*. Albany: SUNY Press, 2001.

Baudrillard, Jean. *Simulacra and Simulation*. Translated by Sheila F. Glaser. Ann Arbor: University of Michigan Press, 1994.

Benjamin, Walter. "Critique of Violence." In *Reflections*, edited by Peter Demetz, 277–300. New York: Schocken, 1978.

Biesecker, Barbara. "Rhetorical Studies and the 'New' Psychoanalysis: What's the Real Problem? Or Framing the Problem of the Real." *Quarterly Journal of Speech* 84 (1998): 222–59.

Bormann, Dennis R. "Some 'Common Sense' about Campbell, Hume, and Reid: The Extrinsic Evidence." *Quarterly Journal of Speech* 71 (November 1985): 395–421.

Bourdieu, Pierre. *Language and Symbolic Power*. Cambridge, Mass.: Harvard University Press, 1991.

Brockmann, Stephen. "Bitburg Deconstruction." *Philosophical Forum* 17 (1986): 159–74.

Bruner, M. Lane. "Carnivalesque Protest and the Humorless State." *Text and Performance Quarterly* 25 (2005): 137–56.

————. *Democracy's Debt: The Historical Tensions between Political and Economic Liberty.* New York: Humanity Press, 2009.

————. "Global Constitutionalism and the Arguments over Free Trade." *Communication Studies* 53 (2002): 25–39.

————. "Global Governance and the Critical Public." *Rhetoric & Public Affairs* 6 (2003): 687–708.

————. "Norm Revolutions and World Order." *Rhetoric & Public Affairs* 9 (2006): 153–81.

————. "Rationality, Reason and the History of Thought." *Argumentation* 20 (2006): 185–208.

————. "Rhetorical Criticism as Limit Work." *Western Journal of Communication* 66 (2002): 281–99.

————. "Rhetorical Theory and the Critique of National Identity Construction." *National Identities* 7 (2005): 309–28.

————. "Rhetorics of the State: The Public Negotiation of Public Character in Germany, Russia, and Quebec." *National Identities* 2 (2000): 159–74.

————. *Strategies of Remembrance: The Rhetorical Dimensions of National Identity Construction.* Columbia: University of South Carolina Press, 2002.

————. "Taming 'Wild' Capitalism." *Discourse & Society* 13 (2002): 167–84.

Bruner, M. Lane, and Noemi Marin. "'Democracies' in Transition in the New Europe." *Controversia* 5 (2007): 15–22.

Bruner, M. Lane, and Viatcheslav Morozov, eds. *Market Democracy in Post-Communist Russia.* Leeds, England: Wisdom House Academic Publishers, 2005.

Burke, Kenneth. "The Rhetoric of Hitler's Battle." *Southern Review* 5 (1939): 1–21.

Carrier, Peter. *Holocaust Monuments and National Memory Culture in France and Germany since 1989.* New York: Berghahn Books, 2005.

Charland, Maurice. "Constitutive Rhetoric: The Case of the *Peuple Québécois.*" *Quarterly Journal of Speech* 73 (1987): 133–50.

Debord, Guy. *Comments on the Society of the Spectacle.* Translated by Malcolm Imrie. 1988. Reprint, New York: Verso, 2002.

————. *The Society of the Spectacle.* Translated by Donald Nicholson-Smith. 1967. Reprint, New York: Zone Books, 1995.

Derrida, Jacques. *Rogues: Two Essays on Reason.* Translated by Pascale-Anne Brault and Michael Nass. Stanford, Calif.: Stanford University Press, 2005.

Dewey, John. *The Public and Its Problems.* Athens: Ohio University Press, 1954.

Eckermann, Johann P. *Conversations with Goethe.* Cambridge, Mass.: Da Capo Press, 1998.

Foucault, Michel. *Fearless Speech.* Edited by Joseph Pearson. N.p.: Semiotext(e) Foreign Agents, 2001.

————. *History of Madness.* Translated by J. Murphy and J. Khalfa. New York: Routledge, 2006.

————. "What Is Enlightenment?" Translated by Catherine Porter. In *The Foucault Reader,* edited by Paul Rabinow, 32–50. New York: Pantheon Books, 1984.

Fraser, Nancy. "Rethinking the Public Sphere." In *Habermas and the Public Sphere,* edited by Craig Calhoun, 109–42. Cambridge, Mass.: MIT Press, 1992.

Goffman, Erving. *The Presentation of Self in Everyday Life.* New York: Doubleday, 1959.

Hartmann, Geoffrey, ed. *Bitburg in Moral and Political Perspective.* Bloomington: Indiana University Press, 1986.

Holton, Robert. "Bourdieu and Common Sense." *Substance: A Review of Theory and Literary Criticism* 26 (September 1997): 38–52.

Hudson, Michael. *Super Imperialism: The Origin and Fundamentals of U.S. World Dominance.* Sterling, Va.: Pluto Press, 2003.

Kant, Immanuel. "An Answer to the Question: What Is Enlightenment?" In *What Is Enlightenment?* edited by James Schmidt, 58–64. Berkeley: University of California Press, 1996.

———. "*Beantwortung der Frage: Was ist Aufklärung?,*" *Berlinische Monatsschrift* 4 (1784): 481–94.

———. *Kant: Political Writings.* Edited by Hans Reiss. New York: Cambridge University Press, 1991.

Klein, Noemi. *No Logo.* New York: Picador, 2002.

Laclau, Ernesto. *On Populist Reason.* New York: Verso, 2005.

———. "Why Constructing a People Is the Main Task of Radical Politics." *Critical Inquiry* 32 (2006): 646–80.

Laclau, Ernesto, and Chantal Mouffe. *Hegemony and Socialist Strategy.* New York: Verso, 1985.

Lippmann, Walter. *Public Opinion.* New York: Simon and Schuster, 1997.

Loewen, James W. *Lies My Teacher Told Me: Everything Your American History Textbook Got Wrong.* New York: Simon and Schuster, 1996.

Lyotard, J. F. "Sensus Communis: The Subject in *Statu Nascendi.*" In *Who Comes After the Subject?* edited by E. Cadava, P. Conner, and J. Nancy, 217–35. New York: Routledge, 1991.

Martin, Jane R. "Methodological Essentialism, False Difference, and Other Dangerous Traps." *Signs* 19 (1994): 630–75.

Marx, Karl. *The German Ideology.* Amherst, N.Y.: Prometheus Books, 1998.

May, Todd. *Gilles Deleuze: An Introduction.* New York: Cambridge University Press, 2005.

Mayhew, Leon H. *The New Public.* New York: Cambridge University Press, 1997.

McConnell, Douglas, and Grant Gillett. "Lacan for the Philosophical Psychiatrist." *Philosophy, Psychiatry and Psychology* 12, no. 1 (2005): 63–75.

McGee, Michael C. "In Search of 'the People': A Rhetorical Alternative." *Quarterly Journal of Speech* 61 (1975): 235–49.

Morgan, Edmund S. *Inventing the People.* New York: W. W. Norton, 1988.

Mouffe, Chantal. *The Democratic Paradox.* New York: Verso, 2000.

Olson, Kathryn. M. "The Controversy over President Reagan's Visit to Bitburg." *Quarterly Journal of Speech* 75 (1989): 129–51.

Perelman, Chaim. "The Rational and the Reasonable." In *Rationality Today,* edited by T. F. Geraets, 213–14. Ottawa: University of Ottawa Press, 1979.

Phillips, Kevin. *American Dynasty: Aristocracy, Fortune, and the Politics of Deceit in the House of Bush.* New York: Viking, 2004.

Rajchman, John, ed. *The Identity in Question.* New York: Routledge, 1995.

Remarque, Erich Maria. *All's Quiet on the Western Front.* Translated by A. W. Wheen. New York: Fawcett Columbine, 1996.

Sandoval, Chela. *Methodology of the Oppressed.* Minneapolis: University of Minnesota Press, 2000.

Schaeffer, John D. *Sensus Communis: Vico, Rhetoric, and the Limits of Relativism.* Durham, N.C.: Duke University Press, 1990.

Schopenhauer, Arthur. *The World as Will and Representation,* Vol. 1. New York: Dover, 1969.

Sennett, Richard. *The Fall of Public Man*. New York: W. W. Norton, 1992.

Silverman, Kaja. *The Subject of Semiotics*. New York: Oxford University Press, 1983.

Sloterdijk, Peter. *Critique of Cynical Reason*. Minneapolis: University of Minnesota Press, 1987.

Stavrakakis, Yannis. *Lacan and the Political*. New York: Routledge, 1999.

Warner, Michael. *Publics and Counterpublics*. New York: Zone Books, 2005.

Weintraub, Jeff. "The Theory and Politics of the Public/Private Distinction." In *Public and Private in Thought and Practice: Perspectives on a Grand Dichotomy*, edited by Jeff Weintraub and Krishan Kumar, 1–42. Chicago: University of Chicago Press, 1997.

Žižek, Slavoj. "Against the Populist Temptation." *Critical Inquiry* 32 (2006): 551–74.

———. "Schagend, aber nicht Treffend!" *Critical Inquiry* 33 (2006): 185–211.

———. *Welcome to the Desert of the Real*. New York: Verso, 2002.

Rhetorical Engagement in the Cultural Economies of Cities

JOHN M. ACKERMAN

"The power of place—the power of ordinary urban landscapes to nurture citizen's public memory, to encompass shared time in the form of shared territory—remains untapped for most working people's neighborhoods in most American cities."[1]

"Civic engagement," as a policy realm and educational scene, appears to accurately name the rhetorical investments of citizen-scholars in the public life of their cities. "Civic" is a keyword in rhetoric,[2] as it is synonymous with "city" and thus recalls the venerable claim that rhetoric once had over public life in the polis, located physically and symbolically in the public space of the agora. As many have noted, throughout antiquity the achievement of civic virtue by the (exclusively male) citizenry was measured by the health and vitality of the polis,[3] and the agora was the preeminent site for both policy and economic deliberation and, as such, a daily commemoration to the identity and power of the city. The word "civic" also, and to this day, is synonymic with civility,[4] indexing a cultural investment in consensual discourse, the rule of law and logic, and a "republican" political style that features open debate, oratory, agreement, and tolerance.[5] Civic engagement taken at its word(s) gestures to the endemic nature of rhetorical practice in the polis because citizens engage each other through words and actions to rewrite the symbolic terrain of public life, recorded in the material artifact of the city.

The word "engagement" connotes less of rhetoric's civic legacy, but its claim to keyword status is in its gesture to the indispensable role of the interlocutor in public deliberation and the indispensable role of public deliberation in a participatory democracy. Democracy in civic life, as a centrist ideal, regenerates itself through an inclusive, poly-vocal, and capricious *poiêsis* (that is, a *bringing forth* in craft and nature), in essence the polis as *vita activa* as Hannah Arendt describes it,[6] capable of populating any corner of public life with the rudiments of democratic action. Civic engagement, then, would appear to complement the sorts of rhetorical engagements presented in this collection, but the coin of the realm of "civic engagement"—as anyone employed by a public or private university would know—far exceeds that of rhetorical practice in civic life. Civic engagement (and not rhetoric) has achieved brand-name status through a burgeoning policy industry, amassing great cultural capital in interrelated fields of influence. It operates as a disciplinarily transcendent educational policy that presents engagement, service, and community outreach as cornerstones of a liberal education in the twenty-first century and as pathways between institutions of higher learning and their public constituencies. As a result, civic engagement is now a centerpiece in strategic planning exercises at public and private colleges and universities. With gathering momentum through the latter moments of the twentieth century, the university has made its own *public turn* through civic engagement and as an educational policy. Civic engagement has joined innovation, entrepreneurialism, and global economic competitiveness to guide university planning. Coincidental with this rise in institutional prominence, civic engagement linked with economic progressivism has become an instrument for partisan and postpartisan political policy debates. Civic engagement (and its variants) increasingly is featured in political arguments for economic solvency and geopolitical power in the United States and abroad in the twenty-first century.

This essay begins with a sketch of interrelated policy spheres aligned with civic engagement—in educational policy and in political and economic platforms—to show why civic engagement no longer simply identifies the motives and context of an isolated classroom or off-campus learning event. As soon as civic engagement jumps the track from experiential learning for the causes of progressive education to planning and political spheres, it is implicated in global economic policies. Because public policy is inherently economic in Western society, and because public life is determined by the marketplace more than the democratic ideal, our rhetorical engagements—as pure as we believe them to be of spirit and purpose—are fundamentally political and economic. When the logic of fast capitalism subsumes the logic of progressivism in the name of civic engagement, there is rhetorical work to be done to unravel this discourse and its material consequences and to rescue from purely political ambition the commonplace economies of the city—to reclaim, in Harry Boyte's words, "the interplay of distinctive, unique interests and perspectives to accomplish public purposes."[7] Rhetorical analysis and participation, attuned to the economic tableau of the polis, can point us toward the locations and locutions where economic equity has been denied through false promise or cultural misstep and where economic futures can be revitalized.

CIVIC ENGAGEMENT ACROSS EDUCATION,
PLANNING, AND POLITICAL SPHERES

For most academic readers, the "scholarship of engagement" is familiar in name and in practice, encompassing a growing set of academic policy initiatives. Coined by Ernest Boyer, the term strives to connect "the rich resources of the university to our most pressing social, civic, and ethical problems, to our children, to our schools, to our teachers, and to our cities."[8] In principle, it is woven into the fabric of campus life, often with direct ties to experiential and service learning, to Campus Compact, and to outreach programs offering service, internships, and undergraduate research opportunities. Engaged scholarship is now ubiquitous in public and private schools, colleges, and universities, growing exponentially through the 1990s and into the twenty-first century. Nearly every major policy agency of higher education promotes and tracks it, and examples abound. The Association of American Universities (AAU) began in 1996 to compile a directory of community service and outreach programs that now account for nearly 100 percent of AAU membership.[9] The Campus Compact began in 1985 and has grown to 1,100 colleges and universities.[10] The American Association of State Colleges and Universities, in partnership with the *New York Times,* hosts the American Democracy Project and the Civic Engagement in Action series with 229 member institutions.[11] The Association of American Colleges and Universities, representing 1,150 institutions, claims that civic engagement has become "an essential learning goal throughout higher education."[12] And the Higher Learning Commission of the North Central Association lists "Engagement and Service" as one of the five criteria guiding reaccreditation.[13] With so much information and interest in circulation, major clearinghouses have emerged such as the National Center for Public Policy and Higher Education.[14]

Now that civic engagement and service are centrally part of innovation and review at the university, it is not surprising to find "engagement" written into the strategic vision of postsecondary institutions as a vehicle to strengthen the collegiate experience, to compete for the best students, and to ensure a university's economic future. As a Google search of "civic engagement strategic planning" reveals, civic engagement and global economic competitiveness intertwine in the strategic plans of most colleges and universities. The Flagship 2030 strategic plan at the University of Colorado, my employer, seeks to redefine the "flagship university of the 21st century," as one that is

> intellectually inspiring, a dynamic global force,
> promoting cultural understanding, and civic and community engagement,
> moving the state of Colorado forward, an international crossroad,
> with a sense of responsibility, a commitment to learning,
> with the financial and operational models to its vision and mission.[15]

Kathy Chaput charts how universities historically have remade themselves for the demands of capitalism. With the implosion of the nation-state and the explosion of digital communication, universities have had to compete for regional and national recognition by attracting the best students and by providing increasingly "bite-size" portions of the university experience that imitate the outsourcing and downsizing of other consumer commodities.[16] With more and more university services delivered on-line, and as they temporally align themselves with consumer culture, universities are complicit in the growth market for more "casual" labor. Chaput's critique is that "ostensibly benign" university programs that deliver "service learning, peer instruction, and unpaid internships" contribute, however inadvertently, to a global economy hungry for free or replaceable labor. This critique extends the horizon of rhetorical criticism whenever "self improvement and civic engagement" for global citizens are intoned along with global competitiveness and economic redevelopment.[17]

As pervasive as civic engagement has become in educational and university policy, it has also risen in prominence in the discourse of U.S. political policy and economic reform. January 2009 marked the end of the George W. Bush presidency, an era when almost all domestic and foreign policy was shaped by an "age of terror" linked to the events of September 11, 2001. Terror and national security, however, are now being usurped by a global economic crisis, and national service has been elevated to a presidential priority for the twenty-first century. On September 11, 2008, ServiceNation and Columbia University hosted the first presidential forum on "service and civic engagement," following the Democratic and Republican conventions."[18] ServiceNation is affiliated with Be the Change, a nonprofit consortium of community and financial leaders, many from the Boston area, which promotes "a bold and innovative policy agenda that is rooted in the practical experience of social entrepreneurs and civic leaders . . . [with] better public polices . . . active citizenship and citizen democracy."[19]

ServiceNation seeks a coalition of "100–million Americans" to elevate community involvement in the public consciousness and policy on a scale never seen before and required, it claims, in the wake of failed "conventional strategies" to address "systematic problems" such as poverty, the environment, sickness, and a faulty economic system. ServiceNation espouses a service agenda with "meaningful opportunities for service at every key life stage, and for every socio-economic group" to address the failures of our national system and to share "American ideals and idealism with the rest of the world."[20]

As the public face of Be the Change, ServiceNation is building a nonpartisan action group, and its Leadership Council lists members as politically diverse as Caroline Kennedy and Mike Huckabee. Many on the council are affiliated with the Democratic Party, however, and their civic and service agendas are sympathetic to the platform of the Democratic Leadership Council

(DLC), which in turn is affiliated with the Progressive Policy Institute (PPI), whose membership and philosophy grew out of the Clinton presidency. The PPI proposes to "adapt progressive values to the new challenges of the information age."[21] *The Hyde Park Declaration: A Statement of Principles and a Policy Agenda for the 21st Century* is one of the DLC's charter documents, and it captures the interlacing frames of influence I sketch here. It seeks a transcendent political identity for U.S. politics; it strives to replace partisan politics with a "third way" policy agenda that rests upon "three cornerstones: equal importunity through government, shared responsibility, and an empowered citizenry."[22]

Both the DLC and the PPI tie a revitalized democracy for the global citizen to civic engagement and to the tenets of what proponents of transnational capitalism and globalization refer to as the "new economy." The new economy champions digital technology, affluence, centrism, and "a new social structure" led by a new "learning class." Global expansion, free enterprise, increased productivity, entrepreneurship, and fiscal discipline promise to "expand the winner's circle" through "economic security" and "lifelong learning for everyone."[23] Third-way politics are not limited to the Clinton wing of the Democratic Party; they are based on the philosophies of Tony Blair and those who promoted the "'Clintonization' of European social democracy."[24] As a geopolitical strategy, the third way erases nation- and class-based definitions of citizenship and harnesses civic life to transnational economies and free-market expansion. The third-way policies of the DLC and PPI can clearly be traced to the Clinton presidency, but these doctrines are not exclusive to the Democratic Party in the United States. Republican and conservative policy groups consider the free-market system sacrosanct, and civic engagement is promulgated to reduce the influence of government over the polis.[25] The church and the family are heralded as the social institutions most responsible for and receptive to civic life.[26] As the Obama presidency unfolds, we will see whether his experience with and investment in community organizing will influence the policy spheres related to civic engagement.

TOWARD A POLITICAL AND ECONOMIC REFRAMING OF RHETORICAL ENGAGEMENT

These spheres depict the depth and breadth of the overlapping policy areas of civic engagement. As Bennett and Entman discuss in *Mediated Politics*, policy and public spheres are interdependent, with the former a "subset of [the] public sphere where ideas and feelings explicitly connect with—are communicated to, from, or about—governmental officials, parties, or candidates for office who may decide the outcome of issues or conflicts facing society."[27] They point out that though policy spheres are overtly political and hierarchical in nature—power continues to travel up to those who decide—these spheres tolerate and sometimes openly court local, civic activism. Those citizens who are able to participate in a policy sphere may on balance achieve a higher degree of political influence when compared with participation in other areas of public life because policy debates tend to be less encumbered by public participation in the form of noisy protests or the quieter forms of representative government, such as voting. Policy spheres are constituted and enacted differently than either the idealized official or vernacular spheres articulated by Gerard Hauser[28] because they tend to rely on digital media to spread their message, sometimes disguising their funding streams and political affiliations, and tend to invent through the velocity of their distributions new mechanisms for limiting local political involvement. They comprise "a relatively unregulated and highly commercialized media economy . . . aimed at containing the scope and setting the terms of public involvement."[29]

Policy spheres in practice are not inherently evil, as they can be instrumental for causes on the left, right, and center of political life.[30] They are, however, one of the factors in a radical reconfiguration of power in everyday life in the (so-called) knowledge economy and information age. In their digital form, they are difficult to track, and participation in them can be limited by their constitutive bias. The question I raise is where and how does the citizen-scholar, through individual or collective action, enter into those policy spheres that influence the political and economic consequences of civic life? How might rhetorical practice alter the linguistic, deliberative, and material terrain that a policy sphere presumes to address, particularly in postindustrial cities? Policy studies, the subfield of political science open to this question, appears to be addressing this question by announcing an "argumentative turn." Policy occurs fundamentally as persuasive action that aggregates and then disaggregates through discursive deliberation.[31] This argumentative turn has two benefits: more accurately than positivist models, it reveals where and how policies accumulate; in doing so, it potentially opens more doorways through discourse and rhetoric for wider participation. As in the many other instantiations of the rhetorical turn,[32] rhetoric is granted the tertiary status of a complement and not a primary instrument in public life. The roles granted to rhetoric and public policy must be reversed. Rhetoric must reclaim its authority in public life by confecting its own "policy turn" aided certainly by the recognition that policies are ubiquitous, discursive, and thus potentially rhetorical but more centrally by locating our practice somewhere in the "middling" range between everyday life in our communities and the regional economic policies that influence them.[33]

To do so will require a reversal of analytical frames, a reversal of the symbolic figure and its economic grounding. It will require that the pursuit of civic engagement be infused with economic justice and political inquiry. We can no longer pretend, in Ronald Greene's words, "that rhetorical agency exists outside the domain of capitalist command."[34] Coincidentally, a similar call to reframe civic engagement away from active learning and toward civic renewal is coming from one of its strongest advocates. Harry Boyte reports that the overwhelming tendency in service programs, sponsored by the university, is to "neglect the dynamics of power and politics" in society obscuring both the ordinary "talent" in local communities and the "craft" nature of academic disciplines that has been diminished by technological specialization and balkanization. Though civic engagement has gained national status as a public policy, the movement has stalled, and it requires, according to Boyte, a reinvention of "civic politics" as "public achievement" to produce "lasting civic goods, material or culture" in "free spaces" defined as public settings where groups gain confidence as "agents of constructive change."[35] This mode goes against the grain of higher education, mostly because it refuses "bite-size" increments of institution practice. It does so by embracing the constitutive nature of civic engagement through a robust model of the civic life construed as "public work" that "builds the power and political acumen of citizens."[36]

Taking nothing away from those in academia or public life who volunteer, serve, or teach under the mantel of civic engagement,[37] this enterprise has risen to prominence coincidental with the rise of transnational capitalism and its proselytizing discourses of globalization and the new economy.[38] The civic reality does not always match up with the civic rhetoric of the new economy. Doug Henwood illustrates how the new economy has risen and fallen as a discursive phenomenon: whereas the usage of the terms "civic engagement" and "globalization" grew exponentially from the mid-1980s to the early 2000s, actual economic prosperity declined during that time.[39] Henwood challenges both the qualitative and quantitative claims supporting the "scripture" of the new economy, including a revisionist history of the 1990s as our contemporary golden age. Regarding the gross domestic product, he states that "the 3.4% average of the 1990s is considerably lower [than the average between 1850 and 1914 of 3.9%], little different from the growth rates . . . in the much-maligned 1970s and well below the 1960s."[40]

For Richard Sennett, new capitalism masks the older social capitalism of the twentieth century, once engendered through education and special skills, with a "specter of uselessness" as a reduction in the need for labor in global markets and a revision of the "moral prestige of work itself."[41] There is a grotesque contradiction between the civic progressivism of third-way, new-economic policies and such sobering and sometimes apocalyptic projections that are today being matched by economic reality.[42] For the rhetorical critic and citizen, what is truly grotesque is the imaginative distance that lies between new economic progressivism and the human costs borne by the planet and the "people" in unbridled, transnational capitalism and the erasure of precisely those stark contrasts in everyday life that could lead residents and critics to challenge the status quo. Chantal Mouffe insists that a disingenuously "radical" centrism underlying the third-way political agenda promotes harmony through dialogue while it is "unable to grasp the systematic connections existing between global market forces and the variety of problems—from exclusion to environmental risks—that it pretends to tackle."[43] Her charge is to reactivate political struggle to highlight the discursive and material terrain between the oxymoron of transnational progressivism found in third-way politics and the abject dissolution of pubic life in a global age. Civic and political forms of engagement in policy spheres (for example, service versus voting) are blurring, largely because more than twenty years of conservative political influence has led to federal and state governments "devolving" and outsourcing their powers and responsibilities to private and nonprofit sectors of society.[44] ServiceNation's goal of enlisting and organizing 100 million Americans to serve their communities may be a powerful corrective for the erasure of public life in a global democracy—or precisely the kind of systemic devolution for which neoliberal economic policies thirst.

To frame rhetorical engagement in economic terms, we must return to the city, because it opens our analysis and participation up to the discursive and material elements of the economic predicaments of our communities. The economies of the city precede and thus predetermine the success and sustainability of our engagements, reminding us that our communities are in constant dialectic with the global economy. If knowledge and information are the new currencies of the global economy, they are being remade each day in our neighborhood schools, offices, streets, and playgrounds as well as our mosques, synagogues, and churches—all of which are shaped by policy spheres. There is a uniquely powerful position for rhetorical agency as it sorts through the economic myth and reality of civic engagement in the polis. A cultural economy is a critical antidote for the utopian excesses of the new economy, because it features the arts, creativity, social action, built space, and local culture, and by implication it includes rhetoric as a civic, urban, and deliberative art. There are multiple economies that must be disentangled to disinter the cultural economy of a city or region: the *new economy,* which is presumed to replace the orthodoxy of fading economy regimes and which is deeply tied to political interests; the *cultural economy,* which is an emerging analytical tool to disrupt both old and new economic models; and then the *creative economy,*[45] which has attributes of both old, new, and cultural economies—offering a topoi to invent new policies for neighborhoods caught in the middle of economic decline, euphemistic policy, and the local need for civic and economic renewal.

As Paul du Gay and Michael Pryke summarize, culture and the economy have invaded each other's intellectual and policy terrain to the point that efforts to determine an actual economy for a people in an organization, city, or region will invariably lead us to critically determine not *the* economy so much as the "assemblage" of cultural agents, artifacts, policies, institutions, and beliefs that arguably constitute a visible, working economic system.[46] They point out that culture industries (film, art, media) are among the most profitable and adaptive, partly because they are fully equipped to participate in the information streams of a digital world. Du Gay and Pryke note that more static service and production-oriented industries have learned to brand their organizational ethos—their culture—leading them to higher efficiencies and profitability. A cultural economy is fundamentally rhetorical because it is fundamentally "contingent." To capitalize on contingency, they advise us to reject all binaries of *the* culture and *the* economy, as we embrace both the attributes of a cultural analysis (for example, discursive systems, ideology) and the attributes of orthodox economies (for example, marketing, sales, accounting) for their persuasive power. The efficacy of a cultural economy, much akin to rhetoric, is determined by its relevance to the circumstance from which it was derived: "while one can profess a cultural or discursive view of economics and continue to make strong economic assertions, one cannot necessarily do economics in a way that follows from one's convictions concerning its cultural constitution."[47] I end this essay with a brief example of my collaborative efforts to divine the cultural economy of a city, under the mantel of civic engagement, which requires a rejection of cultural binaries to produce the best rhetorical effect.

The Cultural Economy of Kent/State

The orthodox economics of Kent, Ohio, are unavoidable to most residents and visitors, because the city does not exhibit the vibrancy of a generic college town. It does not look or feel right in comparison with other university cities and in comparison with neighboring municipalities in what is becoming the exurban network of Cleveland and Akron. Too many storefronts are boarded up, too many businesses have changed hands, and the commercial district does not hum with the street life of a university community. The city is also silent about its past. Visitors remark on the difficulty of finding the commemorative site of the May 4, 1970, shooting on campus, and the downtown district offers little to no public record of the events that led to the city's iconic status in the public imagination.[48] In conversations with students, neighbors, and colleagues, I found a coincidence in the city's tragic past and the artifice of its economic plight, a coincidence and geography that led me to question the detachment of civic engagement as a university-sponsored learning event from the economic solvency of the city. Recent forecasts of the educational and economic futures of public research universities all claim that universities cannot ignore their urban and regional hosts, because growth depends on regional coexistence.[49] The publicized economic health of this city bears little witness to a cultural economy that would embrace a tragic past, as an embodied geography that one can experience in Kent by looking northwest to the city's central business district and then southeast to the grassy hill where National Guard troops shot dead four students and wounded nine others.

In orthodox economic terms, the city's economic future by 2005 was not bright.[50] The consumer price index had increased at a rate of 3.3 percent, while the city's average increase in income tax receipts was 1.5 percent. The 2005 Financial Report for Kent decries the loss of the "buying power" of the city and its residents. Adjusted and actual revenues were drifting farther and farther apart, due in part to the nation's "jobless economic recovery." Kent is a postindustrial city, and like many others in Ohio, it has struggled to adapt to the new competitive environments of a global economy. In a town with few economic engines, Kent State University, and the innovation and entrepreneurialism located there, appeared to many to be the best financial solution if new investors could not be found. Private-sector income tax contributions dropped significantly from 1989 to 2005, while the university's share grew from 31 percent to 35 percent, by far the largest contributor. Manufacturing's contributions were cut in half.

The city's economic past was also troubled. The price of oil quadrupled in the early 1970s, and real wages, fueling economic expansion, were usurped by inflation after World War II and the consumer price index.[51] Kent, once a thriving river town, from World War II forward, had to adjust to the demise of the railroad and the invention of a highway system that helped some communities but hindered Kent with no easy passage to Akron or Cleveland. Local businesses faced more and more competition, while corporations extended their influence through commodity pricing. Local economies in small towns sometimes turn on a few cataclysmic events, and so it was for Kent. The Commerce Building burned down in 1972, displacing numerous businesses in the downtown district. Davey Tree Service, now a national corporation and one of the most lucrative businesses in the community, along with the U.S. Postal Service, moved away from the downtown district. Haymaker Parkway, conceived in the early 1970s, cut a new pathway through the downtown and between the city and the university. Even the university's decision to become a full-service campus offering financial services, food, recreation, learning, and medical aid further isolated the university community from the city. Alcohol was always an incentive to go downtown, and that, too, diminished when the drinking age was raised to twenty-one. To gauge the impact of these times, I turned to the Kent State University Archives and the Portage County Planning Commission. Using 1970 as my benchmark, it took seventeen years for the number of students and twenty years for the city's population to return to the 1970 levels. In Portage County, Kent ranks highest in individual poverty and is one of the highest in poverty among the elderly and families with children. The median income in Kent was nearly $15,000 below the county median of $44,000, which was well below the state and national averages.

If a cultural economy has the capacity to subvert orthodox and new economies by authorizing a prognosis based on the economic attributes of local culture, then the rhetorical analysis of those attributes must be critically multimodal. We must look beyond the symbolic to determine the material attributes of a cultural economy because symbolicity naturalizes an affinity between the aesthetic object and its representation. Walter Benjamin, much earlier in the twentieth century, foresaw this problem, whenever the cultural economy of the city is confused with an aesthetic object that renders symbolic its lived appreciation or critique.[52] Recent studies of the symbolic economies of cities still suffer from the interpretive habit that subsumes culture under the domain of symbolic representation. A symbolic economy may include a wide range of abstract and concrete properties from information and culture to the "spaces in which they are created and consumed," but John Allen insists that we go further to break apart all logics that assign either symbol or space to a specific sphere, for example, as "food, fashion, music, or tourism."[53] The critic must search for novel "registers" that result from productive "entanglements" of aesthetic, material, representational, and discursive elements in a site's cultural economy. Yet critical entanglements do not give license to postmodern confusion. To the contrary, critical entanglements search for a meaningful dissonance in the cultural milieu that defeats the bias of textuality over materiality or the bias of the aesthetic over the quotidian.

The cultural economy of Kent resides most poignantly in the legacy of the public tragedy of May 4, 1970. Cultural memory as an economic attribute differentiates across individual, social, collective, and public memories.[54] As I have written elsewhere, this differentiation allows for vibrant forms of civic reflection, dialogue, and planning if a stage is provided by the city. People not only remember the events of May 4 differently, but their ability to recall those times depends upon the way they revisit the terrain of commemoration. It matters deeply that residents of Kent and employees of the university experience the city differently according to their exposure to the geography of the protests in the streets of the downtown district in 1970 and the eventual location of the May 4 memorial, some twenty years later, on the university campus. Students and newcomers to Kent rely on different degrees of collective and public memory, the memory troves that transcend direct experience and social (community) awareness. Local residents draw upon individual and social memory and at times resent the ideologies sustained by collective and public memory, the memory troves that bind Kent State to a collective consciousness (if you were alive in 1970) and the public imagination. The city is a latent interlocutor in this dissonant, mostly silent, deliberation. There are no commemorative sites or events in the downtown district. The geography and *kairos* of commemoration are overwhelmed by a tragic cataclysm that has been restricted to a few days on the Kent Campus in early May and to an inconspicuous memorial site on campus.

My contention that memory is material and that memory reinscribes a dissonant cultural geography in the economy of the city rests on the assumption that memory and place are intertwined, an assumption fully explored by Edward Casey and many others.[55] "What is contained in place is well on its way to being well remembered," with the reverse equally true that what is contained in memory is well on its way to emplacement.[56] Not only do people recall differently the events of May 4, they assign praise and blame differently according to their ideological bias and geographical wherewithal. This bias— for example, many living residents still blame the students for the actions of the National Guard—corresponds with different explanations of the economic plight of the city. Some recall the broken windows downtown and assign economic decline to political unrest, and others do not, explaining the economic predicament through economic orthodoxy. Everyone, therefore, reads the artifice of the city differently.

Memory reinscribes the city, and the artifice of the city reinscribes memory. Working from that premise, a juxtaposition of orthodox and cultural economies in Kent would suggest that we study the territorial boundaries and proximities of different social institutions. The space between the city of Kent's downtown business district and the west and north sides of the university is bisected by the Main Street Bridge and Haymaker Parkway, a construction project conceived long before the May 4 shootings but completed just shortly thereafter. The bridge and parkway comprise the epicenter of the cultural economy of Kent for several reasons. Haymaker Parkway in its current form inscribes the territorial boundaries of both the city and the university. Haymaker was designed to bring new economic life to the downtown business district, but in my analysis the coincidence of the parkway with the shootings and unrest in 1970, and with what one resident called a "violation of the 50-year commitment to the university as a cultural anchor," meant that the city built a wall in the form of a boulevard. In doing so, it slowed the reconciliation of dissonant points of view on a public tragedy by ensuring that the artifice of the city, owned by all residents and employees, was broken in two.

The legacy of the city's efforts to reimagine and build a positive economic future is cataloged in cycles of urban planning. Figure 1 compresses the material history of the city and its need to cross the Cuyahoga River to promote commerce. The image displayed on the following page illustrates the city's fixation from 1970 to the present on Haymaker and the downtown business district and the desire to correct what it has wrought. Excerpts from planning documents show how the city's artifice inscribed over time has left an indelible geography of the city and university's epicenter. The full history of economic development, the artifice of the city, and an interweaving of public tragedy goes well beyond this essay, but this illustration shows how ordinary urban landscapes, as Deloris Hayden states in the quotation that opens this essay, reveal much more than mere cycles of urban renewal. They exhume a city's cultural economy from its artifice to remind us that culture can never be

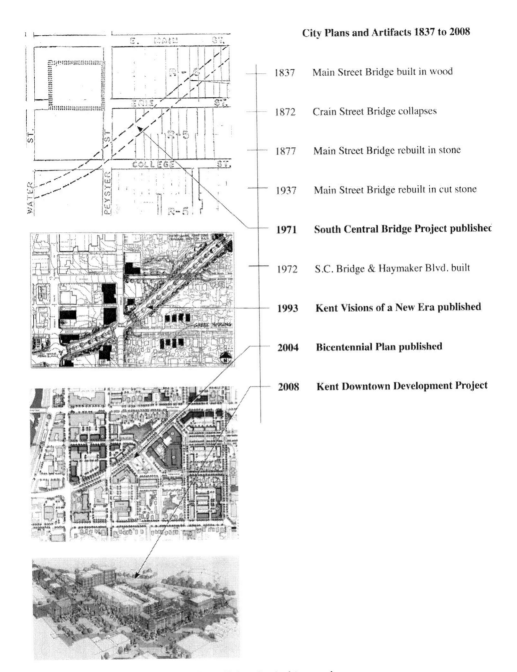

City Plans and Artifacts 1837 to 2008

1837	Main Street Bridge built in wood
1872	Crain Street Bridge collapses
1877	Main Street Bridge rebuilt in stone
1937	Main Street Bridge rebuilt in cut stone
1971	**South Central Bridge Project published**
1972	S.C. Bridge & Haymaker Blvd. built
1993	**Kent Visions of a New Era published**
2004	**Bicentennial Plan published**
2008	**Kent Downtown Development Project**

City plans and artifacts. From Kent State University Archives and
from Ruller, "Kent 360," http://www.kent360.com

explained through orthodox economic accounts alone or by virtue of a city's monumental structures or public record. The city planners of Kent sought the expertise and involvement of the university, and the 1993 and 2004 planning cycles present Haymaker as an urban corridor that must be beautified, rezoned, bisected, tempered by traffic-calming devices, crossed on foot and by bicycle—anything but let the 1970 manifestation stand. One idea was to lower the parkway to decrease the noise and to improve visibility so that the campus and the community would see each other more clearly. The zone that Haymaker created is one of the more economically blighted in the city. Haymaker severed two key arteries in the city, Erie Street and College Avenue, and in doing so invented "college park," consisting of high-density student rental properties further buffering the downtown business district from the customer base of the university and its professional schools.

Each community in which civic engagement occurs can be represented through frames of orthodox, new, and cultural economies. Kent's history is iconic, but all communities inscribe their cultural economies through the design and redevelopment of the urban artifice; the design of cities has never been the sole province of architects.[57] The practical aim of a cultural economy is to recapture the interworkings of public life across discursive, embodied, and material terrain. Kent through the prisms of orthodox and new economies appears to be doubly impoverished: its orthodox economic indicators report depressions in tax and income revenue, and there are few resources in the city, beyond the walls of the university, that are poised to reinvent a vibrant public life fueled in the new economy by digital technology, innovation, a new learning class, and global economic expansion. Kent's cultural economy, however, suggests a different resource for its economic future. Tragedy is by its rhetorical nature epideictic, and the interrelationship between memory, artifact, policy, and discourse in my analysis can assist in plotting a different deliberative future. The city through its cultural economy can become a mezzo-structural commemorative event, the place where reconciliation and entrepreneurialism coexist if steps can be taken to disrupt the institutional memories and urban artifice that calcify the past. It may sound simple, even crass, to suggest the May 4, 1970, must be reconceived as an economic catalyst, as a brand redistributed to the downtown business district, but those proposals are beginning to surface in discussions of the city's future.

RHETORICAL ENGAGEMENT IN THE CULTURAL ECONOMY

Thus far in this essay I have gestured to an affinity between civic and rhetorical engagement, if the economic plight of a region can opportunistically embrace its cultural past. I suggest that it is unwise to deny the economic pretense for civic engagement, either as an extension of university planning or as a political policy. As I have tried to describe in the preceding section, the inadequacies of both orthodox and new economic prisms can be confronted by determining what can *arguably* function as the cultural economy of a city. Civic engagement as practice and policy cannot escape its economic circumstance, and thus our rhetorical engagements will, by necessity, return us to the city to learn how the past calcifies and how our futures can be renewed.

Gerard Hauser concludes his studies of the vernacular with this caution: "Before we can rehabilitate public life, we first must understand the way actually occurring discourses shape it."[58] As I have argued here, we should add actually occurring cultural economies and a transposing of figure and ground— in Hannah Arendt's words, "the transformation of the intangible into the tangibility of things."[59] The cultural economy of Kent differs from other cities in degree but not in kind. It consists of a constellation of public memory, urban artifact, public and institutional policy, design discourse, and human geography. In keeping with the critical impulse in cultural economy theory, our first step is to reject those "technologic" limits that remove rhetorical practice from matters of economic policy. We then gather the once disparate, now contingent pieces of public life that reassemble culture from orthodoxy to supplant the disquieting inequities that unchecked globalization fosters. We must disambiguate orthodox and new economies, and cultural economies, from what I now refer to as "creative" economies that have enough material and discursive metal to alter the policy spheres of local communities.[60]

To translate a cultural economic analysis into a creative economic argument, we in rhetoric must forestall the aesthetic and ideological preference for cultural analysis and critique, and embrace, when the occasion allows, new kinds of sponsorship. Said differently, our critical entrance into the cultural economies of cities (and universities) may well yield the best "register" for public policy deliberation when we look for atypical partners for rhetorical collaboration. As essays in this collection illustrate, sponsorship is multivariate in public life open to residents, students, the arts community, and the university. Rhetorical engagement can also emerge through partnerships in economic redevelopment.

The illustration on page 88 presents four images that coincide with cycles of urban planning in Kent, culminating with a 2008 architectural drawing that portrays the economic future of the city. My foray into Kent's economic future occurred between 2004 and 2008, and in 2005 Right Dimensions, a California developer, proposed to the city a $40 million mixed-used "lifestyle" development lodged in the triangle of urban decay bordered by Haymaker Parkway. This project eventually failed, according to the developers, because neither the city nor the university stepped forward to anchor the development. From the city's point of view, the developers did not attract an anchor retail client to strengthen their financial due diligence.[61] The lessons learned from the Right Dimensions proposal are many with regard to city planning and economic speculation, but the lesson relevant to my analysis is that there are clients in urban communities who are open to rhetorical analyses of cultural economies and who fully comprehend the relationships among orthodox, new, cultural, and creative economies as the coin of the realm for public policy.

Outside developers, city officials, local business owners, and residents of the city and the university learned that we have more in common than the conventional boundaries of economic policy, civic engagement, and rhetorical theory would suggest. I proposed, as did the developers, that downtown development was an opportunity to coalesce many of the attributes of the cultural economy of Kent into an economic future and a site for reconciliation of a tragic past. The location of what is now referred to as the Kent Downtown Development Project reconnects the city and the university by bicycle, by foot, by history, and by artistic and deliberative tradition—all toward economic renewal. Though the Right Dimensions development plans eventually failed for lack of financial stakeholders, the economic futures represented by those plans remain and are carried forward in the more recent city drawings. The illustration compresses the design history of Kent, with focal attention on Haymaker, to convey that the artifice of the city is an archive for both epideictic and deliberative discourse. With the cultural economy in mind, regional economic planning commingles orthodox and new economic futures to produce a creative economic solution heterotopias, where place and event coincide, that embraces tragedy and social division as elements for renewal. The city conducted its own Cool Cities Survey of Kent in 2007 and determined that "lifestyle" was one of the most desired attributes of a livable city, along with biking, outdoor gathering spots, safety, and economic growth.[62] The city has now embarked on a new planning exercise, this time triangulating in a more forceful and economically feasible way the cultural and economic heritage of the city, the university's interests, and those of a new developer, Fairmount Properties.[63]

The rhetorical engagement that I have pursued in my research and through my residency in Kent, and that I briefly summarize here, exploits the economic preconditions of civic engagement. The power of place, as Deloris Hayden reminds, is in the shared time, shared territory, and shared resources that can coalesce for a better future. When university residents venture forth into local communities and in the name of civic engagement, we are wise to open our methods and dispositions to the economies of practice and culture outside of the academic milieu. What I argue for, and have tried to illustrate through my public work, is that culture as an economy operates as both commodity and critique, leading the rhetorician to surprising partnerships and objects of analysis. Our rhetorical engagements must thirst for such opportunities.

NOTES

1. Hayden, *Power of Place,* 9.
2. This comment is inspired by the absences in Bennett, Grossberg, and Morris, *New Keywords.*
3. For example, see Kohrs Campbell, "Promiscuous and Protean"; Crowley, *Toward a Civil Discourse.*
4. WordNet, "A Lexical Database for the English Language," is a corpus-linguistic project at Princeton University that determines denotation through the contiguous usage of words.
5. Hariman, *Political Style,* 3–4.
6. Arendt, *Human Condition.*
7. Boyte, "Different Kind," 12.
8. Boyer, "Scholarship of Engagement," 21.
9. Association of American Universities, "Campus Community."
10. Information retrieved from the Campus Compact Web site
11. American Association of State Colleges and Universities, "American Democracy Project."
12. Association of American Colleges and Universities, "Civic Engagement."
13. Higher Learning Commission, "Institutional Accreditation."
14. National Center for Public Policy and Higher Education, "Links."
15. University of Colorado, "CU-Boulder's Vision for 2030."
16. Chaput, *Inside the Teaching Machine,* 143.
17. Ibid., 129.
18. Columbia University, "ServiceNation." The presidential forum coincided with *Time*'s September 22, 2008, Second Annual Service Issue, A Sense of Community.
19. Be the Change, "Be the Change."
20. ServiceNation, "Executive Summary."
21. Progressive Policy Institute, "About."
22. Progressive Policy Institute, "About the Third Way."
23. Democratic Leadership Council, "Third Way."
24. Mouffe, *Democratic Paradox,* 113.
25. Since the 1970s the conservative movement has built an enduring and a well-coordinated philanthropic apparatus to forward its interests and that of private enterprise. This philanthropic apparatus has fostered federal policies that include deregulating business and cutting social services. Liberal philanthropic organizations have scrambled to address the humanitarian needs that these cuts have created.
26. For example, the Heritage Foundation or the American Enterprise Institute.
27. Bennett and Entman, "Democracy," 4.
28. Hauser, *Vernacular Voices.*
29. Bennet and Entman, "Democracy," 5.
30. Examples are plentiful: Americans for Tax Reform has influenced the Federal Communications Commission (FCC); MoveOn.org has influenced digital political networking and arguably domestic and foreign policy; and DividedWeFail.org connects the AARP with business interests to support bipartisanship.
31. See Fischer and Forester, *Argumentative Turn,* 3–4.
32. Simons, *Rhetorical Turn.*
33. The positionality of such a "middling" rhetorical stance was outline by Lucaites and Condit, "Epilogue."

34. Greene, "Orator Communist," 86.

35. Boyte, "Against the Current."

36. Boyte, "Different Kind," 16.

37. At the University of Utah in the early 1990s, I developed a multisection course titled "Professional Writing: Business," which featured a consultancy model of instruction. As a variant of service learning, groups of students found their own client, established a working relationship with the client, built an assessment model of the client's writing and communication, and decided whether to stop with the assessment or to propose new services. Flower and Ackerman, *Writers at Work*.

38. During the Clinton presidency, the North American Free Trade Agreement (NAFTA) was introduced, welfare disintegrated, and the FCC gave public air space to the telecommunication industries.

39. Henwood, *After the New Economy*. Tables to support this point can be found on pages 4 and 146, with analysis of actual economic growth and equity throughout the book. See also Gee, Hull, and Lankshear, *New Work Order*.

40. Henwood, *After the New Economy*, 4–5.

41. Sennett, *Cultural*.

42. Captured by Appadurai, *Fear;* Attali, *Millennium*.

43. Mouffe, *Democratic Paradox*, 110–11.

44. Zukin et al., *New Engagement?*, 53.

45. With my focus on local policy spheres, I am particularly interested in how a "creative economy" is used in regional planning, for example, by Christopherson, *Creative Economy Strategies;* Douglass and Wassall, *Creative Economy;* and Markusen and Johnson, "Artist's Centers."

46. Du Gay and Pryke, "Cultural Economy."

47. Ibid., 6.

48. See Hariman and Lucaites, "Dissent and Emotional Management."

49. See, for example, Freeland, "Universities and Cities." A broader discussion can be found in Brint, *Future;* Hoeger and Christiaanse, *Campus and the City*.

50. Office of the City Manger of Kent, Ohio, "2005 Financial Report." This report was made available to all residents of Kent through the City of Kent Web site and other venues.

51. Newman, *Declining Fortunes*.

52. See the discussion of Benjamin in Boyer, *City*.

53. Allen, "Symbolic Economies." Allen cites Zukin, *Culture of Cities*, 826.

54. Casey, "Public Memory."

55. Casey, *Fate of Place*.

56. Casey, *Remembering*, 214.

57. See Alexander, "Fifteen Properties," in his *The Phenomenon of Life*, Book 1 of *The Nature of Order;* Rossi, *Architecture*.

58. Hauser, *Vernacular Voices*, 273.

59. Arendt, *Human Condition*, 95.

60. When the term "creative economy" enters into city and redevelopment planning, the writings of Richard Florida often surface. See Florida et al., "University," and compare with Shorthose, "New Cultural Economy."

61. The narrative of the Right Dimensions proposal and its demise can be found in Ruller, "Kent 360," the city manager's blog.

62. Cool Cities Survey Results, "Voice of the Next Generation."

63. Ruller, "Kent 360."

WORKS CITED

Alexander, Christopher. *The Nature of Order: An Essay on the Art of Building and the Nature of the Universe.* Book 1, *The Phenomenon of Life;* Book Three, *A Vision of a Living World.* Berkeley, Calif.: Center for Environmental Structure, 2002, 2004.

Allen, John. "Symbolic Economies: The 'Culturization' of Economic Knowledge." In *Cultural Economy: Cultural Analysis and Commercial Life,* edited by Paul du Gay and Michael Pryke, 39–58. London: Sage Press, 2002.

American Association of State Colleges and Universities. "American Democracy Project." http://www.aascu.org/programs/adp/index.htm (accessed August 10, 2008).

American Enterprise Institute. http://www.aei.org/ (accessed September 4, 2008).

Appadurai, Arjun. *Fear of Small Numbers: An Essay on the Geography of Anger.* Durham, N.C.: Duke University Press, 2006.

Arendt, Hannah. *The Human Condition.* Chicago: University of Chicago Press, 1998.

Association of American Colleges and Universities. "Civic Engagement." http://www.aacu .org/resources/civicengagement/index.cfm (accessed August 10, 2008).

Association of American Universities. "Campus Community Service Directory." http:// www.aau.edu/about/default.aspx?id=3992 (accessed August 10, 2008).

Attali, Jacques. *Millennium: Winners and Losers in the Coming World Order.* Translated by Leila Conners and Nathan Gardels. New York: Times Books, Random House, 1991.

Banning, Marlia. "Manufacturing Uncertainty: The Politics of Knowledge Production, Emotion, and Public Deliberation in the Contemporary U.S." Unpublished manuscript, University of Colorado at Boulder, 2009.

Barnet, Richard J., and John Cavanaugh. *Global Dreams: Imperial Corporations and the New World Order.* New York: Simon and Schuster, 1994.

Bennett, Lance W., and Robert M. Entman. "Democracy in the Public Sphere." In *Mediated Politics: Communication in the Future of Democracy,* edited by W. Lance Bennett and Robert M. Entman, 1–32. Cambridge: Cambridge University Press, 2001.

Bennett, Tony, Lawrence Grossberg, and Meaghan Morris, eds. *New Keywords: A Revised Vocabulary of Culture and Society.* Malden, Mass.: Wiley-Blackwell, 2005.

Be the Change, Inc. "Be the Change." http://www.bethechangeinc.org (accessed September 28, 2008).

Boyer, Christine. *The City of Collective Memory: Its Historical Imagery and Architectural Entertainments.* Cambridge, Mass.: MIT Press, 1994.

Boyer, Ernest. "The Scholarship of Engagement." *Journal of Public Service and Outreach* 1 (1996): 11–20.

Boyte, Harry C. "Against the Current: Developing Civic Agency of Students." *Change,* May/June 2008, 1–11.

———. "A Different Kind of Politics: John Dewey and the Meaning of Citizenship in the 21st Century." Dewey Lecture, University of Michigan, November 1, 2002.

Brint, Steven, ed. *The Future of the City of Intellect: The Changing American University.* Stanford, Calif.: Stanford University Press, 2002.

Campus Compact. "About Campus Compact." http://www.compact.org/about/ (accessed August 10, 2008).

Casey, Edward. *The Fate of Place: A Phenomenological History.* Berkeley: University of California Press, 1998.

———. "Public Memory in Place and Time." In *Framing Public Memory,* edited by Kendall R. Phillips, 17–44. Tuscaloosa: University of Alabama Press, 2004.

———. *Remembering: A Phenomenological Study.* Bloomington, Ind.: Indiana University Press, 2000.

Chaput, Kathy. *Inside the Teaching Machine: Rhetoric and the Globalization of the U.S. Public Research University.* Tuscaloosa: University of Alabama Press, 2008.

Christopherson, Susan. "Creative Economy Strategies for Small and Medium Size Cities: Options for New York State." New York Creative Economy Progress Report, Cornell University, 2004. www.nycreativeeconomy.cornell.edu/reports/arts.mgi (accessed October 10, 2008).

Columbia University. "ServiceNation Announces Columbia University to Host 'ServiceNation Presidential Candidate Forum.'" http://www.columbia.edu/cu/news/newyorkstories/servicenation.html (accessed September 28, 2008).

Cool Cities Survey Results. "The Voice of the Next Generation." http://www.kent360.com/files/University/StudentSurvey.pdf (accessed September 15, 2008).

Crowley, Sharon. *Toward a Civil Discourse: Rhetoric and Fundamentalism.* Pittsburgh: University of Pittsburgh Press, 2006.

Democratic Leadership Council. "The Third Way: Key Documents: The Hyde Park Declaration." http://www.ndol.org/ndol_ci.cfm?kaid=128&subid=174&contentid=1926 (accessed September 28, 2008).

DeNatale, Douglass, and Gregory Wassall. "The Creative Economy: A New Definition." New English Foundation for the Arts. www.nefa.org/pubs (accessed September 28, 2008).

du Gay, Paul, and Michael Pryke. "Cultural Economy: An Introduction." In *Cultural Economy: Cultural Analysis and Commercial Life,* edited by Paul du Gay and Michael Pryke, 1–20. London: Sage Press, 2002.

Fischer, Frank, and John Forester, eds. *The Argumentative Turn in Policy Analysis and Planning.* Durham, N.C.: Duke University Press, 1993.

Florida, Richard, Gary Gates, Brian Knudsen, and Kevin Stolarick. "The University and the Creative Economy." Creative Class. http://creativeclass.com/article_library/ (accessed September 20, 2008).

Flower, Linda, and John Ackerman. *Writers at Work.* Oxford: Oxford University Press, 1994.

Freeland, Richard M. "Universities and Cities Need to Rethink Their Relationships." *Chronicle of Higher Education,* May 13, 2005, B-13.

Gee, James, Glynda Hull, and Colin Lankshear. *The New Work Order: Behind the Language of the New Capitalism.* Sydney, Australia: Westview, 1996.

Goodman, Lee A. Phillips. Kent Ohio: Visions of a New Era. Kent, Ohio: Urban Design Center of Northeast Ohio, 1993. KSU Archives: NA9127.K43 K43x 1993.

Greene, Ronald W. "Orator Communist." *Philosophy and Rhetoric* 39 (2006): 85–95.

Hariman, Robert. *Political Style: The Artistry of Power.* Chicago: University of Chicago Press, 1995.

Hariman, Robert, and John Lucaites. "Dissent and Emotional Management." In *No Caption Needed: Iconic Photographs, Public Culture, and Liberal Democracy,* 137–70. Chicago: University of Chicago Press, 2007.

Hauser, Gerard. *Vernacular Voices: The Rhetoric of Publics and Public Spheres.* Columbia: University of South Carolina Press, 1999.

Hayden, Dolores. *The Power of Place.* Cambridge, Mass.: MIT Press, 1995.

Henwood, Doug. *After the New Economy: The Binge . . . and the Hangover That Won't Go Away.* New York: New Press, 2003.

Heritage Foundation. "Leadership for America." http://www.heritage.org/ (accessed September 4, 2008).

Higher Learning Commission. "Institutional Accreditation: An Overview." http://www.ncacihe.org/index.php?option=com_content&task=view&id=83&Itemid=111 (accessed August 10, 2008).

Hoeger, Kerstin, and Kees Christiaanse, eds. *Campus and the City: Urban Design for the Knowledge Society*. Zurich, Switzerland: GTA Verlag, 2007.

Kent State University. "President's Strategic Plan." http://www.kent.edu/Administration/President/strategicinitiatives/StrategicPlan/ (accessed September 27, 2008).

Kohrs Campbell, Karlyn. "Promiscuous and Protean." *Communication and Critical/Cultural Studies* 2 (2005): 1–19.

Lucaites, John L., and Celeste M. Condit. "Epilogue: Contributions from Rhetorical Theory." In *Contemporary Rhetorical Theory: A Reader*, edited by John L. Lucaites, Celeste M. Condit, and Sally Caudill, 609–13. New York: Guilford Press, 1999.

Lynch, Kevin. *The Image of the City*. Cambridge, Mass.: MIT Press, 1960.

Markusen, Anne, and Amanda Johnson. "Artist's Centers: Evolution and Impacts on Careers, Neighborhoods, and Economies." Humphries Institute of Public Affairs, University of Minnesota, www.hhh.umn.edu/projects/prie (accessed October 3, 2008).

Mouffe, Chantal. *The Democratic Paradox*. London: Verso, 2000.

National Center for Public Policy and Higher Education. "Links." http://www.highereducation.org/links/links.shtml (accessed August 10, 2008).

Newman, Katherine S. *Declining Fortunes: The Withering of the American Dream*. New York: Basic Books, 1993.

Office of the City Manger of Kent, Ohio. "2005 Financial Report." http://www.kentohio.org/dep/manager.asp (accessed October 3, 2008).

Progressive Policy Institute. "About." http://www.ppionline.org (accessed September 28, 2008).

———. "About the Third Way." http://www.ppionline.org/ppi_ci.cfm?contentid=895&knlgAreaID=85&subsecid=109 (accessed September 28, 2008).

Rossi, Aldo. *The Architecture of the City*. Cambridge, Mass.: MIT Press, 1984.

Ruller, David. "Kent 360." http://www.kent360.com (accessed October 3 and 30, 2008).

Sennett, Richard. *The Culture of the New Capitalism*. New Haven, Conn.: Yale University Press, 2006.

ServiceNation. "Executive Summary." http://www.bethechangeinc.org/servicenation/about_us/policy (accessed September 28, 2008).

Shorthose, Jim. "The New Cultural Economy, the Artist and the Social Configuration of Autonomy." *Capital and Class*, Winter 2004. http://findarticles.com/p/articles/mi_qa3780/is_200401/ai_n9366243 (accessed October 2, 2008).

Simons, Herbert W., ed. *The Rhetorical Turn: Invention and Persuasion in the Conduct of Inquiry*. Chicago: University of Chicago Press, 1990.

Terry, Daniel A. "The South Central Bridge Project—Problems for the Central Business District." In Urban Studies Workshop, Summer 1971, papers by Pete Alterkruse, William Burns, and others. KSU Archives: HT168.K5 K45x.

University of Colorado. Flagship 2030 Strategic Plan. "CU-Boulder's Vision for 2030." http://www.colorado.edu/flagship2030/strategicplan/ovision.html (accessed September 27, 2008).

University of Minnesota Center on Public Engagement. "About." http://www.engagement.umn.edu/cope/about/index.html (accessed September 27, 2008).

University of Utah. "Mission." http://www.admin.utah.edu/president/mission.html (accessed September 27, 2008).

Wordnet. "A Lexical Database for the English Language." Princeton University. http://wordnet.princeton.edu/ (accessed August 7, 2008).

Zukin, Cliff, Scott Keeler, Molly Andolina, Krista Jenkins, and Michael X. Delli Carpini. *New Engagement? Political Participation, Civic Life, and the Changing American Citizen.* New York: Oxford University Press, 2006.

Zukin, Helen. *The Culture of Cities.* Oxford: Blackwell Press, 1995.

Democracy and Its Limitations

RALPH CINTRON

"After the general idea of virtue, I know no higher principle than that of right; or rather these two ideas are united in one. The idea of right is simply that of virtue introduced into the political world."[1] The subject of this essay is our current political era, what I call democracy's post–Berlin Wall moment. Francis Fukuyama in his well-known 1989 "End of History?" and subsequent commentators from the Left and Right have plowed the same field. Although my orientation is considerably left of his, I want to recall some of Fukuyama's more dramatic and insightful claims as an introduction to some of my own: "What we may be witnessing is not just the end of the Cold War . . . but the end of history as such: that is, the end point of mankind's ideological evolution and the universalization of Western liberal democracy as the final form of human government. . . . The victory of liberalism has occurred primarily in the realm of ideas or consciousness and is as yet incomplete in the real or material world. But there are powerful reasons for believing that it is the ideal that will govern the material world in the long run."[2]

I quote his 1989 essay, as opposed to his later book with the expanded title, and more recent writings because the Berlin wall fell in November 1989, only a few months after the prescient essay's publication. At that moment it seemed indeed that liberal democracy's "universalization" had established itself as the ideal form of governance. But Fukuyama was merely reiterating one of the major premises that makes democracy massively compelling—namely, that democracy is on a teleological trajectory: history's "final form." This is not to say that democratic theorists from Locke to Kant, to De Tocqueville, to John Rawls, to Fukuyama have whitewashed democracy's shortcomings. They, too, have their occasional reservations, but in the main these thinkers have helped to "virtuize" democracy so that, for the most part, the popular imaginary can no longer analyze democracy, as Aristotle may have, as just another form of governance. Nor can we, like Plato, articulate a deep suspicion of democracy.

There are probably numerous reasons for explaining the emergence of this enthusiasm—or, phrasing it more conceptually, the ontologization of democracy. By describing democracy as now "ontologized," I mean to say that over a number of centuries democracy has acquired a certain primordial value, an automatic virtue, a kind of fundamental, nearly metaphysical rightness. Among the reasons why, here are two:

1. Democracy from the early Enlightenment until now has defined itself against its negatives: monarchy, the uncivilized, Fascism, Communism, and, more recently, religious fundamentalism and terrorism. That is, the negative functions as a structural placeholder for incompleteness or vice. The positive functions as another placeholder, namely, democracy as virtue, and virtue accumulates with each successive victory until virtue begins to look innate to democracy.

    The central point is that our post–Berlin Wall moment offers a remarkable opportunity. Democracy is now a global or transnational phenomenon, meaning that it is the "only game in town," as political theorists of eastern Europe have phrased it.[3] There is no serious contender against which to measure it. What is necessary, and indeed what may happen in our post–Berlin Wall moment, is democracy's sobering encounter with itself because the structuring negative has dissipated. And with that dissipation, will not the ideologies that helped to dismiss the structuring negatives also in time dissipate? My hope is that in encountering itself—truly encountering itself: brutally, acidly—democracy will undergo a kind of purifying ritual.

2. From the early Enlightenment, democracy has been imagined within a context of limitless material resources. Some exceptions to this view are, perhaps, those of Thomas Malthus and other reactionaries. In the main, however, there is an analogy between democracy as a kind of open-endedness of rights, freedoms, and so on, and the open-ended abundance of nature waiting to be harvested—or, phrasing it differently, the first was conceived within the imaginary of the second. The point is that democracy through such devices as property rights awards the whole of nature to the abilities of individuals. Today's problem is that nature itself has become the restricting agent. If we are technologically unable to solve the impending exhaustion of nature, if we cannot distribute nature to the new billions who also have a right to their share of property and commodities, democracy as open-ended rights and freedoms will need serious adjustment.

Given that rhetorical studies and democracy are so often paired as loving companions, it makes sense that any deep critique of the ambitions of democracy will include a deep critique of the ambitions of rhetoric. That is, contemporary rhetorical studies often imagines itself as furthering democracy, and in so doing it acquires a rationale and perhaps, as well, a kind of innate virtue. Because I do not wholly share these assumptions, I fear, then, that some readers of this essay will regard this piece as perverse, cynical, or even despairing. I do not think that is a correct reading. Those who know me best know that between the lines, for good or ill, there is a kind of radical, mystical poetics of egalitarianism driving everything, one that senses the insufficiency of the Right but also of the Left and even the radical Left. Hence the best reading will understand this essay as ultimately about the energy of topoi and things, about the depletion of energy, about the ever-moving, anarchistic power of energy.

TOPOI AND SOCIAL ENERGIES

Let me turn to rhetorical theory to begin my argument, for at the heart of my discussion of democracy is the notion of topoi (commonplaces) as storehouses of social energy. The basic claim here is that topoi organize our sentiments, beliefs, and actions in the lifeworld.

There are two terms in the phrase "topoi as storehouses of social energy" that have long histories in rhetoric. The first, of course, is "topoi," or commonplaces, and the second is "energy," or *energeia*. The first term moves through a long, remarkable history, one that I cannot here explore in detail.[4] Aristotle and many of his later followers, for instance, tended to exploit the ratiocinative potential of topoi in order to unpack a possible universal method for making arguments. Hence their concern with universal topoi empty of specific content led them to explore such categories as similarity, comparison, definition, difference, cause, effect, and so on. In using these topoi, the goal was to establish a flexible set of mental procedures that could be applied to any issue at hand so as to generate a more rigorous dialectics and better logic and, if possible, proof in different disciplines. But this same tradition also had the goal of improving the much less rigorous arguments of rhetorical practice.

Cicero and others shifted the emphasis from matters of logic to matters of invention in the sense that topoi as seats for arguments could be exploited in the production of discourse, that is, invention. The method here was far more practical in the sense that topoi with content had at least as much value as topoi stripped of content. If emphasizing Aristotle's contentless topoi could serve a dialectician's need to produce valid arguments and proofs, an emphasis upon content-filled topoi served the rhetor's need to amplify discourse by piling up ideas. A third tradition, which more properly might be considered an extension of the second, was the emergence of commonplace books enabled by the invention of the printing press. These collections of quotations, excerpts, moral sentiments, aphorisms, fables, proverbial expressions, verbal ornaments, and so on—sometimes organized under separate disciplines of inquiry or heads of argument—served the elite classes and their need to produce discourse. The point is that in rhetorical theory the study of topoi as templates of argument has emphasized the generative dimensions of topoi, generative for both the logician as well as the public rhetor.

As for energy, or *energeia,* my claim that topoi are storehouses of social energy parallels Kennedy's point as he writes in the introduction to Aristotle's *On Rhetoric:* "Rhetoric, in the most general sense, is the energy inherent in emotion and thought, transmitted through a system of signs, including language, to others to influence their decisions and actions."[5] Aristotle's own references to *energeia* in the *Rhetoric* appear, for instance, in Book 3, chapter 11. Energeia here is associated with figures of speech, not topoi. He describes Homer as being able to make the lifeless live via the power of metaphor or analogy. The key concept seems to be a "bringing-before-the-eyes," that is, actualizing things or making them appear to be engaged in an activity. "He [Homer] makes everything move and live, and energeia is motion."[6]

But why limit *energeia* to metaphors? If the point is emotion, motion, action, and actualization—and most important if our subject is politics—we might look to verbal and nonverbal crystallizations that have sufficient umpf to actualize the body politic. For the body politic, too, is in need, collectively, of a bringing-before-the-eyes before it can act. And through what means does that get accomplished? If topoi as described earlier are generative, it is because they are the starting points, the seed crystals that get things moving.

All of this suggests that topoi, in order to move things, must preexist the motion itself, which suggests, to me at least, that the body politic can be described as already organized around its topoi. Topoi do not emerge out of the blue. If they did they would not be recognized, and it is their recognizability, a bringing-before-the-eyes, that makes them potent. So the ability to get things moving collectively is dependent on the fact that topoi constitute the body politic in a visible and highly public sort of way.

Let me offer seven considerations regarding topoi: (1) If rhetoric has traditionally treated topoi as a method for the production of discourse on the part of rhetors, before they become rhetorically useful they must exist in social life. (2) Topoi are not the narratives but the bits and pieces from which narratives are made. (3) Topoi organize or constitute our imagining of social life; indeed they help to generate it. (4) Topoi are energy filled in the sense that they are invested with the contradictory, collective passions and convictions that constitute a people. (5) Topoi can be both verbal and nonverbal; consider the symbols of an ear of corn or a cow at a county fair, the now iconic no-smoking symbol, the wealth of iconic symbols at any protest rally. (6) The relationship between topoi and the material conditions of social life are complex. For instance, changing material conditions create an urgency to generate appropriate topoi by which people tame the new conditions into a possible understanding. But "understanding" here names the process by which the new enters a system of language that "socializes" new topoi with old. As such, the new is never quite new, neither materially nor topically. (7) The phrase "storehouses of social energy" is both topos and metaphor (hopefully one with sufficient *energeia*) and is the consequence of an improvisation. Any collection of topoi is a field of improvisation.

DEMOCRACY AS TOPOS

Thus far I have been speaking about technical matters within rhetorical theory. My analyses, overly brief and perhaps trivial, constitute the barest beginnings of an analytic foundation that might support the following claims: if we think of topoi as storehouses of social energy, we might also think of topoi as organizing our lifeworlds—including our economies, our very materiality— according to social energies. This section suggests that the topos of democracy and its field of related terms (freedom, equality, rights, transparency, the citizen, and so on) organize in particular ways our subjectivities, social relations, and material conditions.

Frankly, I am not certain how far to take the concept of social energies as organizers of our lifeworlds, for the idea itself trespasses into materialist theories, which have always preferred concepts such as social structures as the "true" organizers of social life. Herein, it seems to me, lies an enormous theoretical debate that lacks final answers: Is material life organized around structures? Are our lifeworlds organized around social energies that are stored within topoi? What is material life versus lifeworld, social structures versus social energies?

I sense a rabbit hole opening up that I do not want to enter, but remaining silent is not wise either; hence I feel compelled to add a brief point: is the term "social structure," seemingly, a bit of rhetorical artifice, an attempt to move a term appropriate in material domains (an architectural structure, geological structures) to less material domains (economic relations, social relations)? Inert matter is one thing, but economic and social relations are so bound up with topoi (that is, so bound up with movement) that we might best think of them as processes that are deeply improvisational.

And this is precisely the pivot point upon which arguments by Weber and neo-Weberians turn against Marx. We might describe the Weberian position, then, as exposing the Marxist notion of structure as "mere" metaphor and offering a countermetaphor based on action: "People do not belong to a class but do engage in multiple class actions."[7] For Weber, then, class is not a thing or even a process. At most it is a set of actions. Moreover, people's actions are not limited to any class position; hence actions from different political persuasions might occur from within a specific class position. And if we want to extend the Weberian position and make it also rhetorical, we might further add that the actions themselves are deeply bound up with topoi produced from and furthering the *energeia* of collective passions and convictions.

Consider all that a preamble for the task at hand, a discussion of democracy and its key terms as topoi containing sufficient energy to organize the perspectives and actions of very large communities. In order to get a sense of how this functions, we might turn first to rhetorical theorists, for they tend to deploy the topos of democracy in unexamined ways, which is a remarkable fact given the deconstructive skills that characterize the discipline. Rhetorical scholars use such topoi as democracy, equality, and egalitarianism (to name only a few) as an unstated, unexamined value system that enables them to unpack the shortcomings of institutions, individuals, and rhetorics.

Two examples come to mind: Sharon Crowley in her *Toward a Civil Discourse*[8] and James Aune in his *Selling the Free Market*.[9] Both can be described as attempts to preserve democracy against more exclusionary forces.

What I find interesting about these texts and all similar positions that advocate greater inclusivity of peoples and arguments is how authors imagine their positions as having automatic virtue—as if inclusion itself were not a topos to be examined. What has made it a sacrosanct topos? Is inclusion a realistic possibility—or does any and every inclusion entail an exclusion? My own view is that idealized versions of democracy, those that implicitly or explicitly depend on democracy as automatic virtue, do so by ignoring material limitation. That is, advocacy in the name of equality seems to ignore material limits that shrink the good intention to include. Political organizers know this especially well, and this is why they shoot for more benefits or higher wages than can be achieved because they know that restrictions will eventually curb their aspirations. Moreover, and this is closer to the heart of the matter, we need to be wary of both the practices of democracy as well as its ability to mobilize social energies, for ultimately we might ask, to what purpose are those energies being mobilized?

Let me make my point by turning to some ethnographic work, namely lengthy conversations with a Chicago Latino alderman whom I admire. One day he smirked, "Democracy, what democracy?" For some time he had been making the point that democracy, for him, is a ritual to be manipulated by the power that he has collected so that he might have even more power to do what he thinks is right. In short, he uses power to slow down real estate developers who demand greater transparency from his office and the democratization of his ward. Of course, behind these calls on the part of developers for an expanded democracy are opportunities for profit. By removing him, the developers could then replace a poor Latino population with a wealthy white one. Moreover, he forcefully shapes the will of his Latino constituents so that they continue to legitimize his actions and marginalizes the wills of a smaller group of Latino owners who are potentially sitting on fortunes. Because his "right" has also been my "right," I have supported him, but clearly the "rights" of others have been stymied—and forcefully so.

How does one make sense of the Crowley/Aune deployment of the topoi of democracy versus the alderman's deployment of the same topoi? What would the legitimization of developer voices and the creation of a more inclusive public sphere at the ward level lead to in this corner of Chicago? When does inclusion lose its automatic virtue? As stated, I agree with the alderman's actions, and hence I do not subscribe automatically to democratic values, for they seem meaningless and even harmful in the midst of specific material conditions.

AN ANTHROPOLOGY OF DEMOCRACY

Anthropologist Julia Paley in a 2002 article constructs an emerging tradition in her discipline that documents actual existing democracy in different parts of the world. Her claim, consistent with the skepticism of political theorist Barbara Cruikshank, is that democracy has no a priori understanding, hence no automatic virtue.[10]

My own ethnographic fieldwork in Chicago and, as I describe later, Kosova, also suggests that there is no a priori understanding of democracy. In contrast, the rhetorical theorists discussed earlier mobilize the topos of democracy as if it did have some a priori understanding. This belief allows them to use the topos to mobilize automatic virtue. Moreover, in the heated disputes that characterize real public discourse (see Rai in this volume), interlocutors seem to act also with considerable conviction that some a priori understanding is available—an understanding that precedes all other interpretations—and that that a priori is identifiable, or nearly so, with their own position. This is what gives their arguments force. As a result, opposing positions are seen as subjective, biased, overly narrow, unjust, noninclusive, or undemocratic. Conviction of this sort allows adversaries to not see themselves as self-interested and to see others as mostly, if not utterly, self-interested and subjective. The point is that all adversaries work from the same rhetorical spine, which is nothing less than the democratic organization of social order.

In order to get some understanding of how liberal democracy acquired its virtuous core, we might consider Habermas and his many critics. Remarkably, both Habermas and those who deride his theories as idealistic describe the public sphere as a social space that ought to mitigate violence and human suffering by increasing the amount of inclusive, rational, and empathetic communication. In short, there is general agreement, even among intellectual adversaries, that a working public sphere is desirable, and that it represents, if realizable, a remarkable increase of goodness and justice.

It seems that this virtuous core took distinctive shape during the seventeenth and eighteenth centuries when it dialectically battled monarchical authority. From liberal democracy's perspective, monarchies were imagined as hierarchical, unjust, and corrupt, a social order that fundamentally violated rightness and inappropriately monopolized rights. This particular fusion of moral and political order was overturned by the bourgeois democratic revolutions of the eighteenth century when a different sort of fusion of rightness and rights became organized according to democratic or republican constitutions.

It is hardly surprising that the leaders of a specific social order, no matter what kind, derive their power from some notion of rightness, virtue, or higher calling. As Giorgio Agamben suggests, politics can never be mere politics but must be infused with a degree of metaphysics.[11] Consider: if a king has divine right, then the "people" who are on the verge of overthrowing such a king must argue that they have similar or equivalent credentials: dignity, equality, inalienable rights.

The consequences of these revolutions are obviously very much with us and become rearticulated when groups, minorities or majorities, left or right, demand greater justice, civil rights, autonomy, or participation in decision making. Demands made under these conditions are thought of as innately virtuous or answering a higher purpose. And when the wrong is redressed, the credibility of democracy becomes amplified. Such groups wage what they deem "the good fight" because of their conviction that the inclusion of previously excluded groups or views is good for democracy. This historical "common sense," shaped by both empirical research and social movements, has served to "virtuize" the revolutionary character of most actions taken in the name of democracy.

In short, this ontological attribution of a specific character or ethos to democracy itself constitutes mainstream political theory, which emphasizes rational discourse and consensus as constitutive of the public sphere.[12] I prefer to postpone any such attribution and to claim instead that "democracy" is a concept open to inquiry, a rhetoric whose substance and meaning are opaque until the motives behind its deployment are understood. Democracy and its attendant terms (transparency, rule of law, rights, equality, and so on) are quintessential topoi that exhibit sufficient malleability to mobilize the most disparate collective desires and actions, and as a result have competing meanings. That is, democracy and its attendant terms lack any specific telos, meaning that democratic governance, like all governance, is a relation of power that can only be understood through an analysis of motive since the same terms can mobilize both humane and inhumane actions.

Readers at this point may reasonably demand that I brake my thinking. Have I not conflated democratic rhetorics with the institutions of democracy, and is such a conflation warranted? Even if democratic rhetorics are, indeed, unclear at their moment of use, what, if anything, does this imply about democratic governance itself? Does an analysis of the former tell us anything about the "nature" of the latter, such as the myriad ways by which checks and balances become institutionalized? Moreover, is not democratic governance itself what we want to illuminate, as opposed to just democratic rhetorics?

The relationship between democratic governance and democratic rhetorics is nothing less than the battlefield upon which our civil structures, social relations, and subjectivities are shaped. On this battlefield, contending democratic rhetorics make their moves, which eventually give rise to laws, judicial decisions, and "democratic" institutions (in short, democracy's mechanical operations). But here is the inevitable failure: these operations cannot balance the overproduction of mass desire, which democratic rhetorics incessantly generate, against power's need to manage that desire. In sum: the proliferation of investments represented by contending parties wielding the same democratic rhetorics is a permanent condition; these investments/positions/desires are incompatible and insatiable, and yet, legitimate, for democracy itself warrants a boundless, sovereign self limited only by other sovereign selves; eventually some concrete mechanism (a law, an institution, a principle) must be formulated to adjudicate competing claims over the same bounty; we may ask (demand) that the mechanism and adjudication be "fair" or "democratic," but fairness is not only difficult to determine, but, in the final instance, only a certain amount of "fairness" can be permitted. That is, fairness, because it is an innate threat to power, is permitted only up to the point that it jeopardizes the stability of the social system, for if it oversteps this boundary, the system will respond with its even more rightful claim to "fairness."[13] It is through such means and logics that the mixed system of oligarchic-democracy comes into being.[14]

Let me at this juncture speculate about the future by elaborating a point made in the introduction: one of the emerging crises for this new century may be the widening of a disjunction between the limitlessness that democratic subjectivity implies, through rights talk and all other mobilizations of democratic rhetorics, and the limitedness that material life represents (for instance, the sustainability of resources). My guess is that material life will force a severe readjustment of democratic rhetorics that will cause them to lose their original enthusiasm, become pale and gray, and finally to dissipate into bureaucratic management whose main function will be to preserve hierarchy in the name of public order that will be translated as synonymous with the public good. It will be, in effect, the exhaustion of democracy, which has been long in the making, and the first signs will be laws, democratically passed, that respond to the constriction of resources. This last point is important because social contract models traditionally ignore material resources and instead talk rather simply of liberties as limitless or limited: for instance, individual liberties are constricted only by the need to preserve someone else's individual liberties. In this sense, liberties have no connection to real material resources and thereby invent an unreal world of limitless progress and optimism. But as the nature of constriction shifts increasingly to material resources, liberty as a founding politics will more than likely be forced to adjust. Of course, such adjustments have always been a part of the history of democracy. That is, power has always tampered with the demos by resisting, via laws and other means, equitable distribution of resources while allowing, as a kind of escape valve, the discourses of liberty to foster its distracting ideology. But that game is narrowing—particularly if we cannot find new technologies to replace the wastefulness of current technologies.[15]

In short, a discussion of democratic rhetorics as profoundly suspect takes us to the threshold of questioning democratic governance itself, its mechanical operations—and here we ask the disturbing questions: To what extent are the linchpins of democracy, such as checks and balances, the rule of law, and so on, comparably suspect? Why does the demos as deep artifact never arrive? The answer is simple enough: power protects its accumulated advantages and capital through laws of exclusion and inclusion. And even when one power bloc is replaced by another, it is because that replacement was permissible, posing only a minor threat to the continuity of power, and perhaps even aiding the concentration of power by eradicating antagonistic and/or anachronistic elements. I do not have the space here to examine what may be a classic case in point: post–World War II American civil rights legislation. Such legislation seemed to break up entrenched power blocs based on segregation and Jim Crow laws, which enabled northern capital to more easily invest in the South. The result was an economic boom in the Sun Belt even as the economic crisis in the northern Rust Belt deepened. The point is that just laws, whatever else they might be, also participate in the consolidation of specific power blocs and the dismantling of others in the infinite game of inclusion/exclusion.

OUR POST–BERLIN WALL MOMENT

At the beginning of this essay I suggested that the fall of the Berlin Wall marked a dramatic spread of democratic rhetorics. In my view, these rhetorics have been unable to organize just actions. It is this idea that I hope to now deepen because, if it is true, it helps to further explain the dis-ease that underlies this essay and the consequent emergence of an anthropology-of-democracy perspective focusing simultaneously on democratic rhetorics versus the actual operations of democracies.

It is easy to overstate the point, but it is possible that the entire Cold War period represented a steady hollowing out of whatever "virtuous core" remained as democracy, or at least the United States' variety, pragmatically but duplicitously encountered a variety of Latin American, Middle Eastern, and Asian insurgencies. In effect, the Cold War steadily corroded the two competing idealisms, exposing how deeply the need to grab national security, advantage, and power had taken precedence over the maintenance of "virtuous" idealisms. During the struggles over Korea, Guatemala, Cuba, Vietnam, Chile, Nicaragua, Iran, and Afghanistan, to name only some of the better known examples, competing visions of what constitutes liberty for all were quickly sacrificed to the pressing needs of national interest. The fall of the Berlin Wall, then, marked the funeral of one idealism and became a shot across the bow for the other. At first, however, only the funeral of Communism seemed clear, for the fall of the wall simultaneously rebirthed a particular kind of political enthusiasm regarding democracy and capitalism insofar as all other models for the organization of social, political, and economic life seemed to be effectively defeated—hence Fukuyama. In the United States, both neoconservatism and neoliberalism were distinctive outbreaks of this enthusiasm.

But the triumph was elusive and quickly unraveled. As democracy scattered everywhere, it became evident that all sorts of newly emerging movements and constitutions merely made use of democracy as a topos. Even as the United States negotiated military bases inside the old Iron Curtain, democratic rhetorics in these newly emerging states became organized around older structures of power because these were the only rhetorics permissible if one wanted to preserve power or aspired to power. In short, democracy as the "only game in town" was, in effect, "democracy without democrats."[16] Democracy was circulating and morphing at such speed that it was no longer identifiable; distortions of some vague original democracy seemed to be accelerating. That is, the enthusiasm that democratic rhetorics always generate could not do much more except skim the surfaces of different body politics because underneath other sorts of actions were shaping social structures. In a place such as collapsing Yugoslavia, where I have been doing fieldwork for some time, the disjunction between democratic rhetorics and forces of exclusion/inclusion became glaringly apparent. Democratic rhetorics were tethered to very little.

Let me elaborate this last point by turning to my Kosovar fieldwork, particularly to a local political analyst who makes a fascinating claim in one of his books: "I argue that a democratic Serbia will be impossible with a majority Albanian population Kosova [sic]. In this context, following their national ideology, the Serbs had only three alternatives: 1. To expel the whole Albanian population from Kosova, 2. To expel the Albanian population from part of Kosova (partition Kosova), or 3. To recognize the independence of Kosova."[17]

Most interpretations have blamed the Balkan wars of the 1990s on the intensification of Serbian nationalism, which after the death of Tito crystallized as a kind of anti-Communist liberation ideology.[18] The strength of this interpretation is that it acknowledges how one strand of Serbian populism framed the problem: it demonized and rebelled against Communism, and as an antidote argued for a return to Serbia's roots as well as the territorial unification of the Serbian people. Other interpretations, however, emphasize less the perversities of Serbian nationalism and more "a ruthless activation of the logic of 'sovereignty' in the name of the 'nation,' both of them central concepts of European modernity."[19] This last interpretation is appropriate, for it emphasizes how mass sentiment is itself a consequence of a modernist historical logic that effectively countered problems of monarchical order even as it launched another set of problems that would later be realized. And one might note, again, that the topoi of "sovereignty" and the "nation-state" as embodied by the "will of the people" are storehouses of a particular kind of social energy.

But Spahiu argues still another dimension of this modernist fantasy. Serbia had begun to cultivate democratic institutions such as elections, and many of the leading political parties attached democracy to their names. Call this, if you wish, another instance of "democracy without democrats" or, as many readers of this essay will claim, a hijacking of democracy by nationalists. But be aware that in these phrasings nationalism corrupts the virtues of democracy, and what gets obscured is democracy's dependence on some version of nationalism in order to realize its own project. Democracy needs the coherence that nationalism provides, a sense of We the People, though of course this coherence can emerge from milder forms of nationalism. But Spahiu's point is that when democracy is put under stress and strain, the nationalist ingredient that is part of its makeup cannot be stuffed back into its box. Spahiu argues that Serbian democracy as a representation of the will of the people realized that it would be permanently confronted by restless, highly demanding recalcitrants of another faith comprising approximately one-third of its body politic. For the Serbian state to function democratically, that portion had to disappear or the democracy would face paralysis from a plethora of rights demands that could not be granted, a funneling of resources that could not be afforded, and waves of massive protest that would have eventually led to civil war.

So democratization would have legitimized all these actions and made Serbian life miserable. Serbia wanted to keep Kosova, but keeping it meant the potential destruction of its state. Granting Kosova independence was not acceptable, but bending to its needs was also not acceptable. The only real solutions were to partition it or drive the Albanians out. Consider what the American civil rights movement would have become if African Americans would have constituted 40 percent or more of the American population. Minority rights may be permissible only to the extent that the material conditions permit, that is, when minority differences or numbers do not significantly challenge the hegemonic structure. When liberal democrats genuinely feel their hegemony or security threatened, they will no longer advocate democratic toleration. Hence the dubiousness of democracy when its material limitations are not acknowledged. I am, of course, not defending a shrinking of minority rights but presenting the material conditions, or root conditions, that allow—or disallow—people to think and act according to "democratic virtues."

Spahiu's analysis raises some further issues. It seems that democracy can only be understood as some sort of mixed system. In the case of Serbia, the immaturity of its democracy allowed it to mix readily with forms of totalitarianism. Readers might recognize here Agamben's analyses of the state of exception and the sort of equivalence that it makes between democracy and totalitarianism.[20] This latter point, which may disturb many readers since it opens the door to certain forms of unrestrained power, simply acknowledges that democracy as a set of conceptual ideals cannot be easily materialized in a real state with real needs facing the push and pull of internal and external forces. That is, no state can wear the ideals of democracy comfortably, for the state is a remarkably different animal. Democracy is a thought system that many have tried to institutionalize but has yet to arrive; the state, in contrast, wields pragmatic power, and if its self-preservation becomes desperate enough, it will break the shackles of restraint, including those imposed by democracy, and it will do so "democratically" with the full permission of the "people." A people struggling under the raw anxiety of survival will look first for a cure to their material desperation and will modify and even dismiss with easy abandon the niceties of their ideals. From this perspective, there are no aberrations, distortions, or perversions of democracy; these darker conditions are simply part of the potential of any democratic power, even if only rarely deployed.

And if a state should claim that it observes a set of principles, such as the rule of law or democratic transparency, but acts in wholly opposite ways, it is strange to call such a state hypocritical. The charge is strange because it misperceives the nature of the state as wielder of pragmatic power. That is, it misperceives the gap between theory and practice. Theory attempts to control practice by giving it meaning, high purpose, a telos in order to curb its potential brutality. Practice will abide by theory and more or less follow its rules as long as conditions permit. It is the breaking point, then, the state of emergency, that always proves most interesting, that moment when practice must overthrow whatever theory gives it meaning in order to save the theory itself. In other words, the unseemly practices that at the breaking point suddenly become sanctioned are given full reign because they can be dressed with the last vestige of hope: the salvation of our virtuous theory. But this breaking point simply tells us what has been in place all along, namely, that theory is constantly under assault because it disables and hinders the power of human desire and real needs.

This conundrum is faced by Kant in his essay "On the Common Saying: 'This May Be True in Theory, But It Does Not Apply in Practice.'"[21] His goal here is to embody the transcendental principles of moral order, reason, and justice inside republican constitutions. Through such means natural law (theory) can become human law (practice) that will tame the all too human proclivity for force and cunning. Via a number of brilliant arguments—such as the fact that incessant violence exhausts a people, which brings them back to reason—he makes his case that humans have and will continue to wend their way toward a morally superior state, that is, a public sphere based on reason and empathy, not coercion. This model, in which theory and practice come into reasonable alignment, is picked up by Rawls and Habermas in their own models of a just society but also by their critics who patch up the injustices overlooked by both authors in order to offer an even fuller, more encompassing justice. Theory and practice, then, in all these models can be brought together, and from this perspective the calling out of shortcomings and hypocrisies are legitimate strategies by which the virtues of democracy can be widened and improved and brought back into practice; that is, these theorists and defenders of the public sphere claim that more democracy can repair the damage that democracy has created if we can just point to who or what caused its virtue to slip and fall in the first place.

The reason why I maintain a genuine fondness for Kant, Rawls, and Habermas is because these writers know the potential human tragedy that their arguments try to keep at bay. Nevertheless, the approach taken here regarding the anthropology of democracy and the analysis of democratic rhetorics foregrounds material conditions. It does not background them, as does the idealist tradition. Perceived need or real need, perceived fear or real fear—when people feel subject to these lacks, they assume that material conditions are the causes of their woe, and from that base rhetors search for the available arguments that have the power to win what is needed or defeat what is feared. And those topoi that carry a history of virtue have particular power; hence rhetors evoke democratic rhetorics in the hope of locating some irrefutable sense of goodness and justice—*Recht,* as Kant called it—that will defend their claim. But this irrefutability is often checkmated by arguments and virtues derived from the same democratic rhetorics.

FINAL THOUGHTS ON THE "PUBLIC GOOD"

How, then, do we determine the public good? A related question: how might we improve the quality of the public sphere? These are some of the more common questions raised within liberal democracy. My earlier discussions of Sharon Crowley and James Aune indicated also their deep interest in revitalizing the public sphere. Similarly, in a talk titled "The Lure of Extreme Rhetoric," political theorist and president of the University of Pennsylvania Amy Gutmann, well known for her work with Habermas, examined the "increasing allure of extremist rhetoric in public discourse and its perils for democracy." The central peril was the erosion of a sense of compromise and mutual respect that tends to distort and corrupt democracy. The cure? An "economy of moral disagreement" in which advocates stand passionately for what they believe but do not argue down their adversaries or argue for more than what is necessary.[22] But can democracy be distorted, corrupted, or put into peril? And how does one encourage advocates to stand passionately for what they believe but also to restrain themselves from arguing down adversaries and arguing only for what is necessary? My answers to these questions will hopefully be a fitting conclusion to this essay.

I have been arguing from the beginning that democracy is too large and too abstract to be institutionalized. If anything, democracy is a topos along with a whole host of related topoi that act as storehouses of social energy. They are particularly powerful topoi because they reflect a history that has become sacrosanct, and hence they evoke an instant or automatic virtue to be deployed by rhetors in whatever scene or for whatever cause they choose. Of course, one rhetor's deployment may seem utterly unacceptable to another's, but because the topoi themselves are packed with virtue both camps will probably rely on the same topoi.

If this first point is trivial enough, perhaps the second one is less so. For what is even more at stake is not just how democratic rhetorics are available equally to all parties in the public sphere but to the extent to which democratic governance, because it is not realizable except as an *energeia*, represents a mixed system that I am calling oligarchic democracy. If democracy is, indeed, a mixed system, then it cannot be distorted or corrupted because, in effect, whatever the critic is complaining about is integral to the system itself. Returning to Gutmann's example, the boorish voices that want to trample the voices of opponents and to claim much more than is necessary are not examples of a distorted democracy but part of the expectations and desires that have been unleashed by a special subjectivity that is now filled with the topoi of rights, freedoms, and individual will that mark democracy. Democracy, of course, does not in all cases give birth to boorish passions, but it provides an interpretive lens that can rationalize and legitimize actions and words that I too find reprehensible. Gutmann idealizes democracy because there is no alternative that can realize the sort of public good and public sphere that she desires. She is right that no other alternative has been theorized, but why should she also ignore the ways in which democracy generates the very world that makes her uncomfortable?

Let me inquire more deeply into the motives for asking questions like "how do we determine the public good?" or "how do we improve the public sphere?" First, I cannot imagine a program that could in any pragmatic way improve public deliberation. Second, I suspect that most calls to improve the public sphere reflect the specific motives of some group that feels shut out of the deliberative process. That is, a call to improve the public sphere, whether from a left-leaning or right-leaning group, is a synonym for "let me in" and not really a call to *genuinely* improve the public sphere. In most cases, the group in power, whether left or right and very much like the Chicago alderman described earlier, seeks to stymie the other, while the group out of power calls for improvements to the public sphere. Such calls, then, sound the tones of virtue, but if either group should come to power it may cease to believe its former words if such calls should lead to political suicide. Third, such questions as "how do we determine the public good?" or "how do we improve the quality of the public sphere?" idealize the concept of the public good by suggesting that there is some determination or improvement that will somehow escape the paradoxical conditions of exclusion/inclusion. Certainly there are on occasion win-win conclusions to a public dispute, but the public sphere, particularly when deliberating the most serious of social issues, is mostly a space of limited inclusion and not one that excludes exclusion.

Finally, a more significant, if controversial, point is that such calls are in some instances false emergencies built on a mistaken conflation of democracy with the interests of the nation-state. Conjecture: When we say that democracy is in peril or that our freedom or the constitution or the public sphere is in danger, are we thinking metonymically, that is, substituting the term "democracy" for the state itself? If so, then to call for the preservation of democracy is actually a call to preserve the social order as embodied by the state. I suspect that false emergencies are manufactured out of metonymic magic and that calls to action in the name of saving the constitution or democracy or the public sphere mobilize subjects to rise up in defense of the state by using the bullhorn of virtuous democracy. Such calls are meant to stymie the revolutionary, unruly, destabilizing "red" spirit, whether right-leaning or left-leaning, that constitutes much of the history of democratic movements in order to emphasize the more conservative defense of the status quo interests of the state.

Perhaps a keener way to explore this point is to observe that democratic rhetorics, as suggested earlier, overproduce expectations and desires that generate unrealistic claims of equality, freedom, and rights that are difficult for any social order to realize and manage. The questions "how do we determine the public good?" and "how might we improve the public sphere?" are, particularly in Gutmann's case, about the management of that proliferation, the fear that something has gotten out of hand and now must be righted. That is, they apply one kind of brake on the enthusiasms that democracy births; for most "threats" to the constitution or democracy or to the public sphere are the result of someone's claim to excessive freedom and the like. The social order typically manages this proliferation by working double time to produce an economy of material abundance that substitutes for the abstractions and desires that its politics cannot satisfy. As long as this material abundance constitutes the norm and dire necessity does not threaten, the human propensity for fairness works.

A HESITATION AT THE END

Even as this essay deontologizes democracy, it seems to ontologize power by putting it at the center of politics, particularly the mixed system of oligarchic-democracy. All contemporary governance, I suspect, is a ratio of these two terms, these two forces. Curiously enough de Tocqueville saw some of this: "American society has . . . a surface covering of democracy, beneath which the old aristocratic colors sometimes peep out."[23] I do not have the space here to elaborate the proposition of the mixed system. But it should be clear that my argument relies on a strong reading of that proposition as well as a strong reading of human anxiety as seen in statements like "fear rules." Consider: contemporary rhetoricians favor social theorists who shatter the social order via radicalized versions of the topos of democracy—from Marx and Nietzsche to Foucault, Derrida, Habermas, and the most recent work of Rancière, Agamben, Negri, Badiou, and others. Such work requires an idealized version of democracy, one that rests on a fundamental cleavage between actual existing democracy and democracy itself. My own version of this cleavage has been to call actual existing democracy oligarchic-democracy, a more revealing term, and the other democracy an *energeia* that functions largely in the symbolic and rhetorical. As an *energeia,* democracy is not meant to be realized, and that is what provides it with propulsive force. Up to this point, then, my analysis remains within this specific tradition, but then I seem to be raising questions about the "other" democracy as well, for I am wondering about those instances when the *energeia* of democracy does little to cure perversity but actually instigates it (the Serb case mentioned earlier) or raising questions about an era that we may be entering, namely, the exhaustion of democracy strapped to an exhaustion of nature. The end of my essay hesitates, then, because I do not like this reappearance of determinism.

NOTES

1. De Tocqueville, *Democracy in America,* 244.
2. Fukuyama, "End of History?"
3. Linz and Stepan, *Problems of Democratic Transition,* 5; Trimcev, *Democracy;* Nodia, "How Different," 10.
4. Moss, "Commonplaces."
5. Kennedy, Introduction, 7.
6. Aristotle, *On Rhetoric,* 249.
7. Hall, Introduction, 21. See also Weber, *Economy and Society.*
8. Crowley, *Toward a Civil Discourse.*
9. Aune, *Selling the Free Market.*
10. Paley, "Toward an Anthropology"; Cruikshank, *Will to Empower.*
11. Agamben, *Homo Sacer;* Agamben, *State of Exception.*
12. Habermas, *Between Facts and Norms;* Rawls, *Theory of Justice.*
13. These last four points have been greatly aided by conversations with Candice Rai. They began as her marginal comments to my paragraph.
14. See Canfora, *Democracy in Europe;* Cintron, "Democracy as Fetish."
15. For a more optimistic scenario, see Sachs, *Common Wealth.*
16. Linz and Stepan, *Problems,* 5; Trimcev, *Democracy;* Nodia, "How Different," 10.
17. Spahiu, *Serbian Tendencies,* 7. As Yugoslavian Communism collapsed, a variety of internal struggles wracked the region. Internally, the political leadership in Serbia was unable to articulate a replacement ideology for Communism (say, a version of democratic socialism resting on civic identity as opposed to ethnic and/or religious identity) that might keep nationalist forces at bay. Externally, the independent entities that had constituted Yugoslavia began to assert their statehood. Serbia, which saw itself as the natural inheritor of the old federation, struggled against the centripetal forces through a resurgent nationalism strongly inflected by religious (Orthodox) sentiment. In some cases, such as Slovenia, the Serbs did not put up much of a fight, but in other cases, such

as Bosnia and later Kosova, where sizable numbers of Serbs lived, Serbian paramilitaries, aided by the Serbian army, began to claim territory by expelling non-Serbian populations. In Kosova, the majority Albanian population developed parallel and underground political and social institutions as the Serbs clamped down on a province that they considered theirs. The Albanians also adopted a pacifist ideology advocated by their leader, Ibrahim Rugova, in order to avoid the "ethnic cleansing" occurring in Bosnia. The stalemate was ruptured with the emergence of the Kosovar Liberation Army and increasing repression from the Serbs. By 1998–99 the Serbs, in their hunt for the KLA, initiated massacres and forceful expulsion. The KLA retaliated with their own nastiness, and the growing war quickly became unacceptable to the international community. A combined NATO and U.S. force launched an air war that encouraged even more Albanian refugees but defeated and eventually ended the Milosevic regime in Belgrade. Starting in June 1999 Kosova became a protectorate of the United Nations. In February 2008 Kosova became independent but still under international supervision.

18. Thomas, *Serbia under Milosevic.*
19. Ananiadis, "Carl Schmitt," 152.
20. Agamben, *Homo Sacer;* Agamben, *State of Exception.*
21. Kant, *Kant.*
22. Gutmann, "Lure of Extreme Rhetoric."
23. De Tocqueville, *Democracy in America,* 45.

Works Cited

Agamben, Giorgio. *Homo Sacer: Sovereign Power and Bare Life.* Translated by Daniel Heller-Roazen. Stanford, Calif.: Stanford University Press, 1998.

———. *State of Exception.* Translated by Kevin Attell. Chicago: University of Chicago Press, 2005.

Ananiadis, Grigoris. "Carl Schmitt on Kosovo, or, Taking War Seriously." In *Balkan as Metaphor: Between Globalization and Fragmentation,* edited by Dusan I. Bjelic and Obrad Savic, 119–61. Cambridge, Mass.: MIT Press, 2002.

Aristotle. *On Rhetoric: A Theory of Civic Discourse.* Translated by George A. Kennedy. New York: Oxford University Press, 1991.

Aune, James A. *Selling the Free Market: The Rhetoric of Economic Correctness.* New York: Guilford Press, 2001.

Canfora, Luciano. *Democracy in Europe: A History of an Ideology.* Translated by Simon Jones. Oxford: Blackwell, 2006.

Cintron, Ralph. "Democracy as Fetish." *Politicum* 1, no. 2 (May 2008): 9–12.

Crowley, Sharon. *Toward a Civil Discourse: Rhetoric and Fundamentalism.* Pittsburgh: University of Pittsburgh Press, 2006.

Cruikshank, Barbara. *The Will to Empower: Democratic Citizens and Other Subjects.* Ithaca, N.Y.: Cornell University Press, 1999.

De Tocqueville, Alexis. *Democracy in America.* Translated by Henry Reeve. Edited by Phillips Bradley. New York: Everyman's Library, 1994.

Fukuyama, Francis. "The End of History?" *National Interest* (Summer 1989): www.wesjones .com/eoh.htm.

Gutmann, Amy. "The Lure of Extreme Rhetoric." Craig S. Bazzani Lecture in Public Affairs, University of Illinois at Chicago, November 2006.

Habermas, Jürgen. *Between Facts and Norms: Contributions to a Discourse Theory of Law and Democracy.* Translated by William Rehg. Cambridge, Mass.: MIT Press, 1998.

Hall, John R. "Introduction: The Reworking of Class Analysis." In *Reworking Class,* edited by John R. Hall, 1–40. Ithaca, N.Y.: Cornell University Press, 1997.

Kant, Immanuel. *Kant: Political Writings.* Edited by H. S. Reiss. Translated by H. B. Nisbet. Cambridge: Cambridge University Press, 1991.

Kennedy, George A. Introduction. In *Aristotle on Rhetoric, A Theory of Civic Discourse,* 3–22. Translated by George A. Kennedy. New York: Oxford University Press, 1991.

Linz, Jaun J., and Alfred Stepan. *Problems of Democratic Transition and Consolidation: Southern Europe, South America, and Post-Communist Europe.* Baltimore: Johns Hopkins University Press, 1996.

Moss, Ann. "Commonplaces and Commonplace Books." In *Encyclopedia of Rhetoric,* 119–124. Edited by Thomas O. Sloane. Oxford: Oxford University Press, 2001.

Nodia, Ghia. "How Different Are Postcommunist Transitions?" In *Democracy after Communism,* edited by Larry Diamond and Marc F. Plattner, 3–17. Baltimore: Johns Hopkins University Press, 2002.

Paley, Julia. "Toward an Anthropology of Democracy." *Annual Review of Anthropology* 31 (2002): 469–96.

Rawls, John. *A Theory of Justice,* rev. ed. Cambridge, Mass.: Belknap Press of Harvard University Press, 1999.

Sachs, Jeffrey D. *Common Wealth: Economics for a Crowded Planet.* New York: Penguin Press, 2008.

Spahiu, Nexmedin. *Serbian Tendencies for Partitioning of Kosova.* Budapest: Central European University, 1999.

Thomas, Robert. *Serbia under Milosevic: Politics in the 1990s.* London: Hurst, 1999.

Trimcev, Eno. *Democracy, Intellectuals and the State: The Case of Albania.* Tirana: Albanian Institute for International Studies, 2005.

Weber, Max. *Economy and Society: An Outline of Interpretive Sociology.* Edited by Guenther Roth and Claus Wittich. New York: Bedminster Press, 1968.

[**PART 2**]

Rhetorical Interventions

Rhetorical Engagements in the Scientist's Process of Remaking Race as Genetic

CELESTE M. CONDIT

On July 30, 2002, a *New York Times* headline read, "Race Is Seen as Real Guide to Track the Roots of Disease."[1] The credibility of this article rested squarely on the research of a biologist. Neil Risch, of Stanford University, is cited as the source of the claim that "genetic differences have arisen among people living on different continents and that race, referring to geographically based ancestry, is a valid way of categorizing these differences."[2] This article is part of a substantial trend in current genetic research, which links differences in human social groups to differences in genetics.

Here we go again. Every other generation or so, a group of scientists masks flawed methodology and self-aggrandizing assumptions with the latest scientific trend in order to produce "data" showing that other races are inferior[3]: phrenology bolstered slavery in the nineteenth century;[4] the poorly conceived and biased data of Charles Davenport bolstered eugenics in the Progressive Era;[5] Cyril Burt's manufactured intelligence test of twins backed up segregationism in the mid-twentieth century.[6] All of these, of course, pale in comparison to the Nazi physicians' brutal "experiments" and their broad-reaching claims to superiority in the blood of their Volk.[7] Most rhetoricians readily condemn this recurrent tendency, but is there anything that rhetoricians can do to preclude scientists from constructing these racist statements in the guise of scientific truth?

Rhetorical theorists have, no doubt, long been entangled in efforts for social change. Cicero was both the foremost rhetorical theorist of his era and an active Roman politician, elected Consul in 63 B.C. Like Cicero's activism, most efforts by rhetoricians to participate in social change processes have been directed at the public sphere. Humans, however, have become a thoroughly technologized species, and recent research in science and technology studies have highlighted the powerful influences exerted by the technical sphere upon paths of social change.[8] An enormous variety of scholars have shown that the technical sphere, like the public sphere, is at least partially shaped by rhetorical factors.[9] It might similarly, therefore, be susceptible to intervention through discursive efforts guided by rhetorical theory.

Even when addressing topics raised by science and technology, however, most rhetoricians have directed their discourse at other rhetoricians or at a presumed reading public inhabiting the public sphere. With regard to the topic of race and genetics, there are, for example, numerous analyses that show the problematic metaphors and categorizations of genetics,[10] or reveal the rhetorical strategies by which the linkage between "race" and "genetics" is constructed in scientific discourses or reportage on science.[11] While there are some exceptions to the tendency to focus on technical communication as it plays out in the public sphere, the heavy publication slant suggests that it is likely that more activist interventions are also directed at the public sphere rather than involving engagement *within* the technical (or scientific) sphere.[12] To try to enter the scientists' own conversations, to argue with them within the venues and rubrics of science, is a somewhat different enterprise. To broach the feasibility of the practice and some of the challenges, I recount four different episodes in which I engaged geneticists in scientific venues on the subject of the relationships between "race" and "genetics." I describe some of the major reasons for the varying levels of success I had in each different situation. I conclude that, if my own experience is at all representative, then the fundamental variables influencing persuasiveness in the scientific venue are remarkably similar to those in the public sphere: you persuade people if you talk their language, but it is more difficult to persuade someone the more his or her highly interested worldviews are at stake.

MY COMING TO TERMS WITH RACE AND GENETICS:
The Human Genetic Variation Consortium

Until I moved to New Orleans, I reacted to race in most of the ways the average white professional American today reacts to race. I wanted to be "liberal" and "tolerant," not a "racist," but these were mere platitudes with no depth or breadth of meaning. When I moved to New Orleans, however, I moved to an area called "the black triangle" because I did not want to commute an hour each day to teach at Tulane University, because I was a teacher who could not afford to live in a "white" area, and because my liberal platitudes told me that there was no reason to be prejudiced and avoid a "black" area of town. Living there gave me experiential lessons about the meanings of racialization in America, and it also led me to modify my research agenda to focus on race. Periodically I have become overwhelmed and despondent and "stopped working on race." But race in contemporary America is not something you can ever really walk away from.

Consequently, though I had "stopped working on race" half a dozen years earlier and turned to studying genetics, in 1998 I found myself submitting a proposal to the National Institutes of Health (NIH) to study how laypeople, especially African Americans and Whites, understood the relationship between race and genetics. When that proposal was eventually funded, I was included in a group called the Human Genetic Variation Consortium. This was a group of researchers working in various ways on social, ethical, or legal issues related to race and genetics. Most notably, the group discussed the "Haplotype Map" project (described below) and advised some of that project's advisers. At the close of the term of my cohort of members, a group of its members published a position paper in the *Journal of the American Medical Association* on the lack of relevance of genetic research to the amelioration of health disparities.[13]

The consortium meetings during the first year were devoted to familiarizing ourselves with the new trend in genetics toward taking account of race in genetics and health studies. We were told that there were two major forces generating this trend. The first was a need for geneticists to account for population substructure in their work. Through several expensive and embarrassingly errant studies, geneticists had discovered that differences among the geographic ancestry of control and experimental populations could produce spurious findings that "a gene" was related to a particular health condition.[14] The simplest way of correcting that problem appeared to be to provide relatively rigorous controls on the boundaries among the "racial" groups that composed research populations.

The second concern was more compelling to the humanists and social scientists in the consortium. It was the issue of health disparities. There can be no denial that there are clear health disparities between groups that are understood as "racial" groups in the United States. Compared to people who self-identify as "White," people who self-identify as Black or African American, American Indian, or Hispanic American die younger and suffer more and worse disease across many common diseases, including cardiovascular diseases, diabetes, and several kinds of cancer (the situation is more complex for Asian Americans due to different historical and economic positionings of different nationalized subpopulations.)[15] Many doctors and researchers, including minority physicians, have come to believe that a part of these disparities is due to differences in biology, specifically in genes.

This rationale for attending to the possibility that "race" is "genetic" was compelling to many members of the consortium, because it meant that dismissing biological accounts of race was not a move with positive, or even merely neutral effects, but might be positively harmful to minority groups. For example, ignoring race results in the recruitment of predominantly white populations to research studies, and it produces medicine that is tailored to white bodies and therefore may be less helpful to the bodies of members of other groups. If there is substantial biological variation among the bodies of ethnic or racial groups, then to ignore that variation is to promote "the invisibility of whiteness," which is simply the contemporary route to privileging white people.[16] It is to mistake whiteness as the universal version of humanity.

The members of the Human Genetic Variation Consortium exhibited a range of reactions to these presentations. My own reaction was to be deeply troubled and indecisive. On the one hand, I was profoundly skeptical of the idea that race was biological. As a rhetorician, I understood that words made categories, and that the structure of material reality in the world did not simply and neutrally require a particular set of labels. I wrote, and continue to write, rhetorical analyses designed to show the constructedness of race with regard to human genetic variation.[17] On the other hand, I had come to take seriously the fact that race could not be simply ignored, denied, or swept under the carpet. Health disparities were undeniable, and minority researchers and physicians I respected insisted that they saw important differences between average members of different groups. While it was clearly true that the "average" member of a group was an imprecise construct, it might also be true that denying such average differences would merely reinforce a medical system that served white people well and other people not so well. Moreover, I had something of a consistency problem, as my own research required me to explicitly invite people to participate based on something like their "race." If I were to be able to provide a sufficiently robust input from people other than white southerners, then I had to *explicitly* invite people into my research project based on their identity as "African Americans." If this was a good, even essential, practice for the research I thought I should pursue, then how could I insist that it was not a good thing for people doing other types of research?

I took this profound uncertainty as an initial question for my research process. I decided to trust the community of people who would be most affected by a race-based medical research endeavor, African Americans. So, in conjunction with a fabulous group of graduate students and coresearchers, I designed and conducted focus groups to find out what ordinary people thought of these possibilities.[18] The answer African American participants in this research gave was overwhelmingly opposed to race-based medical approaches. White participants tended to oppose them as well, though not as vehemently. Having learned to distrust my own white-based instincts on issues of race, I determined to trust these people's judgments. The effort to amplify their voice became the basis of my first attempt at engagement with the scientific community.

ENGAGEMENT #1: Publish Data About the Challenges and Costs of
Race-Based Medicine in Scientific Journals on Genetic Medicine

My goal was to engage medical geneticists who were being encouraged to participate in a paradigm of race-based medicine. It seemed to me that the flow of medical science was such that it was better to prevent the formation of an errant consensus by these experts rather than to contest that consensus once it reached the public sphere, so I determined it best to engage in the process by which the medical consensus on race and genetic medicine was being formulated. All I had to offer by way of argument, however, was the fact that a substantial group of laypeople did not like the idea. How could that fact be made of relevance to the medical community?

Medical research in genetics, like all medical research, is largely bereft of attention to many of the issues of how a particular medical regime will be implemented in practice. Medical research is conducted in highly selective locations under near-ideal conditions. When a medical procedure or drug is approved, it is diffused for use under very different conditions. This, I thought, was exactly the problem for a race-based medicine. In an ideal world, where everyone was enlightened, using a social grouping such as "race" as shorthand for mild tendencies for human biology to vary might be acceptable. In the real world, as my participants clearly indicated, it just would not work. Since race-based medicine was being promoted primarily as an economic necessity—due to the presumed expense of doing individualized genetic testing—showing the economic and other barriers to implementation seemed like a reasonable line of argument.[19]

So I and my research team wrote "Attitudinal Barriers to Delivery of Race-Targeted Pharmacogenomics among Informed Lay Persons," and we were successful in publishing it in *Genetics in Medicine*.[20] The article and its companion article were written and published within the generic norms of a scientific article.[21] Its sections are "methods," "data," and "discussion." It uses quantitative presentation of findings and employs the objectivating procedure of intercoder reliability assessments. As Kenneth Burke has noted, you persuade a person insofar as you speak his or her language, and because we wanted to be persuasive to an audience of scientists, we presented our research in the language and conventions of science (even though we were mostly a group of rhetoricians).[22]

The contents of the article indicate that the effectiveness of a race-based medical approach would have to be assessed based on a variety of costs and challenges not presently included in the arguments in favor of its implementation. These additional costs included the inability of doctors to assign people to discrete and accurate ancestries, the lack of knowledge of the biology of one's grandparents especially among African Americans, and very high levels of distrust of such medicines by their users, which is likely to lead to low compliance with prescriptions as well as a potential backlash against prescribers, pharmaceutical companies, and medical research institutions if ever such a drug turns out to have serious harmful side effects (which seems probable over the long run, especially given the contemporaneous tragedy of Vioxx and related cox-2 inhibitors). In other words, we gave the medical experts scientific evidence that race-based medicine was unlikely to be cheap or particularly effective.

The impact of this pair of articles was, so far as we can tell, virtually zero. Citation indexes showed only three citations of either article. A wide variety of sources that should have cited it because they were addressing costs of race-based medicine or feasibility did not. My first intervention was apparently a total failure.

ENGAGEMENT #2: Going Live to Genetics Researchers on the Harmful Impact of "Race as Genetic"

The opportunity for a second intervention presented itself as a matter of both serendipity and foresightful preparation. One of the major arguments that humanists and social scientists use for arguing against geneticization of racial categories is that such geneticization makes race appear absolute and permanent. The technical term for this is that it tends to "reify" race. In contrast, a nonreified understanding of existing labels for groups sees these labels as leaky and imprecise and as a temporary product of historical and social confluences. Indeed, the historical evidence is quite clear that racial group labels and racial groupings vary considerably through time and space.[23] In contrast, assigning a scientific basis for a grouping is believed to suggest that such groupings are permanent and absolute, because we tend to think of scientific categories as universal and rigid. Therefore, a scientific grounding for race should produce more "racism" than would an understanding of race as a product of social and historical forces.

Is this presumption correct, however? Having become skittish about the link between genes and racism, I wondered whether we humanists were really right to claim that people who saw health as differentially distributed by race and who saw race as distributed by genes would be more racist than people who did not. If ignoring race was tantamount to universalizing whiteness, perhaps recognizing race was necessary to overcome racism. And if that were true, then perhaps people who thought of health disparities as a simple matter of biological difference would not therefore conclude that everything about racial groups (for example, class distribution or IQ scores) was a matter of genetics and was therefore fixed forever.

I continue to puzzle over this issue. However, one way of addressing the question, and of addressing it in a way that would have credibility with the scientifically based genetics community, is to run an experiment to see if people exposed to messages linking health, race, and genetics increase the racism level of their attitudes as composed to people who do not hear such messages. So this is what my research team did. The results of the experiment seemed to me shocking and frightening. We exposed people to a very tame message about health disparities, one that simply mentioned genetics in passing as one possible basis for health variation. People who heard this message increased their level of racism an average of almost a full point on a five-point racism scale.[24] We had expected no effect at all, because we had used a very mild message. We were quite concerned about the ethics of increasing people's levels of racism through an experiment, given that we were not sure that the debriefing message we would give them at the end would actually return their levels to preexperimental levels, so we had decided to start below the level where we thought we would create change and inch our way upward to a modest level of effect. The effect of a 20 percent increase that occurred from our first modest level message is unusual in message-design research, so this very large effect convinced us that messages about race, genes, and health most certainly would cause "reification" of attitudes about race and would amplify racism.

So that was the foresight. Serendipitously, around this time, because of my work with the Human Genetic Variation Consortium, I was invited to make a presentation to the sixth International Meeting on Single Nucleotide Polymorphism (SNP) and Complex Genome Analysis.[25] This is a meeting of a group of researchers who participate in projects designed to track down details of variation in the human genome in order to produce the basis for identifying genes that are associated with common diseases and identifying medicines that might address those genetic variations. I presented the results of the message experiment in my fifteen-minute presentation close to the beginning of the conference.

The impact of the talk was, I believe, relatively substantial—among those present, for the duration of the conference. The audience was attentive, and later speakers evidenced awkwardness, discomfort, and attempts at circumspection in labeling groups in their presentations. Moreover, the award-winning poster for the conference was one that indicated that apparent clusters of human genetic variation by continents was an artifact of sampling procedures that left large gaps in samples between continental groups rather than using a continuous sampling procedure. I heard the winner being told that "as soon as I heard that talk, I knew you were going to win."

I might well be exaggerating my own influence here. At the least, my presentation was one straw on a growing pile on an invisible camel (though there were no other presentations of this sort at the conference). I have to admit to being heartened and hopeful. It is important, however, to note the audience that evinced this effect. Most of these researchers do work that is well "upstream" from actual medical applications on live human beings. They might gather DNA from people, but after that they sift and search among single bases, comparing dozens of genomes on computers, looking for variations among millions of base pairs. They are highly mathematical scientists, doing statistical tests and creating statistical tests to assess what might actually count as an association in such large and complex data sets. Their main stake in the "race is genetic" debate is merely the ability to control for population structure. Population structure can be controlled simply through geographic distance. It does not need current racial labels.

This audience also consisted of a very smart and northeastern-biased group of scholars, trained at excellent schools. Not only do these scholars not want to appear to be racist, they really do not want to be racist, and they were trained in an understanding of racism that indicated calling out difference meant racism. They would probably have been completely at a loss if one tried to suggest that one problem of racism *is* the invisibility of whiteness. Therefore, my presentation did not cost the audience much in terms of their scientific goals, and it fit well with their understanding of what "not being a racist" meant. Moreover, short-term ripples do not necessarily make long-term impacts, as the third intervention was to make clear.

ENGAGEMENT #3: Relabeling the HapMap

During the second year of my stint on the Human Genetic Variation Consortium, some personnel of the National Human Genome Research Institute's Ethical, Legal, and Social Implications (NHGRI/ELSI) unit presented the consortium with plans for the "Haplotype Map Project" (or HapMap). In short, the project was designed to gather samples of human DNA from different groups in order to produce a tool for more rapidly and efficiently looking for variations in human genes that are associated with diseases. Various NIH personnel and researchers associated with the project were concerned about the public response to it. A few years earlier a "Human Diversity Project" had gained harsh worldwide negative publicity when it had sought to sample DNA from global cultures that are threatened with extinction. The ELSI researchers wanted the HapMap to be done in an ethically responsible fashion, and other project personnel either wanted that or, at the least, recognized the need to avoid generating another hostile international response. Some members of the Human Genetic Variation Consortium were on the ELSI consulting group for the project, but NIH officials also presented the project to us to get our reaction.

The discussion within the consortium was intense, extended, and challenging. The HapMap is a technically complex project. Understanding it requires careful explanation of detailed scientific information. The consortium included people ranging from an almost knee-jerk antiscience, antigenetics, antirace position, to medical researchers who were opposed to the use of race, to conflicted humanists, and to social scientists from several disciplines. Although I took notes, I make no claim to be able to represent objectively the process. It is my impression, however, that my role in the conversation was to insist that if the HapMap needed to sample across broad geographies merely in order to assure that a broad range of SNPs (genetic variations) be included, then their populations should not be labeled so as to imply that what was being sampled was "race." In other words, instead of labeling one population "Africans" or "sub-Saharan Africans," they should be labeled as coming from the narrowest precise geographic locale—for example, Ibadan, Nigeria. I was quite insistent that the HapMap should not reify the idea that the genetic variation that needed to be sampled was racial groupings, given the project scientists' claim that they were merely trying to obtain diversity, sampling people from geographical regions that were far from each other. As a rhetorician, I focused intensely on the word choices in the labels, operating from the belief widely shared in rhetorical studies that particular word choices matter.

Other people made similar arguments. Moreover, the conduit we had for making an impact was extremely indirect. We had the ear of one NIH scientist and one NIH (ELSI) program director and the ear of those members of the Human Genetic Variation Consortium who would participate directly in the HapMap project. In other words, I have no idea whether my personal arguments had any impact at all. Nonetheless, there is some clear evidence of adoption of the labeling practices we were promoting. On the HapMap Web site, the three groups are not labeled as "Africans," "Caucasians," and "Asians," as was a fairly predictable labeling structure given previous conventions in the scientific literature.[26] Instead, the "recommended descriptors" are "Yoruba in Ibadan, Nigeria (abbreviation: YRI), Japanese in Tokyo, Japan (abbreviation: JPT), Han Chinese in Beijing, China (abbreviation: CHB), and CEPH (Utah residents with ancestry from northern and western Europe) (abbreviation: CEU)."[27]

This novel labeling, and the official Web site's explicit attention to the rationale behind it, suggests that my intervention, or co-occurring interventions by others, had some impact. It was, however, a negligible impact, because in the major article presenting the HapMap project in *Nature,* almost all the data combines the groups JPT and CHB and pits them against the other two groups.[28] This combining of the groups, presented without any rationale, indicates that the authors are still thinking of and presenting these samples as representing "Asia."[29] Furthermore, in later articles that cite and apply these findings, the HapMap data is relabeled with conventional race labels and is explicitly taken to support the idea of continent-based racial groupings.[30]

This does not demonstrate that the labels researchers choose are irrelevant. It merely indicates that getting scientists in a key locale to adopt a particular (nonracial) label set does not necessarily have very large ripple effects. Absent a clear understanding of the novel labels, those who encounter them merely translate them back into more familiar categories. In addition to simple familiarity and inertia, a major force behind the maintenance of the old labels arises from those who have a stake in maintaining those labels. It was this group that my fourth intervention engaged.

ENGAGEMENT #4: The NIH Roundtable on Race

The NIH has relatively recently attended to the ethnic disparities in health and in science in a variety of ways, including structural requirements for researchers to include diverse populations in their research, outreach and financial support for minority researchers, bureaucratic components devoted to minority issues, calls for research projects that are likely to generate information of relevance to nondominant sectors, and a variety of conferences and workshops. The NIH Roundtable on Race was convened as one such conference. It specifically focused on issues surrounding the implications of genetics for race and for race-based medicine. Invitees and presenters included both medical researchers pursuing race-based medical or other projects and social scientists and humanists, most of whom were in some way skeptical of those projects. Minority scholars were included in both groups. Many of the scholars from minority groups, but not all, were favorable to race-based research and practice.

At this conference, I presented the same data I had presented at the SNP conference, as well as descriptive data characterizing the mass media's coverage of race-based genetics research and practice.[31] I would have to call the response of the audience cold, if not hostile. An older female minority scholar told me to "think about the parable of the sun and the wind, trying to get the person to take off their coat. You are the wind." In the parable, the wind fails because it only makes the person pull the coat tighter. The sun succeeds by making the person so warm they take off their coat. In light of the experimental results I had gotten, I was at a loss to figure out how to make people be less racist by applauding their assumption that race was genetic, so in spite of this chastisement I more or less continued a sustained argument against that view in the interactive discussion periods. Nonetheless, I learned a good deal from the people there about their motives, their sincerity, and the source of what seem to me to be their rhetorical blind spots.

I take as an example a researcher named Esteban González Burchard, a well-published scholar as well as a medical researcher dedicated to improving the health of Puerto Ricans. He has special interest, even passion, for addressing the high rates of serious asthma in the Puerto Rican population. He and I had civil, mutually respectful interchanges, but from my perspective Dr. Burchard is fundamentally wrong. At this conference, the warrant he articulated for maintaining race-based approaches and for insisting that race had a genetic basis was the fact that Puerto Ricans have a high asthma rate and a low response to the available medications (much lower than other groups). However, "Puerto Ricans" is not a race, even according to the standards of Dr. Burchard's own published research, and Puerto Ricans are not typical of "Latin Americans" or "Native Americans" or "African Americans" (or any other of the groups geneticists describe as "racial") with regard to their asthma susceptibilities.[32]

Nonetheless, as we talked, I gained additional depth of understanding about the ways in which the increasingly prominent version of antiracism that attacks "color-blind" approaches and the "invisibility of whiteness" applies in health disparities. Dr. Burchard's perspective worked within this vision of anti-racism. Additionally, however, my perception became that Dr. Burchard was unwilling to entertain environmental or cultural explanations for evident differences because such accounts in some sense place blame, or at least responsibility, upon Puerto Ricans for their health problem. In contrast, a genetic explanation places the cause of the health disparity beyond the personal, social, or even cultural control of the population at risk.

There are, of course, other ways to avoid "blaming the victim." The most common is to attribute the cause to the health care system or to environmental factors that are the result of economic forces and structural discrimination. But Dr. Burchard, like many other minority physicians, appears to be in a position that makes it difficult to blame the medical system for health disparities. Minority medical personnel are part of that system, and they are working very, very hard to serve their populations through it. They are disinclined to blame the systems that do indeed provide extensive positive services to their populations, and certainly they should not blame themselves, even though they must serve at least in part as agents of that system, its faults included.

Their acceptance of the system's perspective is not merely due to the social status it provides them. It also seems to result from the adoption of the subject position of "physician," which, as many scholars have suggested, entails seeing patients in certain lights—as bodies, not as products of social systems.[33] Indeed, the medical orientation that all physicians are trained into—even minority physicians—runs to an even more deep set of biases in this regard than has generally been recognized.[34] Physicians are trained into the scientific worldview. The contemporary version of this worldview understands human beings almost exclusively through animal models. No other animal is subject to the variety and complexity of social, economic, and symbolic forces to which human beings are subjected. Thus the animal models provide no reason to factor social structures into health outcomes.

Dr. Burchard has heard extensive, detailed critiques of "race" (at this roundtable as well as at the "Defining Race" NIH In-House Conference in 2006), but these have moved him only to restate more adamantly what he already "knew," not to step back and reconsider the ways in which he was using the term "race." I assert that this sense of certainty arises from at least three causes—his passionate commitment to helping Puerto Ricans, his highly contemporary view that helping Puerto Ricans entails a stance that highlights difference rather than ignores it, and an understanding of what counts in science as a source of causation (that is, genes, not social structure).

I have used Dr. Burchard as an example here not to belittle him, for I have the greatest respect for his intelligence, his hard work, and his dedication to the health of Puerto Ricans. If there is error here, it is the paradigm that is errant, not the individual, and the relevant paradigm is the paradigm of science as currently constituted and as passed through the medical school filter.

I have come to believe that there is nothing I could write or say that would convince someone who cared passionately about the health of a minority group, and who accepted the current discursive framework of medical research, that he or she should abjure the utility of "race" in the study of medical genetics.

SCORECARD

I have undertaken four major engagements with medical geneticists in an effort to get them to eschew the claim that race is genetic. I did so with the hope that by engaging rhetorically in the scientific realm, I could help stop the formation of a scientific consensus that would then be translated into the public realm as the indisputable scientific fact that race is genetic. I harbored no illusions that my efforts, on their own, would be sufficient. The scientific realm is large, with many players, and my voice is just one, able to be heard in few spaces. It is therefore difficult to evaluate these efforts. Who knows how things would have gone if many more people had engaged in a similar way at many more scientific venues? Nonetheless, a tenuous effort at evaluation is required for making any recommendations to others.

It appears to me that of the four engagements, two had some success. The engagement with the SNP consortium was as successful as I could have wished. Those who heard the argument appeared to make on-the-spot choices about what constituted "good science" that were, I believe, different than if I had not spoken. Individual speakers seemed to exhibit some uncertainty about their own labeling choices after listening to my presentation. It seems hard to ask for more from a single fifteen-minute speech. The engagement with the HapMap project achieved some visibility for a different way of labeling genetic variation data, and did so in a large, highly visible project, even if that visible alternative was overwritten elsewhere by the older vocabularies we were trying to replace. One might hope that sustained efforts from multiple voices might ultimately be sufficient for normalizing the new ways of labeling.

These two positive results appear to be enormously encouraging for a program of rhetorical engagement in science, but that optimistic conclusion would overlook the fact that the audiences for these somewhat-successful engagements were scientists with little at stake in the racial labels. Both the HapMap and the SNP consortium truly could achieve their initial objectives with different (non-race-based) vocabularies and assumptions. Race was relatively tangential to the core of their research objectives, so they were willing to enact what they saw as good intentions to avoid what they were already convinced were racist ways of speaking. I simply provided a stimulus to breaking with inertia.

In contrast, with audiences who had more at stake—the medical researchers working with minority communities—there appeared to be no success at all. These individuals defined their practice precisely in terms of what they understood to be "race." Although other people working with minority communities can shift to culturally based concepts of ethnicity that are more historically fluid and more open to social forces as a causative factor, medical personnel are not free to do that because their practice, their medical training, and their science are defined in terms of bodies. They hold to the concept of race because it gives attention to the people about whom they care, and they impose upon race a genetic definition because biology is the only causal force their training permits them to employ.

The implication of this conjuncture is one that is not wholly novel, but perhaps deserves restatement—that scientific projects are neither simply universal nor merely ideological, but task focused. Rhetorical efforts directed at correcting errors in such projects face the greatest difficulty when they interfere with central tasks to which a scientific research stream has been put. This task-focus has daunting implications with regard to the linkage between science and racism. Whenever science engages tasks that might be enhanced by grouping humans, the contemporary version of science may be predisposed to promote racism, because the contemporary version of science can only present groups as fixed physical entities that are genetically based, and such a version of human groups will, at the least, give aid and comfort to racism. This does not mean that the scientific project or goal is, in itself, racist. The task of ameliorating health disparities makes that point clear. It does mean, however, that the inability of science to envision categorical systems for humans that take account of changing socioenvironmental inputs to human biologies, and to treat the impacts of those socioenvironmental inputs on bodies as seriously as it treats genes, makes the current, restricted version of science prone to reproducing support for racism.

BROADER RECOMMENDATIONS

In pursuing these rhetorical efforts, my team and I employed many of the classical tools of rhetorical theory, and we especially employed many of the insights of rhetorical studies of science. We focused on definitional processes[35] and attended to audience's motives,[36] to identities,[37] and to subcommunity boundary marking.[38] Most important, we were scrupulously aware of generic constraints.[39] Rhetoricians have an almost anaphylactic reaction to doing experiments or using numbers, but this is the currency of the scientific realm, and to participate in the scientific sphere may require some use of these languages and methods. At the least, using such methods and vocabularies may facilitate a hearing. If I had spent my fifteen minutes at the SNP conference using historical examples or ideological analyses to tell the conferees that their use of the term "race" might have bad effects promoting racism, I do not think it would have had nearly the impact that presenting them experimental results did. They believe experiments, so using experiments is probably the kind of proof that will have the greatest impact. In a broader sense, this is to say that even in the technical or scientific sphere, one should argue, as Wayne Brock-riede put it, like a lover, not like an enemy.[40]

This may be particularly crucial in technical fields because the zeitgeist of scientific argument is less welcoming of open conflict than that of many public venues. Furthermore, as Douglass Ehninger pointed out, the most authentic form of argument is one where you put your own beliefs at risk.[41] Throughout this engagement, I was never absolutely certain that my own beliefs were right. I always entertained the possibility that to end health disparities required outing "whiteness" and that a genetic diagnosis for "race" might do this. Although the engagements I undertook did not convince me of that, being open to the arguments of scientists like Dr. Burchard led me to understand the dynamics of the use of "race" in medicine in ways I would not have otherwise fathomed.

A second recommendation addresses the question of choice of audiences. I believed that I wanted to persuade the medical researchers themselves not to use constructions that linked genetics to race, but this was the most difficult audience to persuade, and I was not successful at all with them. Perhaps the direct route is not always the best route in science (as it often is not in other realms). A more useful rhetorical strategy may consist of building allies within the scientific establishment from credentialed but less task-involved groups. Such experts are called by reporters to comment on such issues; they lead grant review groups, train students, and hire colleagues. Sometimes one cannot persuade the people on the other side of the boulder to stop pushing, but one can get others to jam up efforts on their side a bit. I am currently engaging in other activities of that sort.

Entering the largely alien scientific sphere to intervene "upstream" of the appearance of scientific products in the public sphere is a daunting endeavor. Understanding the scientific vocabularies and statistics with the level of knowledge necessary to be a credible conversant takes a substantial amount of time and effort. However, once these basics of common communication with the target community are absorbed, the rhetorical dynamics resemble strongly those in the public sphere, as rhetoricians of science have previously suggested. This means that activists trained in rhetorical theory wanting to shape scientific constructions already have many tools to draw upon. I hope that more rhetoricians will take up this task, as technological and scientifically based factors will inevitably continue to shape our futures.

NOTES

1. Wade, "Race Is Seen."
2. Risch et al., "Categorization of Humans," 1–12.
3. Gould, *Mismeasure of Man;* Marks, *Human Biodiversity.*
4. Hamilton, "Am I Not a Man?"
5. Bix, "Experiences and Voices"; Hasain, *Rhetoric of Eugenics.*
6. Tucker, "Burt's Separated Twins."

7. Berger, "Nazi Science"; Frank, "Rhetorical History."

8. Farrell and Goodnight, "Accidental Rhetoric"; Killingsworth, "From Environmental Rhetoric"; Segal, *Health and the Rhetoric.*

9. Ceccaeralli, *Shaping Science with Rhetoric;* Fahnestock, *Rhetorical Figures;* Gross, *Rhetoric of Science.*

10. Hedgecoe, "Transforming Genes"; Rosner and Johnson, "Telling Stories"; van der Weele, "Images."

11. Condit, "How Culture and Science"; Happe, "Rhetoric of Race"; Smart et al., "Standardization of Race."

12. Peterson and Horton, "Rooted in the Soil."

13. Sankar et al., "Genetic Research."

14. Condit, "How Culture and Science."

15. Smedley, Stith, and Nelson, *Unequal Treatment.* I use capital letters to designate the noun "White" as a racialized term, but do not capitalize it when it is an adjective or adverb. Failure to capitalize "White" and "Black" when other racial designations are capitalized (African American or Asian American) introduces an asymmetry that can be read as effacing the racial quality of whiteness.

16. Nakayama and Krizek, "Whiteness."

17. Condit, "'Race' Is Not"; Condit, "How Culture and Science"; Condit, "Race and Genetics."

18. Bevan et al., "Informed Lay Preferences"; Condit et al., "Attitudinal Barriers."

19. Nguyen, Desta, and Flockhart, "Enhancing Race-Based Prescribing Precision."

20. Condit et al., "Attitudinal Barriers."

21. Bevan et al., "Informed Lay Preferences."

22. Burke, *Rhetoric of Motives.*

23. Lee, Mountain, and Koenig, "Meanings of 'Race.'"

24. Condit et al., "Role of 'Geneticis.'"

25. This meeting took place November 20–23, 2003, in Chantilly, Virginia.

26. See the HapMap Web site at www.HapMap.org.

27. See http://www.hapmap.org/citinghapmap.html.en for further information.

28. International HapMap Consortium, "Haplotype Map."

29. This occurs in spite of the fact that the sole graphic presenting separate JPT data seems to be quite different from the other groupings. Ibid., Figure 6.

30. Montpetit et al., "Evaluation."

31. The latter data is now published. Lynch and Condit, "Genes and Race."

32. Risch et al., "Categorization of Humans."

33. Joralemon and Cox, "Body Values." Note especially page 32.

34. Segal, *Health and the Rhetoric.*

35. Lynch, "Making Room"; Taylor, *Defining Science.*

36. Reeves, "Owning a Virus"; Mitchell, "Sacrifice."

37. Keller and Longino, *Feminism and Science;* Happe, "Rhetoric of Race."

38. Sullivan, "Keeping the Rhetoric"; Taylor, *Defining Science.*

39. Ceccarelli, *Shaping Science;* Miller, "Genre as Social Action."

40. Brockreide, "Arguers as Lovers."

41. Ehninger, "Argument as Method."

WORKS CITED

Berger, Robert L. "Nazi Science—The Dachau Hypothermia Experiments." *New England Journal of Medicine* 322, no. 20 (1990): 1435–40.

Bevan, J. L., J. A. Lynch, T. N. Dubriwny, T. M. Harris, P. J. Achter, A. L. Reeder, and C. M. Condit. "Informed Lay Preferences for Delivery of Racially Varied Pharmacogenomics." *Genetics in Medicine* (2003): 393–99.

Bix, Amy Sue. "Experiences and Voices of Eugenics Field-Workers: 'Women's Work' in Biology." *Social Studies of Science* 27 (1997): 625–68.

Brockriede, Wayne E. "Arguers as Lovers." *Philosophy & Rhetoric* 5 (Winter 1972): 1–11.

Burke, Kenneth. *The Philosophy of Literary Form.* Berkeley: University of California Press, 1973.

———. *A Rhetoric of Motives.* Berkeley: University of California Press, 1969.

Camus, Albert. "The Myth of Sisyphus." In *The Myth of Sisyphus and Other Essays.* Translated by Justin O'Brien, 119–23. New York: Vintage International, 1983.

Ceccarelli, Leah. *Shaping Science with Rhetoric: The Cases of Dobzhansky, Schrödinger, and Wilson.* Chicago: University of Chicago Press, 2001.

Condit, Celeste M. "La 'race' n'est pas un concept scientifique: Quelles sont les alternatives?" ("Race" Is Not a Scientific Concept: Alternative Directions?) *L'observatoire de la genetique.* October 2005.

———. "How Culture and Science Make Race 'Genetic': Motives and Strategies for Discrete Categorization of the Continuous and Heterogeneous." *Literature and Medicine* 26 (2007): 240–68.

———. "Race and Genetics from a Modal Materialist Perspective." *Quarterly Journal of Speech,* in press.

Condit, Celeste M., and B. Bates. "How Lay People Respond to Messages About Genetics, Health, and Race." *Clinical Genetics* (2005): 97–105.

Condit, Celeste M., D. M. Condit, and P. Achter. "Human Equality, Affirmative Action and Genetic Models of Human Variation." *Rhetoric and Public Affairs* 4, no. 1 (2001): 85–108.

Condit, Celeste M., R. L. Parrott, T. M. Harris, J. A. Lynch, and T. Dubriwny. "The Role of 'Geneticis' in Popular Understandings of Race in the United States." *Public Understanding of Science* 13 (2004): 249–72.

Condit, Celeste M., A. Templeton, B. R. Bates, J. L. Bevan, and T. M. Harris. "Attitudinal Barriers to Delivery of Race-Targeted Pharmacogenomics among Informed Lay Persons." *Genetics in Medicine* 5 (2003): 385–92.

Ehninger, Douglas. "Argument as Method: Its Nature, Its Limitations and Its Uses." *Speech Monographs* 37, no. 2 (1970): 101–11.

Fahnestock, Jeanne. *Rhetorical Figures in Science.* New York: Oxford University Press, 1999.

Farrell, T. B., and G. T. Goodnight. "Accidental Rhetoric: The Root Metaphors of Three Mile Island." *Quarterly Journal of Speech* 48 (1981): 271–301.

Frank, Robert E. "A Rhetorical History of the 1989 Revolution in the German Democratic Republic: Calling for the People." Ph.D. diss., University of Georgia, 1995.

Gould, Stephen J. *The Mismeasure of Man.* New York: Norton, 1981.

Gross, Alan. *The Rhetoric of Science.* Cambridge, Mass.: Harvard University Press, 1990.

Hamilton, Cynthia S. "'Am I Not a Man and a Brother?' Phrenology and Anti-slavery." *Slavery and Abolition* 29 (2008): 173–87.

Happe, Kelly E. "The Rhetoric of Race in Breast Cancer Research." *Patterns of Prejudice* 40 (2006): 461–80.

Hasian, M. *The Rhetoric of Eugenics in Anglo-American Thought.* Athens: University of Georgia Press, 1996.

Hedgecoe, Adam M. "Transforming Genes: Metaphors of Information and Language in Modern Genetics." *Science as Culture* 8 (1999): 209–29.

International HapMap Consortium. "A Haplotype Map of the Human Genome." *Nature* 27 (October 2005): 1299–1320.

Joralemon, Donald, and Phil Cox. "Body Values: The Case against Compensating for Transplant Organs." *Hastings Center Report* 33, no. 1 (2003): 27–33.

Keller, Evelyn Fox, and Helen E. Longino, eds. *Feminism and Science*. Oxford: Oxford University Press, 1996.

Kilingsworth, M. Jimmie. "From Environmental Rhetoric to Ecocomposition and Ecopoetics." *Technical Communication Quarterly* 14 (2005): 359–73.

Lee, S. S., J. Mountain, and B. A. Koenig. "The Meanings of 'Race' in the New Genomics: Implications for Health Disparities Research." *Yale Journal of Health Policy Law Ethic* 1 (2001): 33–75.

Lynch, John A. "Making Room for Stem Cells: Dissociation and Establishing New Research Objects." *Argumentation and Advocacy* 42 (2006): 143–56.

Lynch, John A., and Celeste M. Condit. "Genes and Race in the News: A Test of Competing Theories of News Coverage." *American Journal of Health Behavior* 30 (2006): 125–35.

Marks, Jonathon. *Human Biodiversity: Genes, Race, and History*. New York: Aldine de Gruyter, 1995.

Miller, Carolyn R. "Genre as Social Action." *Quarterly Journal of Speech* 70 (1984): 151–67.

Mitchell, Robert. "Sacrifice, Individuation, and the Economics of Genomics." *Literature and Medicine* 26 (2007): 126–58.

Montpetit A., M. Nelis, P. Laflamme, R. Magi, X Ke, M. Remm, L. Cardon, T. J. Hudson, and Metspalu, J. P. "An Evaluation of the Performance of Tag SNPs Derived from HapMap in a Caucasian Population." *Plos Genetics* 2, no. 3 (March 2006): e27.

Nakayama, T., and R. Krizek. "Whiteness: A Strategic Rhetoric." *Quarterly Journal of Speech* 81 (1995): 291–309.

National Institutes of Health. *Defining Race and Ethnicity in Biomedical and Behavioral Research*. Bethesda, Md.: NIH, April 18, 2006. MPEG. http://videocast.nih.gov/Summary.asp?File=13179 (accessed April 18, 2006).

Nguyen, A., Z. Desta, and D. A. Flockhart. "Enhancing Race-Based Prescribing Precision with Pharmacogenomics." *Clinical Pharmacology and Therapeutics* 81 (2007): 323–25.

Peterson, Tarla Rai, and Cristi Choat Horton. "Rooted in the Soil: How Understanding the Perspectives of Landowners Can Enhance the Management of Environmental Disputes." *Quarterly Journal of Speech* 81 (1995): 139–66.

Reeves, Carol. "Owning a Virus: The Rhetoric of Scientific Discovery Accounts." In *Landmark Essays on Rhetoric of Science: Case Studies*, edited by Randy Allen Harris, 151–65. Mahwah, N.J.: Hermagoras Press, 1997.

Risch N., E. Burchard, E. Ziv, and H. Tang. "Categorization of Humans in Biomedical Research: Genes, Race and Disease." *Genome Biology* 3 (2002): 12.

Rosner, M., and T. R. Johnson. "Telling Stories: Metaphors of the Human Genome Project." *Hypatia* 10 (Fall 1995): 104–29.

Sankar, Pamela, Mildred Cho, Celeste Condit, Linda M. Hunt, Barbara Koenig, Patricia Marshall, Sandra Lee, and Paul Spicer. "Genetic Research and Health Disparities." *Journal of the American Medical Association* 291 (2004): 2985–89.

Segal, Judy Z. *Health and the Rhetoric of Medicine*. Carbondale: Southern Illinois University Press, 2005.

Smart, Andrew, Richard Tutton, Paul Martin, George T. H. Ellison, and Richard Ashcroft. "The Standardization of Race and Ethnicity in Biomedical Science Editorials and UK Biobanks." *Social Studies of Science* 28 (2008): 407–23.

Smedley, Brian D., Adrienne Y. Stith, and Alan R. Nelson, eds. *Unequal Treatment: Con-fronting Racial and Ethnic Disparities in Health Care.* Washington, D.C.: National Academy Press, 2003.

Sullivan, Dale. "Keeping the Rhetoric Orthodox: Forum Control in Science." *Technical Communication Quarterly* 9 (2000): 125–46.

Taylor, Charles Alan. *Defining Science: A Rhetoric of Demarcation.* Madison: University of Wisconsin Press, 1996.

Tucker, William H. "Burt's Separated Twins: The Larger Picture." *Journal of the History of the Behavioral Sciences* 43 (2007): 81–86.

van der Weele, Cor. "Images of the Genome." In *Current Themes in Theoretical Biology: A Dutch Perspective,* edited by Thomas A. C. Reydon and Lia Henerik, 9–31. Dordrecht, Netherlands: Springer, 2005.

Wade, Nicholas. "Brain May Still Be Evolving, Studies Hint." *New York Times,* September 9, 2005. http://www.nytimes.com/2005/09/09/science/09brain.html?oref=login &pagewanted=print (accessed September 9, 2005).

———. "Race Is Seen as Real Guide to Track the Roots of Disease." *New York Times,* July 30, 2002.

Going Public—in a
Disabling Discourse

LINDA FLOWER

A critical assumption in the rhetoric of social change rests on the notion of "publicity" or "publicness." The power of the public sphere is its ability to give visibility to an issue, to create a demand for disclosure and justification (even from a government), and in doing so to exert a powerful if indirect regulatory force. In *Rules for Radicals*, Alinsky says, "The organizer's first job is to create the issues . . . through action persuasion, and communication."[1] And when social categories such as race, sex, class, or disability use the quiet tool of definition to oppress people by "defining them," a critical step in breaking this marginalizing power has been to go public through the literate act of renaming. Freire describes this public reappropriation this way: "to exist, humanly, is to name *the world, to change it. Once named, the world in its turn reappears to its namers as a problem and requires of them a new naming.*"[2] Within the rhetoric of social/cultural critique, this means analyzing the implicit messages naturalized into unquestioned assumptions. Within community literacy studies, it can mean direct action supporting the public voice of marginalized people and perspectives through collaborative research, community-based courses and projects, media development, and public dialogue.[3]

However, in celebrating the work of rhetoric from an enfranchised academic perspective, we have not always considered the difficulties going public might raise for others. In equating empowerment with acts of critique, self-expression, argument, or advocacy, we rarely consider the cost of challenging "dehumanizing societal constructions of difference," when to do is to identify oneself as one of those marginal people.[4] I speak here about the identity of being "learning disabled" (or LD), but the problem is more general. Academic rhetors can address this dilemma by speaking with a powerful double voice—claiming the "stigma" of disability, of speaking Black English, of poverty, of working-class background, of ethnicity, but doing so in an academically recognized voice and successfully mainstreamed work. But for the rhetors of whom I speak, this is not an option. For these urban high school students, going public about their learning disabilities at school or on a job is no easy decision.[5] It pits the option of getting the help and accommodations they may need against the socially hazardous outcomes of being labeled LD. For them, rhetoric is an embodied act that opens them to being co-opted by the discourse of disability in which they become the object of its rhetoric, not a rhetorical agent.[6]

This essay attempts to understand some of the competing forces (the personal goals, public agendas, language, and practices) one must negotiate to go public within a discourse that disables. In such discourses, the already marginalized speaker must not only resist available representations of himself or herself, but also enact an alternative representation. He or she must not only come to voice but also construct and negotiate that voice, that representation within a personally and publicly conflicted space. Second, I consider what this means for educators and supporters, when the work of empowerment is not limited to speaking in our own voices as advocates or to encouraging self-expression in others. What if the goal is rhetorical empowerment, helping others, as Brueggemann and colleagues so elegantly state it, "to be their own best advocates, their own authors, and their own best representatives."[7]

FINDING YOUR SELF IN A DISABLING DISCOURSE

The public discussion of learning disabilities often revolves around whether such learning should be defined in terms of *differences* in how people learn (for example, the time required or the mode of instruction they prefer, whether verbal, oral, or demonstration) or in terms of *disability*, defined as deviance from the norm (or from schools' preferred modes of instruction). It was in the context of this debate that we organized the Community Think Tank on Learning Disability. The "we" in this case was an upper-level college class on the rhetoric of making a difference as well as the director and students from Pittsburgh's Start on Success (SOS)—a public school program for students with learning disabilities.[8] This semester-long project culminated in a public dialogue that brought together nearly sixty teachers, counselors, school administrators, workforce developers, parents, advocates, and high school students with learning disabilities to address the problem we came to call "Naming the LD Difference."[9]

The inquiry, however, began early in the semester when the members of the Think Tank team (eleven urban high school students with learning disabilities and eleven college students in my class) were asked to create two problem scenarios that would document and dramatize some of the difficult decision points that students with a learning disability routinely confront. These brief skits would be included in an advance briefing book sent to participants and then performed at the Think Tank event to focus and jump-start the deliberation. In this initial inquiry, it became apparent that *going public* about the taboo topic of a disability posed an enormous felt difficulty with practical consequences; how you handle the taboo topic of disability makes a huge difference in an urban high school: if you cannot do what is expected in a class, and dare not talk about what you need in order to learn, you probably will not get the help that could, in fact, let you succeed.

In the first problem scenario our high school/college student team created, Joel has just been paired up for in-class work with Shauna, the smart new student on whom he has a major crush. However, Joel's learning disability makes it difficult to read new material quickly, so while she dives into the task, he tries his standard diversionary tactics (from conversation about the weekend to looking around the room) to avoid the problem. Until, of course, the teacher "helpfully" asks, "Joel, are you having a difficult time with the reading?" Joel is on the spot, and "Billy the Bully" cuts off his retreat:

JOEL: Umm . . . I was just . . .

BILLY THE BULLY (*laughing and sarcastic*): Pfssht! Of course he is . . . you know Joel can't read!

Everyone is shocked, while Billy laughs rudely . . .

SHAUNA: What does he mean, Joel?

Despite his best efforts at avoidance, Joel has entered a public deliberative moment, which asks him to answer the definitional question: what does that revelation mean?

Educators who move out of the classroom in their work with socially disempowered students may find themselves in an oddly similar public space. Like Joel, we must decide how does one deal with the discourse of disability? In this case, some standard—and not entirely happy—ways of going public are readily available. How the LD difference is represented—named and interpreted—has already been shaped by discourses over which we have little control.

MEDIATIZED

One way the LD difference goes public is to become a media topic. For instance, a *Newsweek* cover story on children with dyslexia—those "otherwise intelligent children"—makes a point of explaining that "their brains weren't defective, just different." Yet in doing so, such media accounts perpetuate stereotypes and rehearse the obligatory narratives of the victim, the struggle and overcoming, and the "famous and successful dyslexics."[10] The media also offer a deceptively cheery message, which White describes as the relentless narratives of "overcoming"—stories that fail to note that "successful adults with [learning disabilities] are those with less severe impairments, from affluent families, who had a positive educational experience (often in private schools)."[11] Other images are more accusatory. For some educational conservatives, the exponential growth of diagnoses of learning disabilities is a faddish function of political correctness. As the president of Boston University describes it, students "'swaddled for years in the comforting illusions of learning disabled theory' [then] enter higher education and lower its standards."[12] Although language and self-definition have become a central focus of the disability movement, media labeling dies hard and thematic conventions even harder.[13]

MEDICALIZED

Medical diagnosis has emerged as a scientific alternative to older, invidious popular representations. Early-nineteenth-century perceptions of low-achieving children (and/or low literate immigrants) talked about a "dunce," "loafer," or "reprobate," who was not only "stupid" but "depraved," "wayward," and "incorrigible."[14] As Hull and colleagues put it, "some of these labels imply that the students lacked intelligence, but the majority reflect a flawed character."[15] Later, with the growth of the IQ movement, diagnoses based on defects of character were replaced by notions of intellectual deficits and abnormal development. The pseudo-scientific measurement of IQ offered a "unitary measure of cognitive—and human—worth."[16]

Contemporary research has replaced the unitary image of a deficient person with an increasingly local account of specific neurological differences that can produce a variety of difficulties in perception, in integrating information (such as organizing and abstracting), in memory, and in production (such as expressing what you do know on demand).[17] Many students will have labored since third grade (when language-processing disabilities often show up) with the growing burden of an inexplicable, unnamed difference, with seeing their friends in school effortlessly "get it" while they must wrestle jumbles of letters, numbers, or spoken instructions into a meaningful pattern. Soon the process inside one's head turns into a problem in social relations: parents scold, teachers make failure public, peers laugh, and the child copes through the use of withdrawal, silence, attitude, or diverting behavior. A diagnosis or even the recognition that you are not alone can be liberating, relocating the problem from identity to information processing.

However, being appropriated by the professional/medical discourse comes at a cost. The designation "learning disability" is not a medical term, and the diagnosis of conditions such as attention deficit / hyperactivity disorder (ADHD) is a changing and decidedly interpretive process, while old stereotypes linger in the popular and educational press.[18] Although LD is a social construct without a firm scientific base, its standing as a medicalized, neurobiological construct allows it to be used as a political tool. In education, it is invoked to replace holistic models of language learning and functional images of purposive reading and writing with a mandate for teaching fragmented skills through remedial drills and numbing repetition—the dreaded worksheets that fill up Special Ed classes. As White puts it, such "LD specialists are determined to keep meaning making out of their tent."[19] With a medical diagnosis you acquire legal, financial, and institutional support *and* an institutional label—that is, an intensely problematic public identity.

INSTITUTIONALIZED

Going public by going through the process of diagnosis and placement within the public school system confers some significant advantages: your counselors and parents create an Individualized Education Program (IEP), which notes accommodations teachers should give you (like extra time on tests), and if you are really lucky you might make it into special programs like SOS.

But as the college half of the Think Tank team discovered by shadowing our student partners and talking with the school staff, there are equally significant costs to going public under this institutional label. In seems that many teachers simply do not understand learning disabilities: how a learning disability works and what is actually happening when students cannot read in class, do not finish tests, or fail to follow instructions. Teachers often do not read the IEP or report that its generalized list of accommodations does not help them when they do: it simply tells an already overworked public school teacher to create (unspecified) individualized assignments, conditions, teaching plans, and grading rubrics for each diagnosed student. Others teachers we interviewed simply refuse to acknowledge the need for accommodation: they assertively choose to "treat everyone the same," arguing that the LD stigma is the greater evil, and since students will have to make it in the big world without breaks, they better start now.

For the students, what is worse is how the institutional label can get you placed apart from your friends, in a Special Ed history or English class that frequently makes little distinction between a learning disability and mental retardation. The SOS students often dread these classes, which they complain are dumbed down and subject students to endless repetition and a constant, numbing diet of worksheets. But, according to Mooney, the most painful way students go public happens when the bell rings: your friends go into junior English and you look for an excuse to delay, so they will not see you make that long, embarrassing walk down the hall to the Special Ed resource room. The place the "dumb kids" go.[20]

DAMAGE CONTROL

So how do students, as rhetors in a discourse not of their choosing, respond to the dilemma of going public? When the authors of the Joel problem scenario tested their first draft with the whole team, the tension over the issue of going public was palpable. We were not even sure the SOS teens would feel comfortable enough to talk about the subject in the combined group. Here we are discussing what Joel—outed before the cute girl—should say to Shauna. What should he do?[21]

AMBER: Ask her for help.

LAMAR: I think he should tell her. He's got nothing to be ashamed of.

CHRISTINA: I think he should tell her and try to explain what his disability is. And say, could you help me out?

FLOWER: So guys, does that sound like a good idea or do you have a rival to that?

BRANDON: Personally, if I'm in his situation and I like the girl, I'm not going to tell her nothing at all. I'll make up a lie or something.

LAMAR: I don't feel like reading.

BRANDON: Yeah. I'm not going to straight up tell her . . .

LAMAR: Later on.

BRANDON: But like yeah, later on. I'm trying to talk to her. I'm not going to tell her that up front.

Some students challenge that when it "pops out . . . she's probably going to dump you because you lied to her," but a young man, suggesting he speaks for others, replies:

LAMAR: We're not saying that we're never going to tell her, we're just saying that we're probably going to wait.

And when students do go public, it does not appear to create an educative moment. As one student puts it:

CHRISTINA: I think some of us just say that we have a difficulty in the subject but we don't all the time tell our friends that we have a disability. . . . We just make it . . .

TRISTA: So they understand?

CHRISTINA: Yeah. I guess we don't want them to know.

At this point another student asserts that "I just say straight out, I have a learning disability. I'm above average but I have difficulty in certain areas," and another male chimes in, "I tell my school friends 'If you can't accept me for who I am, you shouldn't be my friend.'" But Brandon suddenly moves assertively back into the conversation.

BRANDON: I don't let no one know what my disability is. At any stage. School, teachers, jobs, I don't let them know at all. If you let them know . . . I cannot read that good . . . so if you let them know up front they're not going to put you, they're not going to make you, how do I put this, they're not going to try to help you to do what you got to do . . .

LAMAR: They'll give you easy work.

BRANDON: Yeah. They'll give you easy work.

FRANK: They'll let you slide.

LAMAR: You get slack.

CHRISTINA: I don't think . . .

LaMar: You don't get challenged.

But, Brandon is asked, what if your job has a task that zeroes in on your disability?

Brandon: If I see that I'm going to have to do that more and more, then
yeah I tell them, but if it's just like . . .
Flower: You hold out to the bitter end . . .
Brandon: Yes.

REPRESENTATION AND IDENTITY

Going public about learning disabilities, just like going public about race and racism or about gender prejudices, is one of the most powerful ways we have to expose misrepresentations, prejudices, and discrimination, and to counteract simple ignorance and misguided goodwill. But who would willingly take on the identities that come packaged with media, medical, and institutional discourses? In these professional discourses of disability, the learner rarely figures as an agent or source of expertise, but is instead the object of someone else's definition. The learner is represented as a news topic, a social, educational, and legal problem—a public commodity. The "LD student" exists because he or she has been identified, assessed, diagnosed, labeled, and placed by powerful institutions. In an activity analysis of school placement, Hugh Mehan has shown how the "politics of representation" construct an LD child into a "social fact" through the routine practices of the educational referral process. Here the psychologist's technical representation silences contradictions posed by a parent's and a teacher's narrative and historical accounts of the child.[22] A study by McDermott shows even more vividly how the institutional obsession with testing and the structure of learning activities in school (versus everyday life) are designed to make disability visible—to allow a disability to "acquire" a child. "We might as well say there is no such thing as LD, only a social practice of displaying, noticing, documenting, remediating, and explaining it."[23] Going public in this way (being commodified, represented, and acquired) does not allow a person to represent his or her own sense of self or the problem as he or she experiences it. The discourse of disability enacted at school constructs the student as the object of discussion, not the agent. And learners preoccupied with dodging the bullet have little chance to develop the rhetorical agency to shape these representations.

Since the 1990s, disabilities studies has aggressively challenged what Goodley calls the "discourses of personal pathology, of individual difficulties, and of dependency in the face of care" with what advocates in the U.K. call a "social model" focused on the sociocultural bases of disability.[24] In this counterdiscourse, an individual may have a physical or neurological impairment, but disability is a disadvantage caused by social practices that fail to take such people into account and exclude them from participation in mainstream social activities. "Physical disability is therefore a particular form of social oppression."[25] For example, I may need technical support or face-to-face contact to "hear" you, written instructions or a demonstration to fully "understand" you, wheels to be mobile, or extra time to organize my thoughts in writing, but I am disabled because "normal" buildings are designed with stairs instead of ramps, teachers (who talk to the board) assume oral instruction should be the norm, and schools judge my intelligence, learning, and potential through the social practice of timed tests. "This social oppression," Swain and Cameron argue, is orchestrated through both "techniques of exclusion" and authoritative "discourses on disability" that include "cultural stereotyping; identification of impairment with loss or lack of some attribute necessary to be fully human; and the assumption that treatment or cure, rehabilitation or therapy or control, pity or compensation, is always the appropriate response."[26]

This approach to disability studies suggests two paths for rhetorical work. One is the rhetorical and critical discourse analysis of disabling language and social practices.[27] The other points us to rhetorical action, with implications for both research and community literacy. For researchers/advocates like Goodley, the social model signifies a proactive shift away from "a focus on what people can not do to what people can do"—a shift to self-empowerment and self-advocacy.[28] Concerned with the "meaning and affects of interventions," it leads us to observe what "disabled" self-advocates actually do, often in collaboration, and how others might support this.[29]

Because the discourse of disability-as-a-personal-deficit so forcefully shapes identity and social representation, the metaphor of "coming out" in these discussions often implies public action. "Coming out, then, for disabled people, is a process of redefinition of one's personal identity through rejecting the tyranny of the normate, [through] positive recognition of impairment and embracing disability as a valid social identity. Having come out, the disabled person no longer regards disability . . . as something to be denied or hidden, but rather as an imposed oppressive social category to be challenged or broken down."[30] However, Davies cautions that resistance strategies, from speaking out, to humor, to avoiding confrontation, may not work as "constructive resistances."[31] That is, they fail to dislodge the oppressive discourse practices to which they respond, because "this 'alternative' discourse exists outside the meaning structure recognized and legitimated by the school authorities."[32]

GOING PUBLIC IN A DELIBERATIVE DISCOURSE

If going public with a disability is hazardous for your identity, putting you at risk of being mediatized, medicalized, or institutionalized, how might a speaker stand with the researchers cited above and challenge "the politics of representation"? I suggest that *in theory*, a deliberative discourse in the context of local public dialogue asserts an alternative to disabling discourses. It allows marginalized speakers a way to "come out" that

asserts a "valid social identity" (which includes learning *differences*);
supports self-empowerment through a focus on "what people can do"
  (as knowledgeable analysts and problem *solvers*); and
engages in "a *constructive* resistance" to mainstream practices (drawing
  others into a search for better options).

However, *in practice*, as in the community Think Tank, public discussion alone is not the engine of change. The public work of rhetoric cannot be separated from—it depends upon—the literate practices of the Think Tank and the constructive work of individual speakers. In the remainder of this essay, I look first at the literate practices or techne that create a scaffold for rhetorical agency in this space, and, second, at the way these youthful rhetors actually took such agency.

In theory, the discourse of the public sphere offers a space in which ordinary, concerned people are drawn to *deliberate* in order to understand and respond to a *shared* problem for the common good. In Habermas's influential normative vision, a "public competent to form its own judgments" rose with the tide of eighteenth-century capitalism and its middle class.[33] The power, the glory, and the trademark of this public sphere is a discourse based exclusively on *critical rationality*. That is, people talk as disinterested parties about public matters—which means that advocacy, activism, and the private are inappropriate here. Because the goal of such deliberation is truth and consensus, a policy or idea must be examined from all sides, and the argument that carries the day (because it wins/demands our *warranted assent*) is one that withstands refutation on the basis of a *generalizable* principle (not a local factor). And because critical rationality is the ticket that gets you into the public sphere, it is open to anyone, or at least anyone who is "competent" to engage in this particular rule-governed discourse. Differences in status, Habermas asserts, are temporarily "bracketed" as people deliberate as social equals.

This public sphere, however, could be a problematic place for an urban teenager with an identity as a person with a disability. First, this postulated bracketing does not happen in practice. People do not ignore differences in race, class, gender, status, or (dis)ability.[34] Moreover, excluding "private issues" is not even ideal: it deprives marginalized people of the right to speak about their particular experience and to assert that such status is, in fact, a *public* concern. It prevents people from using public talk to discover shared concerns. Second, the practice of critical rationality dismisses the epistemic potential of narrative, situated knowledge, and embodied rhetoric to create knowledge and new options. Its elite forums deny access to those unprepared or unwilling to play by its deliberative rules.

By contrast, other accounts of how the contemporary public sphere actually operates contend that if you want to understand participation, do not look for it in the single comprehensive public sphere. Look instead in the vibrant network of local rhetorical spaces and the plurality of competing publics, including the subversive, agitating counterpublics we see in feminism and queer studies. Such publics, Hauser argues, do not operate solely by the rules of disinterested critical rationality, but speak in vernacular voices, operating from positions of interests and passions, creating a vernacular rhetoric.[35] Unlike the unified, homogeneous body envisioned as the Public Sphere, these local (small p) publics are called into being by discourse itself. They are created, Warner argues, by the mere act of attention and process of people engaging in the circulation of discourse.[36] Academic sessions and edited volumes, like community meetings, can help create a public around the questions.

In this model of competing local publics, it is the *counterpublics,* from the civil rights and labor movements to feminism and gay pride, that have challenged the elite, male bourgeois public and its claim to be The Public—to be the source of informed opinion that should shape policy. Counterpublics offer marginalized groups and individuals a rhetorical safe house—a place to try out their voices, to grow, to plan, to recuperate, and to regroup. But in asserting their own vernacular rhetorics, these counterpublics frequently insist on renaming the issues and building embodied arguments through narrative and performance. They are not only a place of retreat but also a force seeking to reshape the larger public discourse on their own terms. They are experiments in transformative public rhetoric.

The Community Think Tank could be described as a counterpublic experiment in how to support a local public rhetoric of transformation. Like the discursive bodies described by Frazer, Hauser, and Warner, it creates a public called forth by common concerns. It speaks in vernacular voices in which narrative and situated knowledge share authority with research claims and policy talk. It creates a space for the circulation of ideas *and* identities through scenarios that document and dramatize problems and through the distinctive structure of its public forums. The ideas and identities it draws out are in turn documented as published findings—a multivocal record of rival readings and options for action—which are then circulated back to their creators as tools for operating within their own local publics as students, parents, teachers, administrators, or policy workers.

The Community Think Tank is also a rhetorical experiment in inquiry. Structured as a collaborative problem-solving dialogue, it is first of all a deliberate effort to create what I have described as a *mestiza public*—an intentionally intercultural body that asks its members to collaborate across the boundaries of race, class, status, power, and discourse.[37] It depends on difference to produce a more inclusive kind of knowledge. Like a counterpublic, it has an additional subversive agenda: to translate the concerns of marginalized people from the status of private and therefore excluded issues into shared public concerns, and in doing so to support the performance and transform the representation of marginalized rhetors as rhetorical agents in their own right.

The foregoing is a theorized statement of intentions and aspirations. The performances to which I now return document some ways students can in fact step into such an agentive space and the kinds of representations they can build within a public deliberation structured as an intercultural inquiry.

TAKING RHETORICAL AGENCY

Within the community of people with learning disabilities, self-advocacy is the starting point for changing both one's situation and one's representation.[38] To speak up for yourself and speak out requires both individual courage and a sense of social support. I had seen this over the previous six years of working with SOS scholars in the CMU Decision Makers project as they talked and wrote about making difficult decisions at work, at school, and in their personal lives, reflecting on the options they saw and the strategies on which they relied.[39] But what this experience also revealed was the intensely rhetorical nature of self-advocacy, which demands not only self-expression but also understanding rhetorical situations, constructing new meanings, and creating a dialogic relationship with others.

To begin with, self-advocacy starts with the difficult job of understanding yourself—your strengths and weaknesses. You must figure out what neither the generalized medical nor institutional discourse can give you—a functional understanding of how *you* learn—what causes you trouble, how you work around it, what you need from others, and where your alternative talents lie. Taking ownership of what a disability means (for example, asking for appropriate accommodations when you need them) starts with a reflective, constructive writerly process of meaning making.

In other contexts self-advocacy is even more directly concerned with challenging limiting self-representations (that is, "coming out") and transforming the ways others understand difference and disability (that is, "constructive" resistance). To do this, the urban teenagers I meet from SOS do indeed need personal chutzpah and social support for speaking up. But to go public in this larger sense, they also need what emerges in community literacy as *rhetorical agency*—that is, the reflective power to interpret themselves to a public and to draw that public into deliberative dialogue.[40]

The Think Tank gave us an opportunity to observe how such rhetors—rarely identified as *experts* much less *rhetorical agents* in the public sphere—might in fact contribute to a deliberative analysis of problems and options. Responding to problem scenarios that included encounters with teachers, supervisors, and peers, Think Tank participants were asked to consider first, "What is the problem here?" and "Whose problem is it?" They then began to develop a set of options and project potential outcomes, both supporting and rivaling one another.[41] The six Think Tank participants I focus on in this analysis included two college students, two adult participants, and two SOS teenagers, one of whom was described as a high-performing and the other as a lower-performing student by their teachers.

The transcripts from this forum reveal three significantly different kinds of rhetorical moves used by the SOS speakers: expressive, interpretive, and dialogic. The four adults spent of lot of their time posing questions, so the teenagers often responded with an expressive move—telling their own story or expressing an opinion. In table 1, I have formatted a series of verbatim excerpts from the transcript to highlight the familiar discourse moves named in the left column. The clarifying connective words in brackets are my addition.

[**TABLE 1**] Expressive Moves

1	PROMPT [Agree?]	CMU student: We can move on to the second decision point. Dealing with the teacher when hindered by your [learning disability]. Which one of the story behind the stories would you agree with Don?
	TELL [Story-Opinion]	Don: I really don't think the teacher is mean like that to me.
2	PROMPT [Story?]	Counselor: Do you guys use your IEPs? Do you say, Hey I have an IEP and you need to do what it says.
	TELL [Story]	Don: • That happened to me either this week or last week • and I had a test and I hadn't finished it and the teacher was gonna collect it. • She asked if I was having trouble with it • and I was like yeah. • I said it says on my IEP that I have more time on my work • and he said I could take it home to finish it.
	TELL [Decision] *Conditionalize* *Conditionalize* *Conditionalize*	Brandon: • If they don't recognize it, I don't put it out there. • Until I really need help. • And if I don't really need help, I don't enforce it.

In table 1, "Expressive Moves," the discussion has turned to interactions with teachers. As the schematic representation suggests, Don responds to a "do you agree?" prompt with a counterclaim (disagreeing with both examples in the briefing book). At another point he responds to a narrative prompt with a supporting story. As Belenky, Bond, and Weinstock have shown with other marginalized, typically silent speakers, this first, expressive level of participation can in fact be a significant act of asserting one's identity and a sense of one's self as a knower, a speaker, and an authority on one's own experience.[42] In fact, the evidence of this normally silent student actively speaking out in this public space with strangers was received by Don's teachers with surprise. In example 2, we see Brandon also responding with an expressive move, though notice how in this case it is the story of a decision, embedded in a highly conditionalized account of what he sees as appropriate action.

Our images of marginalized, socially disabled speakers (like those of inexperienced writers) often lead us to expect expressive discourse, but little more. However, the rhetorical performance of these teenagers asserts another level of rhetorical agency in which one responds as the *interpreter* of a problem or a conflict or a question. In table 2, "Interpretive Moves," we see Brandon being asked to respond with a truth claim (Do teachers really care?). He replies not just by offering a yes/no expressive opinion, but by interpreting the situation: they care, but it demands time and effort as well as strategies and knowledge they do not have. His interpretation is laced with the conditions, qualifications, and justifications that mark a reasoned argument. More important, as a contribution to this public discussion of the teacher's role in learning difficulties, Brandon's contribution to the inquiry is a balanced, qualified, conditionalized, and insightful interpretation of the problem itself. Going well beyond a personal experience narrative, he addresses the complex issue of "whose problem is this?" exploring how and why teachers of goodwill participate in turning differences among all into a disability for some.

[**TABLE 2**] Interpretive Moves

3	Prompt [True?]	Parent: Do you think teachers care?
	Interpret	Brandon:
	Claim	• I think they do care,
	Qualify	• but the LD it will take them more time and effort for a strategy and a work plan
	Claim	• Most LD students they have mainstream classes
	Claim	• and mainstream teachers don't know how to handle and LD student.
	Claim	• Most of the time there's only one or two and she don't know how to deal with them.
	Conditionalize	• If she slows down the process for the whole class people are gonna get bored.
	Conditionalize	• And if she speeds it up the LDs are gonna get lost.

Claim	• In a way the teachers care,
Qualify	• but in certain situations they don't enforce it.
Justify Claim	• [Because] There's more students that need her help that she knows how to help in other ways
Claim	• than [there are] LD students who she doesn't know how to help them as well as she would like.

However, not all interpretive moves are equally sophisticated. Should we really expect to see the more fully dialogic, self-conscious, reflective, and strategic moves that we associate with higher levels of literacy and rhetorical agency? Is that not a lot to ask of young students from urban schools who may even be struggling to succeed at what Freire calls knowledge "banking"? What form would such agency take in this public deliberation with unknown adults?[43]

In table 3, "Dialogic, Re-interpretive Moves," example 4, one of the adults tells the story of his own child who flunked his first year of college and then went for help, offering this as a prompt (and implicit advice?) to Brandon. Brandon, however, responds by reinterpreting the other speaker's story (that is, it is just that your son's strategy failed). Brandon then justifies his alternative scenario, and at the same time rivals himself. That is, the Achilles' heel of Brandon's own solution (that is, don't ask for help; don't tell) is that his strategy has not failed—*yet.* By the end, his analysis has connected a conditionalized analysis of when to get help with a reflection on the motivation to remain silent—pride. Once again, this student's situated understanding of a problem has yielded bona fide insight—evidence of expertise. But even more significant is that as a member of a deliberative public, he has contributed a reflective *reinterpretation* of someone else's image of the problem. He has engaged in that essential dialogic move of listening then building on, challenging, qualifying, or expanding our understanding, creating a more complex and negotiated meaning.

[**TABLE 3**] Dialogic, Reinterpretive Moves (Reinterpret the other's image)

4	PROMPT [Opinion-story?]	[Parent: Tells of own child who flunked 1st semester in college; then went back asking for help.]
	TELL [Opinion]	What would stop you from doing that?
	DIALOG [Reinterpret]	Brandon: Pride mostly. • From your son, he actually went through everything • and the strategy that he tried to do it, it failed.

Justify	• So, in other words he had to come straight up front about it.
Rival	• From my point, my strategy hasn't failed yet.
PROMPT [Recap]	Counselor: He tried a way and that didn't work out so he doubled back and tried another way. But you haven't failed yet.
INTERPRET	Brandon:
Rival self / *Conditionalize*	• So when I get to that and my strategy don't work
Claim	• then I'll just have to confront my own self. • My own pride.
Reflect	

My final example, table 4, "Dialogic, Adaptive Moves," takes this dialogic process one step further, demonstrating a dialogic rhetorical agency that not only interprets but also adapts to other speakers. Asked how he might speak to his friend Travis, who is afraid to admit that he has a learning disability, Brandon begins by imaginatively projecting what Travis would be thinking. Then he begins to lay out a rhetorical plan for drawing his friend into this local public, into an inquiry about learning disabilities as both a reflective and physical space. Notice how he is not only planning how to adapt to his audience, but he is considering reasons, justifying his move, and then, in a wise and reflective move, he qualifies his own rhetorical ability: "I can tell him, . . . but until he opens his mouth its not going to happen."

[**TABLE 4**]. Dialogic, Adaptive Moves (Adapt to the Other)

5	INTERPRET	(In discussing going public, Travis gets mentioned) Brandon: • I know Travis
	Claim	• I know that he plays football, • he don't want to get his personal life like his LD out there. • [Because] He plays football
	Justify	• and they'll call him stupid and bring him down.
	PROMPT [Opinion-Act?]	Parent: (How would you coach a peer like Travis who is afraid to admit his LD and get help?)
	Dialog [Plan-Adapt]	Brandon: • I would have him come into things like this, meetings like this.

Justify	• So he can get more comfortable with that.
	• Being one on one with him I can tell him everything he needs to know,
Qualify	• but until he opens his mouth its not going to happen.

Looking back at the Think Tank as an experiment in counterpublic delib-eration, this analysis suggests that taking rhetorical agency in this setting draws on an embedded set of rhetorical moves that build on one another. At the core are *expressive* moves—identity-asserting statements that tell a per-sonal story or opinion. Speakers expand their reach with broader *interpretive* moves that respond to conflict, claims, or questions with new claims, rivals, or contributions that justify, qualify, or conditionalize our understanding. And finally, speakers may rise to what I have argued is the most powerful form of rhetorical agency in community literacy—a fully *dialogic,* knowledge-building engagement with the understanding of others. In acts of complexity and so-phistication, we see these speakers reinterpret the image of another speaker, rival or compare their own points, plan a response, or actively adapt to others.

This supported performance also helps us name three aspects of going public in the face of a disabling discourse. One is the way a structured discur-sive space, such as the Think Tank, can not only enfranchise speakers but also scaffold their rhetorical work—encouraging them to construct rivals and op-tions in response to others. Another is the way these two students use the occasion to grow and achieve in their own ways. Brandon, who had a history of denying he had a learning disability even within the SOS program, is look-ing publicly and reflectively at his own decision. In this public forum, he has found a way to affirm a "valid social identity" that embraces his learning dif-ficulties. But in other ways, it was Don's participation, speaking up in this public room that astounded his teachers. Don does not talk much; he strug-gles with academic tasks more than most students in the program. Yet here he is, to everyone's surprise and delight, volunteering his story and interven-ing in the discussion with the authority of a person with something to con-tribute.

Finally, in Brandon and other students we are seeing evidence of a distinc-tive form of rhetorical agency. The moves made in this Think Tank dialogue demonstrate a thinker who is entering into a public deliberation, choosing to engage with complex problems. Brandon is not only expressing himself (tell-ing his story or opinion) but also entering this event as an interpreter of prob-lems and as a dialogic meaning maker. In doing so, in going public as a rhetorical agent, he is, in his own way, transforming the discourse of disability. That may seem like a big claim, but in casting his bread on the water, throw-ing his words into circulation, he is helping shape a more public dialogic deliberation about a common good, and in joining that public (created in

Warner's sense) *we too* are in turn implicated in the life success of students with learning disabilities. As collaborative-critical activists (as teachers, researchers, and college students) the public work of rhetoric need not be about our own voice, but can rest on our ability to help call local publics into being, to nurture the rhetorical agency of marginalized speakers, and to use the power of rhetoric to document agency and expertise in a way that challenges and perhaps even transforms the discourses it enters.

Notes

1. Alinsky, *Rules for Radicals*, 119.
2. Freire, *Pedagogy of the Oppressed*, 76.
3. For examples of the range of literacy practices, see Coogan, "Community Literacy"; Cushman, "Toward a Praxis"; Higgins, Long, and Flower, "Community Literacy"; Hull and Katz, "Crafting"; Rousculp, "When the Community." For synthetic, critical overviews, see Deans, *Writing Partnerships;* Long, *Community Literacy.* The specific practice of community literacy referred to here supports public engagement through intercultural inquiry. Developed at the Community Literacy Center, grounded in the prophetic pragmatism of John Dewey and Cornel West, it supports rhetorical problem solving through community-university partnerships. See Flower, *Community Literacy,* for a study of this literate practice and a textual archive in the CLC "Snapshot History" at http://English.cmu.edu/research/inquiry/two.html (accessed July 12, 2008).
4. Brueggemann et al., "Becoming Visible," 371. The authors' excellent multifaceted overview of the meaning of disability for composition studies highlights the difficulty of "becoming visible," while I focus here on the hazards of recognition. The problem in both cases is being represented in the language and categories to which you have contributed, to bring about, as they put it, "nothing about us without us." Ibid., 391.
5. Although "claiming disability [is a] a move that will necessarily 'disrupt the social order,' as disabled people come out," that is not a necessary or immediate effect. Ibid., 373.
6. Andrea Lowenstein treats identity-making as a personal narrative of discovery, understanding, and accommodation. Lowenstein, "My Learning Disability." Self-representation shapes many arguments in LD OnLine www.ldonline.org; in Mel Levine's "All Kinds of Minds," www.allkindsofminds.org; and the powerful Mooney and Cole, *Learning Outside the Lines.*
7. Brueggemann et al., "Becoming Visible," 391.
8. Director Stacie Dojonovic's SOS program, which offers support for the transition from school to work for students with learning disabilities, has been recognized as a model by the National Organization on Disability. Most of the SOS students in this Think Tank team had already been scholars in my Decision Makers community literacy program at CMU (Carnegie Mellon).
9. An outgrowth of the Community Literacy Center, the Carnegie Mellon Community Think Tank had already addressed a series of workplace/worklife problems, bringing marginalized employees into problem-solving dialogues with administrative and policy people. Its methods and findings are at www.cmu.edu/thinktank (accessed July 12, 2008).
10. Kantrowitz and Underwood, "Dyslexia."
11. White, "Learning Disability," 727.
12. Ibid., 720.

13. See Haller, Dorrier, and Rahn's description of the partly successful campaign to "replace holistic designations, such as 'the mentally disabled' . . . (that reduce a human to his or her impairment), with modified terms, i.e., 'people with a learning disability.'" Haller, Dorrier, and Rahn, "Media Labeling." See also Morse, Introduction.

14. Hull et al., "Remediation."

15. Ibid., 311.

16. Ibid., 312.

17. Silver, *Misunderstood Child*, 38–55.

18. White, "Learning Disability," 709.

19. Ibid., 717.

20. Mooney and Cole, *Learning Outside the Lines*.

21. All the speakers in this sequence, identified by pseudonyms, are high school students, except for Trista, a University of Massachusetts student, and myself.

22. Mehan, "Beneath the Skin."

23. McDermott, "Acquisition," 272.

24. Goodley, "Locating Self-Advocacy," 373.

25. Swain and Cameron, "Unless Otherwise Stated," 69.

26. Ibid., 79.

27. See Corker and French, *Disability Discourse*.

28. Goodley, "Locating Self-Advocacy," 373.

29. Goodley, "Supporting People," 441.

30. Swain and Cameron, "Unless Otherwise Stated," 76.

31. Davies, "Discursive Production," 239, quoted in Priestley, "Transforming Disability," 97.

32. Priestley, "Transforming Disability," 97.

33. Habermas, *Structural Transformation*, 27.

34. See Nancy Fraser's influential critique of the Habermas ideal. Fraser, "Rethinking the Public Sphere."

35. See Hauser's coherent framing of this new view in his discussion of what he calls the "vernacular voices" of the "reticulate" and "rhetorical" public sphere. Hauser, *Vernacular Voices*, 44–64.

36. Warner, *Publics and Counterpublics*, 114.

37. For Gloria Anzaldua, a mestiza (mixed) voice is one that embraces rather than avoids conflict and contradiction: "I will have my voice: Indian, Spanish, white. I will have my serpent's tongue—my woman's voice, my sexual voice, my poet's voice. I will overcome the tradition of silence." Anzaldua, *Borderlands/La Frontera*, 81.

38. Goodley, "Locating Self-Advocacy," 367–79.

39. For an overview of "The Decision Makers Assessment: A Web-based Assessment Tool for Reflective Decision Making Based on Writer's Planning and Self-reflection" (2006), visit http://English.cmu.edu/research/inquiry/decisionmakers/index.html (accessed June 21, 2009).

40. For an extended discussion of this notion of rhetorical agency and the collaborative, meaning-making processes of urban rhetors, see Flower, *Community Literacy*.

41. For an overview of the rhetorical structure of the Community Think Tank, see Flower, "Intercultural Knowledge Building."

42. Belenky, Bond, and Weinstock, *Tradition*.

43. For Habermas, "strategic" is a manipulative alternative to "communicative" action; in my perspective from classical and cognitive rhetoric, the art of inquiry is itself

a heuristic and strategically self-conscious process. Habermas, *Theory*, 258. Freire, *Pedagogy of the Oppressed*.

Works Cited

Alinsky, Saul D. *Rules for Radicals: A Practical Primer for Realistic Radicals*. New York: Vintage Books, 1989.

Alzaldua. *Borderlands / La Frontera: The New Mestiza*. San Francisco: Aunt Lute Books, 1987.

Barton, Ellen. "Discourses of Disability in the *Digest*." *JAC* 21 (2001): 555–81.

Belenky, Mary Field, Lynne A. Bond, and Jacqueline S. Weinstock. *A Tradition That Has No Name: Nurturing the Development of People, Families, and Communities*. New York: Basic Books, 1997.

Brueggemann, Brenda Jo, Linda Feldmeier White, Patricia A Dunn, Barbara A. Heifferon, and Johnson Cheu. "Becoming Visible: Lessons in Disability." *College Composition and Communication* 52 (2001): 368–98.

Coogan, David. "Community Literacy as Civic Dialogue." *Community Literacy* 1, no. 1 (2006): 95–108.

Corker, Mairian, and Sally French, eds. *Disability Discourse*. Philadelphia: Open University Press, 1999.

Cushman, Ellen. "Toward a Praxis of New Media." *Reflections* 5, nos. 1–2 (2006): 111–32.

Davies, B. "The Discursive Production of the Male/Female Dualism in School Settings." *Oxford Review of Education* 15 (1989): 229–41.

Deans, Thomas. *Writing Partnerships: Service-Learning in Composition*. Urbana, Ill.: National Council of Teachers of English, 2000.

Flower, Linda. *Community Literacy and the Rhetoric of Public Engagement*. Carbondale: Southern Illinois University Press, 2008.

———. "Intercultural Knowledge Building: The Literate Action of a Community Think Tank." In *Writing Selves/Writing Societies: Research from Activity Perspectives*, edited by Charles Bazerman and David Russell, 239–79. Fort Collins, Colo.: WAC Clearinghouse and Mind, Culture, and Activity, 2002.

Fraser, Nancy. "Rethinking the Public Sphere: A Contribution to the Critique of Actually Existing Democracy." *Social Text* 25/26 (1990): 58–60.

Freire, Paulo. *Pedagogy of the Oppressed*. Translated by Myra Bergman Ramos. New York: Continuum, 1985.

Goodley, Dan. "Locating Self-Advocacy in Models of Disability: Understanding Disability in the Support of Self-Advocates with Learning Difficulties." *Disability & Society* 12 (1997): 367–79.

———. "Supporting People with Learning Difficulties in Self-Advocacy Groups and Models of Disability." *Health and Social Care in the Community* 6 (1998): 438–46.

Habermas, Jürgen. *The Structural Transformation of the Public Sphere: An Inquiry into a Category of Bourgeois Society*. Translated by Thomas Burger, with Frederick Lawrence. Cambridge, Mass.: MIT Press, 1989.

———. *A Theory of Communication Action*. Translated by Thomas McCarthy. Vol. 1. Boston: Beacon, 1984.

Haller, Beth, Bruce Dorrier, and Jessica Rahn. "Media Labeling versus the Us Disability Community Identity: A Study of Shifting Cultural Language." *Disability & Society* 21 (2006): 61–75.

Hauser, Gerard. *Vernacular Voices: The Rhetoric of Publics and Public Spheres*. Columbia: University of South Carolina Press, 1999.

Higgins, Lorraine, Elenore Long, and Linda Flower. "Community Literacy: A Rhetorical Model of Personal and Public Inquiry." *Community Literacy* 1, no. 1 (2006): 9–43.

Hull, Glynda, and Mira-Lisa Katz. "Crafting an Agentive Self: Case Studies of Digital Storytelling." *Research in Teaching of English* 41, no. 1 (2006): 43–82.

Hull, Glynda, Mike Rose, Kay Losey Fraser, and Marisa Castellano. "Remediation as Social Construct: Perspectives from an Analysis of Classroom Discourse." *College Composition and Communication* 42 (1991): 299–329.

Kantrowitz, Barbara, and Anne Underwood. "Dyslexia and the New Science of Reading." *Newsweek,* November 22, 1999, 72–78.

King, Martin Luther, Jr. "Letter from Birmingham Jail." In *The Essential Writings and Speeches of Martin Luther King, Jr.,* 289–302. Edited by James Washington. San Francisco: Harper, 1986.

Long, Elenore. *Community Literacy and the Rhetoric of Local Publics.* West LaFayette, Ind.: Parlor Press, 2008.

Lowenstein, Andrea Freud. "My Learning Disability: A (Digressive) Essay." *College English* 66 (2004): 585–602.

McDermott, R. P. "The Acquisition of a Child by a Learning Disability." In *Understanding Practice: Perspectives on Activity and Context,* edited by Seth Chaiklin and Jean Lave, 269–305. Cambridge: Cambridge University Press, 1996.

Mehan, Hugh. "Beneath the Skin and between the Ears: A Case Study in the Politics of Representation." In *Understanding Practice: Perspectives on Activity and Context,* edited by Seth Chaiklin and Jean Lave, 241–68. Cambridge: Cambridge University Press, 1996.

Mooney, Jonathan, and David Cole. *Learning Outside the Lines.* New York: Simon and Schuster, 2000.

Morse, Tracy Ann. "Introduction to Symposium: Representing Disability Rhetorically." *Rhetoric Review* 22, no. 2 (2003): 154–56.

Priestley, Mark. "Transforming Disability Identity through Critical Literacy and the Cultural Politics of Language." In *Disability Discourse,* edited by Mairian Corker and Sally French, 92–102. Philadelphia: Open University Press, 1999.

Rousculp, Tiffany. "When the Community Writes: Re-Envisioning the SLCC DiverseCity Writing Series." *Reflections* 5, nos. 1–2 (2006): 67–88.

Silver, Larry. *The Misunderstood Child.* New York: Three Rivers Press, 1984.

Swain, John, and Colin Cameron. "Unless Otherwise Stated: Discourses of Labeling and Identity in Coming Out." In *Disability Discourse,* edited by Mairian Corker and Sally French, 68–78. Philadelphia: Open University Press, 1999.

Warner, Michael. *Publics and Counterpublics.* New York: Zone Books, 2005.

White, Linda Feldmeier. "Learning Disability, Pedagogies, and Public Discourse." *College Composition and Communication* 53 (2002): 705–38.

Sophists for
Social Change

DAVID J. COOGAN

It began almost casually, on a warm summer evening in Church Hill, Virginia, as a conversation among friends looking for something to do. "Do you want to rob somebody?" asked one boy, according to police. "All right," answered another. It ended, Richmond police say, with four teenagers—ages fourteen, fifteen, sixteen, and seventeen—stripping, raping, and sodomizing an eighteen-year-old Chesterfield woman at gunpoint on a picnic table in Libby Hill Terrace Park, while the woman's boyfriend was forced to sit helplessly at the table throughout the August 4 ordeal.[1]

I found out about the gang rape the day after it happened. I was walking through the park with a visiting relative when I asked the television reporters what they were doing, and they asked if they could interview me. That night at 11:00 I saw myself walking and heard myself saying that the park was well used; that the neighborhood itself had slowly transformed over the last decade, with rising property rates and dropping crime rates; and that yes, I was shocked by what had happened, but no, I had no plans to stay out of the park.

Along with the video footage of fountains and vistas and cutaway shots of nearby row homes, my words helped the journalists articulate commonplaces about progress and community. But when I later read about the rape in the city's major daily, the *Richmond Times Dispatch* (*RTD*), I grew a little uneasy. It was clear that the rape shocked the reporters not simply because it was a rape, but because it took place in a "desirable" place with "restored" homes that have "panoramic views" of the James River.[2] The fear of border crossing was hard to miss. Jim Nolan reported that before the incident, "the teens met at a playground near the park," a place that loosely marks the invisible border between the white, gentrified part of the neighborhood and the predominantly poor, black part to the north. The teens then walked three blocks to the "popular stargazing spot" overlooking the James River and found their target. "'I don't know, man, white people,' Travon Garnet said at the time, according to his statement to police."[3] Garnet seemed conscious of the difficulty here, crossing some sort of invisible line. Nolan seemed conscious of it, too, when he later wrote that "the brutal rape and robbery" had "shattered the tranquility in this historic Church Hill neighborhood."[4] Alan Cooper, a colleague of Nolan's at the *RTD*, extended that imagery to the boys themselves: "Only Travon Garnet had anything close to normal intelligence. The others were said to have street savvy, but Kelvin Lightfoot reads at a second-grade level, and Rashard Garnet at a first-grade level."[5] To conclude, then: the teens brought the "brutality" and the illiteracy of the black community into the "tranquility" and prosperity of the white community.

Only the victim, in an interview with Nolan, attempted something broader. She said she felt sorry for the teens for "messing up their lives." In fact, as Cooper later reported, the teens were tried as adults and received prisons sentences of roughly thirty years all together. "I don't know what made them do such an act," the woman wondered aloud. Nolan, however, dismissed this perception: "Their reasoning didn't matter to the young woman's mother. 'They belong in jail for a long time,' she said. 'They had choices. And they chose to do what they did. You can't feel sorry for someone who chooses to hurt you.'"[6]

The next week I returned to the park and, by chance, met my councilwoman, Delores McQuinn[7] and Jennie Dotts, the executive director of a local advocacy group, the Alliance to Conserve Old Richmond Neighborhoods (ACORN).[8] McQuinn and Dotts were campaigning for McQuinn's reelection to city council. McQuinn's district not only includes the gentrified area where the rape took place but a much larger, predominantly African American community, which has several public housing developments. We talked about the rape, what the police were doing, and what the two women wanted to do to get to the root of the problem. They suggested that a teen center might improve public safety by compensating for the lack of teen-oriented services and institutions in the neighborhood. ACORN and the city of Richmond, in a joint private-public venture, had bought a campus of three old buildings, made plans for renovations, established a board of directors, earmarked some of the city budget, and surveyed the teens about their interests and needs.[9]

After some conversation where I could affirm these values and share stories of addressing similar problems with students and community organizers in a poor, black neighborhood on the south side of Chicago, a place not unlike the east end of Richmond, they asked if I would be willing to help spread the word.[10] I agreed to help advertise the teen center, but I also suggested that we enlist the teens in the process of advertising by running a writing workshop over the summer and then publishing their writings in a book that we could circulate around the city. What I saw was an opportunity to position the teens as rhetors in a public more accustomed to news stories in which they appeared as rapists and criminals. McQuinn and Dotts agreed to this plan. And in that moment, the park I knew had become what Susan Jarratt, in *Rereading the Sophists,* calls a middle space. And I had become a sophist, in search of social change. A "middle space," writes Jarratt, is a space where diverse stakeholders can reformulate "human 'truths' in historically and geographically specific contexts."[11] In her reading of social history in antiquity, middle spaces were both concrete places and cerebral places where rhetors articulated the "codes" to evaluate conduct, entertain political possibilities, and in other ways arrange their affairs.

Though we generally think of democracy as a sixth- and fifth-century B.C. phenomenon, there is evidence that for centuries before this, villagers, each holding under a feudal arrangement a section of land called a *damos,* met in common space perhaps for the purpose of deciding on questions of agricultural practice or on the nature of requests to be delivered to the king and his council.[12]

Middle spaces are productive places to question the commonplaces or ideological statements that, as Sharon Crowley and Debra Hawhee explain in their decidedly sophistic textbook, *Ancient Rhetorics for Contemporary Students,* are "literally 'taken for granted,'" but which can "be subjected to invention."[13] That Jarratt finds evidence of a "contemporary sophistic" in liberatory educators such as Paulo Freire and bell hooks suggests some precedent for what will follow here. The community organizing framework that I present differs from critical pedagogies, though—at least those that allow classroom theorizing about social change to take the place of community action.[14] Just as the early Sophists, those first teachers of rhetoric, rejected philosophical debate about "transcendent truths and eternal values" in order to attend to pressing "social exigencies" in the community,[15] sophists seeking social change resist "unmasking" power for others, as Raymie McKerrow and others seem to recommend in their programs for critical rhetoric.[16] Nor is a sophist seeking social change likely to find it in traditional forums for public debate, such as neighborhood associations or city council meetings, which can exclude people stylistically or substantively, even while professing not to.[17] Coming into the middle also regards issue-oriented advocacy with skepticism, as it tends to succeed not by forming middle spaces for dialogue but by sharpening the struggle between "us" and "them." The heart of what I am proposing, then, if I can borrow a bit from Paula Mathieu, is not a strategic orientation to the public work of rhetoric, but a tactical one.[18] Making a middle space is not generating and then disseminating ideal strategies for rhetorical intervention but generating publics capable of addressing their own social problems.

What was taken for granted as commonplace in the reporters' associations between race, class, illiteracy, and violence was subjected to invention by me, Dotts, and McQuinn. Building a teen center to reduce violence seemed to me a reasonable conjecture—not to mention good campaign rhetoric—and something I would now characterize as a sophistic approach to public life.[19]

It persuaded not by dispensing "facts" but by projecting shared values, which we might loosely collate here under a liberal interpretation of equal opportunity: the idea that every American has a right to pursue knowledge for self-development and that collective action is needed to ensure that this happens for people who have traditionally faced barriers to that development. When we proceed this way, with conjectures about what we share, we proceed not from the university but, as Eli Goldblatt puts it, "from the activist's ground . . . learning before we act, developing relationships and commitments before we organize classes and set up research projects," and only later, once we have helped community partners "identify problems and transform these problems into issues" that can actually be addressed, do we consider "how students in courses fit in and what university resources could be helpful in addressing the issues."[20] What my community partners wanted, at this point, were handbills, banners, and posters announcing the East End Teen Center. They needed relationships with people who could make this kind of public.

The next week in the park, I saw my neighbor John Malinoski, a graphic designer who works with me at Virginia Commonwealth University (VCU) and who happened to be teaching a service-learning course that links graphic design students with community-based organizations. Malinoski knew about the rape and quickly agreed to a meeting with the teen center advisory board and his students. At that meeting, we learned from the teens' representative—the project manager for the East End Teen Center—that the teens, in a collaborative brainstorming session some months earlier, had renamed the East End Teen Center "Teen City." Malinoski and his students, seeking clues about their collaborators and their audience, perked up.

What the teens were telling us with Teen City was they were not clients in need of specialized services in the East End. They saw their teen center as a place to redefine themselves in relation to fellow citizens. The city, they seemed to be saying, belonged to them. Too often, writes McKnight in his critique of social service providers, there is a "failure of integration." This failure "clearly limits . . . the lives of the labeled people themselves. But the exclusion also limits the experience of local citizens." What is needed in situations like this one, McKnight argues, are not more community services but more "community guides" who can "bring the individual into life as a citizen by incorporating him into relationships where his capacities can be expressed; where he is not defined by his 'deficiencies.'"[21] Now I do not want to ascribe firm motives to either the teens or the woman who interviewed them. Teen City was not elaborated as an argument. And the woman who related it did not claim to be a community guide. Yet the phrase was publicly addressed: the teens were asked to name their organization, and it circulated from the "counterpublic" of the neighborhood to this emerging public of college students, politicians, activists, and professors. As Richard Marback explains, the act of naming a place—"placemaking" is his term—is "a material act of building and maintaining spaces that is at the same time an ideological act of fashioning places where we feel we belong."[22]

Placemaking and community-guiding are especially potent in counterpublics. Those who may be identified with counterpublics, Michael Warner elaborates, are "counter" not because they share essential traits or can be located physically in a particular place but because they are aware of their subordinate status to the dominant. For these groups, "it is hoped that the poesis of scene making will be transformative, not replicative merely"; that the aesthetic and cultural dimensions of their rhetoric will "transform" public assumptions.[23] If the twenty-five teens who were surveyed can be safely characterized as a counterpublic, then we might go on to see Teen City not only as placemaking but as "poetic world making." In Warner's terms: an attempt to transform the way the dominant construed them (as truants, criminals, clients), not only through proposition but through style. And so far as I can tell it worked. The phrase enabled us to reflect upon who the teens imagined themselves to be, which, according to Warner, is what makes public discourse *public:*

> Public discourse says not only "Let a public exist" but "Let it have
> this character, speak this way, see the world in this way." It then goes
> in search of confirmation that such a public exists, with greater or lesser
> success—success being further attempts to cite, circulate, and realize the
> world understanding it articulates. Run it up the flagpole and see who
> salutes. Put on a show and see who shows up.[24]

Teen City was "confirmed," as Warner might say, when the students chose to advertise the center by designing a mural. During that brainstorming meeting, I began by reading from the East End Teen Center mission statement— "to create a non-faith based sanctuary where young people will have an opportunity to grow, develop, and acquire life and job skills in a nurturing, safe, and secure environment"—and the word that stood out to the group was "sanctuary." They wanted to paint that word on the building. Months later they did along with half a dozen teens in the neighborhood.

From the point of view of a sophist, the question that the mural raises is not whether it is "true" that this place will become a sanctuary but who believes it and why. To look at this mural (see the dust jacket of this book) is to ask how it happened, what it means, or even if you are implicated in its vision. Anyone can do that. The stakes are rather low, because, as Warner points out, a public can be "constituted through mere attention."[25] It is worth noting as well that this mural was not made through a timely process of rational deliberation, but through a diffused process of cultural interpretation, linking the reported speech of the teens to the materials about the East End Teen Center provided by McQuinn and Dots and then to the painted brick. To Warner, of course, this diffuse, textualized process merely reflects the underlying reality that a public is a "space of discourse organized by discourse." It is misleading "to think of a discourse public as a people and therefore as a really existing set of potentially numerable human beings" who meet and then decide.[26] To conceive of publics this way, as deliberating bodies or parliamentary debaters who have the power to alter reality, is to limit the style and substance of publics and in some ways miss counterpublics all together. What is liberating about public life, Warner argues, is not its accessibility to outsiders—its capacity to integrate newcomers neatly and share power equitably—but its anonymity.

To actually *make* a sanctuary for at-risk teens, of course, you need much more than a public. You need people. Middle spaces cannot—and should not—take the place of traditional forums for organizing people. Just the same, we need sophists to envision inquiries that challenge people to extend their self-interest *in the name* of a public. That, arguably, is what happened here: the teens needed someone to affirm their vision of themselves as citizens; Malinoski's students needed projects to hone their skills as community-based graphic designers; Malinoski and I both wanted a positive way to respond to a crime close to our homes; and the East End Teen Center needed artists and writers to help it elaborate its mission, gratis.

What I have shown in the making of the mural is how the motivating exigency of the rape created a kairotic moment in the public work of rhetoric. Out of the commonplace reasoning in Nolan's and Cooper's reporting, which effectively escalated a fear of contact across the borders of race and class, came sophistic reasoning that invited geographically and culturally dispersed participants—VCU students and professors, neighborhood teens, and community activists—into a "middle space" of public life where it became possible to imagine an alternative future unfolding.

Although the resources that made "sanctuary" possible—Teen City's ownership of the building, the work of the advisory board, and the cost of paint—were essentially in place before the collaboration with VCU began, resources for the writing workshop I had envisioned months earlier had to be created. Teen City is a fledgling organization with uninhabitable property (in the midst of a renovation) and no operating budget for programming. When I fell in with them, they had no resources to run a writing workshop. McQuinn, therefore, invited her colleague, Ernestine Scott of the Richmond Public Schools Title I Program, to choose thirty African American students from one of the middle schools in McQuinn's district to participate in the workshop and to pay for those students to be bussed to VCU. Scott provided two college-student assistants to tutor and financial incentives for the teens to attend each class. She also paid for course readers, printing, disks, and notebooks.

VCU supported the workshop, too, but again, its pathway into the project had to be constructed out of existing mandates at the university—through tactical rather than strategic planning on my part. One mandate came from the Honors College, which had launched a Summer Undergraduate Research

Program (SURP) that paired one faculty member with one student over a six-week period. I applied to this program, outlining my research questions about writing and social change, and was assigned a student who served as a research assistant, classroom tutor, and workshop organizer. I then took the program prospectus to our Office of Community Programs, which was designed to offer meeting spaces, programming, and computing to the predominantly African American community in the Carver neighborhood, just north of campus. I explained the project I had helped put together and asked if we could use their computer lab to teach writing to African American teens from a different Richmond neighborhood. They agreed, only pausing to tell me to bring my own paper and disks. We now had resources to work.

I offer these details about the material conditions of our partnership not because they are especially interesting but because they demonstrate in a concrete way what community organizing really organizes: the opportunity to do rhetorical work. In this second half of the essay, I show more directly than I can with the mural how rhetoric emanating from such arrangements can actually impact material conditions, how the indirect movement of public inquiries can move people to change more than just their beliefs. I do this by describing the writing workshop that I taught for Teen City and some of the publicity that the students' writings generated. I offer this not as a formula for generating social change but as an extension of what William Hart-Davidson, James P. Zappen, and S. Michael Halloran characterize as the "sort of 'vernacular pedagogy' . . . that recalls, and perhaps re-imagines, a Sophistic tradition of situated learning, challenging, and broadening the borders of the polis."[27]

Sharon Crowley, Debra Hawhee, and Susan Jarratt help me generalize such a pedagogy: to darken the lines that I have been drawing between rhetorical inquiries, associational life, and placemaking. Throughout the workshop, I freely mixed genres—news clippings, literature, speeches—again, taking my cue from the Sophists, who Jarratt locates at the intersection of logos and mythos, between the active and rational experience of logos and the uncritical, cultural experience of mythos. Jarratt rejects this dichotomy, which was made even more rigid by critics who linked logos with print literacy. She argues, instead, that the early Sophists who met in the *damos* did not simply nod to the beat of the bards but questioned the way they were placed—politically, ethically—and what they might do to move out of that place. Within a community-organizing framework built on placemaking and poetic world-making, rhetorical techniques for invention such as the common topics are foundational, then, because they enable rhetors to respond from their places: to denaturalize discourses that, left unchecked, will continue to construct them.

My assignment to "describe what you see in your community—people, places, things, events," for example, was based on the common topic of present conjecture, which asks rhetors to name what exists, what does not exist, the size or extent of what exists, and what might exist in the future. Because commonplace reasoning largely determines which things get identified, these questions do not merely elicit description. They provoke—or I used them to provoke—an evaluation of the scene, as we can see in Jennifer Tillery's essay about Church Hill. She said it is a "good place to live," though maybe "a little too quiet for me" because "where I live no one ever comes outside." In fact, her "neighborhood isn't bad because shootings don't happen there as much as they do in other places. Yes, there are some shootings, but there aren't a lot. When I hear a shooting I don't get scared or anything, I just hope that no one tries to run into my house and hide, especially if my family and I are home."

I told Jennifer during a conference that what she described sounded stressful. She just looked at me, blankly. I explained that knowing someone might run into my house during a shooting would stress me out. How could I feel safe? She listened patiently then turned to her screen and started typing: "I know that this sounds stressful, but to me it isn't because I don't worry myself about things like shootings. I know that I am going to die some day." Now it was my turn to look blank. I had expected that the rhetorical power of the teens' writings would be rooted in the cross-cultural dialogue that the community organizing framework foregrounded. But I had no idea how that power would feel. I grew up without gunplay in an upper-middle class suburb of Connecticut. If I had fatalistic ideas at fourteen, they were not rooted in experience, but in moody rock music.

I was surprised by students' determination to articulate their values in this assignment, even when their own evidence seemed to contradict their claims. Sha'keilia Allen, for example, admitted that some might see her community as "dirty, violent, noisy, and boring," and while all this is true (except the noise) she nonetheless insisted that she liked her community. It is true, she conceded, that "some of the kids in my neighborhood make trash" but it's not like the trash collectors never come. In that same spirit, she warded off what some might mistake as a problem with public safety.

> There are some weird people who live where I live. There is a man who spies on the ladies and girls. But this doesn't make me afraid to go outside and have fun, because he is in this thing that looks like a wheelchair but it's not really a wheelchair. I know that he can't get me because his house has steps and, in order for him to get away from his house, one of his family members would have to bring him out on a ramp. But if he does try to get off his porch, then I will run right home.

When I first read this scene, I could not help but wonder what was really happening—or may have already happened—to girls in that neighborhood. I was concerned. But then I reread it and imagined it visually: an athletic-looking fourteen-year-old girl outrunning a man in a wheelchair that is not a wheelchair. That is when I noticed the placemaking. I was unprepared in so many ways: I had forgotten, quite frankly, what fourteen-year-olds like to do to each other, for sport. And I had no idea how race fit in with all of the other topics of teasing. Iman Clayton complained that "the boys at my school call me names such as ugly, black and crispy. I would like to say that this doesn't hurt me but it really does." She then interpreted the boys' conduct and modeled an alternative. "In anything I do, I will love myself and continue to tell myself that I am beautiful in spite of what some mean boys may tell me. Some boys will probably always expect me to be lighter, but that I cannot change. I just expect myself to be a nice person and to get far in life. One of the things that makes me a nice person is that I care what people say and do, but in a good way."

By modeling "a good way" of caring about color, Iman transformed the private experience of racism into a public disposition. I see this as the difference between what Crowley and Hawhee have called the modern concern with personality—an amalgam of private perceptions or feelings—and the ancient concern with ethos or character, knowable only through the repeated actions or habits of public life. Iman has created new terms for being "accepted, even by people who are the same color as me" and, as Warner might say, in doing this made a world, poetically, one that I believe many would want to inhabit.

Trevon Blakely did something similar in the revision of a passage where he characterized his community as a violent place and later admitted to having "an anger problem." When I asked about this "anger problem"—if it meant that he, too, was violent—he shot me a quick squint and asked why I thought that. I explained how "violence" and "anger" seemed similar, then asked if he agreed. His revision—a new opening sentence—addressed the confusion head on: "Although I do get angry, I am not violent like others in the neighborhood." Violent people, he went on to explain, shoot off guns on the Fourth of July and not just "to celebrate." They are "downright mean and cruel." Their public disposition, to be clear, is indefensible. Trevon's "anger problem," by contrast, was about having to babysit his siblings when he would rather do his own thing. The bulk of his essay was about making good grades, liking basketball "more than anything in the world except life and the Lord," and acting "like a smart person and not someone who doesn't care about life and goes around being a fake thug or whatever you want to call it." In this revision, Trevon not only distinguished what Crowley and Hawhee would call his habitual practices of caring and learning from those of the violent people and the "fake thugs," but he also invited his readers to understand that there is more to his community than violence.

There is a subtlety in these students' essays, publicly addressed, but very much rooted in particular places and experiences. We see Iman, Sha'Keila, Trevon, and Jennifer in the midst of that life, constructing their characters aesthetically and rhetorically, in ways that readers can judge. From the vantage point of character, it is harder to generalize on the issues. For every student who complained that there was too much pressure in school to fight, as one girl put it, "over stupid things like a pencil or a boy," there was another testifying that some students "help other students by tutoring and staying back after school to teach them new things." The facts were always open to counterfacts. Darrius Bolling wrote that "some of the teachers can be your best friends because of the way they act by just being themselves and not trying to imitate or act like someone they aren't." But "one day," Trevon confided, "my teacher gave us a test on material that we never even learned. Sometimes she gives us stuff that she doesn't even know." One girl wrote against the idea that "young ladies" should not compete in sports, get sweaty, or "do the more 'MANLY' steps in Step Dancing." But another seemed to affirm that sort of traditional gendered role, dreaming about opening a hair and nail salon so that she could "make people feel happy and to help them to stop thinking negative about themselves."

If all this seems like making the worst case look better, as the usual case against sophistry goes, it also meant honoring Protagoras's dictum that the human is the measure of all things. The task, after all, was not to get it right—to generalize the state of inner-city school teaching, the cleanliness and safety in the neighborhoods, the real causes of racism or gender stereotypes—but to crack the hard shell of commonplace reasoning *as it actually functioned in each rhetor's world.* Honoring individuals this way has an obvious humanistic value, but it also adds value to public inquiry itself. The day we talked about achievement, for example, I began by asking questions about a news clipping they had read about the problems with Richmond public schools. I asked them if they knew what a truant was. They did. I then asked them if they knew what the truancy rate was at the high school that they would be attending in the next year or so. It was just over 60 percent. I would like to say that that quieted them down. But it didn't, at least not until I read aloud Gwendolyn Brooks's poem "We Real Cool." I asked if the kids in that poem were actually cool for skipping school, as Brooks slyly suggests in the first few lines. "It depends," they told me. What they wrote that day elaborated why. They did not talk about standardized tests or tracking. What they were following was far less complicated, but more profound: school was cool when people were nice to each other.

Their statements about their futures were also narrated along these lines, as a contest between people who help and those who do not. There are some people, Jennifer Tillery wrote, who "tell me I can't—and I will not—make it because I will not try hard enough." She told her readers, however, "people like this I call haters," and they are "probably" the ones who "won't make it in life" because "they are so focused on my life instead of their own." Jennifer wanted to make it as a doctor, "to help little children like me," because "three or four years ago" she got bitten by a stray dog, and even though she had to have "four or five needles inside the dog bite" and she "started screaming and couldn't breathe," the doctor was really nice. And so while she admitted it seemed like a "bad experience," it actually was enabling. Denise Alert's desire to have her own hair and nail salon could also be traced back to a desire to contribute something positive to her community. She explained simply that she liked to "make people feel happy and to help them to stop thinking negative about themselves." When she described herself and her friends walking through the park encountering "mean people who talk about others" and who "might not like you," it is plain to see that her goal is to get rid of that negativity.

Positive human relationships were the heart of it. A jock confessed what he learned from his coach, after he and his friends were laughing at a boy who could not catch the ball. "You never tease a fellow player. He's a part of your team!" Another jock confessed that while he likes to "show off in football to boost up" his self-esteem and confidence, it hurts him to hear people say, "You suck." He realized that he does not have the self-esteem he thought he had, and moreover, that the true source of his confidence was not in sports, but in "becoming a scientist." What he wrote about was that moment when he knew: looking through the microscope with one eye and, with the other, at a career in chemistry or gerontology. "In this writing," he confessed, "I am taking off the mask." Like the girls who untangled themselves from gender expectations—LaVarsha Griffin wrote with some resignation, "People always expect me to clean up"—DeJohn separated himself from the masculinity he felt compelled to perform.

PUBLICITY EFFECT

I had high hopes that these essays might stoke these stases in public discourse, and so by the end of the summer, Malinoski and I created a book of the teens' writings that they chose to call *Two Sides of a One Track Mind*. This fit their sense of humor and, from my point of view, their *dissoi logoi*. Many months later, the book was published and distributed to the teens and their parents at an awards ceremony put together by Councilwoman McQuinn. Before that ceremony, which was in the fall, McQuinn released a few of the students' essays to the *RTD* as a press release about the workshop. And that created a middle space of some size and capacity.

Shebony Carrington
Dear Friend,
    I don't know where you live or what you do, but I do know this: you don't want to live where I live. You don't want to see what I see every day. I live in Fairfield Court and I am going to tell you how I feel about it.
    It's true the houses are very nice looking. They just put new ovens in, and a while back they put in new refrigerators. But the place still isn't

'WHERE I'M FROM TO WHERE I'M GOING' ESSAY BY SHEBONY CARRINGTON

Dear friend,

I don't know where you live or

what you do, but I do know this:

you don't want to live where I live.

You don't want to see what I see every day.

I live in Fairfield Court and I am going to

tell you how I feel about it. SEE FULL TEXT ON PAGE A5

"Where I'm From to Where I'm Going." Front page, *Richmond Times Dispatch*,
August 12, 2005, reprintedby permission of the *Richmond Times-Dispatch*

right. Some of the houses are dirty, and they are only cleaned when it's
time for inspection. After that, they go back to being dirty houses again.
The people in my neighborhood don't take pride in how it looks.

Some people feel comfortable sitting on their porches, but now they
can't because of the shooting and the crazy people around the neighborhood. No matter what happens, there are always people arguing. There are
people that walk around the neighborhood looking stupid. In other words
there are people who drink too much liquor and beer and walk around
bent over, smelling like alcohol. That's not a good sight.

In my neighborhood there are some streets that are clean, but there
are some streets that are nasty looking. The area that I live in is clean
because there is always someone picking up the trash. On other streets
there are just people who throw trash on the ground. There are some
people that just sit around and drink and leave their beer bottles/cans
on the ground. Another problem is the drug dealers. They sell drugs
and urinate in front of the children. They just don't care what they do,
so they're just going to do it.

I don't think that the negative things in my neighborhood are going
to stop me from being what I want to be in life. I see the negative things
in my neighborhood but I'm not involved in them. I feel that being on
the outside of the situation looking inside makes me want to help people. I feel really bad because of the people that are being hurt and bruised
from getting beat up. Just because I'm in the neighborhood around these

things, it doesn't mean that anything is going to stop me from accomplishing my goal of being a doctor. When I grow up I want to become a General Practitioner. That is a doctor you go to for everyday needs like if you have a cold or if you are sick. I want to become a General Practitioner because I like to help other people. Darren Thomas, the preacher from the Temple of Judah told me, "To be somebody you have to help somebody." So I'm going to be that person to help somebody.

What might be in my way from accomplishing this goal is my negative attitude toward some situations. What I mean is that someone may come across the wrong way by getting smart with me or getting frustrated with me and I might not know what to do or say to them. Then, I might get an attitude with them. However that's not stopping me from being me. What I mean is that there are some people that expect me to be a young lady and not to play sports. They would rather see young ladies dress up and wear heels and also keep their hair and nails done. But me, I just want to be comfortable for myself. It doesn't matter how I look as long as I'm clean and comfortable. I am going to be me no matter what.

Media General, the owner of the newspaper, later told me that over 9,000 people read the essay online and that it got more hits than any other story in the entire history of the paper online. The editors had also created a blog where roughly 100 people wrote comments, nearly all of them positive. Readers responded well to this strong voice emanating from public housing. Of the ninety-six recorded comments, roughly one-third (twenty-four comments) addressed Shebony's placemaking directly. "You go, girl!" one of them wrote. "Don't let your present dictate your future!" Readers liked the idea of somebody beating the odds of doing well even in public housing. An even greater number of the readers (thirty-seven comments) liked Shebony's Christian sense of how to do it. Some did this simply by telling readers "this child is blessed" or by closing their note, "God's speed." Others offered advice to the writer— "I would like to say to Ms. Carrington, 'Trust God.' He will be there for you as long as you have faith and trust in Him." Readers carefully noted that Shebony had already taken good advice and praised the advice givers: "I also attend Temple of Judah," wrote one, "and its good to know that you took what the minister said and ran with it."

The Christian discourse of redemption through service, along with the defiant appropriation of American bootstraps, warranted the otherwise harsh juxtaposition between herself and the "stupid people" who "just don't care" about the greater good of the community. Shebony does not choose to rise while her community slides, but to make her success her community's success. Ultimately, it is not the drug dealers or drunks that she worries about, then, but the people who spark an attitude in her: "There are some people that expect me to be a young lady and not to play sports. They would rather see young ladies dress up and wear heels and also keep their hair and nails done."

Her own expectation, to be "clean and comfortable" and "to be me no matter what," suggested a contemporary alternative that concretized as it generalized. Who doesn't want to be clean and comfortable? Who doesn't want to steer clear of unreasonable gender expectations? Who doesn't want to help somebody? Who doesn't want "to be me"? Hart-Davidson, Zappen, and Halloran, in their work with young African American teen writers in Troy, New York, noted a similar resistance to "traditional gender roles." But they also saw them temper self-confidence "about themselves and their futures" with "contemporary social and family values," including those found in "the mass media."[28] In this rhetorical performance, however, just as it was in many of the others I discussed in the preceding section, Shebony cut through those commonplaces.

Not everyone was so sanguine about the power of self-determination and faith overcoming structural barriers. The remaining third of the commentators shifted the ground away from Shebony and her situation to the difficult environment of Fairfield Court. One characterized "this young lady" as "just one example of what our City youth experience day to day."

> I hope that the city council members catch this article and Mayor Wilder. She is asking for some help. She may not have said help me, but she painted a picture of a young girl who does not want to be caught up in what she sees in her neighborhood. I too, as a youth in Richmond said that I would not involve myself in those negative things, but because I did not have stable parent figures in my life I lost that hope, because I felt like nobody else cared. I care young lady. Peace and Blessings!!!

In telling her story of getting involved in "negative things" and then regretting it, this commentator made a confession while also inventing a broader argument about teens in need of community guides ("stable parent figures"). Closing the note with "I care," the reader symbolically became that guide. This was part of a larger effort to make a middle space online, but to go beyond it, as we can see in the following comment.

> I have four children who live in Northside. They did not grow up there, but chose to live there. What they have encountered to their dismay is the attitude of city officials that if you live in Northside you have to expect trouble. The result of this attitude is there is no follow up on solving crime here. If young people such as the author of the letter published today wish to have opportunities in life, the problems on their street should take the same priority as in any other part of the city.

These accusations of civic neglect contrast rather loudly to the prior analyses that were premised on Christianity and American opportunity. What stands in the way of opportunity here are "city officials" who shrug their shoulders at crime and tell you to "expect trouble."

Most readers, however, did not waste time debating who was really to blame. They offered to introduce Shebony to medical work through their jobs or their connections, recommended inspiring books, or more mysteriously offered to send gifts. Others generalized the need to help teens like Shebony, counseling readers that "any little thing will help, whether it is volunteering at the schools or giving small donations for school supplies." Then, in what seemed like a conscious response to the title of Shebony's essay, one commentator exclaimed, "We may not live where she lives or have her experiences thus far in her young life but we can help change her environment. I for one will seek her out to help her stay on track to achieve her goals. There are some more out there. Who else will help?" A week later, Rob Rhoden, the pastor at Commonwealth Chapel, answered that call.[29] He invited Shebony to his church to read her essay aloud. Here is how Dena Sloan, in the *RTD* of August 15, 2005, describes the sequence of events: "On Friday afternoon, a local pastor called. Less than forty-eight hours later, Shebony was standing in a church she had never attended, Commonwealth Chapel in the Fan District, facing a crowd of about 150 strangers and reading her essay. . . . The church's pastor, a man Shebony had met just a few hours before, told her that people she doesn't know are setting up a fund for her education. The tall, thin girl seemed at once stunned and pleased at the whirlwind of developments. Wearing a soft, green jacket and skirt, and with her short hair in a tight ponytail, she greeted well-wishers after morning services yesterday. 'It's a very good thing,' she said quietly."

At the time of this writing, Pastor Rhoden's congregation has raised $10,000.[30] The "whirlwind of developments" continued when Habitat for Humanity called to see if Shebony's family might qualify for a home.[31] Months later, Shebony won first prize at the banquet honoring the writers, which was organized by Councilwoman McQuinn and Ernestine Scott. That night she went home with a laptop.

Not all of these whirlwinds blew favorably, though. Lindsay Kastner, in a follow-up piece for the *RTD*, wrote that "in her own neighborhood response has been positive and negative. . . . Some people told her the essay brought tears to their eyes. But Shebony said neighborhood drug dealers also had something to say to her. . . . 'Some said you been talking about Fairfield, you been snitchin.'"[32] Though Shebony did not name any names or even particular places, the snitch reaction indicated that she had provocatively challenged rhetorical decorum in her community, that her placemaking toward mainstream values like hard work, sobriety, and a respect for the law had threatened their move away from it. The *RTD* columnist Michael Paul Williams praised Shebony on these grounds for her "precocious courage . . . to break the code of silence" and dismissed the snitch reaction as something emanating from a "confused code of ethics" condoning irresponsible behavior, illegal activity, exploitation, and violence.[33]

In "Where I've Been, Where I'm Going," Shebony Carrington spoke out against her placement in the city, constructing a scene in which her character could exit. And that is just what she did. She left Fairfield Court rhetorically. Then, with the publication of her essay and the invitation from Pastor Rhoden, she left it physically. She did not do this because I had taught her how to uncover the truth, as I saw it. She did it because I had asked her to orient herself to a reading public.

In these feel-good, Oprah moments, where we can easily see the link between rhetorical cause and material effect, it may be tempting to confuse the sophistic framework that I have been elaborating here with the Angels Network. And while I am certainly proud to have been a part of a process that landed the girl a med-school scholarship (and later landed another student whose essay got into the paper a dance scholarship),[34] I hope I have also shown that sophists, in their capacity as teachers, writers and community guides, do not use rhetoric to target change. They make middle spaces for placemaking and poetic world making. Then they get out of the way.

NOTES

1. Nolan, "Statements."
2. Nolan, "After Rape."
3. Nolan, "Statements."
4. Nolan, "Teens Charged."
5. Cooper, "Four Teenagers."
6. Nolan, "After Rape."
7. For further information on Councilwoman McQuinn and her district, see http://www.ci.richmond.va.us/citizen/city_gov/district7/accomplishments.aspx.
8. For further information on ACORN, see http://www.richmondneighborhoods.org/.
9. Walters, "City Plans."
10. Coogan, "Counter Publics"; Coogan, "Community Literacy"; Coogan, "Service Learning."
11. Jarratt, *Rereading the Sophists,* 42.
12. Ibid., 40–42.
13. Crowley and Hawhee, *Ancient Rhetorics,* 109.
14. Cushman, "Rhetorician."
15. Jarratt, *Rereading the Sophists,* 2.
16. McKerrow, "Critical Rhetoric."
17. See the essay by Candace Rai in this volume for an extended critique of inclusivity in citywide forums.
18. Mathieu, *Tactics of Hope.*
19. See Crowley and Hawhee, *Ancient Rhetorics,* chapters 3 and 4, for more on the rhetorical technique of conjecture.
20. Goldblatt, "Alinksy's Reveille," 283.
21. McKnight, "Redefining Community," 117.
22. Marback, "Speaking of the City," 146.
23. Warner, *Publics and Counterpublics,* 122.
24. Ibid., 114.

25. Ibid., 87.

26. Ibid., 68.

27. Hart-Davidson, Zappen, and Halloran, "On the Formation," 135–37.

28. Ibid., 135–36.

29. For more information on this church, see http://www.comchap.com/started.php.

30. Walters, "City Plans."

31. Kastner, "Essayist."

32. Kastner, "Youths' Essays Honored."

33. Williams, "'Snitch' Shirts."

34. MacDonald, who won second prize at the banquet and who also had his essay published in the *RTD*, received a $360 scholarship for ballet lessons. According to Lindsay Kastner of the *RTD*, "Diontey's mother, Wanda McDonald Cooper, said she would not have been able to pay for his lessons." Kastner, "Teen."

Works Cited

Coogan, David. "Community Literacy as Civic Dialogue." *Community Literacy Journal* 1 (2006): 95–108.

———. "Counter Publics in Public Housing: Reframing the Politics of Service Learning." *College English* 67 (2005): 461–82.

———. "Service Learning and Social Change: The Case for Materialist Rhetoric" *College Composition and Communication* 57 (2006): 667–93.

Cooper, Alan. "Four Teenagers Sentenced in Rape on Probation at Time of Crime, They Get Roughly 30 Years Behind Bars." *Richmond Times Dispatch*, July 20, 2005.

Crowley, Sharon, and Debra Hawhee. *Ancient Rhetorics for Contemporary Students.* 3rd ed. New York: Pearson Longman, 2004.

Cushman, Ellen. "The Rhetorician as an Agent of Social Change." *College Composition and Communication* 47 (1996): 7–28.

Goldblatt, Eli. "Alinksy's Reveille: A Community Organizing Model for Neighborhood-Based Literacy Projects." *College English* 67 (2005): 274–95.

Hart-Davidson, William, James P. Zappen, and S. Michael Halloran. "On the Formation of Democratic Citizens." In *The Viability of the Rhetorical Tradition*, edited by Richard Graff, Arthur E. Walzer, and Janet M. Atwill, 125–40. New York: SUNY Press, 2005.

Jarratt, Susan C. *Rereading the Sophists: Classical Rhetoric Refigured.* Carbondale: Southern Illinois University Press, 1991.

Kastner, Lindsay. "Essay: Where I'm From, Where I'm Going." *Richmond Times Dispatch*, August 12, 2005.

———. "Essayist, 15, Grateful for Encouragement: Her Education Is Getting a Boost; Her Family May Qualify for Habitat." *Richmond Times Dispatch*, August 27, 2005.

———. "Teen Steps Toward Goals: Art Center in Richmond Fosters Student's Love of Dance, Hopes for College." *Richmond Times Dispatch*, January 9, 2006.

———. "Youths' Essays Honored: What Began as a Workshop in Summer Has Led to a Book Showcasing Their Work, Voices." *Richmond Times Dispatch*, October 30, 2005.

Marback, Richard. "Speaking of the City and Literacies of Place Making in Composition Studies." In *City Comp: Identities, Spaces, Practices*, edited by Bruce McComiskey and Cynthia Ryan, 141–55. New York: SUNY Press, 2003.

Mathieu, Paula. *Tactics of Hope: The Public Turn in English Composition.* Portsmouth, N.H.: Boynton/Cook, 2005.

McKerrow, Raymie. "Critical Rhetoric: Theory and Praxis." In *Contemporary Rhetorical Theory: A Reader*, edited by John L. Lucaites, Celeste M. Condit, and Sally Caudill, 441–63. New York: Guilford Press, 1999.

McKnight, John. "Redefining Community." In *Writing and Community Action*, edited by Thomas Deans, 116–22. New York: Longman, 2003.

McQuinn, Delores. "Teen Center Mission." In *East End Teen Center: "Bojangles Block" in Historic Church Hill*. Richmond, Va.: East End Teen Center, 2004.

Nolan, Jim. "After Rape, a Long Healing Process: 4 Teens Will Be Sentenced Tomorrow in an Attack That Shocked the Community." *Richmond Times Dispatch*, July 18, 2005.

———. "Statements Piece Together Rape." *Richmond Times Dispatch*, November 13, 2004.

———. "Teens Charged in Park Attack: News of Arrests Cheers Local Residents Frightened After August Rape and Robbery." *Richmond Times Dispatch*, September 10, 2004.

Sloan, Dena. "'It's a Very Good Thing:' A Richmond Girl's Essay Prompts Church to Fund Her Education." *Richmond Times Dispatch*, August 15, 2005.

"Top 40 Under 40: Rob Rhoden, 36, Lead Pastor, Commonwealth Chapel." *Style Weekly*, September 27, 2006.

Walters, Brandon. "City Plans First Center for Teens." *Style Weekly*, September 3, 2003.

Warner, Michael. *Publics and Counterpublics*. New York: Zone Books, 2002.

Williams, Michael Paul. "'Snitch' Shirts Are a Sad Look." *Richmond Times Dispatch*, September 5, 2005.

Knowledge Work with the Cherokee Nation

The Pedagogy of Engaging Publics in a Praxis of New Media

ELLEN CUSHMAN AND ERIK GREEN

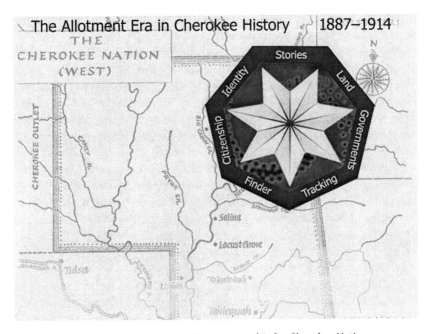

The Allottment Era in Cherokee History. **Opening graphic for Cherokee Nation Web site at http://www.cherokee.org/allotment**

In spring 2005 at Michigan State University (MSU), students enrolled in the Multimedia Writing class, including undergraduate Erik Green, along with instructor Ellen Cushman, produced an educational Web site in conjunction with representatives from the Cherokee Nation (CN): Gloria Sly, the cultural resources director; Richard Allen, the policy analyst for the Cherokee Nation;

and Tonia Williams, the webmaster for the Nation. Our main task was to create a Web site that examined the kinds of rhetorical, literate, and legal struggles experienced by the Cherokees living in Indian Territory during the allotment period (roughly between 1887 and 1914). Gloria, Tonia, and Richard perceived a need for an in-depth and accessible understanding of the period, something that could be disseminated widely and could represent the complexity of competing perspectives at the time. They set this goal for the project in part because Oklahoma was poised to celebrate the anniversary of its statehood and was disseminating histories that de-emphasized the history of Indian Territory. The process of allotment, the individualization and privatization of land among Native peoples who had been removed to Indian Territory, was central to this history of the current state. They also set this goal because they considered the allotment period a time in the Cherokee Nation's history that was equally important to the Trail of Tears, though not often treated in published histories. The Multimedia Writing class I was teaching could produce this history to be distributed as part of the educational resources currently on the Cherokee Nation's site.

And so with their blessings, our class set about reading hundreds of pages of legislation, treaties, Senate reports, pioneer papers, and tribal histories as well as collecting and analyzing drawings, advertisements, documentaries, and photographs. Throughout spring 2005 we met with Tonia and Gloria as well as Ben Philips. Through videoconference and e-mail, we discussed our progress on interface design and content delivery, and secured their continued blessings on this work.

When engaging publics as rhetoricians, these students experienced keen pressure to produce historically accurate, publicly available multimedia educational materials for an audience of Cherokee Nation Web site visitors (some 6,000 hits per day). The screenshot that opens this essay is of the entry portal to the educational resource that we created. The screenshot represents a culmination of learning for students who developed their understandings of authorship, ownership, and representation while working at the intersection of cultural, critical, and digital literacies. In this essay, we situate the story of the Cherokee Nation/MSU Collaborative within a praxis of new media. The kinds of composing students engaged in differed considerably from those they had done throughout their college writing experience, causing dissonance, exacerbation, concern, and ultimately a class meltdown in willingness to continue with the work. Through open discussion, the leadership of three team programmers (Erik was one), and the assurance that this kind of writing product and process is precisely what teams of knowledge workers experience on their job sites, students ultimately completed a project that the Cherokee Nation now hosts at www.cherokee.org/allotment. The entire process was stressful, intense, joyful, challenging, and demanding—everything, we think, learning should be.

While the culmination of learning represented in this screenshot is noteworthy, so, too, were the important lessons we gathered about the differences between authoring and representing a tribe's history and culture from this praxis of new media. Even though we initially strived to produce culturally relevant materials, we found that the Nation bounded the scope of the project as it became clearer to them what information about the tribe they wanted to be publicly available. This boundary between representations of the tribe's history and representations of its culture became apparent to us as we drafted content that was eventually deleted by the Nation's representatives. Ultimately, this screenshot represents one chapter in the Cherokee Nation's history, but it does not represent the tribe's cultural perseverance in the face of allotment. While this partnership and the specific learning outcomes it achieved may be unique and contingent, the intellectual framework that helped structure this learning might well be transportable to other contexts where students do knowledge work as rhetoricians.

THE CHEROKEE NATION/MSU COLLABORATIVE

In collaboration with representatives of the Cherokee Nation in Oklahoma (CN), MSU students enrolled in Multimedia Writing, along with the instructor, developed a Web site and CD titled *The Allotment in Cherokee History 1887–1914*.[1] This collaboration began with a qualitative study of Cherokee language and identity that Ellen continues today. To begin this study, she attended the Cherokee National Holiday in 2004 and learned about the kinds of digital mediations the tribe was undertaking in order to reach its citizens who live away from the tribal cores in Oklahoma and North Carolina where the language is spoken and Cherokee traditions and religion are still practiced. Ellen learned that many people in the Nation were warm and inviting to citizens raised away from Oklahoma, especially since the CN has diverse needs for citizens with skills and education to contribute to the betterment of the tribe.

Fast forward to fall 2004: Ellen enrolled in Cherokee 1 taught by Ed Fields, whom she had also met at the National Holiday. At that time, Sammy Still was the course administrator and long-time insider to both the Eastern Band of the Cherokees and the CN. He and Ellen wrote e-mails often outside of class, exchanging stories and ideas for cultural preservation. Ellen asked if he thought maybe she and her students at MSU could do a multimedia project with and for the Cherokee Nation. He sent her to speak with Tonia Williams and Gloria Sly. To Tonia and Gloria, Ellen described some possible projects, and they saw a place where we could begin.

Together, the three of us agreed that educational materials about the Dawes General Allotment Act of 1887 were needed to show how this federal policy of parceling out Native Americans' commonly held land into individual units of private property has shaped current perspectives on Cherokee citizenship, identity, sovereignty, and the geographic dispersion of the tribe.[2] One of our aims was to recover stories of the allotment process from as many perspectives as possible, to extend the histories that were already told about and from the Nation, and to link these past events to the present. The Nation had three goals for this work:

> satisfy the need for educational materials that present in-depth, accessible understanding of the allotment period in Cherokee history for any learner interested;
>
> distribute widely these digital products to citizens of the tribe, educators, noncitizens of the tribe, and anyone who visits Tahlequah, Oklahoma, during the Cherokee National Holiday; and
>
> relocate the typical histories of Oklahoma from the vantage point of Indian Territory.

The allotment period was a time in the tribe's history that was equally important to the Trail of Tears, though not treated as often in published histories. The allotment era is important because it has shaped the Cherokees' current views on citizenship, identity, sovereignty, and the geographic dispersion of the tribe. As is the case with most federal legislation in relation to Native peoples, this, too, was touted as an effort to "civilize" Native Americans; the Dawes General Allotment Act of 1887 and the Curtis Act of 1898 legislated that all Native American tribes were to split their commonly held land on reservations into individually owned private property. Land that was not allotted was then opened for "settlement." This act was part of the larger story of "the Progressive Era" in U.S. history that included ideologies of manifest destiny, the great westward expansion, and taming the Wild West. U.S. histories of this time are usually told from the urban, eastern-seaboard vantage point—a perspective that looks from the U.S. East Coast outward toward the West, a vantage that sees "wildness," vast stretches of "unused land," and passive, even welcoming, Indians.[3]

Our work for this project tries to re-place the stories of allotment from the vantage of Indian Territory, now Oklahoma, where the Cherokee Nation is based in Tahlequah. This vantage relocates the story of the Progressive Era, showing the detrimental effects of allotment policy for the Cherokees in Indian Territory, who suffered an erosion of sovereignty, land holdings, and economic bases for their tribe, as well as forced assimilation through reeducation and dissolution of their tribal governments. This counternarrative is one that the CN wanted to present to their Web users, teachers, and students as a corrective to the myths of the Progressive Era narrative. We have presented this counternarrative with digital stories, cut-and-paste text, audio recordings, and images, as well as links to primary sources, such as legislation and public documents.

Since this site was launched at the 2005 Cherokee National Holiday, the chief's policy analyst, Richard Allen, joined Gloria, Tonia, and Ellen. The project has grown to include an installment for the Nation's online history that explores the treaties and laws that shaped the tribe from the early 1700s up to the allotment.[4] Together with the MSU Writing in Digital Environments Research Center, this collaborative has exchanged files and collaborated on beta versions of projects through a jointly shared server space that Writing in Digital Environments (WIDE) maintains for our use. Throughout each semester, our collaborative met twice through video conferencing provided by MSU's Writing Center using Avacaster software that the Nation provides to host its language classes. Ellen would then head to Tahlequah over the summer to work through final programming and editing, making necessary revisions to design and content. Though students were not privy to these meetings, their work was impacted by the decisions made at them.

The particular multimedia writing course we describe in this essay is not at all unique in that it has the typical layers of institutional, curricular, and social complexities that have been well documented in research on service learning in rhetoric and composition.[5] In particular, Nora Bacon has focused on the mismatch between the intellectual and rhetorical skills that students bring to class and those required to write in public contexts. She describes how difficult it is for students to learn the genres, content, and styles needed to write well in, for, and with community organizations, let alone being able to understand adequately the context and exigencies within which community organizations do their work. The central problem she identifies has to do with the extent to which students can really become immersed enough in the context of their work to develop a sense of authorship and valid representations. Immersion in the content and context of work should not be mistaken for immersion in a culture.

With Bacon, we have found that students can feel daunted and stressed when trying to meet the authorship, ownership, and representational demands of knowledge work in university and community projects. Their immersion in this particular project involved learning three software packages and file management strategies, in addition to historically appropriate content, styles, and genres needed to produce this educational piece—all this within the infrastructural constraints of this classroom environment. DeVoss, Cushman, and Grabill describe the infrastructure of new media and the ways in which it enables and constrains new media composing. "These often invisible structures make possible and limit, shape and constrain, influence and penetrate all acts of composing new media in writing classes. Though these structural aspects of teaching new media might easily be dismissed as mere inconvenience when they break down or rupture entirely, they are, in fact, deeply imbedded in the acts of digital media composing. [They] argue that infrastructures are absolutely necessary for writing teachers and their students to understand if we hope to enact the possibilities offered by new media composing."[6] In a praxis of new media, students learn the ways in which infrastructures influence their composing. An awareness of infrastructural constraints can be cultivated with students as they press the limits of computing resources in their production processes. A praxis of new media helps students identify the ways in which policies, institutional conventions, and procedures for composing with new media enable and limit their knowledge work.

In a praxis of new media, students also become critically aware of the limits of their immersion in the knowledge bases of the organizations, communities, and tribes with whom they work. In the case of this collaborative, students were able to immerse themselves in the history of the Nation, but were not immersed in the cultural traditions of the tribe. This nuance has everything to do with the ways in which indigenous nations articulate their sovereignty through a political and governmental interface with the wider public and with state and federal governments; behind this interface is cultural tradition that is practiced and maintained at the local level, often protected from outsiders and not often or necessarily mediated (for example, filmed, written about, or photographed).

As one way to understand this difference between Nations and tribes, anthropologist James Clifford, following Stuart Hall, offers the idea that cultural tradition is an articulation. "In articulation theory . . . the process of social and cultural persistence is political all the way back. It is assumed that cultural forms will always be made, unmade, and remade. Communities can and must reconfigure themselves, drawing selectively on remembered pasts. The relevant question is whether, and how, they convince and coerce insiders and outsiders, often in power charged, unequal situations, to accept the autonomy of a 'we.'"[7]

Cultural articulation, then, would be viewed as a place where Native cultures choose which part of their past and current traditions and practices and events to represent in order to enact part of their sovereignty—a process that allows them to name who they are, what makes them autonomous, what practices count, what structures govern, and what technologies allow for adaptation and preservation. Thus Clifford might see the Cherokee Nation's attempts to use the Internet for cultural preservation as the very articulation of reconfiguration; new technologies and popular cultural artifacts, such as the educational piece we developed with the Cherokee Nation, are created in an ongoing process of nation formation; importantly, this formation is distinct from tribal formation or the preservation of tribal practices. The Nation is the political, public face of the sovereign entity, while the tribe is the cultural practices, social networks, and lineal relations that have existed since time immemorial. As a praxis of new media unfolded, it became clear to students that they were immersing themselves in the history of the Cherokee Nation and were not responsible, to their relief and disappointment, for immersing themselves in the culture of the tribe.

As a theoretical framework for public rhetorics, then, a praxis of new media helps to account for the knowledge bases that students will immerse themselves in as they write in university and community partnerships. Working at the intersections of community, critical, and digital literacies in a service-learning / new media course places demands on the intellectual and rhetorical understandings that students bring to writing classes. Because it frames the reflective practices, rhetorical conventions, and infrastructures that enable learning, a praxis of new media offers students a language for understanding their authorship, representations, and ownership. They begin to see praxis as the *phronesis* it is: ethical action that adheres to conventions of behavior that are set forth by stakeholders. These conventions of behavior, in our case, came to light as a boundary limit to our representation of the Cherokee Nation. Said another way, as our collaborators articulated to us the difference between the Cherokee Nation and tribe, we learned the *phronesis*—that is, the ethical action "adhering to certain ideal standards of good (ethical) or effective (political) behavior" necessary to undertake this knowledge work.[8] To illustrate, we offer a brief discussion of what we are calling a praxis of new media as it relates to students' learning in the class.

A PRAXIS OF NEW MEDIA

As a theoretical model for reflective practice, a praxis of new media works at the intersections of critical, community, and digital literacies with the goal of knowledge production. Our notion of praxis has its intellectual roots in Aristotelian rhetoric as *phronesis*, ethical action, and good judgment for the public good, but also in critical pedagogy as it is infused with notions of praxis that is both action and reflection.[9] Stakeholders in this model can include teachers, students, community and workplace members, and scholars. A praxis of new media works from three premises:

all stakeholders have knowledge, critical awareness, and important perspectives on the social problems being addressed;

high-end technologies and multimedia texts need to be interrogated—and produced—with stakeholders; and

a flexibly structured inquiry and problem-solving approach to research and curriculum, one that applies knowledge from various disciplines, can help students address problems that community members have identified.

A praxis of new media can be understood as an expansion of the designs of meaning and kinds of pedagogical practices described in the New London Group's "A Pedagogy of Multiliteracies" and their later book on this topic, *Multiliteracies: Literacy Learning and the Design of Social Futures*.[10] In these works the authors bring together an interdisciplinary understanding of language and literacy to describe what they call designs, or those flexibly structured social organizations, knowledge bases, and cultural practices that influence daily meaning-making practices and life chances.

In "A Pedagogy of Multiliteracies," the authors describe the pedagogies related to multiliteracies.

Situated Practice Immersion in experience and the utilization of available discourses and simulations of the relationships to be found in workplaces and public spaces.

Overt Instruction Systematic, analytic, and conscious understanding. . . . This requires the introduction of explicit metalanguages. . . .

Critical Framing Interpreting the social and cultural context of particular designs of meaning. This involves students standing back from what they are studying and viewing it critically in relation to its context.

Transformed Practice Transfer in meaning making practice, which puts the transformed meaning to work in other contexts or cultural sites.11

A praxis of new media is a theoretical and pedagogical framing of the ways in which community, critical, and digital literacies are combined in community literacy initiatives. It expands upon the practices listed above by including both a notion of audience and infrastructure, as these rhetorical and material conditions are absent from a theory of multiliteracies.

Though the space of possibility that a praxis of new media occupies is difficult to obtain and sustain, it can result in engaging public rhetorics on many levels and is therefore worthy of our attention.

PEDAGOGIES RELATED TO A PRAXIS OF NEW MEDIA

Situated practice Immersion in experience and the utilization of available discourses and technologies for meaning making; purposes, audiences, collaborations are real time, not simulated.

Overt Instruction Systematic, analytic, and conscious understanding. . . . This requires the introduction of explicit metalanguages . . . It also requires introduction and ample opportunity for authentic multimedia and computer tool use.

Critical Framing Interpreting the social and cultural context of particular designs of meaning. This involves students becoming deeply, ethically, involved in what they are studying, having a stake in making new knowledge, and viewing it critical in relation to its context.

| Transformed Practice | Transfer in meaning-making practice based on the real needs and purposes of communities, which puts the transformed meaning to work for real audiences in other contexts or cultural sites. |
| Ethical Practice | Praxis of new media and digital technology is learned as it is used in critical interpretation and production activities that increase students' civic participation and academic preparedness; and teaching and research are conducted with community members and students in collaborative inquiry for problem solving. Respecting boundaries set by stakeholders and adjusting work to suit the limits of representation they set are key. |

A pedagogy of multiliteracies issues a call for transformative practice that scholars around the country are beginning to realize in their curricula. That is, the call for a pedagogy of multiliteracies needs to model ways in which it can be enacted both inside and outside the classroom. How might this model be adopted in and adapted to local purposes, knowledge, and activities? In what ways might rhetoricians and writing teachers and students work at the intersection of digital, critical, and community literacies to develop civically responsible research? We explore these questions below by revising the pedagogies of multiliteracies in light of digital composing for public audiences and their rhetorical exigencies. In the remainder of this essay, we describe this framework, then apply it to the teaching, research, and service related to the Multimedia Writing class in order to demonstrate how a praxis of new media unfolds in the learning practices of students. We find that the learning practices that take place in this particular partnership may well be unique to this project; however, the intellectual framework that guides the critical reflection on learning might well illuminate the work unfolding in other work in public rhetorics.

SITUATED PRACTICE IN A PRAXIS OF NEW MEDIA

Rather than simulating the relationships to be found in the workplace and the experiences of using available discourses as a pedagogy of multiliteracies might, the Multimedia Writing class actually immersed students in a process and knowledge base that created a workplace using an entirely new form of discourse related to Cherokee history. Students initially read, wrote reflections, and discussed hundreds of pages of primary and secondary readings about the allotment period in order to reach their first milestone: a compilation of "research papers" that were to become the content of the online materials.

At the start of the class, the members on this group project had very little knowledge about the allotment period or the Cherokee Nation, and so it was necessary for us to engage in what was described as an immersion process.

Using as many primary documents as possible, we spent the first few weeks of the semester in an intensive reading process where we tried to familiarize ourselves as completely yet efficiently as possible with the history, treaties, reactions, reasoning, and effects of the allotment period.

For Erik, although he had a vague knowledge of historical events like the Trail of Tears or of Native customs regarding land, he had no idea about all the intricacies and nuances of the time period or of the Cherokee way of life. However, he was able to quickly learn and absorb a lot of different ideas in those first few weeks—from understanding the ideas of communal land ownership, to exploring how advanced the cultures of the Five Civilized Tribes really were (in direct contrast to how they were characterized by white settlers), to seeing how important laws and treaties were in the allotment process (such as the infamous Dawes Act), to reading direct stories of people living in Indian Territory.

This immersion was a necessary step before we even began contemplating our project, since so many parts of it—not just the content, but also the design and the way we framed the issue—were dependant on our understanding of the time period and the culture. It also set up a specific pedagogical move of giving our class—a group of white, privileged students with no experience working with the Cherokee Nation—a chance to move from being interested but uninformed students to being content managers who were experts in this historical period (relatively speaking). Aside from building our knowledge, this immersion process also built our confidence.

One of the difficulties with this immersion process, however, was that although we were situating ourselves directly in the written discourses of the time period, there was still the tendency for it to feel disconnected or unauthentic. At this point in the course, our immediate goal was still an academic essay—something that, although required for the institution and useful for our work as university students, was hard to conceptualize as part of our final product. By attempting to break down the readings and responding with a very specific focus, we were able to successfully create a simulated situated practice—especially with the large number of primary documents—which helped to place us within the context of the allotment period. However, the authenticity of the work would not be apparent until later in the course, when we discovered that we could practically cut the content from one genre—our academic papers—and paste it into another—our Web site/CD-Rom, something that felt much more authentic in its creation.

In this situated practice, then, the genre of academic research paper, at first, seemed extraneous, perhaps even arbitrary to students. Their sense of authorship had not yet fully developed because it seemed to them that this paper was merely an exercise meant to prove to the professor they had done their readings or had explored something of interest to them, as is the case with many of the research papers. The practice of immersing in the historical knowledge base still seemed simulated, a simulation that felt disconnected to the final project and the people it was meant to represent. This immersion also seemed to give some students the impression that they were learning about the culture of the tribe as opposed to the history of the Nation. Certainly our readings covered ways in which Cherokee culture changed as a result of allotment, but reading a text about the history of a culture does not translate into a license to represent cultural knowledge. This key difference in representational authority would become more apparent to us as the semester progressed.

OVERT INSTRUCTION IN A PRAXIS OF NEW MEDIA

In a praxis of new media overt instruction includes a systematic, analytic, and conscious understanding and introduction of metalanguages related to software and means of production. It also requires introduction and ample opportunity for authentic multimedia and computer tool use and is in line with an infrastructural approach to composing in new media. In community and institutional settings that rely on new media, infrastructural constraints both enable and limit the knowledge work possible. Unfortunately, these infrastructures remain largely invisible until they break or their limits have been reached. The when of new media composing came to the foreground as issues with accessibility and transportability of our work emerged. Here the immersion in the infrastructural limits and knowledge needed to circumvent these moved from being simulated to an actual exigency—our collaborators' needs became apparent at the receiving end. At the same time as we were determining the naming conventions and boundaries of our file production, we were also determining the boundaries of our representational authority. While file-naming conventions might feel simply technical in nature, they were rhetorical and had everything to do with our audience's goals for content and establishing the nature of our authoritative and representational limits.

Overt instruction in how to manage projects moved to the foreground as students began to see that they did not own this work, but were producing pages that would eventually be uploaded, changed, and resaved at the CN. File management lessons were crucial to this process as teams took these lessons and developed naming protocols for the site's architecture. Their naming protocols made explicit the ways that knowledge work must be handled within class and were created with an upstream audience in mind—the webmaster and her team at the Cherokee Nation had to be able to make sense of the file structure and naming conventions. While instruction in file management came at the beginning of the semester, it was encountering infrastructural constraints of having to transfer and reclaim so many files that made this a practice that took into consideration the transportability and life of the files outside of class.

File management is rhetorical at another level: we were developing and naming content areas, tracing out for our collaborators the scope and nature of what we were to represent. Some students became uncomfortable with their lack of tribal knowledge as they were bringing together the content of the papers into what would become the files developed for content nodes. They were concerned that, as outsiders, they were not getting it right and worse that they had no right to be talking about how family structures changed, for instance, because they did not know what family structures were like before allotment and now.

By happy coincidence, we had a visit by Craig Howe, a speaker brought to campus and a new media developer who worked with the Lakota to create multimedia educational resources about their winter counts. When some students voiced their concerns about the limits of their knowledge of the tribe, he assured us all that we were representing the history of the Nation and not the tribe. He explained that he was not allowed to show many of his multimedia works outside of the Lakota tribe because they represented tribal knowledge. However, when a nation commissions a work, and much of that work is drawn from historical documents, it is not likely to be representing tribal knowledge so much as a nation's history. While Ellen had assumed students would inductively understand this distinction from the nature of the historical documents we were using, Craig's explicit instruction put to rest students' initial concerns by pointing to the ways that indigenous peoples articulate a difference between nations and tribes.

In both their authoring of the content and saving it under conventionalized file structures, students were developing their sense of authoring and ownership to include audiences and exigencies beyond this class. Importantly, this critical reflection would not have been prompted had the infrastructural constraints presented themselves and the rhetorical boundaries of their work became evident to them. In a praxis of new media, then, the technical is often rhetorical and the instrumental subject to exigencies of audiences.

CRITICAL FRAMING IN A PRAXIS OF NEW MEDIA

In a pedagogy of multiliteracies, critical framing results from interpreting the social and cultural context of particular designs of meaning. This interpretation and critique means applying a critical theory to whatever problem, issue, or object is under study. Rather than asking students to enact disinterested critique of the content they were developing, as a pedagogy of multiliteracies might ask, a praxis of new media demands that students have deep immersion in and commitment to the products they are producing. Their analysis is done from the perspective of becoming ethically involved in what they are studying, having a stake in making new knowledge, and viewing it critically in relation to its context. For students, their positions as stakeholders in the project emerged in various instances of strong responses that they had when they increasingly took hold of the authoring responsibility, ownership of the structure of their learning, and initial representations of this learning.

One of the unexpected results of our work was the very emotional response that we had with the material. We remember one student in particular who broke into tears when we were sharing our research papers with each other. For the most part, no one in the class had any extensive background in Cherokee history, but through our immersion process at the beginning of the class we were all situated as "experts" by the time our research papers were finished and we were preparing to create our multimedia project. Although no one in the class, outside of the instructor, was Cherokee, as a result of our immersion in the history, and as we prepared to try to tell that story through our project for others, there was a distinct emotional connection that was made—one that rarely happens with other traditional research assignments. This emotional connection to the work increased the sense of authorship we had as we moved from knowing little to being immersed in the topic enough to see ourselves as novice-experts.

Finally, after immersing ourselves in two very different discourses of learning content, then the software to present this content, and becoming proficient in them (although it was to varying degrees how much the students personally felt like they had become "experts"), we were able to tackle the actual issue of creating our project. At first we had to consider the overall representation of the materials we thought would work best for the Nation and users who came to the site. We visually arranged the topics of our papers using Post-it notes on a whiteboard and as a class discussed the generalized topics and overarching areas we envisioned for the major categories of our project— what we dubbed "nodes," which eventually became the hotlinks around the septagon as seen in the image that opens this essay. We presented a wire frame of the interface to the Cherokee Nation that included a node for religious practices, among others, and they agreed that the design, potential content, and navigational structure of the wire frame was strong.

We were simultaneously balancing ideas of organization, rhetoric, and design as we considered the ways that our categories could successfully cover all the topics we wanted to talk about, the ways that our written research papers could be the starting point for each of those topics, and the ways that our design would fit the rhetoric we designed for the project as a whole. As all of the pieces of the class came together then, the sense of being a stakeholder in the project emerged from immersion that went beyond disinterested critique to a commitment to the purpose, content, and scope of the knowledge work. This critical framing of course included interpretation and analysis in the content of our papers, especially as we each tackled one aspect of Cherokee history and culture and tried to reveal how the allotment process changed it, but it also included an ethical commitment to the ownership and authorship of the work. One student in particular became deeply interested in the Cherokee stomp dance as a tradition that has been maintained despite allotment and the increased importance of the Cherokee Baptist church to the tribe. He created a digital video describing the stomp dance, piecing together additional research on the Internet and books to describe the dance. Because the CN representatives had already endorsed the inclusion of religious practices and the placeholder content that indicated we were going to talk about Cherokee Baptists as well as stomp dance, we thought it would be strong content to add. However, as the next section shows, the critical framing and immersion in the project brought about thornier issues in representation.

TRANSFORMED AND ETHICAL PRAXIS OF NEW MEDIA

Transfer in meaning-making practice is based on the experienced needs and purposes of communities. To this, a praxis of new media adds the component of public writing for purposes and within exigencies designated by stakeholders. New media and digital technology are learned as they are used in critical interpretation and production activities that increase students' civic participation; and teaching and research are conducted with community members and students in collaborative inquiry for problem solving. The praxis of new media hit home for students how their authorship, ownership, and representational practices were being changed as they engaged in this knowledge work.

The final challenge to our understandings of representation could not be foreseen in the content we developed. One of the surprising results of working with a partner outside of our group and gifting them with a rhetorical creation was some of the final content management that the Cherokee Nation did. In particular, we had a section outlining some of the religious practices of the Cherokees, especially in regards to the way these were used as a form of resistance. However, the Cherokee Nation decided that they did not want this sort of information published since it dealt a little too closely with practices that they considered sacred and private, so whole pages of that subnode were removed—including the video file describing the stomp dance that one student had spent weeks developing. It was his main contribution to the entire node. Especially given the time and effort that the individual who created that subnode and video spent in making his section, it was tough to imagine having parts of it removed, but we realized that it was necessary to understand and respect the reasons for doing so.

In this way, even though we had taken pride in the work and our authoring of the best site possible, we understood that our representations may not be as culturally relevant as they should have been, or in this case, that they were too culturally relevant and the CN did not want this tribal knowledge to be widely disseminated.[12] This became evident to Ellen as she worked with the CN collaborators in Tahlequah. They debated for some time the possible inclusion of this stomp dance video and the text surrounding it in this node. Recognizing the hard work the student had done, they still were not comfortable with the level of nuance in the video—stomp dance differs from ground to ground, and it seemed that this representation was both revealing too much and not enough. In the end, when the project was handed over to the Nation, our ownership of it ended though our responsibilities for representing their history did not. The historical representations were strong and accurately reflected the immersion that students had in the history of the Nation, but the ways that the Nation articulated itself to us as a public face for the tribe had to be learned the hard way—by developing content that ultimately could not be included despite initial green lights for inclusion.

We learned firsthand and the hard way the difference that Howe explained: we were immersed in and representing the history of the Nation and the history that the Nation wanted us to represent; we were not immersed in or representing the culture or the tribe's cultural practices. This rhetorical and ethical boundary emerged as the work progressed and the Cherokee Nation's representatives articulated the difference between the Nation's history and the tribe's cultural practices, a difference we were ethically bound to respect. While we had immersed ourselves in the historical representations of the Nation, we mistook this immersion as knowledge of cultural practices.

IMPLICATIONS

As these examples illustrate, students' previously held notions of authorship, ownership, and representation shifted as this course progressed and even after the final project had been delivered. All of these aspects of learning in a praxis of new media reveal the ways in which it is important to press boundaries of conventional writing classroom practice, but also point to the limits of knowledge work with community partners.

With so many shifts in learning contexts—from the content of the course, to the tools used to represent it, to the exigencies and purposes for learning, to the audiences who read this writing—the effect can cause strong emotional response and dissonance. If students and professors understand the ways in which a praxis of new media revises knowledge work, then perhaps some of the dissonance might be mitigated. In subsequent iterations of this course, the ways in which the work would unfold were expressed upfront, placed into the syllabus for the course, and repeated frequently so that students could at least anticipate the challenges this class content and tools present to their previous forms of learning, writing, and reading. Ellen has been especially careful to make explicit for students how they will be immersing themselves in the history of the CN that is for the most part publicly available, as opposed to immersing themselves in the culture of the Cherokee tribe.

The lessons we learned are important for work that engages students in participating in public rhetorics. First, the technical is often rhetorical. Knowing infrastructural limits and working within and against these is a rhetorical process that must take into account the needs, purposes, capacities, exigencies, and work activities of audiences beyond our classrooms.[13] Second, stakeholders in public writing collaborations set the representational boundaries that often articulate the autonomy of themselves as a "we" that protects cultural knowledge while producing historically accurate materials. Students learn to compose the public face of an organization or tribe from historical texts and/or highly selected texts that the stakeholders want to be used. Their immersion in and with texts does not equate to immersion with a culture; writing a valid history is powerful work that is quite different from writing a valid ethnographic representation.

The knowledge work taking place at the intersection of critical, digital, and community literacies is certainly complex and complicated, at times dauntingly so. A praxis of new media is an intellectual framework for scaffolding active work; rather than disappearing into the work once a project begins, the framework always allows one to see, critique, and adjust practice throughout the development and iterations of that work. This framework provides a metalanguage for learning how to learn, and may offer a buoy to help professors and students understand the changing nature of the learning unfolding in the class. The intellectual framework of a praxis of new media will be useful to describe the knowledge work unfolding in public rhetorics.

NOTES

1. Cherokee Nation, *Allotment.*

2. Ellen's family went through this process of allotment and enrolled on the Dawes roll, a kind of census for the Cherokee Nation and other tribes. Because they went through that seven-year-long process, today's generations of Drews (my Cherokee family's name) are able to maintain our citizenship with the tribe.

3. While helping the Cherokee Nation produce a counternarrative is an important topic that Ellen has explored elsewhere, this essay focuses more on the transformative learning for students understood within a praxis of new media. Cushman and Ghosh, "Mediation."

4. To view the second installment, visit http://www.cherokee.org/cultures/treaties/toc.htm.

5. See Deans, *Writing Partnerships;* Crooks and Watters, Writing in the Community; Flower, Long, and Higgins, *Learning to Rival;* Herzberg, "Community Service"; Flower "Partners in Inquiry"; Flower, *Problem Solving;* Peck, Flower, and Higgins, "Community Literacy"; Bacon, "Building a Swan's Nest"; Grabill, *Community Literacy;* Coogan, "Counterpublics"; Cushman, "Public Intellectual"; Cushman, Special Issue; Cushman, "Sustainable Service"; Cushman and Emmons, "Contact Zones"; Schutz and Gere, "Service Learning"; Carrick, Himley, and Jacobi, "Ruptura."

6. Devoss, Cushman, and Grabill, "Infrastructure," 16.

7. Clifford, "Indigenous Articulations," 479.

8. Warry, quoted in Cushman, *Struggle,* 28.

9. Freire, *Pedagogy.*

10. Cushman, "Toward a Praxis"; Cazden et al., "Pedagogy of Multiliteracies"; Cope and Kalantzis, *Multiliteracies.*

11. Cazden et al., "Pedagogy of Multiliteracies," 88.

12. Cushman and Ghosh, "Mediation."

13. See Grabill, *Writing Community Change;* Simmons and Grabill, "Toward a Civic Rhetoric."

WORKS CITED

Bacon, Nora. "Building a Swan's Nest for Instruction in Rhetoric." *College Composition and Communication* 51 (2000): 589–609.

Carrick, Tracy, Margaret Himley, and Tobi Jacobi. "Ruptura: Acknowledging the Lost Subjects of the Service Learning Story." *Language and Learning across the Disciplines* 14, no. 1 (2000): 56–75.

Cazden, Courtney, Bill Cope, Norman Fairclough, James Gee, Mary Kalantzis, Gunther Kress, Allan Luke, Carmen Luke, Sarah Michaels, and Martin Nakata (The New London Group). "A Pedagogy of Multiliteracies: Designing Social Futures." *Harvard Educational Review* 66 (1996): 60–93.

Cherokee Nation. *Allotment in Cherokee History 1887–1914.* www.cherokee.org/allotment.

Clifford, James. "Indigenous Articulations." *Contemporary Pacific* 13 (2001): 468–90.

Coogan, David. "Counterpublics in Public Housing: Reframing the Politics of Service Learning." *College English* 67 (2005): 461–82.

Cope, William, and Mary Kalantzis. *Multiliteracies: Literacy Learning and the Design of Social Futures.* London: Routledge, 2000.

Crooks, Robert, and Ann Waters, eds. *Writing the Community: Concepts and Models for Service Learning in Composition.* Washington, D.C.: American Association for Higher Education, 1997.

Cushman, Ellen. "The Public Intellectual, Activist Research, and Service-Learning." *College English* 61 (1999): 68–76.

———. "Service Learning as the New English Studies." In *Beyond English Inc.*, edited by D. Downing, M. Hurlbert, and P. Mathieu, 204–18. Portsmouth, N.H.: Heinemann, 2002.

———, guest ed. Special Issue on Service Learning. *Language and Learning Across the Disciplines* 14 (2000).

———. *The Struggle and the Tools.* Albany: SUNY Press, 1998.

———. "Sustainable Service Learning Programs." *College Composition and Communication* 64 (2002): 40–65.

———. "Toward a Praxis of New Media: The Allotment Period in Cherokee History." *Reflections on Community-Based Writing Instruction* 4, no. 3 (2006): 124–43.

Cushman, Ellen, and Chalon Emmons. "Contact Zones Made Real." In *School's Out*, edited by Glynda Hull and Katherine Shultz, 203–31. New York: Teachers College Press, 2002.

Cushman, Ellen, and Shreelina Ghosh. "The Mediation of Cultural Memory: Digital Preservation in the Cases of Classical Indian Dance and the Cherokee Stomp Dance." *Journal of Popular Culture.* Forthcoming Spring 2010.

Deans, Tom. *Writing Partnerships: Service Learning in Composition.* Urbana, Ill.: National Council of Teachers of English, 2000.

DeVoss, Danielle Nicole, Ellen Cushman, and Jeffrey T. Grabill. "Infrastructure and Composing: The *When of New Media Writing*." *College Composition and Communication* 57 (2005): 14–31.

Flower, Linda. "Partners in Inquiry: A Logic for Community Outreach." In *Writing the Community: Concepts and Models for Service-Learning in Composition,* edited by Linda Adler-Kassner, Robert Crooks, and Ann Watters, 95–118. Urbana, Ill.: National Council of Teachers of English, 1997.

———. *Problem Solving Strategies for Writing in College and Community.* Fort Worth, Tex.: Harcourt Brace College Publishers, 1998.

Flower, Linda, Elenore Long, and Lorraine Higgins. *Learning to Rival: A Literate Practice for Intercultural Inquiry.* Mahwah, N.J.: LEA, 2000.

Freire, Paolo. *Pedagogy of the Oppressed.* New York: Continuum, 1972.

Grabill, Jeffrey T. *Community Literacy Programs and the Politics of Change.* Albany: SUNY Press, 2001.

————. *Writing Community Change.* Creskill, N.J.: Hamptom, 2007.

Herzberg, Bruce. "Community Service and Critical Teaching." *College Composition and Communication* 45 (1994): 307–19.

Kassner, Linda Adler, Robert Crooks, and Ann Watters, eds. *Writing the Community.* Urbana, Ill.: National Council of Teachers of English, 1997.

Peck, Wayne, Linda Flower, and Lorraine Higgins. "Community Literacy." *College Composition and Communication* 46 (1995): 199–222.

Schutz, Aaron, and Anne Gere. "Service Learning and English Studies: Rethinking Public Service." *College English* 60 (1998): 129–49.

Simmons, Michele, and Jeffrey T. Grabill. "Toward a Civic Rhetoric for Technologically and Scientifically Complex Places: Invention, Performance, and Participation." *College Composition and Communication* 58 (2007): 486–99.

Wide Research Center Collective. "Why Teach Digital Writing." *Kairos* 10 (2005), http://English.ttu.edu/Kairos/10.1/binder2.html?coverweb/wide/index.html (accessed March 26, 2009).

On Being Useful

Rhetoric and the
Work of Engagement

JEFFREY T. GRABILL

It is commonplace to think that when we are doing the work of rhetoric, we are speaking or writing. Certainly when we teach students to be rhetors, we are teaching *them* to speak or write purposefully. The speaker, writer, composer, performer is the center of our attention. In similar fashion, it is common to think about community engagement in terms of ourselves—the work that we are doing, the impact that we hope to have, and the way that our presence changes a community. As rhetors we speak; as engaged scholars we act. I begin this way to highlight the fact that the agencies with which we most concern ourselves are the agencies of writers, researchers, and activists, and that when we consider these agencies, we focus mostly on ourselves or those we train to be like us. In this essay, I want to take us in a somewhat different direction. I want to explore the notion that the public work of rhetoric might be to support the work of others—to help other people write, speak, and make new media and other material objects effectively.[1]

To be able to support the work of others requires ways of researching, acting, and otherwise performing in communities that are carefully considered. My procedure in this essay, therefore, will be to outline elements of what I think of as a methodology of engagement, or elements of a theory of how to act that stands a good chance of being useful to others engaged in the "knowledge work of everyday life," a concept I develop in *Writing Community Change*.[2] I discuss two methods that are fundamental to rhetorical engagement. These are methods that are well known under a number of names, but they lack, in my view, the attention and visibility they deserve. These two methods—assembling a public and supporting performances—are essential to effective public rhetoric and fundamental to the notion that rhetoric might more usefully be understood as enabling the work of others.

Assembling a Public, Community, Group, or Other Aggregate

I do not mean the title to this section to sound flippant. Scholars and activists argue passionately about the differences between these terms and their meaning for their work. And they should. Nor do I think that these terms are substitutable. Rather, because I am trying to work at the level of methodology, I highlight the theoretical problem of assembly, a problem that is shared by those working with various forms of "groupness."

The difficulty of understanding the public (or various publics) and locating it with precision and usefulness is a common and recent concern. Even if we attempt to locate a rhetorical public instead of defining it, we are still left with multiple places and terms in the literature: public space, public sphere, civic/civil society (and space), and civic culture.[3] Each of these terms means something quite different, both in terms of what a rhetorical situation looks like and in terms of what a particular rhetoric looks like. While it is true that recent work in rhetoric theory on the problem of the public is full of possibility, it does not typically concern itself with what I understand to be empirical questions of how people create public spaces, forums, or what I will soon call "things."[4] My purpose here is to focus on the activity of making a public, of understanding who we are together when we are doing rhetoric, because this type of activity is required for public engagement.

In his recent essay in *Critical Inquiry*, Bruno Latour argues for a new kind of criticism, one that is both closer to facts and positive—by which he means a criticism concerned with making. Latour wants criticism to be a "multifarious inquiry launched with the tools of anthropology, philosophy, metaphysics, history, sociology to detect how many participants are gathered in a *thing* to make it exist and to maintain its existence."[5] What Latour understands as a "thing" is what I would like to understand first as both a group (including, conceivably, "a public") and the ideas and activity that give a group a reason to exist. Latour's project has a descriptive component to it ("to detect") but also a strategic component. The critic—the rhetor—offers participants places to gather and cares for gatherings. This essay by Latour provides something conceptually powerful given my experience helping to make things in communities: a purpose for contemporary public rhetorical work—to gather and care for things.

Based on my own experience as a community-based researcher, I have never found it useful, either empirically or conceptually, to understand the collectives with which I was working as fixed or in some cases preexisting entities. The implications of this sentence are significant, not obvious, and at the very heart of my argument. Latour is useful in helping to visualize these implications. In *Reassembling the Social*, Latour's most recent and explicit treatment of what is commonly known as actor-network theory, his target for criticism is social theory and the social sciences.[6] He writes that with normative social science, the concept of "the social" is a domain asserted to exist and given, depending on the sociology, certain defining characteristics. Sociologists of the social are therefore able to use "the social" to explain other activity. The basic question for Latour is this: does the social exist or is it something that we create? Latour writes, "Whereas sociologists (or socio-economists, socio-linguists, social psychologists, etc.) take social aggregates as the given that could shed some light on residual aspects of economics, linguistics, psychology, management, and so on, these other scholars [like Latour], on the contrary, consider social aggregates as what should be explained by the specific associations provided by economics, linguistics, psychology, law, management, etc."[7] Latour's point is that social aggregates must be explained and also that the social is "a type of connection between things that are not themselves social."[8] The social, then, is not a domain or realm but a "very peculiar movement of re-association and reassembling."[9]

As a matter of methodology, Latour's assertion that the social is best understood as a type of connection that is visible because of movement (activity) is true as well for what we call "community" or "public," an argument that I have made in more detail elsewhere.[10] Each must be assembled and continuously reassembled. But Latour's claim is true for that which we call "the rhetorical" as well. The study of the rhetorical, therefore, is the study of particular kinds of associations that are actively created and re-created. The rhetorical is and creates particular kinds of connections. Furthermore, to be useful as a public rhetorician or engaged researcher is to become one who understands associations and, in understanding them, becomes a creator of associations. To associate, therefore, becomes a method and strategy for a methodology of engagement. It is true that the sociologist and the rhetorical scholar study different kinds of associations—or just as often make visible similar associations but understand them differently. But associations of what? If the work of the rhetor is to help gather and care for these gatherings, then what, exactly, is to be gathered and cared for—and in what ways?

To illustrate this methodological argument, let me turn to two examples from recent work that I have been a part of. The first example comes from a project Stuart Blythe and I worked on in a community we call "Harbor."[11] Stuart and I were part of a Technical Outreach Services for Communities (TOSC) team, funded by an Environmental Protection Agency (EPA) grant, to complete independent technical reviews of science and engineering and to conduct community education workshops around those technical reviews. Our presence in Harbor was a function of a proposed U.S. Army Corps of Engineers plan to dredge a canal linking an industrial area with a large lake. The canal at Harbor is one of the oldest industrial corridors in the country. The canal was designed to service the petroleum-based and steel industries in the region. The canal must be dredged in order to enable heavier barge traffic to reach the industry along the canal. The Corps plans to scoop out millions

of cubic yards of sediment and deposit them in what is called a confined dis-
posal facility (CDF), or a raised landfill, which is located near two schools and
residential areas in this densely populated area.

This is a situation in which there is significant community concern. The
industrial uses of the harbor and canal have left the waters heavily polluted.
Some of the toxins found in the sediment include arsenic, cadmium, chro-
mium, dioxin, toluene, lead, mercury, oil, polychlorinated biphenyls (PCBs),
and polyaromatic hydrocarbons (PAHs)—all bad stuff for plants, animals, and
humans. Some stretches of the canal are so toxic that they cannot sustain
life. Therefore, this navigational dredge is also necessarily an environmental
cleanup project, but it is an environmental cleanup project that results in the
deposit of toxic sediments in a landfill located in an urban area. Cleaning the
canal therefore creates new risks as it mitigates existing risks. Some in Harbor
are quite concerned about the dredging project; others are strongly opposed
to it. Citizens have raised two concerns about the Corps' plans: whether the
dredge will be characterized as an environmental or navigational project, a
distinction governed by differing regulations and which type of dredge technology will be used. The distinction between the two dredging characteriza-
tions is meaningful. To call the dredge "environmental" means the ability to
tap into new sources of revenue to fund the project and being governed by
regulations that some in the community thought more stringent. Naming the
project "environmental" carries significant symbolic value as well as certain
material changes in the project.

Stuart and I focused on trying to understand how people in Harbor conducted their own science (their inventional activities) and communicated
those understandings to others. Our goals were to use these understandings
to help TOSC with its work, and, if possible, enhance the capacities of the
community to do its work. To this point I have left a number of loaded terms
scattered throughout my description, and it is precisely the danger of these
loaded terms that occupied much of our work in Harbor. If we were to be of
use to "the community"—indeed, if we were to conduct "community-based"
research—what, exactly, does this mean, and who, precisely, constitutes "the
community" with which we were engaged? Figure 1 is a figure from our field
notes of April 2004, and in reproducing this figure here, I mean to signify a
number of things: it is one of many such maps that we created (though a relatively stable one); it is an artifact of our research and not "true" in any other
sense; and in publishing this map (now twice), we have given the public space
of Harbor a type of rhetorical stability *with respect to our work there* that is both
useful and also only one type of connection possible in that same geographical, cultural, political, and social space at that time—or at any given time.

The community map of Harbor, then, is an answer to the question "who/
what is the community" in Harbor. In terms of the functional details, there are
two significant issues represented by this map. The first is that the community

is a collection of organizations, institutions, and individuals. Some of these organizations are large and highly structured, like a government agency, while others are more loosely structured, such as a neighborhood association. The second issue is the connection between groups. Some groups have more formal associations by way of funding or people who are members of multiple organizations. Some groups are networked by their communication practices. If we return to Latour and to my methodological argument that to engage is to assemble, then the activity of assembling this map is a key engagement activity opening up a range of agencies. We were able to assemble this map by paying attention to activity; that is, the connections between organizations and the relative positioning of organizations are a function of those organizations doing things: meeting, writing, collaborating, coordinating, and so on. Of course, the activity that enables this map is the activity generated by the dredging project itself, so if we were following different work, then we would see different activity, alternative connections, and therefore new groupings at this same time and in this same space. In other words, a different map, a different community.

A map like this yields patterns that are actionable. The community organization with which we worked most closely is labeled "CEC" on this map. It was not the first organization that TOSC worked with, nor was it the only organization with which TOSC sought to work. But it emerged as the most important organization because it was often at the very center of citizen-driven activity in Harbor. For our work in Harbor to have an impact, therefore, it was clear that we needed to learn from CEC and support its work as best we could. While the organization is small and relatively unstructured, its members are highly effective communicators: they write frequently and with impact; they have multiple, effective communication channels; and they use these to share what they learn and to hear from others what they are learning. In methodological terms, to be useful in Harbor as an engaged partner, we had to assemble—from the first to the last moment of our time there—a "public," which in this case we understood as a "community." There is no question that there was a spatial and political entity known as Harbor before we arrived on the scene. The organizations existed. The people were there. The ideas and issues, for the most part, were surely in evidence. But in arriving on the scene, we changed things, and so there existed in that time and space a new community dynamic, which we systematically tried to account for from our point of view. We assembled the community of Harbor with respect to this project as a way to account for possible agencies. For us, this work was called "research," but it is no different as an issue of methodology if the work is called "community organizing" and the agents called "activists" or "rhetoricians." In identifying CEC as important, therefore, we were also locating finer-grained patterns of activity that we thought mattered, and so we sought to support that activity (more on this in the next section). The map, then, is simply a research artifact, but it represents the more complex work of assembling and caring for that assembly.

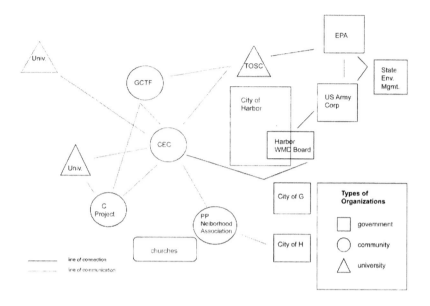

A community map of "Harbor"

Example two comes from work I have been doing to help build a community media center in Lansing, Michigan. The original story for me goes back to the Capital Area Community Information research project, an action research project funded by Michigan State University's University Outreach and Engagement.[12] This three-year effort focused on understanding how people used information technologies to do the work of community organizations, and on the Capital Area Community Voices Web site as a key resource for this knowledge work. One outcome of this project is a newly redesigned Capital Area Community Voices Web site. As a part of that project, we began to think about the larger community infrastructure supporting community computing, and through this conversation I ended up as part of a small, ad hoc group of people who have now incorporated and are making progress in terms of building this media center. Nearly three years ago, while sitting in an early meeting of this group, one of our graduate students turned to me and said that we really needed to read *Aramis* because she thought that we were engaged in making a sociotechnical system.[13] She was correct, and as I have always understood making a media center as a project of assembly, let me unpack the example of the media center in these terms. Let me pull two threads to follow: the making of the media center as the making of a thing; and the (re)making of a research center (WIDE) into a community media center (or: when activity is what is required to be real, how to act like a media center).

The first of these threads is more abstract. There is no reason why Lansing must have a community media center. The Lansing area functions today without one, and most people in the Lansing area, it is fair to say, have no idea what a media center is and what it affords to those who may use it. To make a media center, therefore, requires argument, the establishment of an exigency in "the community." In other words, while folks get along just fine now, current work could be facilitated by a media center, new work could be imagined, and that which is impossible now might be possible with a media center (and so: perhaps we are not getting along very well at all).[14] The most persistent activity that we have engaged in as part of making a media center is rhetorical. It is also mundane: community groups, neighborhood organizations, issue groups, and others must always and persistently make arguments through activities like writing letters, holding meetings, and proposing ideas, and in making these arguments, gather participants in what Latour would call a "thing."

Like many who work with "thing theory," Latour works through Heidegger to derive basic concepts of a thing.[15] A "Thing," in this view, is a certain type of assembly and could refer to a meeting as much as to an object. As an assembly, one of Latour's references is the old Icelandic assembly called a "Ding" (thing).[16] In Latour's resurrected Ding, people assemble not because they are like each other or agree but because they share matters of concern about which they do not agree. A "Thing" is the issue—the matter of concern— that brings people together and also the assembly itself. In many ways, this notion of assembly alludes to traditional and stable ideas of public space, namely the forum, the legislature, the visible and well-bounded public. This trajectory in Latour's thinking is much less interesting to me as a matter of methodology. Much more important is the idea of matters of concern as exigencies for gathering and the role of an engaged public rhetoric in assembling that gathering.

To make a community media center, therefore, we had to assemble it, and that assembly is a rhetorical practice. We were required to make arguments for the need for a community media center rooted in two discourses: one about digital divides and the other about innovation and entrepreneurship. We were required to make arguments of possibility rooted in ideas about creativity, community capacity building, and educational innovation. We were required to make arguments about feasibility rooted in needs analysis, market studies, financial analyses, and inventories of various kinds. And we were required to make arguments of expediency based on a declining political economy in Michigan. To assemble these arguments required a great deal of invention on the part of groups of people working both collaboratively and in coordination. That invention, of course, required inquiries of various kind—historical, empirical, philosophical—and knowledge work of this kind requires an infrastructure: people, time, machines, networks, and various forms of capital. As we began to have success with our arguments, our assembly began to grow as more individuals, organizations, and eventually government institutions joined, as best they could given their own interests and capacities, this thing we call the Capital Area Community Media Center.

The arguments that I describe here are invented and distributed in a highly diffuse manner, which is one of the messages of this essay. These arguments also continue to be invented and distributed (and so reassembled). To locate "public rhetoric" in a single speech or text produced by a single author—understood in either an orthodox or reformed fashion (that is, acknowledging other people)—is to make a mistake in understanding how the work of rhetoric gets done. I was present when some of these arguments were invented, most often in a series of meetings over time. Yet there are remarkably few documents associated with this project: a business plan, two one-pagers, and some proposals. Most of the arguments were invented and delivered orally. I delivered a few at a cocktail party (the mayor being one audience), in an associate provost's office, over dinner, and in many meetings in which the media center was not on the agenda. And I was just one of many who did so. One project that has been persuaded of the media center's value is the Information Technology Empowerment Center (iTec) in Lansing.[17] We hope that this becomes the center's home. It is possible to see in the vision and mission of iTec some of the same arguments made in support of the Media Center, in part because the projects have some people in common. They are different assemblies composed of some like elements.

The process of assembly that I have just described is abstract only in that we were assembling an *idea*, and as that idea took shape, necessarily the material, cultural, institutional, and human agencies that are part of any idea that becomes a thing. Accordingly, the second thread that I want to follow is more pragmatic and concrete and entails assembling elements of the media center's infrastructure. The methodology of engagement that I have been developing here is rooted in activity. That is, if there is no activity, there is no engagement, no thing (this is also a principle of actor network theory, a fact that is coincidental in this case). Therefore, if we wanted to assemble a community media center, then we needed to act like a community media center. To do this, we took a portion of the infrastructure of the writing program at Michigan State University and turned it into the community media center.

The WIDE Research Center is a basic research center that examines what it means to write (and learn to write) in digital environments.[18] I direct this center with Bill Hart-Davidson, and since its beginning, we have always understood WIDE as a community-based research center, by which we mean that WIDE is open and responsive to the needs of community partners and tries to solve problems with those partners. To generate the activity of a media center, we devoted resources to infrastructure (servers, networks, phones, offices, desks, chairs, mailboxes, and so on), human beings, and programming.

We conducted a number of workshops at various locations in the area on topics ranging from basic tool use to podcasting (we also utilized computers from the Writing Center). And we marketed this activity under the name of the Capital Area Community Media Center, not WIDE or Michigan State University. Therefore, we have been able to make the argument that we *have* a community media center that is effective, that is engaged, and that needs to grow. In other words, when I write of the requirement to assemble as part of any methodology of engagement, I also mean this quite literally. Rhetoric is always material, and it is most powerful when it makes things that enable others to perform persuasively. The two examples used here actually demonstrate three methods of assembly: research to assemble a group in order to discern patterns of activity and their possible agencies; rhetorical assembly of ideas toward the making of a Thing; and the related and always material assembly that must be gathered into any thing. All of this assembly work is required in order to be useful to others. In the next section, I turn to more fine-grained examples of supporting the knowledge work of others and to my related claim that this is a proper goal for public rhetoric and community-based research.

SUPPORTING THE KNOWLEDGE WORK OF OTHERS

In chapter 4 of *Writing Community Change*, I write about the inventional activities of a citizen environmental group at various levels of granularity. Below is a data display from that chapter that represents the finest level of analysis, that of the infrastructure supporting the writing of a woman named Barbara (a pseudonym). Barbara and her group routinely produce four-page documents for distribution to others in Harbor. In that fourth chapter, I call the reader's attention to a few features in the figure: the elements of infrastructure that support the work of writing a document, such as computers, computer networks, interfaces, databases, phones, chairs, desks, paper, pens, people; the elements of infrastructure that connect to larger, more distributed infrastructures, particularly data and other computer networks; and elements of more local infrastructures, such as the resources of a local public library or city government and, in this case, a local repository of documents related to the current environmental project. I argue that even at the level of a relatively simple four-page document, the activity required to write it is complex and that the writing done in Harbor to enact community change is impossible without the infrastructure to support it.

I believe in that analysis, but there is too much missing from it, namely the deeper rhetorical value of this situation. Here, therefore, I want to understand the work of this organization as the making of a thing and not precisely in terms of writing a document.

To do this, I need to zoom out from our view from the writing of a document to the situation in Harbor that I detailed earlier. Barbara is a key member of CEC. It is the work of individuals like Barbara, or more properly the

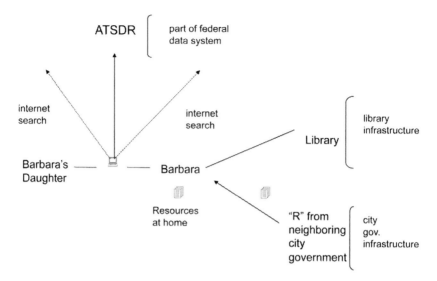

Distributed work and infrastructure supporting the writing of a document

various groupings that she is a part of and that enable her work, that are worth supporting. Before I get to this, however, let me take the time to revisit my own understanding of the activity represented in illustration above. As a writing researcher, I understand Barbara (and CEC's) activity in terms of writing, and so not surprisingly, the public rhetorical activities of CEC that consumed my attention were written practices and literacies. As a researcher, I attach significant value to the analytical power that comes from drilling deeply into composing practices, but as an analytical matter, I have always struggled to place these ways of understanding writing into a larger chain of agencies that might clearly be called "public rhetorical work." In other words, as an analytical matter, it has long been difficult for me to trace with precision a chain of activity that connects the writing of an issue summary to a given public action or impact. The ability to do so seems terribly important as a matter of research and in terms of our ability to be convincing when we say that writing and rhetoric matter to public life.

In all of the work that my colleagues and I have done to understand our work in Harbor, we have not focused on the primary rhetorical problem of this situation for community organizations, and therefore one of the key goals of a mundane document like an issue summary. The primary problem, and thus the focus of public work for citizen environmental groups in a situation like Harbor's, is to make the dredging project a matter of concern. The primary rhetorical work involved is the assembling of the participants necessary to make a thing. This is work that Barbara and her colleagues are good at and have been doing in Harbor for some time. Let me unpack this situation a bit more fully.

It may seem obvious that dumping polluted sediments in a heavily urbanized area is "concerning" if not a full-blown matter of concern. But let me describe this situation somewhat differently by assembling another set of actors in this public who seek closure (it is their job, their work, to seek closure, and they do so for reasons that are reasonable and understandable). The scene I describe here is constructed from real situations I observed in Harbor. In this scene, we assemble a government board room—intended as a public meeting room—with a particular design that enables some participants to sit in certain places that command attention and other participants to sit in places where attention is not forthcoming. Some participants stand, and others occupy spaces outside the room. Participants include human actors such as scientists, engineers, government officials, concerned citizens, each dressed (as well as positioned) in ways consistent with their status or role. The scientists, who are the heroes of this assembly, bring with them their disciplines, professions, data, and tools. Most visible in this scene are a computer, a projector, and a set of slides that show the economic costs of a canal not accessible to certain kinds of barges and an aerial photo of contaminated sediments (brown) flowing into the lake (blue). The story told here is that the canal needs to be dredged: jobs are at stake, money is being lost, and the situation is environmentally intolerable. The weight of authority insists on it, as does the cold rationality of science. A massive array of participants are here assembled to make the following argument: dredge this canal. And there is no reason not to, is there?

What does it take to make a thing here, to open up a matter of concern and resist the closure of fact, of a decision, of silence? That is, what must Barbara and others do to assemble a matter of concern? The irony is that they must break their backs to make something as delicate as a thing. The illustration on p. 202 is, for me, a tiny fragment of the work of that assembly, and the issue summaries a key participant. It is the mediating activity of the issue summaries that Stuart and I were able to see. We were able to see how these texts made others act. They were referenced by other community groups, were used in meetings, and were one of the trusted sources for "science" in this community. Aside from this particular genre of writing, we were also able to see the related elements of infrastructure assembled to facilitate the work of Barbara and her organization, and, just as important, we were able to see how they assembled participants—how they *invented*—in order to maintain the dredging project as a matter of concern.[19] "The dredging methodology is safe!" claims the U.S. Army Corps of Engineers in deploying its massive assembly, and so let us now move on to our implementation plan. "It is not safe!" claims the citizens' group, deploying a ragtag assembly of people, machines, voices, bodies, and simple little texts. So far, the dredging has been delayed. And so the dredging project is not closed down, fixed, and decided. Closure has been refused as Barbara and her group reveal to the world as best they can the particular assemblages of environmental toxicology, civic engineering, politics, and other such things. The public work of rhetoric is therefore visible. Rhetoric makes things.

All of that is well and good and makes for a nice story. It might also be analytically productive and serve as a useful metaphor for connecting some elusive dots for me from the writing of mundane documents to the making of public arguments.[20] In terms of the methodology of engagement that I am starting to build with this essay, however, a key problem is how best to support Barbara's work. If part one of this emerging methodology is the imperative to assemble, part two is the imperative to support the assembling of others. In many ways, the second part is something we do very well as a field. We research and teach performances like writing, speaking, making new media, and other such material rhetorical objects. When we teach or otherwise build capacity with others to act effectively in these ways, then we are certainly supporting the rhetorical activity of others. I want to underline, in other words, our own work as teachers in particular. We are good at it, and the work that we do matters and should matter as an issue of methodology for community engagement. But there are ways that we are not effective as well. We tend to orient more toward individuals than groups, and so as a field we would focus on Barbara's skills and performances and not necessarily on Barbara as a member of a group and that group as the writer or rhetor. As a field we tend to orient more toward the great speech, text, or the known and bounded public sphere—the rhetorical situation, the known forums of public media, the visible public conversations among our visible public intellectuals (including ourselves). We tend to miss, therefore, the mundane, the technical, the routine, the Barbaras, and the CECs of the world. We miss the issue summaries, the research required to understand what a PCB is and how many parts per million is dangerous (and how to even imagine that metaphor in a useful way), and the endless meetings that must be attended and attended to in these less visible public moments. Transformative rhetorical work takes place in these scenes as well.

Why, then, do some assemblies come together, persist over time, and have value? Why do others not? I do not really know, in part because I do not believe it is common to see and understand rhetorical work in the way that I have argued for it here. What rhetorical research does not do very well is detect rhetorical activity as coordinated and distributed, as human and non-human, as performative in the ways that I have suggested it is performative, as a chain of agencies that is not bounded in the ways we have historically bounded rhetorical agencies. Likewise, we do not measure rhetorical outcomes much at all (including an interrogation of indicators that would help us distinguish—or not—between the rhetorical and the arhetorical). Aside from not detecting very well in a way that might provide better evidence, the reasons for the success and failure of assemblies—at least as I have been able to determine from my own work—are due to the ability of groups to form and effectively assemble the infrastructure necessary to do the work of rhetoric. There is a tautology here, I know—to assemble effectively requires one to assemble effectively. But the requirements for successful assembly are why I root my work in technical and professional writing and have used the notion of "knowledge work" when describing what I see in communities. Rhetoric is work, a type of discursive work that is difficult to do and which is taught, often, in conjunction with what we understand as "professional work"—managing projects, coordinating activity, learning and using information technologies, working well with others, communicating effectively. These are the skills of assembly.

I am not aware of much work that is focused in quite this way on supporting the work of others and calling it rhetoric. Grace Bernhardt's recent work describes what it takes to build an infrastructure to support the proposal writing and content management of a small nonprofit focused on advocacy for women.[21] In order for members of the organization to advocate effectively and provide the services they promise, they need to write effectively, or more properly, assemble effectively that which they need to be persuasive. To fail at the tasks that Bernhardt was able to see is to fail, eventually, as an organization. To the extent that Bernhardt's work supported the work of this organization, she was engaged in a type of research and public rhetorical work that I want to value and make visible as methodology. To return to Latour, a methodology of engagement asks the researcher/activist/rhetor to attend to and follow the performances of group formation (the ongoing construction of boundaries, of a we); to allow actors to make sense of their social (rhetorical) world; to pay attention to the range of agencies (not precisely to who or what is the agent); to trace, with precision, "the string of actions where each participant is treated as a full-blown mediator [actor]," actions that can be used to describe rhetorical work; and to interrogate the agencies at play in order to distinguish between matters of fact and matters of concern.[22] The results of such attention are useful to others because they render visible and actionable the scene of rhetoric. More important, the work described by this methodology is necessary to *do* public rhetoric.

NOTES

1. My reference to material objects is intended to reinforce the fact that most rhetorical work results in a material object of some kind, and while I do not have the time to explore a rhetoric of objects here, the role of objects in rhetorical work is important. More important and directly relevant is work on material rhetoric—specifically indigenous material rhetoric—that has been influential for me. See Driskill, "Yelesalehe Hiwayona"; Haas, "Rhetoric of Alliance." Sometimes rhetoric produces baskets, wampum, and other such objects. Rhetoric theory must account for them.

2. Grabill, *Writing Community*.

3. Simmons and Grabill, "Toward a Civic Rhetoric."

4. See Asen, "Imagining"; Asen and Brouwer, *Counterpublics;* Banning, "Truth Floats"; Dahlgren, "Internet"; Edbauer, "Unframing Models"; Goodnight, "Personal."

5. Latour, "Why Has Critique Run Out of Steam?," 246.

6. Latour, *Reassembling.*

7. Ibid., 5.

8. Ibid.

9. Ibid., 7.

10. Grabill, *Writing Community.* For the original, see Latour, *Aramis.*

11. Blythe, Grabill, and Riley, "Supporting Invention"; Grabill, *Writing Community.*

12. Grabill, *Writing Community.*

13. Latour, *Aramis.*

14. The politics around community media in Lansing are long and complicated. Some community media people associated with schools and government have been trying to argue for a media center for twenty years. Our most recent effort is part of that history. Of late, the media center has been part of a larger conversation about how to transition to a postindustrial economy and about the public value of community media infrastructure. This conversation takes place in a context of declining public revenues for public projects, and so the media center must compete with other good ideas. There are also differing visions of what a community media center might become and how it might best serve the public interest.

15. Latour, *Reassembling;* Latour, "From Realpolitik"; Heidegger, *What Is a Thing?*

16. Latour, "From Realpolitik."

17. Information Technology Empowerment Center, http://www.iteclansing.org/ (accessed (March 22, 2009).

18. I use the term "basic" research center to identify WIDE as an organization that seeks to identify and solve fundamental research problems associated with writing in digital environments. We identify explicitly with the notion of "basic" research and with research centers in the sciences, which is useful to us inside our university and with outside funders. We also use this language to distinguish WIDE from similar centers in rhetoric and composition that have a teaching, service, or combined mission more than a research mission.

19. In this regard, the meeting itself should not remain invisible as both technology and rhetorical performance. In some ways, this is obvious. What else do meetings do other than "assemble"? While potentially true, this is not necessarily true. But more to the point, there are genres of meetings, and when done well, they serve an ongoing function as ways of assembling, as spaces and practices for invention, and serve other communicative functions—reporting, for instance. The meeting as material rhetorical performance is completely invisible in work on public rhetoric, and this is an indicator of a problem in how we understand what it means to do the actual work of rhetoric.

20. Connecting the dots remains a serious concern of mine. Reviewers of this essay asked me about impacts and audience response to some of the documents, like the issue summaries, that we saw produced in Harbor. As I have mentioned here, we did find other groups and individuals who referenced the issue summaries produced by CEC, but in this particular project, we did a poor job of connecting the dots in this way (in part because it was not our focus). Most writing researchers concern themselves with production, not reception. To pay attention to reception and outcomes requires attention over time, and it also requires serious thought about indicators—and indicators are difficult to work with. Indicators—what we can actually see and how we understand them to mean—entail questions of politics and power, questions like what should we

look for and at when trying to research rhetoric? What are we actually seeing when we notice what we think is rhetorical activity? Whose interests are served by measuring (or not) rhetorical activity? For some types of rhetorical analysis, this is a relatively easy problem. Judgments are made all the time based on an interpretation of an artifact like a text or a speech. With such an interpretation, we can determine what techniques and strategies are used, the likely audiences, and, based on this, it is not uncommon to make a judgment on effectiveness. Of course, these are, at best, indirect measures of rhetorical agency. They are also limited in terms of the number of agencies accounted for. I am not opposed to the use of indirect indicators—they are often all that we have—but I am suggesting that we have poor indicators to account for the rhetorical work that people do in their lives, and that we have paid scant attention to the impacts of that work. Traditional textual/rhetorical analysis does not help us much with this problem, as we need a different set of indicators and methods to render them visible to us. I am interested in more robust indirect indicators, and this is a project that currently occupies my time.

21. Bernhardt, *Moving Beyond*.
22. Latour, *Reassembling*, 129.

WORKS CITED

Asen, Robert. "Imagining in the Public Sphere." *Philosophy and Rhetoric* 35 (2002): 345–67.

Asen, Robert, and Daniel C. Brouwer, eds. *Counterpublics and the State*. Albany: SUNY Press, 2001.

Banning, Marla. "Truth Floats: Reflexivity in the Shifting Public and Epistemological Terrain." *Rhetoric Society Quarterly* 35, no. 3 (2005): 75–99.

Bernhardt, Grace. "Moving Beyond Single Sourcing to Single Organizations: Understanding Content Management in Small Nonprofits." Master's thesis, Michigan State University, 2007.

Blythe, Stuart, Jeffrey T. Grabill, and Kirk Riley. "Invention: Action Research and Professional Communication as Public Discourse." *Journal of Business and Technical Communication* 22 (2008): 272–98.

Dahlgren, Peter. "The Internet and the Democratization of Civic Culture." *Political Communication* 17 (2000): 335–40.

Driskill, Qwo-Li. "Yelesalehe Hiwayona Dikanohogida Naiwodusv/God Taught Me This Song, It Is Beautiful: Cherokee Performance Rhetorics as Decolonization, Healing, and Continuance." Ph.D. diss., Michigan State University, 2008.

Edbauer, Jenny. "Unframing Models of Public Distribution: From Rhetorical Situation to Rhetorical Ecologies." *Rhetoric Society Quarterly* 35 (2005): 5–24.

Goodnight, Thomas G. "The Personal, Technical, and Public Spheres of Argument." In *Contemporary Rhetorical Theory: A Reader*, edited by John L. Lucaites, Celeste M. Condit, and Sally Caudill, 251–64. New York: Guilford Press, 1999.

Grabill, Jeffrey T. *Community Literacy Programs and the Politics of Change*. Albany: SUNY Press, 2001.

———. *Writing Community Change: Designing Technologies for Citizen Action*. Cresskill, N.J.: Hampton Press, New Directions in Computers and Composition, 2007.

Haas, Angela. "A Rhetoric of Alliance: What American Indians Can Tell Us About Digital and Visual Rhetoric." Ph.D. diss., Michigan State University, 2008.

Heidegger, Martin. *What Is a Thing?* Translated by W. B. Barton Jr. and Vera Deutsch. Chicago: H. Regnery, 1968.

Latour, Bruno. *Aramis, or the Love of Technology.* Translated by Catherine Porter. Cambridge, Mass.: Harvard University Press, 1996.

———. "From Realpolitik to Dingpolitik: Or How to Make Things Public." In *Making Things Public: Atmospheres of Democracy,* edited by Bruno Latour and Peter Weibel, 14–41. Cambridge, Mass.: MIT Press, 2005.

———. *Reassembling the Social: An Introduction to Actor-Network-Theory.* Oxford: Oxford University Press, 2005.

———. "Why Has Critique Run Out of Steam?" *Critical Inquiry* 30 (2004): 238–39.

Simmons, W. Michele, and Jeffrey T. Grabill. "Toward a Civic Rhetoric for Technologically and Scientifically Complex Places: Invention, Performance, and Participation." *College Composition and Communication* 58 (2007): 419–48.

PART 3

Remaking Rhetoric in Universities and Publics

Finding a Place for
School in Rhetoric's
Public Turn

DAVID FLEMING

George Kennedy may have coined the term "secondary rhetoric," but the belief that the extended language produced by children and young adults in school—prototypically written, narrative, and personal—is inferior to and separate from the "primary rhetoric" of the public world outside—paradigmatically oral, persuasive, and civic—is widely held and of long standing, and it is nowhere more firmly entrenched than among professors of rhetoric and composition, most of whom make their living, of course, from the language of school.

Kennedy's main reason for distinguishing primary and secondary rhetoric was to trace the historical drift from the former to the latter, a process he termed *letteraturizzazione* and which he always figured as a loss.[1] From this point of view, the story of rhetoric is the story of how the virile practice of Greek public discourse in the direct democracies of the classical era became the literary simulations of public discourse in the classrooms of the Hellenistic period and beyond. At almost every juncture, the villain in this story is *school*.

Marjorie Curry Woods, for one, has questioned Kennedy's influential denigration of school and claimed that our willingness to accept so readily his account of the relationship between the "real world" and the classroom is evidence of our "academic self-hatred," our tendency to belittle those parts of our work that take place in school and involve children and young adults.[2] The problem with Kennedy's position, writes Woods, is that it employs a "postromantic 'unteachability' topos, which assumes that what is most important about education is what least resembles the classroom."[3] But it can also be faulted for perpetuating traditional rhetoric's sexism and ageism, since, as Woods shows, stories of disciplinary decline in our field privilege the civic rhetoric of men and demean the school-bound rhetorics of women and children.[4]

I follow Woods here in asking us to resist such easy denigrations of school. And, like her, I argue that, in some respects, it should be the *classroom* that is primary, prior, and superior in our understanding, and the "real world" that is secondary, subsequent, and inferior. But I also acknowledge that there are good reasons for our usual ordering of affairs. Let me begin, then, by examining two of the more devastating critiques of traditional schooling.

THE PROBLEMS WITH SCHOOL

The most prevalent critique of school from the point of view of rhetoric's public turn is that it is inauthentic, a place set apart from society and given over to mind-numbing busy work, useless trivia, impractical abstractions, and empty formalisms. In school, students learn not to be better thinkers, citizens, workers, or human beings, but only to be better *students*. They learn, that is, to "do" school. According to this interpretation, the most important characteristics of school are a function of the institution itself—namely, its appetite for order—rather than the needs of society or the dreams of individuals. Large numbers of age-segregated children and young adults sit in ordered desks inside boxlike classrooms reading bland textbooks, writing insipid essays, and doing endless problems under the direction of solitary authority figures—not because any of this prepares them for meaningful, fulfilling, engaged future lives but because that is the cheapest and most efficient way in a (post)industrial society to process the young masses through their immaturity.

In the context of contemporary composition studies, unease about the inauthenticity of school can be seen in our field's continuing embarrassment about "current-traditional rhetoric," the small-minded writing pedagogy that most of the public still associates with what we do. The classic account of such pedagogy remains Janet Emig's 1971 study of twelfth-grade writers in Chicago-area public schools, which portrays school writing in this country as a thoroughly stultifying, even "neurotic," activity.[5] In the book, no one discerns more acutely the shortcomings of current-traditional rhetoric than the students themselves, one of whom says of her teachers, "They seem to have this thing about spelling."[6]

The problem with school writing from Emig's point of view was not the students—it was their *teachers*, who were "interested chiefly in a product [they] can criticize rather than in a process [they] can help initiate through imagination and sustain through empathy and support."[7] Emig complained, in fact, of widespread "teacher illiteracy" in U.S. high schools and described educators who did not themselves write and who thus "underconceptualize and oversimplify" the process of composing so that "planning degenerates into outlining, reformulating becomes the correction of minor infelicities."[8] Through such devices as the five-paragraph theme—"so indigenously American," Emig writes, "that it might be called the Fifty-Star Theme"—teachers set rigid parameters for writing that "students find difficult to make more supple."[9] The result? "Outward conformity but inward cynicism and hostility."[10] It is no wonder that, in devising a more authentic educational experience in writing and rhetoric, one that can help our students develop into more self-actualized, engaged citizens and individuals, school is often the last place we look.

Of course, in many contemporary writing classrooms, students are allowed to pick topics about which they care and write papers that seem at least to reflect genuine purposes, genres, and audiences—a letter to one's representative about gun control, for example. But even this attempt to make school writing more like "real world" public discourse ultimately fails, according to Susan Wells: "in such assignments, students inscribe their positions in a vacuum since there is no place within the culture where student writing on gun control is held to be of general interest, no matter how persuasive the student or how intimate their acquaintance with guns. 'Public writing' in such a context means 'writing for no audience at all.'"[11]

In a penetrating essay published a few years ago, Joseph Petraglia called this kind of writing "pseudotransactional," discourse that, rather than actually transacting business with the world—informing, persuading, instructing others—only *appears* to do so, discourse in which any authentic purpose is an illusion.[12] According to Petraglia, pseudotransactionality is a function of school itself and has its origins in the teacher's role as evaluator rather than reader. The purpose of rhetoric in school, according to this argument, is not, and cannot be, to actually get something done, make things happen, alter an attitude. It is to get a grade.

A second, equally devastating problem with traditional school from the point of view of its critics is that it reproduces the unequal socioeconomic structure of the surrounding society and is thus both symptom and cause of economic and cultural hegemony. What students learn in school from this point of view is their place in the stratified order of the "real world," which thus does not change through education but is instead perpetuated by it. Emig saw forty years ago that school's obsession with trivialities like spelling did not prevent it from having enormous social power. She does not dwell on this in her critique, but she clearly shows that schools reward students who are willing to play by the schools' inane rules.

Of course, the connection between the language of school and the levers of power is not just a modern phenomenon. Roland Barthes, in fact, defined rhetoric in general as "that privileged technique (since one must pay in order to acquire it) which permits the ruling classes to gain *ownership of speech*" and noted how, as a metalanguage and thus an object of schooling, rhetoric was born in legal conflicts surrounding property.[13] It emerged "from the baldest sociality, affirmed in its fundamental brutality, that of earthly possession: we began to reflect upon language in order to defend our own."[14]

Today, ideological analyses of schooling are common, and they have shown us how our classrooms perpetuate the status quo by teaching children and young adults to assume their predetermined subject positions.[15] But, according to this critique, the curriculum not only stratifies young speakers and writers socioeconomically; it obscures that that is what it does, disempower-ing critique of unequal education, mystifying and distracting students and their guardians from the "real" power of language to effect change in the world.

In a sense the two critiques just summarized contradict one another: the first portrays school as essentially "busy work," a simulation of real activity that is a waste of resources for all concerned; the second, by contrast, depicts school as extraordinarily effective at what it does, reproducing the social order "outside" without making it at all obvious that that is what it is doing, training students to take on their preassigned roles with astonishing efficiency. But the two critiques are actually closely related, different interpretations of the same phenomenon: school's failure to promote students' self-actualization and improve the world in any appreciable way. It is just that one sees that situ-ation as a case of ineptness; the other, as the design of the ruling classes.

Given these problems with traditional schooling—pseudotransactionality, on the one hand; reproduction, on the other—any turn from the traditional classroom would seem to be a welcome development for rhetorical education. But in which direction should we turn? After all, nearly everyone acknowl-edges the continuing need for education of the young in speaking and writ-ing, especially given the complexity of such practices, the important role they play in our communities, and the long immaturity of our offspring. The ques-tion is, what should such education look like?

At a theoretical level, if the problem of traditional composition pedagogy has been its reliance on what Petraglia has termed "General Writing Skills Instruction," which involves explicit instruction in decontextualized reading and writing skills, the solution would seem therefore to involve the educa-tional dispersal, particularization, and implicitization of writing.[16] From this point of view, "real world" written discourse is irreducibly diverse, inextrica-bly situated, and always already interested; the way to effectively, and ethi-cally, develop fluency in a given writing practice is thus to immerse oneself in a world where that practice makes sense.

A pedagogy based on such a belief would involve a literal (and not just a conceptual or metaphoric) move away from school and toward society, away from the classroom and toward the community, away from solitary, imprac-tical exercise in decontextualized skills and toward situated, collaborative, concrete, human action. It would involve, that is, a new dedication to prac-tice, whether that is seen as culturally embedded, inescapably ethical action;[17] insistently reflective engagement with the materials of the world;[18] or "free, universal, creative and self-creative activity through which man creates (makes, produces) and changes (shapes) his historical, human world and himself."[19]

The public turn in rhetoric and composition studies is clearly aligned with such a recasting of education. Recent work in service learning, activist research, community literacy, and public discourse studies has helped the field reclaim an outward-looking profile, making learning both more authentic—because it is oriented to the particular, local, and embedded—and more radical—because it encourages students to question and change the world rather than merely reproduce it.

But I worry that in turning so definitively toward "society" and away from "school," we may be neglecting aspects of classroom education that are not necessarily antithetical to a genuinely *practical* mission for rhetoric and composition, aspects of schooling that, in fact, could contribute in important ways to a public turn in the field. The problems of school are many and obvious. But there are virtues as well, virtues that might be especially pertinent for rhetoricians of public life.

THE VIRTUES OF SCHOOL

Let us take two prototypical features of traditional schooling—its emphasis on factual knowledge and its preference for theoretical abstraction—and ask whether they might harbor learning opportunities for a praxis-oriented rhetorical education. My goal here is not to mount a comprehensive defense of school but to suggest that we reconsider the easy denigration of the classroom that has sometimes accompanied rhetoric's public turn.

IN DEFENSE OF FACTS

We are accustomed now to malign traditional schooling's emphasis on—or obsession with—the transmission of "inert" facts, and with good reason. But even a writing pedagogy focused on "real world" activity, on authentic, socially embedded, potentially transgressive practices, needs to reserve a place for the development of substantive knowledge in its students. In fact, it could be argued that a truly *civic* rhetorical education in a complex society like ours cannot work without some kind of common schooling in the shared histories, beliefs, and values of the various worlds to which its students will graduate.

Since the late 1960s, of course, conventional wisdom has held that formal education plays an insignificant role in the development of good citizens. But political scientist William Galston has summarized a compelling body of recent research that supports an important role for traditional, classroom-based education in fostering democratic attitudes and habits in young people.[20] These studies, writes Galston, have shown surprisingly positive effects for coursework in political life and classroom-based discussion about politics; political scientists now increasingly acknowledge that, though citizens do not need to be policy experts to be engaged in their community's affairs, they do need basic political knowledge to be effective in and fulfilled by public life, knowledge that is perhaps best transmitted *in school*. The evidence shows, according to Galston, that substantive political knowledge affects acceptance of democratic principles, attitudes about politics, and political participation rates. Controlling for race, class, and other variables, he argues, citizens with more knowledge have less fear of immigrants, are less likely to feel mistrust and alienation, more likely to participate in politics, less likely to vote on the basis of their own circumstances and interests, and more likely to express tolerance for unpopular groups. There appears to be, in other words, a link between years of formal education and prodemocracy attitudes. Though Galston also admits that the results of other kinds of civic education—service learning, for example—remain mixed, he does not conclude from his summary that we should simply return to a political pedagogy based on rote learning of facts and principles. The evidence shows instead that traditional formal education in politics needs to be combined with regular discussion by students of current events, opportunities to practice democratic skills in school governance, exposure to social science methods and findings about political life, training in such practical skills as the decoding of charts and tables, and treatment of non-American political structures.

A recent essay in *CCC* by David Coogan would seem to support just such an integration of classroom- and community-based methods in writing and rhetoric education.[21] Coogan recounts a two-semester service-learning course he taught in 2002 at the Illinois Institute of Technology in Chicago, in which a dozen undergraduate students worked with a Bronzeville-area nonprofit organization called Urban Matters to increase parent involvement in the local school councils (LSCs), which help govern neighborhood schools in the Chicago public school system. Unfortunately, despite the effort and resources put into the yearlong course, the students' work had limited impact: they were unable to significantly increase attendance at the parent meetings they organized, the brochures they painstakingly produced went largely unread, and the advocacy they tried to sponsor among their clients was practically ineffective.

Coogan uses this "rhetorical failure" to argue for a new approach to service learning that pays as much attention to "rhetorical scholarship" as to "rhetorical activism."[22] "What really went wrong in the project," he writes, "was that the students and staff were thrust into rhetorical production . . . before they had done any rhetorical analysis."[23] They did not know enough about the history of the school reform movement in Chicago, were unfamiliar with the "style and substance" of parent involvement in schools, and misread the dominant "ideographs" of the rhetorical environment around them, failing to understand, for example, the historical shift in local discourses about education that now privileged "local responsibility" and "accountability" over "local control."

Coogan advocates here a greater role for relatively formal, even classroom-based instruction and analysis within service-learning projects, an integration of school and society, an oscillation between classroom and community, that may well turn out to be a pronounced feature of the next generation of community literacy initiatives. And he proposes an educational sequence that would move students from discovery to analysis to production to assessment, in which really only the third step—admittedly the heart of any such project—would be nontraditional in the terms I have been using here.[24]

IN PRAISE OF THE ABSTRACT

Another feature of traditional schooling that deserves reconsideration is the focus on abstract, theoretical knowledge. Since at least the rise of the "situated learning" movement of the 1980s, there has been a concerted move in educational circles away from the teaching of general, abstract knowledge and toward contextualized, embodied, concrete learning, especially apprenticeship-style projects in which explicit instruction in general knowledge is replaced by immersion in particular communities of practice.

But in turning toward such informal education, is it possible that we have overlooked the continuing *practical* possibilities of theoretical abstraction? In a persuasive defense of such knowledge, and the relatively traditional pedagogies by which it is usually transmitted, John R. Anderson, Lynn M. Reder, and Herbert A. Simon concede that "much of what is learned is specific to the situation in which it is learned" and that there is often a "mismatch" between school situations and "real world" situations such as the workplace.[25] They cite such well-known studies as the one that portrays Orange County homemakers doing poorly at schoollike mathematics problems but well at supermarket "best-buy" calculations. They dispute, however, the conclusions usually reached on the basis of this research: that all learning is context-bound and that the abstract knowledge that school often emphasizes is largely useless. They suggest instead that knowledge gained in school *can* transfer across contexts in powerful ways if the learning situation is well designed. For example, knowledge taught in multiple contexts turns out to be less context-bound than knowledge not so taught.

The authors also contest the claim of the situated learning movement that "training by abstraction" is of little use, an argument that has been used to support projects like apprenticeship programs that turn their back completely on the classroom.[26] The alleged irrelevance of school-based "theory" is supported by stories like that of Los Angeles police officers who are told, upon leaving the police academy, to "now forget everything you learned." Though there is obviously some justification for this advice, the real problem, according to Anderson, Reder, and Simon, is not school but our tendency—on both the Left and Right—to belittle what school in fact does well. What police recruits learn in the classroom about not violating subjects' civil rights, for example—education that is hard to imagine *outside* of a classroom context—needs to be not "forgotten" but constantly reinforced. In this case, the better advice would be "now *remember* everything you learned!"

Research on writing acquisition has sometimes found similarly large effects for explicit instruction, despite the manifest superiority in many cases of practice over theory and implicit over explicit instruction.[27] Students have been shown to revise better, for example, when explicitly instructed to do so. In one study, young writers improved their performance significantly when told "Add five things to your essay to improve it," rather than simply "revise your essay to improve it."[28] Though they do not deal specifically with writing instruction, it is for reasons such as these that Anderson, Reder, and Simon argue for a more nuanced approach to the relative role of situated and abstract knowledge in pedagogical design. "Numerous experiments show combining abstract instruction with specific concrete examples is better than either one alone."[29]

Finally, the authors deal with the claim of situated learning advocates that learning should always take place in complex, social environments, those that mimic the "real world," rather than the simplified, often solitary contexts of school. Again, there is often good reason for reforming school to make it more like society in these ways. But Anderson, Reder, and Simon find ample evidence for the usefulness of solitary learning methods and the decomposition of tasks into parts. A student learning to play violin in an orchestra, for example, requires training *both* inside *and* outside of that context.

But what does any of this have to do with the kind of political or civic goals associated with the public turn in rhetorical education? Well, one of those goals is usually to help develop in students a more critical sensibility about their society, an oppositional stance toward socioeconomic inequality, for example. While it is true, as I argued above, that school is often a place where the status quo is naturalized and reinforced, and while "extracurricular" organizations and activities can be fruitful sites for learning and practicing counterhegemonic discourses, it is also true, as scholars of service learning like Bruce Herzberg have shown, that classroom work—reading, writing, analysis, discussion, and so forth—can edify practical action by helping students question the theories with which they operate in their daily lives and which can distort their interpretations of what they see and hear outside of school.[30] Coursework in women's studies programs has demonstrated for more than thirty years now the transformative power of relatively traditional classroom work.

It may be, in fact, that counterintuitive knowledge, that which goes against students' prior beliefs, can only reliably be acquired through overt instruction, the way effective textbooks often teach new concepts by first explicitly refuting students' misconceptions. In fact, one of the hallmarks of expertise is the prominence of abstract knowledge that is not readily accessible in "everyday" life. Cheryl Geisler describes how novices studying physics tend to rely on concepts close to everyday, literal understanding; experts, on the other hand, use discipline-specific understandings that are more abstract, nonliteral, specialized, and learned. Clearly, expert knowledge comes, in part, from long immersion in a community of practice; but it also comes from *study*, often of a fairly traditional kind. The very power of that kind of expertise—its practical effectivity in the world—is further reason to reappraise our tendency to denigrate classroom-based education.[31]

We might see in both of these features of traditional schooling—the emphasis on factual knowledge and the preference for theoretical abstraction—a defensible role for *explicitness* in progressive education. In fact, though we often associate explicitness with legalism, authoritarianism, even repression, compelling arguments have been raised in recent years about the liberatory potential of *some* kinds of explicit instruction. In writing studies, this reappraisal has been most persuasively advanced by Lisa Delpit, who has argued that there are rules for participating in power, and "if you're not already a participant in the culture of power, being told explicitly the rules of that culture makes acquiring power easier."[32]

I have focused so far on the potential role of traditional educational *content*—facts and theories—in authentic, even counterhegemonic, learning. But what about the *structure* of traditional education, the prototypical organization of classroom life itself? Is there something there that a public turn in rhetoric might take advantage of? By structure, I mean the way school is usually so dramatically set off from the rest of society: the way it segregates and isolates aged cohorts of children and young adults in institutional settings, often under compulsion of some kind; the way it organizes their time together into artificial chunks, like the "courses" of postsecondary education; the way such chunks are conceived on a narrative basis, each with a beginning, middle, and end through which students move and, ideally, become transformed; the way participants—teachers and students alike—are asked constantly to reflect on that movement, to imagine, represent, contemplate, and assess their progress, or lack thereof, in the story of learning. If education can take many forms, school itself is hard to imagine, even in the early twenty-first century, without calling up such specific spatial and temporal images.

These images also point, of course, to what makes traditional schooling so susceptible to the critiques I summarized at the beginning of this essay. The segregation of students by age, class, "ability," and so forth deprives young learners of the "real world" diversity they need to grow as thinkers and citizens; the physical arrangement of the typical classroom encourages docility among students and authoritarianism among teachers; the isolation of school from everyday life makes student learning so often irrelevant and ineffective; the division of educational time into units like the semester, as Mathieu has shown, gives students an artificial and solipsistic view of the phenomena they are studying; and so forth.[33]

But the classroom, *as a classroom*, can also be a site of genuine discovery and enlightenment, with transformative potential not readily or reliably available anywhere else. Outside of school, after all, people rarely have the chance to gather with unfamiliar peers, in dedicated spaces, at regular intervals, and devote themselves to courses of study meant to facilitate their individual and collective growth.

To illustrate what I mean by these *structural* possibilities of formal education, I want to end this essay by looking at an example of educational reform during a period of dramatic cultural crisis, when a group of energetic young teachers at a large public university in the United States, teaching freshman composition, tried to reimagine school in terms of freedom, growth, and change. What is most crucial about this example, I believe, is the teachers' refusal to give up on the classroom even as they sought to imbue their students' experience with a radically new set of methods and goals.

REIMAGINING THE CLASSROOM

On November 18, 1969, after two months of stormy meetings and impassioned memos, during one of the most turbulent periods in local and national history, the faculty of the English Department at the University of Wisconsin (UW) in Madison voted twenty-seven to twelve to cease offering English 102, the second semester of its required Freshman Composition program. Coupled with a 1968 decision to remedialize the first-semester course (English 101), the move effectively abolished the university's seventy-five-year-old first-year writing program for the next quarter of a century.

The official reasons given by the faculty for this decision were first, that first-year students' writing skills at UW no longer warranted a universally required general composition course; and, second, that whatever writing instruction students still needed was better provided by their major departments.[34] The unofficial reason, however, was that senior faculty in the department had lost confidence in their own graduate teaching assistants (TAs), believing them to be more interested in politically indoctrinating students and disrupting the university than in teaching writing. This explanation can be heard in taped interviews with English faculty collected over a thirty-year period by the UW-Madison Oral History Project.[35] Former chair Walter Rideout argued in 1976, for example, that the main reason English 102 was abolished in 1969 was that "the TAs were not teaching the course as it was intended to be taught. . . . They felt that it was more important to liberate the students from old fashioned ideas, to argue against the war than to proceed with . . . writing as such."[36]

Minutes of departmental meetings at the time confirm this explanation. At a meeting two weeks before the vote to eliminate English 102, Freshman English director William Lenehan argued that TA misconduct was resulting in too much variation in the course, "ultimately destroying" its value.[37] He gave two examples of deviation from the approved syllabus, "one of which involved a TA's shuffling cards for grades, another involving a TA's discussing the 'pigs' for three solid lectures, causing some of the students to become very upset." Lenehan noted, however, that "usually the deviation was the result of sheer incompetence, the TAs not knowing how to teach composition."[38]

In 1999 this TA-centered explanation for the abolition of Freshman English at UW received scholarly imprimatur when the fourth volume of the *History of the University of Wisconsin* was published. According to its authors, the "unstated" reason for the decision to drop English 102 in 1969 was that "senior members of the department believed they had lost control of the Freshman English course to . . . radicalized . . . TAs staffing [its] numerous sections. Most of the tenured . . . faculty objected to unauthorized grading experiments and indications that . . . freshmen were getting more exposure to Karl Marx and Che Guevara than to the writers and poets . . . specified in the departmentally approved reading lists."[39] Clearly, it was a time of stark ideological conflict and dramatic cultural confrontation. And, in fact, what seemed to have most impressed, and disturbed, many of the TAs at UW, what motivated them to work so hard toward change, was the gulf they perceived between the world outside of school—a world of injustice, repression, and war, on the one hand; youthful freedom, experimentation, and protest, on the other—and the staid nature of the course they were assigned to teach, concerned as it was with formalisms and trivialities and completely disconnected from the world described above.

Now, one place where direct engagement by these teachers in life outside their classrooms can be found was in their persistent call for more "relevant" classroom materials, reading and writing assignments pertinent to the pressing issues of the day. Though the faculty at the time often read "relevance" as code for lack of standards and loss of control, the TAs believed that "the demand for relevance [was] a mortal challenge to [the] imagination . . . to ensure that knowledge [was] related to human fulfillment rather than human destruction," as an "Anonymous" English TA put it in the fall 1969 issue of *Critical Teaching,* a journal written, edited, and published by UW TAs in the late 1960s.[40]

Former UW TA Ira Shor was especially intent at the time on transforming the course into a space where social and political problems in the real world could bear directly on students' thinking and writing in school. "We were tossing [the syllabus] aside," Shor commented in an interview. "For example, I was trying to figure out a way to raise the issue of social inequality and to pose it as a thinking problem. So I remember bringing in the Gross National Product of America at that time. And then I asked students to divide it by the number of Americans living in the country and come out with a per capita figure. So . . . then I said, okay, now here's the median family income in America, which I got from some census source, and I put it on the board. It was very low, . . . and so I asked them to write, or something like that, to give a context to inequality and base it in data."[41] There is other evidence of TAs at the time incorporating problems from the outside world in their Freshman English classrooms.[42]

But if devising *relevant* reading and writing assignments was key for these TAs, they also tried to reform Freshman English by taking seriously its internal logic: this low-enrollment, content-less, activity-oriented course, required of all students at the university, taken at the beginning of their college careers, taught by teachers who were themselves still students, all embarking together on a journey of individual and social discovery through reading, writing, thinking, and talking.

Research by Rasha Diab, Mira Shimabukuro, and myself suggests that the English TAs at UW in 1968 and 1969 engaged especially vigorously in three kinds of pedagogical experimentation, all of which seemed designed to take advantage of freshman composition's inherent structure.[43] First, they tried to develop what we might call a *teacherless* writing class, in which authority was dramatically de-centered and the students' responsibility for their own reading, writing, and thinking—their own lives—radically heightened. One source of inspiration for such a teacherless class in the late 1960s was an article that appeared in the winter 1968 issue of *Daedalus* by Princeton history professor Martin Duberman, who in the fall of 1966 tried to empty one of his undergraduate seminars of all authoritarianism.[44] In the course, Duberman required no readings, assigned no papers, held no exams, and gave no grades. Instead, he provided students with a list of topics and books and then turned the class over to them, letting them determine together what they would study, as well as how, when, where, and why. In its egalitarianism and stress on self-directed learning—"The young have their own interests and timetables," Duberman wrote—the essay is a classic story of 1960s pedagogical experimentation.[45]

It clearly influenced UW Freshman English TA Bob Muehlenkamp, whose account of a student-run writing course, titled "Growing Free," appeared in the first (1968) issue of *Critical Teaching*. Muehlenkamp wrote that he had no problem with the official goal of English 102, "to develop skill in writing logical and convincing essays," but he did have a problem with its methods: the focus on style, the analysis of models, the classification of essays by mode—in short, the tyranny of form. "The development of 'effective' writing involves having something which you want to say and seeing the necessity of saying it in certain ways."[46] To accomplish this, Muehlenkamp turned the course over to the students themselves, asking them what *they* wanted from Freshman English. They then began to look for other subject matter and methods, following the technique of "evolving ideas and alternatives" for all course matters and developing an attitude of maximum *flexibility* with regard to composition itself.[47]

This idea of "maximum flexibility" brings us to the second "structural" feature of the TAs' pedagogical experiments. They were interested not just in a *democratic* writing class but an *emergent* one as well, imagining a curriculum driven not by a prior and externally imposed syllabus but by the constantly evolving desires of its actual participants, reflecting day to day on the meanings they wanted to explore and construct, in conversation with one another and in dialogue with the surrounding world.

"Becoming a Radical Teacher," written by an anonymous English TA for the second (1969) issue of *Critical Teaching*, tells the story of a syllabus-less writing course at UW. The piece opens with a critique of the English 102 curriculum, including its very reliance on a syllabus, "this giving and receiving of lectures and grades, requiring attendance three times a week at a given hour, etc." "We decided . . . that a syllabus and the lecture system taught submission to authority, acceptance of an authority figure's decisions about topic, method, questions, and answers; that grades taught competitiveness, placed top value on measurable products, and atomized people from each other; and that the three lectures a week taught machine production mentality and submission to bureaucracy."[48]

But the best example of an "emergent" curriculum at UW in the late 1960s comes from English 101, the old first-semester course that was remedialized in spring 1968. In designing the new course, TAs asked that classrooms be made available five days a week at the appointed time so that they could have more flexibility in scheduling: meeting with their students daily at the beginning of the semester, for example, and less often later. The rooms could also be made available for individualized instruction and small group meetings. As for a course syllabus, the group wrote that "no common calendar is possible since instruction must depend completely upon the needs of the students, which will vary widely."[49] Similarly, no specific texts were prescribed, so that TAs could be free to experiment in this area.

Hand in hand with their advocacy of decentered, emergent curricula was an insistence among English TAs at UW in the late 1960s that Freshman English move away from formal evaluation of student writing by teachers and toward informal evaluation by the students themselves, who would thus—it was hoped—be *internally* motivated to write, and improve their writing, rather than be driven to do so by external compulsion and fear. Now, "de-grading" was a practical matter at this time: early in the Vietnam War, male students were at greater risk to be drafted if they had low or failing grades. In fact, the very birth of the Teaching Assistants' Association at UW, one of the first graduate student employee unions in the country, was connected to TAs' refusal there to participate in an educational system in which the evaluation of classroom performance was used in such a deadly manner. The tie between grades and the draft was eventually weakened, but opposition to traditional evaluation only increased during this period. English TA Inez Martinez wrote in "The Degrading System," a short essay in the first (1968) issue of *Critical Teaching*, that grades stood in the way of a society of self-realized persons—they reinforced a value scheme that equated acceptability of self with performing better than others.[50]

What is clear from all this is the continuing attraction, in the late 1960s, of a decidedly modern belief in the possibilities of personal growth. As Marianne DeKoven has recently shown, even the most radical political and cultural movements of the 1960s were dependent on a narrative of the unified self, capable of resisting the alienations of modern society and progressing toward freedom.[51] This explains the rather remarkable faith in self-discovery, self-exploration, and self-generating inquiry that animates these pedagogical experiments, experiments less notable for *what* students read, wrote, and talked about than *how* they went about such activities. And it explains as well, I would argue, the rather remarkable faith that these teachers had in the classroom itself.

Freshman composition was especially amenable to these experiments because of three features that it *still* possesses in North American higher education: universality, generality, and liminality. By "universality," I mean the way the course is typically designed to meets the needs of *all* students on campus, to be an experience common to all, one that brings together a diversity of students. And at UW in the late 1960s, it was a course whose universal requirement, its teachers thought, could work against the fragmentation of the U.S. economy, the segregation of its social and physical landscape, the privatism of its society, and the vocationalism of its universities.

By "generality," I mean the way freshman composition is almost by design a course without "content" in the academic sense of that word, a course that practices students in processes, habits, and dispositions rather than transmitting substantive knowledge to them. It is a course, that is, based on *activity*— and the trick has been to imagine an activity-based course that is not therefore *empty,* a course without content that is not therefore about *nothing.* In fact, the content-less nature of freshman composition, rightly understood, can be seen as its original and abiding genius. As Richard Ohmann once put it, the thinness of the first-year writing class is what makes it "socially useful."[52]

Finally, by "liminality," I mean the way freshman composition seems to be always and everywhere on the border or threshold—a course suspended between other, better-known and better-understood educational states. In fact, it is hard to imagine a more "liminal" course in higher education: its students positioned between high school and the major, its instructors (at least when the course is staffed by graduate TAs) positioned between their own studenthood and their professional responsibility as teachers, the course itself cast midway between a tutorial and a seminar, oriented toward neither skill nor content but rather experience, passage, change.

My point in all this is not that freshman composition is the only educational space harboring those possibilities, or that the TAs at UW in the late 1960s actually achieved in their classrooms the transformative potential they imagined there. But I do think the example highlights how the classroom can be redeemed even when school itself deserves criticism. The episode should remind us, in other words, that a public turn in rhetoric need not always involve denigration of school, that there are ways to think about formal education that are compatible with our goals for a just society and genuine learning of discourse practices.

Finally, the episode suggests to me how rhetoricians might usefully engage with social movements by *indirection*, designing classrooms that are sensitive to the world outside, cognizant of and oriented to it, but also, in a sense, protected from it. What was most powerful, and most dangerous, about Freshman English in the hands of radical TAs at UW in the late 1960s, after all, was not that their students were reading Karl Marx and Che Guevara, which in fact we never found any evidence of, or that those students were throwing down their textbooks and marching outside to live truly free and democratic lives, but that they were given the space, time, and encouragement to find their own voices.

CONCLUSION

Now, admittedly, the pictures of "school" and "society" I have presented in this essay have been painted with rather broad strokes. The latter has been portrayed as practical but unforgiving; the former, as inauthentic but thoughtful. Part of this has been purposeful: to make sure that those of us excited about the public turn guard against academic self-hatred. But I acknowledge that the exaggeration is potentially problematic. My hope, after all, is that we avoid all forms of binary thinking about school and society, regardless of which term we privilege. In making the public turn that this collection celebrates, in other words, I propose that we adopt a more Janus-faced attitude to school and society, focused on what each does best educationally.

But I have dwelled here mostly on problems associated with the denigration of school. And I have tried to suggest that in our embarrassment about the bad things that school sometimes does, we should not blind ourselves to the good things that also happen there. Some types of traditional classroom activity *can* serve the progressive purposes many of us have for rhetorical education.

What I hope to have done, then, is remind us that school need not be, in Jane Tompkins's words, the enemy of what we want to learn and teach.[53] In turning our gaze outward, in other words, we should not lose sight of what, as teachers, we do well and can do better. Because as much as we would like our classrooms to be more like our best publics, there are publics out there that we should wish were more like our best classrooms.

NOTES

1. Kennedy, *Classical Rhetoric*, 1–5.
2. Woods, "Teaching"; Woods, "Among Men," 18.

3. Woods, "Among Men," 18.

4. Ibid.

5. Emig, *Composing Processes*, 99.

6. Ibid., 70.

7. Ibid., 98.

8. Ibid.

9. Ibid., 97, 93.

10. Ibid., 93.

11. Wells, "Rogue Cops," 328.

12. Petraglia, "Spinning Like a Kite."

13. Barthes, "Old Rhetoric," 14.

14. Ibid., 17.

15. See Anyon, "Social Class"; Bloom, "Freshman Composition"; Heath, *Ways with Words*.

16. Smit, *End of Composition*.

17. MacIntyre, *After Virtue*.

18. Schön, *Reflective Practitioner*.

19. Petrovic, "Praxis," 435.

20. Galston, "Political Knowledge."

21. Coogan, "Service Learning."

22. Ibid., 669–70.

23. Ibid., 687.

24. Perhaps the best-known recent attempt to integrate traditional and praxis-oriented pedagogies in literacy education is the 1996 proposal of the New London Group, which argues for a pedagogy comprised of four parts: situated practice, overt instruction, critical framing, and transformed practice. See Cazden et al., "Pedagogy of Multiliteracies."

25. Anderson, Reder, and Simon, "Situated Learning."

26. Ibid., 8.

27. See Freedman, "Show and Tell?"

28. Hayes et al., *Reading Empirical Research*, 355. See also Wallace and Hayes, "Redefining Revision."

29. Anderson, Reder, and Simon, "Situated Learning," 8.

30. Herzberg, "Community Service."

31. Geisler, *Academic Literacy*.

32. Delpit, "Silenced Dialogue."

33. Mathieu, *Tactics of Hope*.

34. William T. Lenehan, Memo to English Department Teaching Assistants, November 19, 1969. Archived in the files of the University of Wisconsin–Madison (UW-Madison) English Department, Helen C. White Hall. Copies of this and other primary texts cited here are in the author's possession.

35. UW-Madison Oral History Project at http://archives.library.wisc.edu/oral-history/overview.html.

36. Walter Rideout, interview by Laura Smail (Madison: Oral History Program of the UW-Madison Archives [#88, First Interview], 1976); see http://archives.library.wisc.edu/oral-history/guide/1–100/81–90.html#rideout.

37. UW-Madison English Department, Minutes of the Departmental Committee, November 4, 1969, 1.

38. Ibid., 2.

39. Cronon and Jenkins, *University of Wisconsin,* 290.

40. Anonymous, "Becoming a Radical Teacher," 51ff.

41. Ira Shor, interview by Mira Shimabukuro, July 13, 2005, transcript in author's possession.

42. Fleming, "On the Hinge of History."

43. Ibid.

44. Duberman, "Experiment in Education."

45. Ibid., 321.

46. Muehlenkamp, "Growing Free," 44.

47. Ibid.

48. Anonymous, "Becoming a Radical Teacher."

49. Thomas, Ednah, with Jeanie Peterson, John Pirri, Mary Richards, Michael Stroud, and Sharon Wilson, *Report on English 101* (Madison: University of Wisconsin English Department, February 5, 1969).

50. Martinez, "Degrading System."

51. DeKoven, *Utopia Limited.*

52. Ohmann, *English in America,* 160.

53. Tompkins, *Life in School.*

WORKS CITED

Anderson, John R., Lynne M. Reder, and Herbert A. Simon. "Situated Learning and Education." *Educational Researcher* 25, no. 4 (1996): 5–11.

Anonymous [Sea Unido]. "Becoming a Radical Teacher." *Critical Teaching* 2 (1969): 51ff.

Anyon, Jean. "Social Class and the Hidden Curriculum of Work." *Journal of Education* 162 (1980): 67–92.

Barthes, Roland. "The Old Rhetoric: An Aide-Mémoire." In *The Semiotic Challenge.* Translated by Richard Howard. New York: Hill and Wang, 1988.

Bloom, Lynn Z. "Freshman Composition as a Middle Class Enterprise." *College English* 58 (1996): 654–75.

Cazden, Courtney, Bill Cope, Norman Fairclough, James Gee, Mary Kalantzis, Gunther Kress, Allan Luke, Carmen Luke, Sarah Michaels, and Martin Nakata (The New London Group). "A Pedagogy of Multiliteracies: Designing Social Futures." *Harvard Educational Review* 66 (1996): 60–93.

Coogan, David. "Service Learning and Social Change: The Case for Materialist Rhetoric." *College Composition and Communication* 57 (2006): 667–93.

Cronon, E. David, and John W. Jenkins. *The University of Wisconsin: A History.* Vol. 4, *1945–1971: Renewal to Revolution.* Madison: University of Wisconsin Press, 1999.

DeKoven, Marianne. *Utopia Limited: The Sixties and the Emergence of the Postmodern.* Durham, N.C.: Duke University Press, 2004.

Delpit, Lisa. "The Silenced Dialogue: Power and Pedagogy in Educating Other People's Children." *Harvard Educational Review* 58 (1988): 280–98.

Duberman, Martin. "An Experiment in Education." *Daedalus* 97 (1968): 318–41.

Emig, Janet. *The Composing Processes of Twelfth Graders.* Urbana, Ill.: National Council of Teachers of English, 1971.

Fleming, David, with Rasha Diab and Mira Shimabukuro. "On the Hinge of History: Freshman Composition at the University of Wisconsin–Madison, 1967–1970." Unpublished manuscript.

Freedman, Aviva. "Show and Tell? The Role of Explicit Teaching in the Learning of New Genres." *Research in the Teaching of English* 27 (1993): 222–51.

Galston, William A. "Political Knowledge, Political Engagement, and Civic Education." *Annual Review of Political Science* 4 (2001): 217–34.

Geisler, Cheryl. *Academic Literacy and the Nature of Expertise: Reading, Writing, and Knowing in Academic Philosophy.* Hillsdale, N.J.: Lawrence Erlbaum, 1994.

Grafton, Anthony, and Lisa Jardine. *From Humanism to the Humanities: Education and the Liberal Arts in Fifteenth- and Sixteenth-Century Europe.* Cambridge, Mass.: Harvard University Press, 1986.

Hayes, John R., Richard E. Young, Michele L. Matchett, Maggie McCaffrey, Cynthia Cochran, and Thomas Hajduk, eds. *Reading Empirical Research Studies: The Rhetoric of Research.* Hillsdale, N.J.: Lawrence Erlbaum, 1992

Heath, Shirley Brice. *Ways with Words: Language, Life, and Work in Communities and Classrooms.* Cambridge: Cambridge University Press, 1983.

Herzberg, Bruce. "Community Service and Critical Thinking." *College Composition and Communication* 45 (1994): 307–19.

Kennedy, George A. *Classical Rhetoric and Its Christian and Secular Traditions.* 2nd ed. Chapel Hill: University of North Carolina Press, 1999.

MacIntyre, Alasdair C. *After Virtue: A Study in Moral Theory.* Notre Dame, Ind.: University of Notre Dame Press, 1984.

Martinez, Inez. "The Degrading System." *Critical Teaching* 1 (1968): 4–6.

Mathieu, Paula. *Tactics of Hope: The Public Turn in English Composition.* Portsmouth, N.J.: Boynton/Cook, 2005.

Muehlenkamp, Bob. "Growing Free." *Critical Teaching* 1 (1968): 44–50.

Ohmann, Richard. *English in America: A Radical View of the Profession.* 1976. Reprint, Hanover, N.H.: University Press of New England for Wesleyan University Press, 1996.

Petraglia, Joseph. "Introduction: General Writing Skills Instruction and Its Discontents." In *Reconceiving Writing, Rethinking Writing Instruction,* edited by Joseph Petraglia, xi–xvii. Mahwah, N.J.: Lawrence Erlbaum, 1995.

———. "Spinning Like a Kite: A Closer Look at the Pseudotransactional Function of Writing." *Journal of Advanced Composition* 15 (1995): 19–33.

Petrovic, Gajo. "Praxis." In *A Dictionary of Marxist Thought,* 435–40. 2nd ed. Edited by Tom Bottomore. Oxford: Blackwell, 1991.

Schön, Donald A. *The Reflective Practitioner: How Professionals Think in Action.* New York: Basic Books, 1983.

Smit, David W. *The End of Composition Studies.* Carbondale: Southern Illinois University Press, 2004.

Tompkins, Jane. *A Life in School: What the Teacher Learned.* Reading, Mass.: Addison-Wesley, 1996.

Wallace, David, and John R. Hayes. "Redefining Revision for Freshmen." In *Reading Empirical Research Studies: The Rhetoric of Research,* edited by John R. Hayes, Richard E. Young, Michele L. Matchett, Maggie McCaffrey, Cynthia Cochran, and Thomas Hajduk, 349–69. Hillsdale, N.J.: Lawrence Erlbaum, 1992.

Wells, Susan. "Rogue Cops and Health Care: What Do We Want from Public Writing?" *College Composition and Communication* 47 (1996): 325–41.

Woods, Marjorie C. "Among Men—Not Boys: Histories of Rhetoric and the Exclusion of Pedagogy." *Rhetoric Society Quarterly* 22 (1992): 18–26.

———. "The Teaching of Writing in Medieval Europe." In *A Short History of Writing Instruction: From Ancient Greece to Twentieth-Century America,* edited by James J. Murphy, 77–94. Davis, Calif.: Hermagoras Press, 1990.

Mediating Differences

ERIK JUERGENSMEYER AND THOMAS P. MILLER

Like many developing cities, Tucson, Arizona, has experienced growing pains. Unfortunately, increased growth has brought increased conflict and complications in a region already struggling to cope with its contentious geographic positioning. Located just fifty miles north of the southern border with Mexico, Tucson experiences its share of border town issues, while struggling to adapt its own cultural identity. An increasingly large amount of the conflict revolves around the swelling populations confined within the physical borders of the city, so much conflict that the Northwest Police District—one of five in the city—struggles to handle even simple neighborhood disputes. According to Sergeant Ron Thompson, the district receives a call reporting a dispute between neighbors almost every other day. Not only were these calls burdening the district's resources, but after a fatal dispute in June 2006, all calls were approached with the utmost caution and treated as potentially dangerous. On June 22 Wayne Poppin was shot to death in front of his central Tucson apartment by a neighbor who was upset with the amount of noise Poppin was making in the mornings while loading his truck for work. Community members remembered Poppin as an energetic man and good neighbor who was sincerely interested in his community. According to Poppin's widow, "All those people had to do was go and ask him to be quiet and he would have."[1] This unfortunate incident illuminates the desperate need for increased conflict resolution skills within the community.

One site where that need is being met is Our Family Services (OF), a joint venture of Our Town Mediation Services and the Family Counseling Agency. Active in Pima County for over seventy-five years, OF serves more than 35,000 people a year.[2] Providing services ranging from counseling to education to mediation, OF has shaped itself around the needs of Tucson residents. Currently, OF offers fifteen programs in areas such as elder care, crisis management, transitional living, disability services, reunification services, parenting education, community mediation, and school mediation education.[3] Whereas all of these programs contribute valuable services, the mediation program has been especially effective at improving social conditions. Staffed by three full-time employees as well as ten to fifteen volunteers at any given time, the community mediation program provides "safe, neutral and voluntary mediations, in English or Spanish, for a variety of neighbor and family disputes."[4] OF offers comprehensive methods for improving conflict resolution skills using transformative mediation principles. Mediations last approximately two hours, are facilitated by two mediators, and use the "living room" configuration (a spatial organization conducive to community interaction) in order to create an amiable space where community members can comfortably discuss their differences. OF mediations construct important spaces for members of the same community to create productive discussions and preserve relationships.

OF has collaborated with Pima County to establish a transformative mediation program that provides free or low-cost mediation services for property and noise complaints. The most popular collaborative program is with Pima County Animal Care Center and involves individuals who file animal noise complaints toward neighbors. This program creates a great opportunity for neighbors to collaborate on more than just their immediate needs. As the Community Mediation Program director, Andrea Stuart, explains, "Most often it's not about the dogs. There are usually other things that have escalated."[5] Those who file complaints (plaintiffs) can pursue their issues through free, voluntary mediation sessions. If plaintiffs agree to mediation, they contact OF mediation staff, who then contact the animal owners and arrange a mediation session that offers an opportunity for parties to discuss their issues with each other instead of following through with the formal complaint process. The ensuing mediations follow a process conducive to successful collaboration—a process that attempts to transform what Tucson city prosecutor Alan Merritt describes as "the lines of communication [that] are not open between the dog owner and the complainant."[6] An important aspect of the process is that mediators often change parties' attitudes by shifting the frame of reference away from securing agreement, a shift that encourages disputants to feel more in control and begin to listen and learn from each other in new ways.

While the democratic applications of rhetoric continue to provide popular justifications for its teaching, applications to public discourse often end up being reduced to writing letters to the editor, criticizing political propaganda, or critiquing popular ideologies. Our continuing concentration on academic discourse positions our work at a critical distance from rhetoric's professed concern for collective action. Our increased involvement with service learning and community literacy work has been complemented by work with action research and social movement studies. This renewed concern for collective agency has been pivotal to the civic turn in rhetoric and composition that is the subject of this collection of essays. As scholars and teachers, we need to build on these opportunities to consider new ways of thinking about how rhetoric relates to civic participation. We will contribute to this line of discussion by exploring a deliberative domain where we may be able to develop more broadly based engagements with the conflicts that people work with every day. Conflict mediation is one such mode of deliberation in which we may be able to rearticulate a civic vision of rhetoric that makes productive use of the differences that we have come to see as integral to public deliberations.

Conflict mediation provides a purposeful but open-ended mode of engaging with practical deliberations on issues ranging from barking dogs to toxic waste dumps. In "Rhetoric and Conflict Resolution," Richard Lloyd-Jones called for rhetoricians to consider how conflict mediation might help us become more broadly engaged with how people "contextualize conflict so that its energies can be directed toward positive ends."[7] A mediator is a third-party facilitator who does not have the authority to judge opposing arguments and pronounce a verdict. The judicial model of an expert judge overseeing the making of pro and con arguments before an impartial jury has continued to shape our thinking about deliberative inquiries even as we have come to question the foundations of disinterested objectivity. Such questions have prompted the development of models of conflict mediation that are less concerned with preserving impartiality than with investigating the heuristic potentials of differences in assumptions. These developments parallel recent trends in rhetoric and composition, and those parallels can help us to see these continuing trends in a different context, as often proves to be the case when community-based inquiries challenge the presumptions of academic researchers. Such moments have a heuristic potential that conflict mediators have learned to value.

The inventive capacities of conflicted situations are one of the points where trends in rhetoric and composition parallel those in conflict mediation. For example, specific resolution practices like principled negotiation rely on rhetorical strategies to explore the dynamic relations among speakers, audiences, and contested situations. The inventive capacities of such strategies become apparent in places like Tucson, where people are pressed to resolve their differences. Much of the power of classical heuristics arises from their ability to make use of contested situations. As we will discuss, such heuristics have been configured in quite complementary ways by various schools of conflict resolution—most usefully by theories of transformative mediation. This school of conflict mediation challenges people who are enmeshed in conflicts to reflect upon how they can mediate their differences in ways that expand their sense of what can be achieved in the situation. Sites of conflict are central to the civic tradition in rhetorical studies, and those of us who are versed in that tradition have much to offer, and to learn, from those engaged in mediating conflicts in community centers, large organizations, and other sites beyond the academy. Rhetoric's traditional concern for the art of discovering the possibilities of contested situations can be reinvigorated by engaging in work with conflict mediation, especially those approaches that look not simply to resolve differences but to open up their broader possibilities.

REDISCOVERING THE INVENTIVE CAPACITIES OF CONFLICTED SITUATIONS

Recent trends in rhetoric, composition, and a wide range of related fields can be benchmarked by the rediscovery of inventive capacities of conflicted situations. Kenneth Burke challenged rhetoricians to expand the locus of their studies from persuasion to "identification," and his "dramatism" became part of the interpretive frameworks of social movement studies in communications and sociology.[8] Scene-act ratios have also been used by compositionists such as Karen Burke LeFevre; her discussion of "resonance" is congruent with how conflict mediators attempt to help disputants reflect upon how their communities' values frame their decision-making possibilities.[9] Collaborative models of invention have reshaped how we think of writing itself, as can be seen in Jim Corder's writings on "generative ethos" as a means to engage in discovering the possibilities of situations with others.[10] In rhetorical studies, as in conflict mediation, these trends of thought have often been identified with the writings of Carl Rogers. Like Burke, "Rogerian collaborative rhetoric," as Nathaniel Teich has termed it, has served as a resource for developing heuristics that can be used to investigate the transactional potentials of conflicted situations in ways that are less tightly scripted than by the traditional emphasis on persuasion in classical theories of invention.[11]

These familiar theories of invention provide a more open-ended framework for exploring the rhetorical dynamics of conflict mediation. "Conflict resolution" can generally be defined as a variable set of practices concerned with helping disputants reach agreement through noncoercive methods of collaborative inquiry. With clear parallels to our traditional emphasis on argument, the *distributive* model treats conflict resolution as a "zero-sum" game that entails "a competition over who is going to get the most of a limited resource."[12] Here, the mediation process is envisioned as a competition for position, with participants focusing on what they want to achieve if they win out over their opponents.[13] As in rhetoric and composition, this model of conflict resolution has been replaced with approaches that have a more open-ended sense of the process—*integrative* theories of mediation, which look to resolve conflicts in ways that can be mutually beneficial. This school of conflict resolution was popularized in Fisher, Ury, and Patton's *Getting to Yes.*[14] A best seller that has sold over two million copies in twenty-one languages, it attempts to enable people to reimagine conflict in order to work through their differences. The invention strategies are similar to those identified with Rogerian rhetoric, for disputants are encouraged to listen and brainstorm together in order to identify mutual goals. Conflict mediation becomes an invention process concerned with discovering the possibilities of differing interpretations. Integrative theories of conflict resolution enlist invention strategies to help disputants break out of the assumption maintained by distributive negotiations that conflicts inevitably arise over a fixed set of resources to be divided between the disputants.[15] In these and other ways, integrative negotiators enlist invention strategies not to help disputants develop opposing arguments but to rethink the situation itself and their purposes in it.

Distributive and integrative approaches to conflict mediation have striking continuities with how theorists such as Burke and Rogers reframed rhetoric's classical focus on audience, situation, and purpose to develop situated models of purposeful interaction that are more open-ended than traditional conceptions of persuasion. As in composition studies, the counterpoised stances of the critic and the advocate have been replaced within discussions of conflict mediation that have adopted an integrative approach that is less intent on winning and more concerned with listening to others and reaching consensus. However, in both areas the tacitly perpetuated assumption is often that conflicts are to be resolved as quickly as possible so that people can move on to better things. This conception of conflict has lost its standing in both composition and conflict mediation. Rogerian rhetoric and an unproblematized faith in collaborative inquiry lost their standing in rhetoric and com position as we became attuned to how liberal models of building *consensus* often function to make a virtue of the power of persuasion. Consensus lost its authority among many practitioners when critics of collaborative learning called upon teachers and researchers to attend to how prevailing hierarchies are perpetuated by pressing diverging points of view to be reasonable and accept the will of the group. Critics such as John Trimbur argued that opposing views can be better sustained and valued for their inventive capacities when "dissensus" is seen as a productive part of a healthy discussion about conflicted issues.[16] In rhetoric and composition, as in conflict mediation, we have become suspicious of the idea that collaborations should work toward consensus as we have learned to value the generative capacities of our differences. Fortunately, conflict mediation offers such models of collaborative inquiry, which have expanded as we have looked beyond the classroom to community-based research projects. The work of Linda Flower aptly documents these possibilities, as we discuss after we consider another school of conflict mediation that provides a complementary model to the concern for "dissensus" in rhetoric and composition.[17]

Transformative Mediation as a Model
for Learning from "Dissensus"

Insofar as we have become suspicious of consensus, we are likely to be critical of the collaborative presuppositions of integrative conflict resolution, such as Fisher, Ury, and Patton's advice on audience or reframing as a process of invention. Such thinking suggests an unproblematized concern for consensus that tends to isolate conflicts from broader contexts that raise complicated issues that may require mediators to confront broader inequities and hierarchies. For example, *Getting to Yes* offers four strategies—such as "separate the people from the problem" and "focus on interests, not positions"—to help disputants reconcile differences in order to reach agreement.[18] Even though these suggestions are oriented to mediating differences rather than winning out over others, these collaborative strategies mirror recent attempts to adapt classical rhetoric to a more liberal orientation on learning. They are concerned with solving problems, not with changing situations or using the collaborative process as an opportunity to explore the potentials of collective action among people who may face problems not of their own making. As a result, integrative as well as distributive mediation strategies tend to manage conflicts in ways that do not challenge prevailing assumptions or help groups develop social capital through productive collaborations, and thereby develop coalitions to advance broader changes.

Such mediation practices may help people improve their immediate situations but may not help them understand the conditions that led to the conflicts. In fact, some resolution strategies are specifically intended to help people focus on the immediate problem and ignore broader factors. Concern for solving immediate problems is pushed to the forefront, eliminating chances to learn the broader contributing factors. Because agreement is the main goal, mediators do not focus on developing disputants' abilities to develop a sense of common cause. Some mediation practitioners, however, do attempt to address underlying inequities by envisioning conflict resolution not as a means to an immediate end but as part of a broader process concerned with enabling communities to discover the inventive capacities of their shared traditions and build up social capital by working through collaborations.

The most popular alternative approach is known as "transformative mediation." It is guided by a vision of collaboration as a means to help people gain more control over their situations and create alternative resolutions. This school of conflict mediation was developed by Robert Bush and Joseph Folger and articulated in their *The Promise of Mediation: Responding to Conflict through Empowerment and Recognition* and their revised version, *The Promise of Mediation: The Transformative Approach to Conflict*. These texts redefine the mediation process and mediator roles and provide case studies and commentaries concerned with helping mediators to serve as collaborative educators by emphasizing relationship building over settlement. Bush, Rains Distinguished Professor of Alternative Dispute Resolution Law at Hofstra University School of Law, and Folger, professor of Adult and Organizational Development at Temple University, offer a vision of mediation that moves beyond contemporary mediators' desires to increase satisfaction with dispute resolution or provide collective opportunities for community members. Transformative mediators treat conflict not as something that must be solved but as an opportunity to change disputants' interpretive schema. This approach opens up opportunities for mediations to position the particular problem in broader contexts and try to provide a constructive atmosphere where disputants can air shared needs.

Perhaps the most important characteristic of transformative mediation is its redefinition of the purposes at issue in conflicted situations. The goal is not resolution, or agreement, but transformation. According to Bush and Folger, "transformation" does not refer to a general reallocation of resources or restructuring of schema but a "change in the quality of social interaction, in and beyond conflict."[19] Transformative mediators attempt to change the way people understand conflict from negative and destructive to instructive and creative. Once disputants recognize conflict as "an emergent, dynamic phenomenon, in which parties can—and do—move and shift," they are more willing to participate in generative invention processes.[20] Disputants learn to appreciate the mediation process as an opportunity to expand inventive strategies by collaborating with others. Consistent with this framework, transformative mediation offers a practical framework for improving people's strategies for addressing conflicts. Similar to problem-solving mediators, transformative mediators follow a general outline; however, transformative mediators expand invention strategies by pursuing four different goals: released process control in which disputants learn how to learn from conflict, expanded information gathering that may open up broader avenues of thinking about the issue, improved collaboration through recognizing mutual constraints and shared needs, and personal shifts in viewpoint that may arise as people learn that what may have appeared to be interpersonal conflicts arise from the structures of situations or the assumptions imposed upon them.

By beginning with questions about how the mediation process should proceed, transformative mediators seek to enable the sort of collaborative invention processes that LeFevre has studied. Whereas problem-solving mediators begin by setting out a formal multistage process, transformative mediators delegate control of the process to disputants. As explained by Bush and Folger, mediators "let the parties know that they can design the process as it unfolds."[21] Much as critical pedagogues begin by challenging students to become more actively involved in shaping assignments and expectations, disputants are encouraged to envision the situation as they see fit and bring in cultural values and social practices from their backgrounds that might foster a more collaborative environment. For example, because disputants control introductions, they can frame a conflict by acknowledging significant moral beliefs that affect their perspective and the purposes they envision. By creating a participatory environment, transformative mediators attempt to open up the situation to encourage participants to articulate how their stance is consistent with the beliefs of the groups with which they identify. Through these broader identifications, participants can tap into commonplaces and topoi that may serve as productive resources for rethinking the issues at hand. Reframing conflicts in these ways can enable people to understand how others think and why they have acted as they have. At the same time, the speakers are presented with opportunities to reflect upon how well their traditional assumptions speak to the situation and their changing needs.

The four transformative criteria—released process control, expanded information-gathering, improved collaboration, and personal shifts—expand disputants' discovery processes: by gaining control of the mediation process, disputants can identify concerns and topics specific to their situation; through expanded information-gathering processes, disputants include personal and community values; empowerment and recognition help disputants both regain control and acknowledge others; and increased collaboration parallels the dialectic nature of communication. These criteria provide a "rhetorical" sense of mediating differences that has heuristic power in thinking about work in the community and its relevance for broader trends in rhetoric and composition. Instead of simply attempting to resolve disputes, transformative mediation attempts to create a space where disputants can think through their differences to put them to practical use, and not simply to rise above them (as presumed by traditional civic models). This approach has been highly successful in the U.S. Postal Service's national REDRESS mediation program— a program that has been described by the *New York Times* as "one of the most ambitious experiments in dispute resolution in American corporate history"— by creating opportunities for postal employees to control their disputes and participate in the outcomes.[22] Practiced across the country in many of our communities, transformative mediation offers a proven method being that can lead to an improved connection between rhetoric and social change.

A PLACE FOR RHETORIC—TUCSON'S OUR FAMILY COMMUNITY MEDIATION CENTER

Whereas academic scholarship in rhetoric and composition locates places for rhetoric in community writing centers and various genres of public discourse, academics find difficulty speaking the same language as community members. Linda Flower and Julia Deems explain how rhetorical principles from sources such as Aristotle or Perelman carry an "air of book learning" in community settings that can make the principles seem impractical.[23] Additional distractions can arise from class projects and service-learning programs that have a missionary ethos of helping out those in need.[24] Those in rhetoric and composition who are involved with community outreach have struggled to overcome such presuppositions to develop reciprocal relations with varied community members. The language problems involved can be usefully addressed by principles of transformative conflict mediation, which are grounded in concerted efforts to help communities not just resolve but also learn from their problems. Beyond improving interpersonal understanding, transformative mediation can enable collective action by providing skills that can be applied to situations other than the immediate conflicts. People who develop transformative skills like empowerment, recognition, and increased data collection can help their communities develop practical deliberative capacities. Transformative mediation provides valuable transferable skills, not simply to persuade others but also to listen and work with neighbors and members of one's communities in order to act on their shared problems.

Community centers that practice transformative conflict mediation can help to develop people's capacities for collective action. Following upon the landmark Pound Conference of 1976, "Neighborhood Justice Centers" were established in Atlanta, Los Angeles, and Kansas City to put transformative mediation into practice.[25] Following the cities' success, mediation centers and organizations like the National Association for Community Mediation (NACM) became more involved in promoting community interests by strengthening individuals' collaborative skills. NACM's mission is "to preserve individual interests while strengthening relationships and building connections between people and groups, and to create processes that make communities work for all."[26] Over 550 community mediation centers are currently mediating some 50,000 cases a year.[27] This direct connection to communities creates opportunities for mediators to improve social invention strategies. It creates spaces where community members can learn how to better understand differences while focusing on immediate issues. Because transformative community mediators facilitate improved interpersonal interactions, disputants learn how to create similar spaces for working with differences.

After observing several animal noise complaint mediations in the spring of 2006, we witnessed firsthand how community members have gained skills helpful to better negotiating in their daily lives because they have developed rhetorical strategies that empower them to create change. Disputants transformed their conflicted experiences into constructive opportunities to create change. Whereas each mediation session was distinct—ranging from the close quarters of a mobile home park to the homogeneity of suburban gated communities to the isolation of open ranch lands in the foothills—and the varied sessions required different skills, several common characteristics enabled participants to be successful. Mediations succeeded when people overcame misunderstandings of invention, utilized positive physical spaces in which to interact, and developed framing strategies that increased their ability to negotiate differences.

First, disputants learned to work beyond narrow conceptions of the inventive possibilities of conflicts. When explorations of assumptions and needs are confined to the initial stage of the collaborative process, disputants tend to assume that they have thought through the problem and the issue is how to get others to agree with them, as is the case in distributive models of conflict mediation. This narrow conception of invention has been perpetuated, as Jim Corder suggests in *Uses of Rhetoric*, by assumptions that invention precedes deliberation. If the process is divided into five phases (invention, arrangement, style, memory, and delivery), then people tend to assume that one phase precedes the others. People do not anticipate that the process is recursive and not linear. For Corder, such assumptions of "sequentiality" limit people's ability to improve communication by rethinking their intentions.[28] Prior to meeting at OF, disputants tended to assume that the purpose of mediation is to support and defend specific arguments. For example, in a lengthy and contentious mediation between a young couple and a retired U.S. serviceman about three large dogs, disputants had a difficult time working together because they were obsessed with assigning blame. They constantly referred to evidence such as tape recordings, photographs, and personal research, and they read prewritten narrations of their experiences. Once they realized that the process of arguing back and forth was leading nowhere, they become more interested in rethinking their positions.

Second, disputants learned the values of the using the mediation process to step back from their conflicted relations and interact more constructively. The mediation space enabled them to assume different roles and relations. Because boundaries such as property lines and privacy walls often separate people's public and private lives, people are accustomed to dividing their interpersonal interactions. In a growing metropolis such as Tucson, residents are often separated from their immediate communities. Be it on open ranch lands or in trailer parks, disputants often understand private space in ways that limit their opportunities to interact productively. Using the "living room" model of spatial organization that places disputants on equal footing, transformative mediation sessions take place in a comfortable room where participants sit close to each other and chairs are arranged in a semicircle with no structures or tables acting as dividers. Consequently, brainstorming sessions are highly interactive and foster collaboration. When a whiteboard is used, mediators do not dichotomize issues by dividing sides but instead use writing as a collaborative product. For example, during collective brainstorming sessions, mediators record disputants' suggestions in the middle of the board, without dividing the sides. In one vertical column, disputants' ideas exist together as they share the process of invention.

Within their communities, individuals can collaborate in spaces where they can mutually discuss issues and create change. In these spaces different ideas gain capital through what LeFevre describes as "resonance," a term she borrows from Harold Laswell.[29] As LeFevre explains, "Resonance comes about when an individual act—a 'vibration'—is intensified and prolonged by sympathetic vibrations . . . when people provide a supportive social and intellectual environment that nurtures thought and enables ideas to be received, thus completing the inventive act."[30] Resonance, therefore, results from direct and indirect communication. OF mediators create environments that support resonance by establishing collaboration. Oftentimes this involves reminding individuals of who their audience really is—*each other*. For example, within several minutes of a mediation session involving retirees who had severed all communication among each other, OF mediators often reminded the disputants that they should talk to each other instead of talking to the mediator. Once people begin addressing each other, they become more capable of working together. Recognition of the other party immediately changes people's tone as they begin to take control of their own situations.

Finally, disputants learned the importance of framing and reframing conflicts. In conflict mediations, analyses of frames and efforts to reframe issues can help people construct more productive ways of seeing a problem. Reframing, as explained by Kovach, helps mediators explain "the disputed issues of the parties in more neutral manner, in such a way that the parties begin to focus on potential outcomes."[31] OF mediators reframe issues in order to clarify points and help people gain alternative perspectives, to filter out negative language and select more neutral terms so that disputants can see a situation differently. Successful reframing helps disputants shift their interpretive schema, and such shifts often form turning points in collaborations. As Beer and Steif discuss, at such a point disputants gain new perspective and begin to see through a different lens: they "shift from presenting their conflict as stories and positions to viewing the situation as a set of specific interests, principles, and mediatable issues."[32] As linguist George Lakoff explains, reframing is an important step in creating change because reframing changes how people see the world: "It is changing what counts as common sense."[33] Community mediation centers are important sites for creating such change. Community centers like OF help people develop skills that they can use in their public lives. Transformative mediation—as it is practiced at OF—helps participants reenvision rhetoric as a mode of collective deliberation and conflict mediation. Such sites have much to teach us about how to reframe our own concerns in ways that might be more broadly useful to our students, for the collaborative inquiries at OF provide frameworks for thinking about argument, inquiry, and purpose in ways that can help us break out of the constraints that have come to be assumed in rhetoric and composition classes.

TRANSFORMATIVE MEDIATION IN THE CLASSROOM

To contribute to efforts to integrate outreach into instruction, we want to sketch out how scenario-based classroom assignments can help students develop strategies to engage in conflict mediation and other community learning processes. Working with scenarios in the classroom is not an alternative to service-learning assignments, but it can be a useful complement to them. By centering the class on a shared deliberative process, teachers and students can gain experience in working with the practical strategies and ethical issues that are likely to come up in community-based learning activities. By work-ing with each other in collaborative learning scenarios, students can gain skills such as empowerment and recognition while developing improved invention strategies vital to their academic success and civic literacies. Based on experi-ences from OF mediations, these two scenarios provide students with oppor-tunities to collaborate and practice important rhetorical skills, which can then be developed through service-learning assignments, internships, and other collaborations beyond the classroom.

"Showdown in Superior!"

"Showdown in Superior!" was a set of course-long assignments developed with three collaborating classes at the University of Arizona in the fall of 2005.[34] Several writing instructors created a scenario to have students work together to resolve a community dispute. Codesigned by Erik Juergensmeyer, David Reamer, and Brian Jackson, the unit combined an honors first-year composition class with business and technical writing classes to deliberate upon a regional mining issue in Superior, Arizona, a town that is two hours away from the University of Arizona campus. The curriculum asked students to work together and research, present, and deliberate upon how the mining issue will affect the town's residents. Students wrote such assignments as researched essays, letters to the editor, pamphlets, Web sites, and so on. These writings were circulated among the three classes in preparation for a mock town hall meeting. At the end of the semester, all three classes met together in a large lecture hall, presented their cases through PowerPoint presentations and public speeches, discussed the different issues and affected groups, and eventually voted on whether to support the copper company's mining pro-posal.

All three classes had distinct roles in the project. The technical writing class represented a local copper company looking to extract copper from Superior's vast reserves. As representatives of the mining company, they pre-pared Web sites, brochures, newsletters, and oral presentations that blended technical information with reasoned arguments encouraging the townspeo-ple to approve the mining project. Students who took on these roles were put in the position of defending their positions amid opposition from special interest groups and demonstrating their goodwill. Students in Erik's business writing class took on the role of several special interest groups that opposed the mining company's bid. Role-playing as local and national groups, stu-dents prepared professional documents arguing against permitting the min-ing project in Superior. They discussed their sides with employees of the copper company and attempted to convince town residents that they too were concerned with the town's best interests. Finally, the first-year honors class assumed the role of the townspeople of Superior. As townspeople, they wrote imaginary letters to Superior's newspaper, speeches for the town hall meeting, and researched reports advocating that the town pursue a specific course of action.

During the semester, the students' deliverables were both engaged and specific. In Erik's business writing class, for example, student groups created fictitious organizations and focused on realistic viewpoints within a community. One group interested in studying law established the RACB (an acronym derived from students' first names) law firm, "a local law firm that has been serving the citizens and businesses of Superior since October 2005," "a small agency with a big mission and a lot of ground to cover." After researching the specific geographical and environmental components of the mine proposal, RACB immediately identified their focus on a brochure intended for indifferent townspeople: "We are committed to preserving Oak Flat Campground, Devil's Canyon, Queen Creek Canyon and Apache Leap for the benefit of this and future generations." RACB espoused a mission of equal importance: "We are working in the best interest of the city of Superior, providing knowledge and education to its citizens."

Another student group, operating under the acronym SAERG (Southern Arizona Economic Resources Group), focused on citizens of the town of Superior opposed to the mining project. In an informational brochure, students of SAERG implored citizens to be more active in their community beliefs. Under a section entitled "What you can do," they provided several steps:

> If you believe that RCC [Resolution Cooper Corporation] has no business in your town, then vote "No" in the town hall meeting next week. Now is the time to take a stand and fight. Here are a few things you can do:
> *Spread the word!* Tell your friends and family about the economic dangers of the RCC project. Urge them to spread the word.
> *Make your voice known.* There are many ways in which you can partner up with local or national interest groups that will side with you against RCC. Rally your fellow citizens, start a petition, do whatever it takes.

For students in SAERG, civic participation involves both negotiating through community interests and developing integrative skills that can help town citizens mobilize their interests. It also involves actively participating in community discourse and conflict.

The semester-long project culminated in a mock town hall meeting where all three groups, who had been exchanging research and documents, met for the first time and discussed their differing positions. Following PowerPoint presentations from the students role-playing as the mining company and special interest groups, members from all three classes joined small group collaborative sessions to discuss the issues in further detail. These groups of approximately twenty-five students (roughly one-third from each class) offered physical spaces for people to discuss the different positions and further explain why they took their specific views on the mining proposal. Similar to the mediation rooms at OF, these spaces created opportunities for role-players both to collect data and recognize others' needs. After deliberations, all classes reconvened, and the townspeople took the stage, where they discussed what they had learned from talking one-on-one with the interest group and mining company representatives. Attempting to persuade their peers, different townspeople explained their sides and eventually voted for an appropriate course of action—in this case, opposing the mining company's bid.

"Showdown in Superior!" created an opportunity for the transformation of both invention and collaboration strategies. It provided a comfortable environment for students to discuss their different views and listen to their opponents in order to resolve conflicts. With the townspeople serving as mediators, the small group deliberative sessions paralleled transformative mediation sessions where people control the agenda and discuss whatever issues they think are relevant to the case at hand. Modeled after the transformative principle of avoiding caucusing, these sessions created a place where invention is not limited to the beginning of one's arguments and people can work together to actually invent new understandings and resolutions. Students both became empowered through documents and presentations and also recognized others by working together and listening to alternative views on their issues—views expressed by real people seated next to them. They learned conflict resolution strategies that will help them examine and better negotiate their differences.

BREAKING THROUGH THE BORDER

Building on their experiences in "Showdown in Superior!" Erik Juergensmeyer and David Reamer joined with colleague Leslie Dupont to create another scenario designed to foster transformative mediation and rhetorical invention in a border town. Occurring during fall 2006, "Breaking through the Border" asked professional writing students to research, represent, and collaboratively discuss current issues at the Mexico-Arizona border, with particular consideration of how these issues affect Tucson residents. Students confronted challenging issues that were both close to their lives and represented potentially intractable conflicts—scenarios where they could apply transformative mediation strategies to create change. Ultimately, students had to suggest a specific course of action, such as increased border security or humanitarian support, that would influence local and state agencies. Students from Erik's business writing class researched and represented issues from the border debate based on their social impact on Tucson citizens. Representing different groups, these students created mission statements, brochures, and informational letters detailing their claims. Students from David's technical writing class researched and represented issues based on their economic impact on

Tucson citizens. Representing different groups, these students created brochures and Web pages detailing their claims. Student's from Leslie's business writing class, role-playing as professional writers commissioned to write a proposal to the legislature, read and listened to the other classes' sides and created proposals attempting to represent as many interests as possible.

Throughout the semester, students from all classes met in two "forums" where they discussed their different research and attempted to influence final proposals. At the first forum meeting, David's and Erik's students presented on social and economic impacts in the hopes of convincing Leslie's students that their particular views of the border issue were relevant. Following Power-Point presentations, students joined small group deliberative sessions in order to further discuss their presentations and answer any questions that might have arisen. At the second forum meeting, Leslie's students presented their proposals to David's and Erik's students, who hoped to have their views represented. David's and Erik's students voted on which proposal best represented the border dispute. Building on the previous project's strengths and addressing its weakness, "Breaking through the Border" focused more on collaboration and open invention. Most important, we eschewed the town hall model used in "Showdown" because we believed it created a physical space that encouraged division and competition as the townspeople became consumed with critically analyzing each side's research. We instead designed two forum meetings where students presented and discussed their research with the hopes of influencing others' work. Whereas the one meeting of "Showdown" culminated in a thumbs-up or thumbs-down vote, the forums of "Breaking" espoused a generative and informational environment. Students provided research to their peers and used data gathering and collaboration as ways to expand invention. We also realized that assigning sides to the two classes in Showdown (pro- or antimining) was too prescriptive. So, for "Breaking" we let students create their own groups. Whereas we restricted one class to "social" and one to "economic" impact to avoid repetition, we found students more invested in their arguments as they represented their personal beliefs. They were also more creative as they could research different viewpoints and proposals to create their side and proposed course of action. Enabling open invention of groups expanded "the pie" by letting students create possible solutions that were not confined to our categories.

When questioned about the project's strengths in a follow-up questionnaire, students described "a sense of purpose with assignments," an appreciation for "working together in a group and doing good research together," and a "fun atmosphere [that] provided for learning and using collaboration while recognizing a specific audience." Several even suggested the experience was "exciting." Finally, when asked about what was learned in "Showdown," one student noticed an increased ability to "find relevant points in any side I choose to take and different ways of looking at the given information."[35]

Similar to the comfortable spaces of mediation, the nonhierarchical settings of "Showdown in Superior!" and "Breaking through the Barriers"—places where students sat together during presentations and collaborated face-to-face in small group deliberative sessions—created valuable experiences for learning how to be both rhetors and citizens. By creating similar projects, teachers can connect students to community issues, helping them negotiate through the conflicts that often limit collective action.

CONCLUSION

In the realm of public dispute resolution, rhetoric both provides useful frameworks for approaching conflicts as well as specific strategies for improving people's abilities to resolve those conflicts. Looking at mediation through the lens of rhetorical invention can improve conflict resolution strategies. Likewise, similar to many of the most useful dimensions of rhetoric, conflict resolution provides new ways to understand the rhetorical tradition and its applications in the classroom as well as community. Our positions as teachers of rhetoric and composition do more than help us profess important communication and persuasive skills. They provide opportunities for us to reconnect to and participate in our immediate communities. These connections can help us challenge the misconceptions that have limited our ways of discovering solutions to conflicted situations. By focusing on invention and its possibilities for improving conflict resolution practices, we are better equipped to demonstrate how the arts of rhetoric move beyond mere persuasion and create increased opportunities for social change.

NOTES

1. Poole, "When Neighbors Collide."
2. "Our Family Services," para. 7.
3. "Our Family Services, Programs."
4. "Our Family Services, Community Mediation," para. 1.
5. Poole, "When Neighbors Collide."
6. Kelly, "Taxpayer Watch," para. 4.
7. Lloyd-Jones, "Rhetoric and Conflict," 173.
8. Burke, *Rhetoric of Motives.*
9. LeFevre, *Invention,* 65.
10. Corder, "Varieties."
11. Teich, *Rogerian Perspectives,* 3–4.
12. Lewicki et al., *Negotiation,* 74.
13. Kovach, *Mediation.*
14. Fisher, Ury, and Patton, *Getting to Yes.*
15. Lewicki et al., *Negotiation.*
16. Trimbur, "Consensus."
17. See Flower, "Partners"; Flower and Deems, "Conflict."
18. Fisher, Ury, and Patton, *Getting to Yes,* 17–81.
19. Bush and Folger, *Transformative Approach,* 18.
20. Ibid., 55.

21. Ibid., 109.
22. Meece, "Companies Adopting," para. 3.
23. Flower and Deems, "Conflict," 98.
24. Flower, "Partners."
25. Kovach, *Mediation*, 21.
26. NACM, "Overview," para. 1.
27. Ibid.
28. Corder, *Uses of Rhetoric*, esp. 49–50.
29. LeFevre, *Invention;* Laswell, "Social Setting."
30. LeFevre, *Invention*, 65.
31. Kovach, *Mediation*, 50.
32. Beer and Steif, *Handbook*, 113.
33. Lakoff, *Don't Think*, 15.
34. Jackson, Juergensmeyer, and Reamer, "Showdown."
35. Ibid., para. 20–22.

Works Cited

Antes, James. "Ten Years after the Promise of Mediation: A Report from the First National Conference on Transformative Mediation." Mediate.com. http://mediate.com/articles/antesj1.cfm# (accessed October 14, 2008).

Beer, Jennifer E., and Eileen Steif. *The Mediator's Handbook.* Gabriola Island, B.C.: New Society, 1997.

Benford, Robert D., and David A. Snow. "Framing Processes and Social Movements: An Overview and Assessment." *Annual Review of Sociology* 26 (2000): 611–39.

Burke, Kenneth. *A Grammar of Motives.* Berkeley: University of California Press, 1945.

———. *A Rhetoric of Motives.* Berkeley: University of California Press, 1950.

Bush, Robert A. Baruch, and Joseph P. Folger. *The Promise of Mediation: Responding to Conflict through Empowerment and Recognition.* San Francisco: Jossey-Bass, 1994.

———. *The Promise of Mediation: The Transformative Approach to Conflict.* Revised ed. San Francisco: Jossey-Bass, 2005.

Corder, Jim. "Argument as Emergence, Rhetoric as Love." *Rhetoric Review* 4 (1985): 16–32.

———. *Uses of Rhetoric.* Philadelphia: J. B. Lippincott, 1971.

———. "Varieties of Ethical Argument, with Some Account of the Significance of *Ethos* in the Teaching of Composition." *Freshman English News* 6, no. 3 (1978): 1–23.

Fisher, Roger, William Ury, and Bruce Patton. *Getting to Yes.* 2nd ed. New York: Penguin, 1991.

Flower, Linda. "Partners in Inquiry." In *Writing the Community: Concepts and Models for Service-Learning in Composition,* edited by Linda Adler-Kassner, Robert Crooks, and Ann Watters, 95–117. Urbana, Ill.: National Council of Teachers of English, 1997.

Flower, Linda, and Julia Deems. "Conflict in Community Collaboration." In *Perspectives on Rhetorical Invention,* edited by Janet M. Atwill and Janice M. Lauer, 96–130. Knoxville: University of Tennessee Press, 2002.

Hallberlin, Cynthia J. "Transforming Workplace Culture through Mediation: Lessons Learned from Swimming Upstream." *Hofstra Labor and Employment Law Journal* (Spring 2001): 375–83.

Hodges, Ann C. "Mediation and the Transformation of American Labor Unions." *Missouri Law Review* (Spring 2004): 365–439.

Jackson, Brian, Erik Juergensmeyer, and David Reamer. "Showdown in Superior! A Three Class Collaborative Course Design." *Composition Studies* 33, no. 2 (2005). http://www

.compositionstudies.tcu.edu/coursedesigns/online/34-2/Showdown%20in%20
Superior.html (accessed October 14, 2008).

Kelly, Andrea. "Taxpayer Watch: City's Answer to Noisy-Dog Complaints Is Mediation."
Arizona Daily Star, June 4, 2005. http://www.azstarnet.com/sn/ taxpayerwatch/ 91778
(accessed October 14, 2008).

Kovach, Kimberlee K. *Mediation in a Nutshell*. St. Paul, Minn.: West Group, 2003.

Lakoff, George. *Don't Think of an Elephant! Know Your Values and Frame the Debate*. White
River Jct., Vt.: Chelsea Green, 2004.

Laswell, Harold D. "The Social Setting of Creativity." In *Creativity and Its Cultivation*,
edited by Harold H. Anderson, 203–21. New York: Harper and Brothers, 1959.

LeFevre, Karen Burke. *Invention as a Social Act*. Carbondale: Southern Illinois University
Press, 1987.

Lewicki, Roy J., Bruce Barry, David M. Saunders, and John W. Minton. *Negotiation*. 4th
ed. New York: McGraw-Hill/Irwin, 2003.

Lloyd-Jones, Richard. "Rhetoric and Conflict Resolution." In *Beyond Postprocess an Postmodernism: Essays on the Spaciousness of Rhetoric*, edited by Theresa Enos and Keith D.
Miller, 171–84. Matweh, N.J.: Erlbaum, 2003.

Meece, Mickey. "Companies Adopting Postal Service Grievance Process." Indiana Conflict Resolution Institute. http://www.spea.indiana.edu/icri/ nytsepa.htm (accessed
October 14, 2008).

National Association for Community Mediation. "Overview of Community Mediation." http://www.nafcm.org/pg5.cfm (accessed October 14, 2008).

Our Family Services. http://www.ourfamilyservices.org/ (accessed October 14, 2008).

———. "Community Mediation." http://www.ourfamilyservices.org/programs/prog005
.html (accessed October 14, 2008).

———. "Programs." http://www.ourfamilyservices.org/programs.html (accessed October 14, 2008).

Poole, B. "When Neighbors Collide." *Tucson Citizen*, July 14, 2006.

Teich, Nathaniel. *Rogerian Perspectives: Collaborative Rhetoric for Oral and Written Communication*. Norwood, N.J.: Ablex, 1992.

Trimbur, John. "Consensus and Difference in Collaborative Learning." *College English*
51 (1989): 602–16.

U.S. Postal Service. "REDRESS." http://www.usps.com/redress/research.htm (accessed
October 14, 2008).

A Place for the Dissident Press in a Rhetorical Education

"Sending up a signal flare in the darkness"

DIANA GEORGE AND PAULA MATHIEU

A rhetorical education enables people to engage in and change American society—but not always.[1]

Resistance is sending up a signal flare in the darkness.[2]

In 2007 the Council of Writing Program Administrators sponsored a Modern Language Association (MLA) session asking, essentially, "Should academic or public writing constitute the focus of a first-year composition course today?"[3] It is an important question, one that might easily send composition scholars and teachers back to an observation Jim Berlin and others made many years ago, that any rhetoric arises out of a time, a place, and a social context. In that way, a rhetoric is always situated, "always related to larger social and political developments," and so a composition course needs to acknowledge that situatedness, by recognizing that no language, no rhetoric, is ever innocent, ever free of the politics and culture from which it emerges.[4] That question—public or academic—suggests, however, there might be a clear-cut choice: we either teach students to understand and use the language of the academy, or we turn to a different kind of rhetorical education entirely. To a large extent, that concern over what to teach has been the dilemma of first-year composition all along, though at times the proposed opposition has been academic preparedness versus private expression. For our purposes here, then, the question is not so much academic versus public writing but, instead, why is public writing often considered, if not out of bounds, at least not quite worthy of the college classroom? Moreover, if we choose to teach public writing—as many of us do—just what public writing do we teach? Do we teach the rhetoric of electoral politics, the language of corporate structures, the appeal of nonprofits? What about the rhetoric that students are warned against—the bare outrage of radical politics? What is the rhetoric our students need for this time, in this place?

To put all of this in a more direct light: as the two of us write this piece, we are living in a country at war—a war argued for and made possible by *public* debates and shoddy news reporting. (Witness, for example, the *New York Times*'s 2004 apology for not carefully investigating the Bush administration's claims of weapons of mass destruction inside Iraq.)[5] We are in a country where, according to the National Coalition for the Homeless, requests for emergency shelter have increased in some cities by as much as 24 percent in the just this past year (2007), while a number of those same cities (Atlanta and Orlando are two examples) have passed legislation to restrict the distribution of food to people who are homeless. These ordinances were voted on and approved, we presume, after *public* arguments made to legislatures and their constituents about homelessness, the nature of homeless persons, and the need to do something. The National Coalition for the Homeless tells us:

> The motivations behind city food sharing restrictions vary as greatly as the tactics themselves. For instance, some cities view the restrictions as a way to channel charitable activities through designated organizations and institutions that provide services. Other food sharing restrictions seem geared toward moving homeless persons out of downtown areas and away from tourist and business locations. Finally, some cities' restrictions demonstrate an open hostility to the presence of homeless persons anywhere in the city limits.[6]

We are in a country at a time when the general population does not trust its leaders or its traditional sources of news and information. According to the Pew Project for Excellence in Journalism, the number of regular viewers of television news and readers of newspapers who actually trust these outlets to give them reliable news has dropped by 10 percentage points in the past decade. The number of readers who have turned to Internet blogs as their primary source of news has risen almost as sharply. The same report found that even the journalists writing the stories are skeptical of the media's reliability.[7]

Admittedly there is little new in a claim that writing courses, in particular, have typically responded to the pull of contemporary politics, changing classroom demographics, economic down- and upturns, and more. The semantics movement of the 1940s and 1950s, for example, has often been credited to the propaganda-soaked conclusion of World War II, the beginnings of the Korean War, the paranoia of the McCarthy era, and the sudden entrance of television into homes across the country. Later, in the shadow of the Vietnam War, campus protests, and, eventually, the disillusionment of Watergate, it is no surprise that writing classrooms turned to the importance of the individual and individual expression as one primary lesson in this course.[8] As well, a number of scholars have observed that composition took what has often been called a "social turn" in the 1980s.[9] Most recently, perhaps as a logical extension of that social turn, we have begun to hear increased calls for attention to public rhetoric or public writing—calls that might easily be read as a rhetorical turn, or, to put it more accurately, *a rhetorical return*—a turn back to questions and lessons that locate writing instruction at the heart of at least one rhetorical tradition: preparing students for participation in civic life. The question that arises in that rhetorical re-turn, if we might call it that, is how a rhetorical education might embrace not only the social or political structure at hand but also the rhetoric of those outside that structure arguing for change. Is there a place, even or especially in calls for public or civic rhetoric, for a rhetoric of dissent?

We opened this article with a brief passage from Glenn, Lyday, and Sharer's *Rhetorical Education in America*. In that collection of essays, Glenn reminds us that traditionally, a rhetorical education was meant to enable citizens "to engage and change American society—but not always."[10] Glenn's "not always" is a useful caveat in her discussion because she follows it by tracing the historical trajectory of a rhetorical education in the United States geared to enable those already in power—white, privileged, and (for a very long time) male. This was a rhetorical education generally inaccessible to anyone outside the halls of power and privilege. It was also a rhetorical education that would not have drawn upon the kinds of public writing or civic rhetoric that have, for decades, moved the public to action: the dissident press.

When, for example, African American abolitionists Samuel Cornish and John Russwurm wrote, in the 1827 inaugural issue of *Freedom's Journal*, the first African American–owned and –operated paper in this country, "We wish to plead our own cause," they were addressing those very rhetors who (even with good intentions) had for too many years been speaking for and about them.[11] That belief in the power of language to do something—change minds, form coalitions, uncover lies—is at the center of dissident movements throughout history. It is also at the heart of any rhetorical education, and especially one that seeks to engage in public writing or public rhetoric.

It is in this context that we explore the role of what Glenn calls "nontraditional rhetors"—in this case, the dissident press—in a rhetorical education.[12] In what follows, we offer an examination of just what the dissident press is, what constitutes a rhetoric of dissent, and what role the dissident press has played in social and political movements of all sorts. In particular, we focus on *"Hobo" News* (1915–1929 in its initial iteration) as the sort of small, special interest dissident paper that can, as Tony Kushner writes, send up "a signal flare in the darkness," the kind of paper (and rhetoric) often ignored, even reviled in the writing course.[13]

WHAT IS THE DISSIDENT PRESS?

Ordinarily, one particular rhetoric is dominant—the rhetoric embodying the ideology of a powerful group or class—but the exclusion of all other rhetorics is never completely achieved, not even in a totalitarian state where the effort to do so is common. . . . A democracy, however, ordinarily provides political and social supports for open discussion, allowing for the free play of possibilities in the rhetorics that appear— although these possibilities are obviously never unlimited.[14]

According to journalism scholar Lauren Kessler, the mainstream press in the United States has never represented an open marketplace of ideas, where a diversity of opinion is tolerated and circulated.[15] Kessler argues that historical studies overwhelmingly show that the U.S. mainstream press has consistently spoken for the "homogenous middle" and thus has been a closed marketplace of ideas, with access routinely denied to those holding aberrant or unpopular beliefs.[16] This denial of access—especially to blacks, abolitionists, working-class radicals, labor organizers, feminists, utopians, pacifists, gay and lesbian groups, and homeless advocates, among others—results from such groups being excluded entirely in the press or by the press selectively covering their disruptive events (such as demonstrations or strikes) but not their goals or ideals. Such coverage often even ridicules and stereotypes the philosophies and positions of such groups. Mainstream news media tend to focus on events ("if it bleeds, it leads"), not issues, further marginalizing groups seeking to circulate new ideas to a broader public.

Denied access to the established media, a vast and varied assortment of fringe groups initiate publications of their own. Such publications often begin because of the financial support of one or a few people working on a shoestring budget, and many continue to struggle with financial problems throughout their runs. Some writers and editors have faced government harassment or have been ostracized by others in their communities. Many publications have started and stopped suddenly, as funds run out, public pressures change, or the issues begin to receive broader, more balanced coverage in the popular press. Kessler importantly notes that the fringe publications she studied—papers linked to social movements like the New Harmony Community's *New Harmony Gazette* or the agrarian revolt–inspired *National Economist*—were typically as closed to ideas at odds with their own group's beliefs as was the mainstream press.[17]

The difference, it seems, is that dissident publications have embraced their situatedness, never claiming to be broad-based or inclusive. In fact, according to Kessler's study, many dissident press writers were—and are—simultaneously those who lead a movement and who write about it. The dissident press, then, does not pretend objectivity. It does not seek to cover a wide array of issues, nor does it prize disinterest or balanced reporting. In other words, dissident publications are and have always been nakedly rhetorical, with the real and concrete aim of having their words and ideas *do* something, to *make changes* in the broader world.

In order to make changes, dissident publications have sought both to speak passionately to an audience of their believers and to educate and persuade a broader public about their issues and alternative ways of understanding those issues. Achieving these goals of a more focused and a broader readership at once has been difficult, practically as well as rhetorically. In practical terms, reaching a broad audience with limited resources and distribution networks is extraordinarily difficult; rhetorically, writing both for those deeply committed and those indifferent or unaware of a cause represents a tricky challenge. As a result, sometimes the writing in dissident press papers is uneven or inconsistent; some pieces are quite heated and polemical while others seek to introduce issues or provide evidence to argue for a cause.

Despite the ongoing material and ideological problems of circulating unpopular views in what might be called undiplomatic language, the dissident press in the United States has often managed to successfully circulate and eventually normalize issues that once might have seemed radical or out of bounds. Until dissident publications began championing them, for example, causes like the abolition of slavery, women's rights, or education about AIDS received little to no mention in mainstream publications. Because of these and other examples, journalism scholar Rodger Streitmatter argues that the dissident press has "been instrumental in shaping the history of this nation." He goes as far as to assert that "a strong argument can be made that the dissident press has played a more vital role in shaping American history than has the mainstream press."[18] If this is true, then it would follow that studying the rhetorical strategies and force of a dissident press, both contemporary and historical, would and should occupy a central place in a classroom devoted to rhetorical education. What might such study entail?

A Rhetoric of Dissent

Political theorist Iris Marion Young writes that rhetoric—"the way claims and reasons are stated"—occurs in all sorts of public address, including, Young writes, "the affective dimensions of communication, its figurative aspects, and the diverse media of communication—placards and street theatre instead of tabloids or reports. Rhetoric has the important function of *situating* those seeking to persuade others in relation to their audience."[19] Young thus reminds us that rhetoric is inherently *situational*. That is, in responding to a particular need/argument/event and aiming to persuade a particular audience, rhetoric must be grounded in the situation at hand.

While it might seem common sense, then, that anyone trying to persuade an audience to support an unpopular cause or radical social change would want to write with a measure of caution, an ear to a broad audience in need of convincing, the rhetoric of dissent is anything but cautious. What, for example, might we make of a newspaper or magazine that introduces itself in this way:

> This Magazine is Owned and Published Co-operatively by its Editors. It has no Dividends to Pay, and nobody is trying to make Money out of it.

A Revolutionary and not a Reform Magazine; a Magazine with a Sense of Humor and no Respect for the Respectable; Frank; Arrogant; Impertinent; Searching for the True Cause; a Magazine Directed against Rigidity and Dogma wherever it is found; Printing what is too Naked or True for a Money-Making Press; a Magazine whose final Policy is to do as it Pleases and Conciliate Nobody, not even its Readers—A Free Magazine.[20]

With this masthead boast, the *Masses*, an early-twentieth-century socialist magazine, declared itself beholden to no one, a magazine "searching for the true cause," a "revolutionary" magazine presumably uninterested in "reform," a magazine free from the constraints of capitalism. That declaration, if we take it on face value, defies every lesson on audience at least as it is traditionally taught in rhetoric handbooks. The writer violates, for example, several of the rules that Sharon Crowley and Deborah Hawhee have outlined in *Ancient Rhetorics for Contemporary Students* for creating a successful ethos: the claims lack specific evidence, which violates a demand for showing that one has done one's homework; the arrogant tone arguably fails to create goodwill with the reader; and the third-person discourse fails to create a personal relationship between writer and reader.[21] If evaluated on the basis of classical rhetorical appeals within the text, the *Masses*—and many dissident press concerns—might be deemed rhetorical failures. Perhaps this is why, in classrooms where we purport to study the power of language to make change in the world, we pay scant attention to the universe of dissident texts. Ignored or dismissed as "bad rhetoric," dissident texts offer the opportunity to study rhetorical examples that have consistently sought to make changes in the world, and occasionally have succeeded.

Looked at in this way it seems that rather than violating rules of discourse, this passage from the *Masses* seeks to change the rules of the game. In declaring itself free, true, revolutionary, nonconciliatory, arrogant, "against rigidity and dogma," the editors challenge readers to imagine themselves as somehow aligned with a publication that aligns itself with no one and with nothing in particular, save the freedom to print what it wishes as it wishes. The audience that made this magazine so popular in the first decade of the twentieth century was looking, we might assume, for something new, something bold.

The rhetorical importance, then, of examining the workings of the dissident press is to explore how, within such spaces, writers make different assumptions about discourse protocols. Dissident press articles can exemplify how the rules we teach our students—about, for example, constructing a positive ethos—are not universal rules of good writing but rules for writing that operates within certain accepted rhetorical situations. When one seeks to create change, or make something different happen in discourse, the rules might seem to fly out the window.

In examining the rhetorical workings of the dissident press, however, it would be incomplete to look only at the rhetorical appeals made within the texts or to equate its rhetorical force with the composed text itself. How these texts managed or failed to find readers and to circulate both materially and ideologically significantly determines the rhetorical power of any text to create a public appeal.[22] Thus in order to study the rhetoric of dissent, one must also look more closely at the relationship between textual circulation and the creation of a readership, or public. To do this, we turn to the work of Michael Warner on the creation of publics and counterpublics.

Dissident press publications work to create counterpublic spaces, which Warner argues are "defined by their tension with the larger public. . . . Discussion within such a public is understood to contravene the roles obtaining in the world at large, being structured by alternative discourse positions or protocols, making different assumptions about what can be said or what goes without saying . . . it maintains at some level, conscious or not, an awareness of its subordinate status."[23] In other words, counterpublics engage in alternative rhetorical strategies while seeking to effect change in a more-dominant public sphere.

Warner's work, then, allows for an alternative way to evaluate dissident rhetoric: one that goes beyond close inspection at the textual level. Rather than examining internal textual criteria, Warner shows us that a public appeal is successful when people pay attention. He argues that if and when public appeals are successful, they hail a public into being by their discourse. Once readers recognize themselves as the type of person being hailed by a message, and once they pay attention to it, a public is constituted. So the arrogance or lack of evidence in the appeal of the *Masses* is irrelevant if readers feel themselves to be addressed by such words and pay attention to them. The act of readers' paying attention importantly begins the creation of a public.

Warner continues by arguing that a public cannot be constituted by a single text, no matter how compelling or provocative. He describes a public as "an ongoing space of encounters" defined by the "concatenation of texts over time."[24] Thus conversation and circulation are key. A publication can create a counterpublic space only if readers pay attention and if they seek to respond, speak back, or write letters to the editor: in other words, when the discourse reflexively circulates. In that sense, Warner argues, a text must be circulated, not just emitted in one direction. This challenge is key for dissident press concerns, for while it is one thing to give the appearance of people paying attention, creating responsive readers and writers is another matter entirely.

Take a contemporary example: the International Network of Street Papers (INSP) has a goal of creating a global space for circulating underreported news about poverty and homelessness. To this end, they have created the Global Street News Service.[25] At this point, nearly 100 independent antipoverty member newspapers around the world have successfully managed to share content among themselves, so that, for example, a newspaper in Seattle can publish a story about child labor in Argentina reported locally by journalists there. This news service has helped each paper locally engage its readers, to broaden the discussion of poverty, via letters to the editor or local meetings of interested volunteers, to include a global scope. As of yet, however, the News Service itself has not created a public of its own. The Web site is not a large draw for readers; it is more an internal resource for the papers themselves. When readers do happen upon stories there, there is no clear feedback mechanism, so the articles do not readily invite response or the creation of new texts. Going forward, the INSP can decide whether its News Service should remain an internal resource or whether it should seek to create an online counterpublic space for uniting readers around the world interested in antipoverty issues. That would require directing readers to the site, but also making it a site that invites response and textual circulation.

With dissident press publications, response and circulation are always meant as means to change the world in some way, whether it is to change how people think about poverty, for example, or take action on a specific campaign. Warner argues that a public is always created with an aim of "poetic world making."[26]

Public discourse says not only 'let a public exist' but 'Let it have this character, speak this way, see the world in this way.' It then goes in search of confirmation that such a public exists, with greater or lesser success—success being further attempts to cite, circulate, and realize the world understanding it articulates. Run it up the flagpole and see who salutes. Put on a show and see who shows up.[27]

To judge the rhetorical success of a dissident press publication, ultimately, is to examine the situation in which it appears, to consider how it creates an image of the world as well as explore who shows up to salute this image. In the case of the INSP, it is too soon to judge whether it or another antipoverty network can help build global solidarity against poverty and create an alternative image of globalization that will draw significant numbers of people. Still, it is a useful question to ponder and to examine as things unfold.

In that context, looking historically at publications like the *Masses* or *"Hobo" News* can help students of rhetoric see when and how publics form and dissipate, how discourse constitutes a public, whose attention gives life to a public, and how the dissident press creates images of the world that often are utopian but that sometimes have performative force. In the section that follows, we provide a background sketch of *"Hobo" News* as an example of how historical dissident press rhetoric might be used in today's rhetoric classroom.

"HOBO" NEWS AND A RHETORIC OF DISSENT

[James Eads] How's newspaper bridge connected America's migratory workers to one another and to the larger labor movement; today it lies virtually forgotten, in a remote corner of the St. Louis Public Library.[28]

We propose to show you in plain unvarnished language the great truths of things as they are, by the men who are on the bottom of this social system.[29]

By the 1870s most people in the United States were becoming increasingly aware of a growing stream of migratory laborers that later became known and feared as a "Great Army of Tramps." Historian Todd De Pastino, in his book *Citizen Hobo*, attributes the cause of this mass homelessness to economic issues: the post–Civil War shift to a wage-based economy that left many people unemployed, a stock market crash, years of bankruptcies, and an international depression.[30] Even though economic changes primarily caused an unprecedented stream of homeless workers, the mainstream press, academics, and politicians failed to attribute economic causes to the change: "One might have expected the most learned commentators on the tramp crisis to have recognized its roots in the problem of unemployment. Such, however, was not the case."[31] Mainstream journalists, charity workers, and politicians responded in ways that were "not generous. Rather than offer charity, they called for mass arrests, workhouses and chain gangs."[32] Tramps on the road were dismissed as "lazy" and "shiftless."[33]

In the ensuing years, journalists and academics became preoccupied with writing about the individual moral failings of tramps and hobos. De Pastino writes that certain members of the tramp army tried to engage the mainstream press through letters, like William Aspinwall, who sought to establish himself as a credible rhetor and to focus the critique of tramping on problems of social class and unemployment. All the while, his interlocutor, John James McCook, a minister and language professor at Trinity College, steered the questions back toward personal habits and morals. On his own, even a gifted rhetor like Aspinwell could not create a counterpublic force to counter the tide of antihobo sentiment circulating in the United States. But this tide of negative public sentiment did establish the rhetorical exigency for one man to help create a press outlet for hoboes to publicly express their views.

Today, off through a maze of hallways and closed doors, tucked into a tidy corner of the St. Louis Public Library Special Collections, is the fragile, yellowed archive of the 1915–1929 paper *"Hobo" News*, founded and funded by the eccentric, self-effacing James Eads How. How's grandfather (James Buchanan Eads, distant cousin to President Buchanan) had built the first road and rail bridge across the Mississippi—the Eads Bridge in St. Louis. His father (James Flintham How) served as vice president and general manager of the Wabash Railroad. His paternal grandfather (John How) was three times elected mayor of St. Louis. How himself was Harvard and Oxford educated, trained in theology and medicine, and a member one of the most prominent families in St. Louis.

What makes How's life significant for our purposes is a promise he made to use what fortune he had to "publish a newspaper for the benefit of his organization of the unemployed."[34] How did more than that, of course, but his paper, *"Hobo" News,* served as a voice of dissent, written by and about the very men How wanted to help. How's life often was that of the hobo. He rode the rails and frequently lived with hoboes sleeping in makeshift lean-tos along the Mississippi and following the crops as migrant labor. His life was dedicated to serving the poor and unemployed and especially the ever-increasing numbers of men living the hobo life. For them, he began the International Brotherhood Welfare Association (IBWA), established and funded hobo colleges across the country, and was their "guiding spirit and 'angel,'" as an editorial in the first issue of *"Hobo" News* declared. By 1933, at age fifty-six, How was dead, stricken by pneumonia exacerbated, physicians said, by years of starvation and what one *Time* magazine article called the life he had chosen as a "vagrant."[35] His was not a life that went unnoticed. A 1911 *New York Times* feature story called him "The Millionaire Hobo," a "scientific anarchist," and a tireless campaigner for the rights of the unemployed. How called himself a "voluntary anarchist," and told the reporter he probably was not a good socialist.[36]

As with many dissident papers, *"Hobo" News* took its cue from this impassioned leader. The paper began as the official voice of the IBWA and early on broadcast the aims of this new organization: "We are forming brotherhoods of the unskilled and unorganized workers commonly called 'tramps' by newspapers and officials, but who, in reality are usually honest workingmen compelled to shift about like hungry animals in search of work."[37] *"Hobo" News* was established, in part then, as a response to a mainstream press that saw nothing of worth in the ever-growing numbers of people who were homeless and unemployed.

Founded in an era of radical labor movements like that of the Industrial Workers of the World (IWW) and of outspoken anarchists and socialists like Emma Goldman, Ben Reitman, and Eugene Debs, *"Hobo" News* early on established its dissenting voice, often publishing articles and extracts by Debs, Upton Sinclair, and other powerful socialist and leftist leaders. This paper spoke directly to the people about and for whom it was written.

One scholar characterizes the rhetoric of this paper as functioning "primarily as a published version of a more oral format—meaning the campfire tale-telling and political discussion of the 'hobo jungle.'"[38] To some extent, that is the case. The paper did feature stories, poems, and commentary that had the tenor of local talk. Yet *"Hobo" News* went far beyond that campfire tale-telling mode. More than simple folksy talk, *"Hobo" News* was a serious advocate for unorganized laborers and, especially, for the unemployed. As the official publication of the IBWA, the paper published convention notes and organization news. Its greatest contribution, however, had to be the fact that it put a face on America's tramps, hoboes, and those who were homeless, out of work, and impoverished. As the editorial for the first issue states, "The writer admits that he doesn't like the word 'hobo,' but philosophically concludes: 'We have got it and we are going to make it respectable.'"[39]

In a number of issues, the paper challenged the mainstream press, accusing it of not doing the job of a free press. In 1920, for example, one writer quotes Upton Sinclair's account of journalist John Swinton's remarks on "The Independent Press": "There is no such thing in America as an independent press, unless it is in the country towns. You know it, and I know it. There is not one of you who dares to write his honest opinions, and if you did, you know beforehand that it would never appear in print. . . . The business of the New York journalist is to destroy the truth, to lie outright, to pervert, to vilify, to fawn at the feet of mammon and to sell his race and his country for his daily bread. . . . We are intellectual prostitutes."[40]

In that way, *"Hobo" News* separated itself from the mainstream press and claimed, by association if in no other way, that it was a paper willing to write "honest opinions," independent of the "rich men behind the scenes" that Swinton called the puppeteers of New York journalists. How likened his paper to the socialist papers the *Call* and *Appeal to Reason*: "We must have our printed word—our 'Appeal,' 'Call,' our daily press in every town. How else can the masses of the people learn? The hour has struck—the psychological moment is here. It calls for economic education and for intelligent action."[41]

In an attempt to reach a broader audience, as Lynne Adrian notes, *"Hobo" News* did try, at times, to address a double audience: both those it was written for and about and those who were closer to centers of power who might be swayed to use that power to effect change. In 1917, for example, one writer directly addresses that second audience with a challenge: "We care not whether you be an aristocrat or a plebeian, a priest or millionaire, a professional man or worker—it is necessary for your welfare and all your fellow-citizens, that you should be in touch with the evils of the hobo life."[42] In light of the 1917 Espionage Act, the editors might have felt a strong need to address even millionaires as "fellow-citizens" in language that was certainly softened from earlier issues. Like other radical papers, *"Hobo" News* had been affected by that legislation, which threatened, and in many cases closed down, socialist and radical papers throughout the country. The *Masses* stopped publication during this period, for example, as seven of their editors, artists, and writers (John Reed, Max Eastman, Floyd Dell, Art Young, Merrill Rodgers, Josephine Bell, and H. J. Glintkerkamp) were tried for seditious actions under the Espionage Act.[43] Founded in 1897, the socialist paper *Appeal to Reason*, which had published writers like Karl Marx, Friedrich Engels, William Morris, and John Ruskin, had by 1922 closed its operations also under pressure from the Espionage Act. Though never actually shut down, *"Hobo" News* found its second-class mailing status suddenly gone, a real blow to a paper already running on shaky finances. It was also during this time that hoboes selling the paper were harassed, arrested, and beaten by police—their papers confiscated and, in at least one case, destroyed as the prisoner looked on. Under these circumstances, it is not surprising that the paper tempered its rhetorical appeal in what seems an attempt to broaden its base of support and even forestall potential charges of sedition.

Early on, however, the *"Hobo" News* rhetoric was anything but conciliatory. In the April 1915 issue, for example, How freely uses the language of leftist and radical politics. In what he called "The First Letter" to the paper, How addresses the editor as "Dear Comrade." What follows is melodramatic but direct, and reads much like the earlier writings of Jacob Riis and Jack London[44]:

> Dear Comrade:
> Here's welcoming the "Hobo News" and its Editor.
> What a field you should have, O, paper!
> What good you should accomplish!
> What a multitude of sad and lonely lives you should
>   strengthen!
> What a world of economic darkness and gloom you
>   should dispel!
> Oh, Paper of the Masses of the proletariat. May you ever be true to the
>   highest and the best; generous to the adversary and fearless in the
>   championship of the weak and oppressed.[45]

Jack London had written this on watching street people in the city of London picking scraps off the sidewalk to eat: "And, this, between six and seven o'clock in the evening of August 20, year of Our Lord, 1902, in the heart of the greatest, wealthiest, most powerful empire the world has ever seen."[46] Or, from Riis's introduction to *How the Other Half Lives:* "Long ago it was said that 'one half of the world does not know how the other half lives.' That was true then. It did not know because it did not care. The half that was on top cared little for the struggles, and less for the fate of those who were underneath, so long as it was able to hold them there and keep its own seat."[47]

The language in *"Hobo" News* was drawn from these earlier authors, meant to touch the heart and to confront: "What are you going to do about it?" Riis asked in 1890.[48] "What a world of economic darkness and gloom you should dispel!" How writes in 1915.[49] The ample use of pathos, exclamation, and direct address is not a strategy a mainstream press would rely upon in telling the story of poverty. It is, however, a primary tool in dissident press publications as they function in advocacy roles.

In *The Design of Dissent,* Tony Kushner posits four characteristics of successful dissent: "It is shocking, it is clever—even funny in a grim sort of way—and
its meaning is instantly intelligible. . . . It is, or at least it seems to be, samizs-
dat, dangerous, forbidden." "Resistance," Kushner writes, "is sending up a signal flare in the darkness."[50] A paper like *"Hobo" News* does precisely that: it
aims to shock and surprise, to make readers reassess their own roles and, in
the end, consider the extent to which they are complicit in the trouble at hand.

In a rhetoric classroom, one might ask students to read from the *"Hobo"
News* archives alongside De Pastino's work or other historical accounts of the
time period, the rhetorical situation for which *"Hobo" News* journalists wrote.
Understanding the historical situation is complex and would make useful
ground for discussion: What effect did an organized group of homeless men
have on later government policies that offered some safeguards to workers,
policies such as unemployment compensation, the acquiescence to the forming of unions, and later, the GI Bill? In what ways did a publication like *"Hobo"
News* create a counterpublic space for offering alternative causal explanations
of the widespread poverty that Americans were witnessing and undergoing?
To what extent did the specter of an organized, politicized, publishing hobo
army help change the public discourse on hobo culture—which later became
romanticized in popular culture as the last bastion of true American man-
hood? While there are no definitive answers to questions like these, in a rhetoric classroom they would serve to shift the focus away from an exclusive
study of invention, to consider the entire rhetorical situation, including the
historical situation and questions of circulation and performativity, questions
we believe are generative and exciting to pose with students.

These questions are additionally useful in helping students seek a public
for their own work. In this way, students are reading *as writers* the journalists
in the dissident press to consider if and how their strategies and appeals for
creating an audience could be useful. One of us, for example, has twice taught
a course called Writing for Social Change, in which students create their own
advocacy writing projects. When first taught, students read a range of essays
from mainstream new journalists, like Ted Conover, Adrian Nicole Leblanc,
and William Finnegan. While useful in many ways, this work seemed an unrealistic model for students, since these journalists were publishing in venues
like the *New Yorker* and the *New York Times,* and, for them, finding responsive
readers was never in question. The second time this course was offered, students additionally discussed dissident press writings, from contemporary local
writers as well as from historical positions, to help writers think through how
to lend their voices to the creation of a public, rather than being a one-off cry
in the wild. In such a sense that students are trying to write their way into
the publics they seek to join—whether they be academic, political, social, and
so forth—reading the work of outsiders seeking to create a responsive public
can provide the bases for useful conversations.

BUT ARE WE TEACHING BAD RHETORIC?

Even though rhetoricians are interested in the social function of texts and how language makes changes in the world, in what ways might we still be governed by questions of aesthetics instead of performativity? In other words, are we reticent to teach dissident press publications because we think it is just "bad writing"? In a recent discussion on the WPA Listserv, for example, one writer sought help finding examples of "good political writing" and prefaced his request with the caveat that he did not want examples of texts that he thought were "too moralistic or partisan" to engage students. Rather than questioning the writer's assumption that good political writing must not be too partisan or must not moralize, some responders to this thread offered examples of texts that defined "political" as bipartisan writing that took no clear political position: "[the writer] is not running for anything, has no hidden agenda . . . for . . . people . . . on both sides of the aisle." Alternatively, others suggested texts that took no political positions but rather analyzed political rhetoric to help students see that we "get 'fooled' by our culture into seeing every issue as having only two sides." Such analyses of rhetoric are valuable in any class, but we would argue that analysis is not a substitute for strong rhetorical claims that passionately seek to persuade their readers of the justness of a cause. Analysis of political rhetoric is not a substitute for political, or politicized, rhetoric, and we believe a rhetoric classroom can and should be a place to examine and explore rhetoric that can be highly partisan, can be moralizing, can have clear agendas, and not be written for both, or either, side of the aisle.

What, then, might be the reluctance in recommending baldly political texts? One fear, expressed by the original writer of the question, is that students of an opposing political position would be turned off by the strong argument. But if we are trying to show that counterpublic discourses appeal to some readers while not appealing to most readers, would not such a response be an important part of the discussion in understanding how dissident rhetoric works? If an argument were immediately appealing and accepted by all, it would not be dissident, and it might well not be an argument at all. Dissident rhetoric works by appealing to some while turning off many others.

Take, for example, Grant Allen's editorial in the March 1920 issue of "Hobo" News. In it, he sets up a worldview of clear Manichaean opposites of good and evil:

> If you are on the side of the Spoilers, then you are a Bad Man.
> If you are on the side of Social Justice, then you are a Good Man.
> There is no effective test of High Morality at the present day save this.
> Critics of the Middle Class type often explain, of reasoning like this,
>   "What on earth makes him say it? What has he to gain by talking in
>   that way? What does he expect to get by it? So bound up are they in

the idea of selfinterest [*sic*] as the one motive of action, that they never even seem to conceive of honest conviction as a ground for speaking out the truth that is in one.

To such critics, I would answer, "The reason why I write all this is because I profoundly believe it.

I believe the poor are being kept out of their own. I believe the rich are, for the most part, selfish and despicable. I believe wealth has been piled up by cruel and unworthy means.

I believe it is wrong in us to acquiesce in the wicked inequalities of our existing Social State, instead of trying our utmost to bring about another, where Right would be done to all, where Poverty would be impossible. I believe such a system is perfectly practicable, and that nothing stands in its way save the selfish fears and prejudices of individuals. And I believe even those craven fears and narrow prejudices are wholly mistaken: that everybody, even the rich themselves, would be infinitely happier in a world where no Poverty existed, where no hateful sights and sound met the eye at every turn, where all slums were swept away, and where everybody had their just and even share of pleasure and refinements in a free and equal community.

Arguably, this polemical statement might easily be dismissed by many students, because it conflicts with their beliefs or identity or seems too utopian.[51] But as an example of dissident rhetoric, it would not be expected to be embraced by most readers. What would be interesting, when discussing a text like this, is to consider to whom such an argument might appeal. What aspects, if any, of Allen's worldview seem appealing to any students? To whom is he writing if he describes the rich as "for the most part, selfish and despicable"? It would also be important to discuss the ethics and responsibility of such writing: is it ever acceptable to characterize a person or a group as "despicable," "cruel," and "unjust"? Are issues of the relative power and prestige of the writer versus his or her subject germane to the discussion?

Beyond student resistance, we might hesitate to teach dissident writing in a rhetoric class based on aesthetic grounds: despite all its good intentions, dissident publications may not represent very good writing as we typically imagine it. Certainly Allen's article lacks subtlety or nuance. English-department aesthetics generally favor ambiguity over polemics, complexity over clarity.[52] Perhaps we fear we might infect students with "bad taste" if we take up language that aims more to do things than to mean, reverberate, and echo. Perhaps we additionally fear that we already live in a world saturated by "bad rhetoric": blogs, talk radio, and chat rooms that seek more to malign individuals than to argue for ideas or positions. Bringing in rhetoric like Allen's might only add to the cheapening of public discourse. Why give students examples of "bad rhetoric" if we all swim in a sea of it daily?

We would argue that dissident press rhetoric may, indeed, engage in some of the same rhetorical moves of character-assassinating blogs, discussion boards, and so forth, but the aim of bringing this rhetoric into the classroom is not imitation so much as it is a lesson in understanding rhetorical strategy. Moreover, the aim of a piece like Allen's is not to eliminate or ignore opposition. Allen's vision is to take all people—rich and poor—along to a better, more just world. His goal is not to murder or eradicate the rich, but to change hearts and minds. Dissident-press writing, then, might not teach students how to write a model essay in the traditional sense of that word, but it can show them something about focusing on an issue passionately and seeking to bring readers along in the struggle.

Returning, then, to the question that began our discussion: should a first-year composition class teach public or academic writing? Rather than arguing one side or the other—public or academic—we would suggest another tact entirely. Relying on recent discussions of genre theory, we would argue that a first-year composition course ought to take as its focus the question of how language works, within situations, within genres, to consider how writing and speaking can move audiences to action.[53] In such a class one would explore how public or academic arguments are made, arguments that result in, say, ordinances that ban the distribution of food to homeless men, women, and children, and how voices from the margins respond to such changes.

Nearly twenty years ago, when speaking about teaching rhetoric in the age of George H. W. Bush politics, Richard Ohmann, who describes himself as "a dissident intellectual," challenged our discipline with these words:

> As everyone has heard, socialism is now dead, capitalism is triumphant, and history is at an end. Let my irony not be read as a slur on the bold revolutions in Central and Eastern Europe. People there need our hopes and help as they try to shake off the tyrannies and bureaucracies that claimed and tarnished the name of socialism. But they enter a world system whose tensions and crises grow ever more taut, more threatening to a decent future on the planet. Capitalism triumphant needs critical thought and liberatory rhetoric still more than capitalism militant in mortal combat with the Evil Empire. We will have to invent something new, or decay and perish. Can vision become a goal for rhetoric?[54]

That question, "Can vision become a goal for rhetoric?" is one we believe is at the center of our desire to bring a rhetoric of dissidence into the writing classroom. A second Bush era has now come nearly to its end. In its wake, perhaps "vision" is the only appropriate goal for rhetoric today.

NOTES

We thank the many friends and colleagues who encouraged us in this work and read bits and pieces of drafts or listened as we talked through so many of the issues raised by the dissident press. Among them, we especially thank John Trimbur, who is both a good listener and a powerful skeptic; Allison Manuel, who read a late draft of this article and helped put us back on track; Lauren Goldstein, who help us with formatting; and the wonderful and generous men and women working in the basement and in the archives of the St. Louis Public Library. In many ways, this essay was written for Diana's great-great uncle Thomas Scanlon (1855–1938), who lived as a hobo in St. Louis at the turn of the last century, who surely walked under and past the Eads Bridge, and who, we imagine, might well have been one of the thousands of men carrying *"Hobo" News* from one harvest to the next.

1. Glenn, Lyday, and Sharer, *Rhetorical Education in America.*
2. Kushner, *Design of Dissent.*
3. MLA, "Focus."
4. Berlin, *Rhetoric and Reality,* 4.
5. "Times and Iraq."
6. National Coalition for the Homeless, "Feeding Intolerance," para. 13.
7. Pew Project, "State."
8. Berlin, *Rhetoric.*
9. See Trimbur, "Review Essay"; Mathieu, *Tactics of Hope.*
10. Glenn, Lyday, and Sharer, *Rhetorical Education,* viii.
11. Cornish and Russwurm, *Freedom's Journal,* March 16, 1827.
12. Glenn, Lyday, and Sharer, *Rhetorical Education,* ix.
13. Kushner, "Design," 220–21.
14. Berlin, *Rhetoric,* 5.
15. Kessler, *Dissident Press.*
16. Ibid., 155.
17. Ibid., 14.
18. Streitmatter, *Voices of Revolution,* x.
19. Young, *Inclusion and Democracy,* 7.
20. *Masses,* October 1913.
21. Crowley and Hawhee, *Ancient Rhetorics.*
22. See Trimbur, "Review Essay."
23. Warner, *Publics and Counterpublics,* 56.
24. Ibid., 90.
25. For more information, see www.streetnewsservice.com.
26. Warner, *Publics and Counterpublics.*
27. Adrian, "World We Shall Win."
28. *"Hobo" News,* November 1916.
29. Ibid.
30. De Pastino, *Citizen Hobo.*
31. Ibid., 17.
32. Ibid., 4.
33. Ibid.
34. How, "First Letter."
35. "End of an Idealist."
36. "Millionaire Hobo."
37. Ibid.
38. Adrian, "World," 105.
39. "Editor's Statement," *"Hobo" News* 1, no. 1 (1915): 2.
40. O'Brien, "Light," 5.

41. Quoted in "Millionaire Hobo."
42. Adrian, "World," 111.
43. See, for example, "Hard to Get"; Sayer, "Art and Politics," 42–78.
44. See, in particular, London, *People of the Abyss;* Riis, *How the Other Half Lives.*
45. How, "First Letter."
46. London, *People of the Abyss,* 78.
47. Riis, *How the Other Half Lives,* 1.
48. Ibid.
49. How, "First Letter."
50. Kushner, "Design," 221.
51. This is a rhetorical strategy used, for example, by Catholic Worker cofounder Peter Maurin in what he called his "easy essays." In them, he offered straightforward challenges for change:

Better Or Better Off

The world would be better off,
if people tried
to become better.
And people would
become better
if they stopped trying
to be better off.
For when everybody tries
to become better off,
nobody is better off.
But when everybody tries
to become better,
everybody is better off.
Everybody would be rich
if nobody tried
to be richer.
And nobody would be poor
if everybody tried
to be the poorest.
And everybody would be
what he ought to be
if everybody tried to be
what he wants
the other fellow to be.

52. See Newkirk, *Performance of Self.* In it, he argues that writing teachers by and large share a tacit aesthetic about what constitutes good writing, which includes writing that takes tentative or exploratory stances and which is not overly emotional or sentimental.
53. See, for example, Bawarshi, *Genre;* Devitt, "Generalizing about Genre"; Miller, "Genre as Social Action."
54. Ohmann, "Kinder, Gentler Nation," 230.

Works Cited

Adrian, Lynne M. "The World We Shall Win for Labor: Early 20th Century Hobo Self-Publication." In *Print Culture in a Diverse America*, edited by James P. Danky and Wayne A. Wiegand, 101–27. Urbana: University of Illinois Press, 1998.

Bawarshi, Anis. *Genre and the Invention of the Writer: Reconsidering the Place of Invention in Composition.* Logan: Utah State University Press, 2003.

Berlin, James. *Rhetoric and Reality: Writing Instruction in American Colleges, 1900–1985.* Carbondale: Southern Illinois University Press, 1987.

Cornish, Samuel, and John Russwurm. *Freedom's Journal,* March 16, 1827.

Crowley, Shanon, and Deborah Hawhee. *Ancient Rhetorics for Contemporary Students.* 3rd ed. Boston: Pearson, 2004.

De Pastino, Todd. *Citizen Hobo: How a Century of Homelessness Shaped America.* Chicago: University of Chicago Press, 2005.

Devitt, Amy. "Generalizing about Genre: New Conceptions of an Old Concept." *College Composition and Communication* 44 (1993): 573–86.

"End of an Idealist." *Time,* August 4, 1930. http://www.time.com/time/magazine/article/0,9171,740008,00.html (accessed March 22, 2009).

Glenn, Cheryl, Margaret M. Lyday, and Wendy B. Sharer, eds. *Rhetorical Education in America.* Tuscaloosa: University of Alabama Press, 2004.

"Hard to Get Jury for 'Masses' Trial," *New York Times,* April 16, 1918.

How, James. "The First Letter." *"Hobo" News,* 1, no. 1, April 1915.

Kessler, Lauren. *The Dissident Press: Alternative Journalism in American History.* London: Sage, 1984.

Kushner, Tony. "The Design of Dissent." In *The Design of Dissent,* edited by Milton Glaser and Mirko Ilic, 220–23. Gloucester, Mass.: Rockport, 2005.

London, Jack. *People of the Abyss.* London: Echo Library, 2007.

Mathieu, Paula. *Tactics of Hope: The Public Turn in Composition.* Portsmouth, N.H.: Boynton, Cook, Heinemann, 2005.

Maurin, Peter. "Easy Essays." Catholic Worker Movement. Catholicworker.org. http://www.catholicworker.org/roundtable/easyessays.cfm#%3CSTRONG%3ENo%20Recourse%3C/STRONG%3E (accessed March 22, 2009).

Miller, Carolyn. "Genre as Social Action." *Quarterly Journal of Speech* 70 (1984): 151–67.

"Millionaire Hobo Seeks Cure for Jobless Men." *New York Times,* May 14, 1911.

Modern Language Association (MLA). "The Focus of First-Year Composition: Academic or Public Writing?" Modern Language Association Roundtable sponsored by the Council of Writing Program Administrators, December 30, 2007.

National Coalition for the Homeless. "Feeding Intolerance: Prohibitions on Sharing Food with People Experiencing Homelessness." http://www.nationalhomeless.org/publications/foodsharing/intro.html#4 (accessed January 7, 2008).

Newkirk, Thomas. *The Performance of Self in Student Writing.* Portsmouth, N.H.: Heinemann, 1997.

O'Brien, Dan. "Light on the Hobo Problem." *"Hobo" News,* 5, no. 5, March 1920.

Ohmann, Richard. "A Kinder, Gentler Nation: Education and Rhetoric in the Bush Era." *JAC* 10, no. 2 (1990): 215–30.

Pew Project for Excellence in Journalism. "The State of the News Media 2007." http://www.stateofthenewsmedia.com/2007/ (accessed January 7, 2008).

Riis, Jacob. *How the Other Half Lives: Studies among the Tenements of New York.* 1901. Reprint, New York: Digireads, 2005.

Sayer, John. "Art and Politics, Dissent and Repression: The Masses Magazine versus the Government, 1917–1918." *American Journal of Legal History* 32, no. 1 (January 1988): 42–78.

Streitmatter, Rodger. *Voices of Revolution: The Dissident Press in America.* New York: Columbia University Press, 2001.

"The Times and Iraq." *New York Times,* May 26, 2004.

Trimbur, John. "Review Essay: Taking the Social Turn: Teaching Writing Post-Process." Review of *Academic Discourse and Critical Consciousness* by Patricia Bizzell, *Critical Teaching and the Idea of Literacy* by C. H. Knoblauch and Lil Brannon, and *Common Ground: Dialogue, Understanding, and the Teaching of Composition* by Kurt Spellmeyer. *CCC* 1 (1994): 108–18.

Warner, Michael. *Publics and Counterpublics.* New York: Zone Books, 2002.

Young, Iris Marion. *Inclusion and Democracy.* Oxford: Oxford University Press, 2000.

The Community Literacy Advocacy Project

Civic Revival through Rhetorical Activity in Rural Arkansas

DAVID A. JOLLIFFE

This essay analyzes an interesting, yet thorny, case in the public work of rhetoric. It tells the story of an academic office at a public, research university supporting the public, rhetorical work of a small town in eastern Arkansas. All corners of the town are striving to craft a new statement about it. Its citizens are making Herculean efforts to reshape the rhetoric that they employ with one another when they talk about civic survival and, ideally, economic turnaround. Its leaders are offering a whole new perspective when they characterize the town's current status and its potential to prospective citizens and employers. Confronting what many observers would characterize as the hallmarks of civic decay, Augusta, Arkansas—population 2,390, county seat of Woodruff County, population around 7,900—working in collaboration with the Office of the Brown Chair in English Literacy at the University of Arkansas, is announcing to its citizens, to the state, and to others who care to listen that it is the town that reads and writes together, the town where literacy makes a difference.

The thorny aspect of the case emerges from the new message itself. Sitting at the center of Augusta's rhetorical activity is a hotly contested term, *literacy*, and the rhetorical campaign to promote more and better reading and writing in the town has developed without much attention to the historical roots of the issues being addressed and the political and social implications of the work. So what should an academic collaborator in this civic campaign do? As I explain below, my path has been to help the movement grow in the direction it wants to grow and then to use the project as a teaching opportunity to help University of Arkansas students and the citizens involved to understand the deeper ideological issues involved and eventually, I hope, to act in responsible, productive ways about those issues.

In what follows I describe in some detail the rhetorical/revival campaign that Augusta has undertaken since 2005, document its successes in its first

year, and unpack several problematic issues that the project raises, issues that
will eventually need to be addressed as part of an effort to teach an inclusive
definition of literacy. To start, however, let me set out three perspectives that
build a foundation for explaining how municipalities (and community literacy
programs within them) craft rhetorical statements and how those statements
can influence social change and, ideally, economic and material progress.

HOW DO TOWNS, CITIES, AND LITERACY PROGRAMS
MAKE A RHETORICAL STATEMENT?

Both ancient and contemporary rhetorical theories provide explanations about
how towns and cities craft rhetorical statements about themselves. The classical perspective is thoroughly Aristotelian; one contemporary perspective de-
rives from social form theory; another contemporary theory examines the
tropes underlying community literacy programs and, by extension, commu-
nity-building efforts.

   An Aristotelian rhetorician (which I unabashedly characterize myself as)[1]
would contend that towns and cities make rhetorical statements about themselves in essentially the same way any text or any graphic—a picture, a cartoon, a chart, a graph, an advertisement, a billboard, and so on—does: by
developing an argument that, in Stephen Toulmin's neo-Aristotelian terms,
incorporates "data" and makes a claim, with the data and the claim connected by warrants: generally unspoken "because" statements, assumptions
that the author/creator of the text hopes its readers/listeners/consumers share
with him or her.[2] A verbal text manifests organizational patterns, choices of
diction and syntax, imagistic and figurative language that fleshes out its central argument, appealing to the writer's character and credibility and the audiences' emotions and life states all the while. A graphic text does the same
thing, only incorporating actual images—sights and sounds—as well as imagistic language.

   Cities and towns take advantage of verbal and nonverbal texts in both official and unofficial documents to make a statement—that is, to offer an argument about what kind of city or town it is, why people live there, why people
might visit or move there, and so on. Consider this example of an official
document making a rhetorical statement for a city: if one searches for "Little
Rock" on the Internet, one quickly finds a link titled "Little Rock City Limitless." (Notice, even from the outset, that the title's punning intertextuality
with the phrase "city limits" creates a kind of "in" joke between the creator
and the viewer, thus strengthening the former's ethos.) By clicking on the link,
one gets to www.littlerock.com, the homepage of the Little Rock Convention
and Visitors' Bureau. This homepage is dominated by a beautiful photograph
of the Arkansas River as it flows past downtown Little Rock, with the words
"River Magic" superimposed on it. The text on the page describes in detail the
cultural and recreational activities happening in the near future in Little Rock,

and it lists the two dozen or so organizations that are holding conventions in Little Rock over the coming months. Here is the enthymeme, cast in the Toulmin's terms:

DATA: Little Rock has abundant cultural events and recreational possibilities available at all times.
CLAIM: Little Rock is a "magical" city, with "limitless" possibilities.
WARRANT: The greater number and variety of recreational and cultural events that a city makes available to tourists and other visitors, the more attractive, "magical," and "limitless" it becomes to them.

As one processes this enthymeme, one glances at the portrait of President William Clinton over the link to the Clinton Library and Museum, at the graphic representations of local and touring Broadway shows that are coming to theaters in the city, at the announcements of upcoming concerts by the Arkansas Symphony, and the advertisement for the Arkansas Water Sports Association. The *ethos* of the city is strong: it is goodwilled; it is on your side. The *pathos* of the city is strong: it appeals to your sense of adventure, fun, excitement. Little Rock is apparently quite a hip place.

Unofficial "texts" about a town or city also make rhetorical statements. Consider Chicagoans' frequent invocation of the phrase "city of big shoulders," taken from Carl Sandburg's poem about the city. Here is the claim: Chicago is, despite its many cultural and commercial amenities, still a simple, solid, working-class city. Here are the "data": the famous cuisine is deep-dish pizza and hot dogs; the football team is the Bears (*da Bares*), "the monsters of the Midway"; the mayor (*da mare*) for much of the past half-century has been a plainspoken Irish American named Daley who talks tough with the media and makes sure the garbage is picked up. The ethos of the "city of big shoulders" and the pathos that its images conjure up work together to establish the warrant that the best American city is the down-to-earth, unpretentious one, where the work ethic that made America great remains at the center of civic life. The implicit claim is that Chicago is that city.

A second perspective on how cities and towns make rhetorical statements about themselves comes from the work of the contemporary communication theorist David Procter, who studies "how rural communities—read as small towns—communicate in a pattern that enhances their chances to survive and thrive."[3] Maintaining that that "language is a fundamental component in creating a sense of community," Procter explores "the ways citizens in a small town instill a sense of interdependence, fulfillment, and concern for one another" via "symbolic forms and cultural performances used to create those feelings of interdependence, fulfillment, and concern."[4] He explains: "As people talk about their town, they are doing more than expressing their individual support or disgust for their locality"; instead, "citizen rhetoric about locality-oriented events and acts is the materialization of a larger synthesis of community sociopolitical beliefs and values." And, Procter notes further, "this citizen rhetoric functions to create community belief and motivation. Community rhetors . . . enact community by organizing experiences and then naming those experiences, thereby feeling communal with one another."[5]

Central to Procter's analysis is his concept of "civic communions": "specific and significant moments of community interaction directed toward civic issues." Civic communions embody "rhetorical processes and cultural performances that function to build community"; moreover, "they are fundamentally a rhetorical and performative civic sacrament functioning to bond citizenry around the social and political structures—local ways of life, community goals, and political operations—of a specific people."[6] Procter's analogy comparing religious and civic communions is instructive: "Just as church leaders recall important texts and parables that function to connect the faith community and guide religious behavior," Procter explains, "civic leaders recall important historic texts, people, and events that ultimately serve to solidify community identity and offer guides to appropriate civic values and practices." As a result, he argues, "organizers and citizens celebrate some features of community while devaluing others."[7]

Yet another contemporary perspective examines the rhetorical activity specifically of community literacy programs. Since the remainder of this essay describes how Augusta, Arkansas, has placed its Community Literacy Advocacy Project at the forefront of its civic revitalization project, this perspective is relevant to the analytic task at hand. In *Community Literacy and the Rhetoric of Local Publics*, Eleanor Long analyzes community literacy programs in terms of their dominant tropes, their rhetorical situations, their discursive features, and what might be termed their perlocutionary effects—the implications of their rhetorical work. Arguing that community literacy programs represent "symbolic constructs enacted in time and place around shared exigencies"—constructs that Long labels "local publics"—she explains that people develop community literacy programs "around distinct rhetorical agendas that range from socializing children into appropriate language use . . . to eliciting stakeholders' perspectives on a shared problem . . . to demanding respect under conditions that yield little of it."[8] In other words, when a community literacy program has an agenda, as it does in Augusta, Arkansas, to revitalize the community and support economic growth, then that agenda is purposefully rhetorical.

To analyze the rhetoric of community literacy programs, Long creates a five-element "point-of-comparison" model. For any program, Long maintains, one can name its "guiding metaphor," or "the image that describes the discursive space where ordinary people go public"; the "context," or the "location, as well as other context-specific features that give public literacies their meaning"; the "tenor of the discourse," or the "register—the affective quality of the discourse"; the "literacy," or the "key practices that comprise the discourse" or "how people use writing and words to carry out their purposes for going public"; and the "rhetorical invention," or the "the generative processes by which people respond to the exigencies that call the local public into being."[9]

All three perspectives can be used, as I do below, to analyze the new rhetorical work that is ongoing in Augusta—new rhetorical activity that stands in contrast to the tacit, unpromising message that Augusta was communicating about itself in the first years of the new millennium. The work of the Augusta Community Literacy Advocacy Project, a collaborative effort of the White River Rural Health Center and the Office of the Brown Chair in English Literacy at the University of Arkansas, has yielded a sustained and continuing project of rhetorical activity and civic communions designed to promote community literacy and revive the dying town.

Augusta on Life Support

Sitting as it does on U.S. 64, the "old highway" to Memphis for motorists who do not want to fight the truck traffic on Interstate 40, most of Augusta is hidden from the casual driver-through. Entering the town from the west, one crosses over the White River and sees the river port, the Bunge Corporation grain elevator, the liquor store and gas station, a supermarket and two general-merchandise stores, and a branch of the bank. Off the main road where the passer-by does not see them are the turn-of-the-century courthouse, the half-dozen churches, the lovely old homes that overlook the river, and the American Legion hut where civic events are held. The casual motorist also does not see the nearly deserted downtown or the elementary and high school where classes have been getting smaller and smaller.

By all demographic measures,[10] Augusta is in decline. In 2007, 2,390 people lived there, but the town lost 10.32 percent of its population between 2000 and 2007. In 2007, the unemployment rate in Augusta was 8.4 percent, compared to 4.6 percent nationally. In the twelve months between October 2006 and October 2007, Augusta lost 5.5 percent of its jobs, while jobs in the U.S. grew 1.4 percent during the same period. Augusta's per capita income in 2007 was $13,500, compared to $24,200 nationally; the average household income was $24,260, compared to $44,080 nationally. Nearly 82 percent of the households had an income of less than $50,000, whereas nationally 52 percent of the households brought in less than $50,000. In the 2000 census, 23.6 percent of all Augusta families lived below the federal poverty level, as compared to 9.2 percent nationally, and 28.9 percent of all individuals in the town lived in poverty, compared to 12.4 percent nationally. Nearly 22 percent of the population over the age of twenty-five lacked a high school diploma; about half of that number had eighth grade as their highest level of educational attainment. Only 6.4 percent of the population had a four-year college degree. In 2007 the Augusta public schools spent $4,804 per student, as compared to a national average of $6,058 per student.

This was the scenario that confronted a brave group of folks in 2005 who chose to begin reshaping Augusta's statement to the region, the state, the nation, and the world.

THE AUGUSTA RECOVERY INITIATIVE AND THE COMMUNITY LITERACY ADVOCACY PROJECT

One poignant aspect of the Augusta story is the work of the Augusta Recovery Initiative, a citizens' group that assembled to find ways to save the town from decay and death. The group was convened by Dr. Steven Collier, executive director of the White River Rural Health Center, which has its central headquarters in Augusta. Beginning early in 2005, the group met regularly for a year, operating under the assumption that since the consequences of Augusta's decline were economic, the causes must be economic as well. The following notes from a meeting during the first year of operation demonstrate this economic focus: "Today we worked on an action plan, which was for Existing Business and Industry. . . . Economic development will drive everything. It is mandatory to follow action plans. In following an action plan, you will fill in the problems, like workforce availability and capability."[11]

Nine months later the focus of the Augusta Recovery Initiative had shifted. As Dr. Collier told me—and as he repeats regularly in presentations about Augusta—"we realized our problem wasn't economic—it was educational." This shift of emphasis is evident in the Initiative's meeting notes from October 2006: "Last year we started an Augusta improvement plan with brainstorming sessions. The topic of education kept coming up. We are now putting it on the front burner."

I had been introduced to Dr. Collier in September 2006 at a meeting of a group called the Crossroads Coalition, devoted to improving health care in the region. He and I talked at some length about how a community literacy project might provide a center of gravity for the Initiative's new focus on "education." Collier invited me to the Initiative's November 2006 meeting. Seated around the table was an amazing collection of dedicated citizens. Here is the roster of attendees, with my notes about each of them:

> Raymond Bowen: Taught at Augusta High School for 35 years. Now retired but teaching algebra II and advanced math part-time.
> Katina Biscoe: Nurse practitioner for White River Rural Health. Graduated from Augusta High School in 1991 and has children there now. Member of the Augusta School Board and serves on the Woodruff County Literacy Council.
> Janice Turner: Recently moved to Augusta, her husband's hometown, after he retired. An ordained minister, she runs "The J Spot," a Christian book store, and is the new president of the Woodruff County Literacy Council. Has been the principal and administrator of a private school.

Danny Shields: The postmaster in Augusta. Wife and son teach in
  Augusta; daughter teaches in McCrory, ten miles to the east of Augusta.
Evelyn Coles: Farm owner, mother, and grandmother. Husband was on
  the School Board for many years. One son graduated from college and
  is in farming. Two other sons still in college.
Brenda Collins: Longtime resident of Augusta. Two children graduated
  from Augusta High School and two grandchildren still in the Augusta
  schools. Member of the city council and the Woodruff County Literacy
  Council.
Jimmy Rhodes: Lifetime resident of Augusta. Graduated from Augusta
  High School in 1992 and went to Arkansas State in Mountain Home for
  a degree in funeral science. As funeral director, he notes that "I'm bury-
  ing too many young people." Serves on city council and plans to run
  for mayor.
Craig Meredith: Graduated from Augusta High School and joined the
  Navy, serving for four years, where he had the highest security clearance.
  Now working as a computer technician for White River Rural Health.
Regina Burkett: Community Development Coordinator for White River
  Rural Health and a licensed practical nurse.
Steven Collier: CEO of White River Rural Health Center. Graduated from
  Augusta High School. Went to Baylor University and took a degree in
  history. Got his medical degree from University of Arkansas for the
  Medical Sciences and did his residency in Pine Bluff. Was a practicing
  physician in central Arkansas for 20 years before "getting into the busi-
  ness side" and becoming CEO. White River Rural Health now has clinics in 17 towns in the area.

A thought occurred to me: seated around this table were representatives of
all sorts of "constituencies" in this small town: education, health care, small
business, government, religion, agriculture. Each was interested in helping to
save Augusta. Each had bought into the notion that improving "education"
could play a central role in the recovery initiative. Each was completely open
to my argument that improving literacy—improving all citizens' abilities to
read and write to the extent that they can live a rich, fulfilling personal life
and participate in a changing economy—was *the* most vital aspect of the educational improvement plan.

To make this plan work, I argued, we could not simply focus solely on the
schools and hope that they "fix" the literacy problem. Without wanting to
endorse any political candidate, I argued that "it takes a village" to raise the
profile of reading and writing and to improve education. Consider, I asked
them, all the organizations and entities in Augusta that might say, if asked,
that they were interested in helping folks read and write more fully and effectively: not only the schools but also the churches, the library, the local literacy

council, the local economic development council, the health clinics. Why not launch, I asked them, a Community Literacy Advocacy Project that would have a person at its helm who would actively seek out individuals and groups in Augusta who wanted to read and write in fuller, richer ways than they had in the past and who would forge "literacy liaisons" between and among all the constituencies who wanted to raise the profile of literacy in Augusta but who had not known about one another or worked together in the past.

Thus was born the idea for the Community Literacy Advocacy Project. After a quick marshaling of resources by White River Rural Health and the Office of the Brown Chair in English Literacy, Collier identified the miraculous Joy Lynn Bowen, a former teacher in Augusta public schools who knows (and is trusted by) nearly every person in Augusta and placed her on the staff of White River as the community literacy advocate.

THE KICKOFF AND THE INITIAL YEAR

The Community Literacy Advocacy Project got off to a rousing start. A community kickoff event on August 16, 2007, drew seventy-five citizens and featured introductions of the project by Collier, Bowen, and Jolliffe and testimonials of support for the project by Carol Ann Dykes, a former Augusta resident who now works on the faculty of the University of Central Florida, and by Otto Loewer, the former dean of the University of Arkansas College of Engineering who now runs an economic development institute focusing on rural Arkansas. Throughout, our message was consistent. We were going to "celebrate" reading and writing; we were going to bring students, parents, government officials, church leaders, business owners, and not-for-profit workers together; we were going to emphasize the roles that reading and writing play in the twenty-first century. We were not going to berate students and citizens for having poor literacy abilities but instead do all we could to help them acquire those abilities.

Under Bowen's direction, the project sprung into action. Bowen set up or attended four meetings that involved what we came to call "literacy liaisons"— connections between and among local, state, or regional government and not-for-profit organizations that were interested in improving literacy but had not worked together in the past. The project went to work immediately on dealing with a pressing issue in literacy—namely, helping young (often single) parents both to establish a productive literacy environment for the preschool children in their homes and to connect with educational and social-service providers, which would help them in many cases complete their GEDs and move into postsecondary educational and job-training settings. The high point of the young/single parents' initiative was a daylong workshop, "Preparing Your Child to Read and Write in School," led by Judy Fox, a curriculum specialist for the Washington (Maryland) County Schools and attended by fifty-five parents and child-care and health-care workers.

For the elementary school population, the project purchased copies of the elementary school principal's "book of the month" and distributed them in doctors' and dentists' offices throughout the town. In addition, the project helped to sponsor a pep rally to kick off the Augusta schools' "million-word challenge" at the beginning of the year and another rally, deemed "Pump It Up," to prepare students to take the state standardized test.

The project established two connections with local business and industry councils, one of which resulted in a college-and-career-awareness day that seventy-five high school students attended in April, focusing in particular on the reading and writing demands that a college curriculum or a career would place on them. Bowen made contact with one of the largest churches in Augusta to solicit its members' help in working as tutors for students, young parents, and adults who might come to the Woodruff County Literacy Council. Working in collaboration with Jeannie Waller, a doctoral student in rhetoric, composition, and literacy at the University of Arkansas, the project worked with the Woodruff County Literacy Council to compile a book of personal essays written by and about veterans of the armed forces in the region. The volume will be published as part of the unveiling of a new veterans' memorial statue on the courthouse lawn.

The most vibrant site of activity for the Augusta Community Literacy Advocacy Project was Augusta High School. The project set up a joint faculty-student task force, a ten-member group that offered perspectives on why relatively few students in the past had taken the ACT examination and gone to college, what students perceived the college environment to be like, and how the project could help them effect the transition from high school to college. The task force recommended that the project offer ACT-improvement workshops, specifically focusing on the reading challenges the exam poses to test-takers; in response, the project offered three such workshops in 2007–8. To learn more fully about the level of intellectual pursuits in college, about fifteen students, all juniors, from the high school participated with several other schools in the region in the Arkansas Delta Oral History Project, another project sponsored by the Office of the Brown Chair in English Literacy. In the Delta project, about sixty-five students from four schools worked in collaborative Web-based writing groups, each led by a University of Arkansas student mentor, to plan, complete, publish, and perform essays, stories, and scripts that grew out of oral history interviews they conducted in their towns. The Augusta Community Literacy Advocacy Project helped these students find topics and interviewees and brought them to Helena, Arkansas, for the opening and closing events, and to Fayetteville in the middle of the term for a face-to-face working session with their groups. The project sponsored two celebratory luncheons for the Arkansas Delta Oral History Project students, events that were repeated later in the year for any high school student earning a 3.2 grade average or higher and then for all graduates.

The project thus tried to embody an ethos dominated by three terms: challenge, support, and celebration. Bowen and the growing group of citizens and civic leaders she recruited both tacitly and explicitly said to young parents, elementary school students, high school students, and adults who might want to learn to read and write more effectively, "We challenge you to improve your reading and writing; we will do all we can to support you if you take up this challenge; we will celebrate your success when you succeed."

In general, the students and citizens of Augusta caught the buzz of the literacy initiative and responded positively. At the high school level, for example, thirty-three students took the ACT examination, up from twenty-five in the previous year, and the average composite score for these students went up a half a point. Of the forty-seven graduates of Augusta High School in May 2008, eleven had been accepted into colleges or technical schools by the time of graduation, in contrast to six the previous year, and twenty-three had received some kind of scholarship that would help them pursue postsecondary education if they chose to. One graduating student wrote to Bowen: "I don't think I would have even thought I was capable of attending college without the support that has been given to me. Knowing that people outside of school are willing to provide assistance, encouragement, and connections helped me to believe I could dream dreams and achieve them. My plans are now to get a college education, become a teacher, and return to help others."

Among the young, often single parents, the enthusiasm ran similarly strong. One soon-to-be mother, a high school senior herself, said the daylong early literacy workshop made her feel more confident about being a mother and helping her child have fun as they worked on reading together. One participant in the Arkansas Delta Oral History Project described her weekend of work and campus culture at the University of Arkansas as "the best weekend of my life."

ANALYZING THE RHETORICAL ACTIVITY OF THE
COMMUNITY LITERACY ADVOCACY PROJECT

At its base, of course, the tacit aim of the Augusta Community Literacy Advocacy Project is persuasive: Bowen, Collier, the White River Rural Health Center, and the Office of the Brown Chair in English Literacy need to persuade the citizens of Augusta and Woodruff County that improving the "literacy climate" is a necessary, if not sufficient, step to bring the town and region back to life. All three theoretical perspectives set out earlier in this essay can be used to analyze how this persuasion is being effected.

The municipality of Augusta has not, so far, reshaped its Web site to proclaim itself as the town that reads and writes together, and so far no one has moved to hang banners around town like the ones from the Nicaraguan literacy campaign of the 1960s: "Every home a classroom / Every table a school desk / Every Nicaraguan a teacher!"[12] But the events and workshops sponsored by the Community Literacy Advocacy Project do embody texts of various kinds—verbal and material—that can be analyzed from an Aristotelian perspective. For example, at the recent kickoff for year two of the project, held on August 12, 2008, the slogan printed on the program cover was "Shine a Light on Education," and at each seat, for each participant, was a small flashlight, courtesy of White River Rural Health Center. The sessions at the event both highlighted the project's successes in year one and announced the initiatives for year two: continuing work with young parents and their families, now supported by an additional grant from the Dollar General Foundation; a new emphasis on school and family literacy activities designed for youths age seven through fourteen, particularly boys; a continuation of the Arkansas Delta Oral History Project at Augusta High School and a new focus on helping students improve their reading and writing abilities via independent projects in their EAST (Environmental and Special Technology) lab course; an expansion of the project activities into all five major churches in Augusta, helping ministers see how they can build reading and writing activities into their services and outreach efforts; and a new initiative to develop community arts and literacy activities at the Woodruff County Library. If the claim in this Toulmin-model "enthymeme" is that Augusta needs to "shine a light on education" and the data comprise all the activities accomplished in year one and planned for year two, then the unspoken assumptions, the warrant, must be twofold: these activities constitute "the light" needed in the community, and there are still citizens of Augusta and Woodruff County who are in need of enlightenment.

The events and workshops emanating from the project qualify as the types of "civic communions" that Procter describes. The two year-opening kickoff events, the midyear community rally for literacy—at which 600 people showed up for a charity basketball game with "pep talks" about literacy during halftime—and the "celebration" luncheons for the high school students are certainly "significant moments of community interaction," directed toward the purported goal of civic improvement via literacy.[13] Congruent with Procter's analogy of civic and religious communions, the events, rallies, and workshops in Augusta frequently had an air of returning to "the good old days" in Augusta when the town was economically vibrant and the high school, in particular, was the center of intellectual life. These invocations gave the leaders of the project, the town, and the churches the opportunity, as Procter puts it, to "recall important texts and parables" as well as "important historic texts, people, and events that ultimately serve to solidify community identity and offer guides to appropriate civic values and practices."[14]

Finally, it is clear how the Augusta Community Literacy Advocacy Project functions rhetorically in the manner Long describes. In Long's model, the guiding metaphor for the project is embodied in the noun "advocacy" itself: the program as a whole is advocating for the town as it tries to revive its economic base, and the components of the program are blatantly advocating for the clients being served. The various initiatives being developed for Augusta High School—its participation in the Arkansas Delta Oral History Project and the workshops targeted at reading comprehension and time management on the ACT examination—and for young parents and their children openly advocate for the high school students as potentially college-bound and for the parents as effective literacy sponsors and providers in their homes. In Long's model, the location of the Augusta Community Literacy Advocacy Project comprises the material conditions of Augusta and north-central Arkansas—a region marked by economic, employment, and population declines—as well as the institutional leadership of White River Rural Health Center and, in particular, its CEO Collier, of efforts to revive the town and the region. The tenor of the discourse surrounding the Community Literacy Advocacy Project is marked by two adjectives: "supportive" and "nostalgic." Virtually all the activities sponsored by the Community Literacy Advocacy Project are imbued with a "can-do" and "we-can" rhetoric—the young parents' programs embody a "we can raise our children to succeed" rhetoric; the school programs are redolent of such terms as "celebration" and "opportunity"; the local literacy council representatives openly use phrases reflecting rebirth. At the same time, however, a great deal of the discourse surrounding the Community Literacy Advocacy Program has been blatantly nostalgic, reminiscent of the "good old days" when Augusta was prosperous, when students graduating from Augusta High School could find good jobs in the area, when teachers lived in the town and were part of its cultural fabric. The literacies being promoted by the Augusta Community Literacy Advocacy Program are primarily school-based. While some efforts are under way to elicit and support reflective writing among the adult citizenry, particularly in regard to the veterans' memorial story project, the bulk of the work so far has been dedicated to helping young parents build a literacy environment that will prepare their preschool children for academic literacy and for helping high school students develop the literacy abilities to master the ACT examination and get into college. What Long calls in her *Community Literacy and the Rhetoric of Local Publics* the "rhetorical invention" of the program—which she expands to embrace "implications" or "how rhetorical invention translates into choices, practices, and actions"—is highly instrumental: the program aims to get more high school students to apply for and attend college, to get more preschool children ready for school-based literacy, and to get more adults ready for the twenty-first-century workplace.

PUBLIC RHETORICAL ACTIVITY AS A TEACHING OPPORTUNITY

For all its successes—young parents learning how to create environments conducive to reading in their homes, high school students thinking seriously about going to college, adults capturing stories about veterans—the Augusta

Community Literacy Advocacy Project can be the source of intellectual anxiety, particularly for scholars who study literacy theory and the history of literacy movements in this century. As the director of an academic office, housed in the state's flagship university, dedicated to supporting the community literacy project, I could have reacted to this concern by squelching the plans of the project's leaders, by putting the brakes on until we sorted out the historical, theoretical, and ideological issues involved. I have not done that, choosing instead to use the ongoing project as an opportunity to teach the providers and clients in the program, as well as students at the University of Arkansas studying the history and theory of literacy, about how such issues become manifest in specific contexts like Augusta.

In the new argument being promoted about Augusta, *literacy* is a metonym, a single term into which a wide range of semantic and emotional associations are packed, and that metonymy is itself a source of tension. Like most observers of the contemporary educational scene who want to do what they can to improve it, working with the general assumption that better education leads to a better life, the citizens of Augusta who support the project and the various clienteles who benefit from it tend to see literacy as a set of discrete skills, most of them school-based, that are disconnected from the nuances of local social, economic, and political circumstances. This view, of course, corresponds to what Brian Street calls the "autonomous" model of literacy, one that embodies "the apparent neutrality of literacy practices" and one that Street maintains needs to be replaced with an "ideological model" that focuses on "the significance [of literacy practices] for the distribution of power in society and for authority relations."[15] As the project continues, therefore, one goal of its leaders must be to help both the service providers and the clientele to understand that the "literacy climate" they perceive in Augusta and Woodruff County did not simply emerge de novo. It is the outgrowth of a regional culture that has a long history of social stratification, of an educational culture that has not always lived up to the goal of equal access and equal benefits for all students, of an agricultural economy that essentially took from the poor and gave to the rich as family farms gave way to agribusinesses.

The work of Deborah Brandt is instructive in considering how to finesse these tensions. In her magisterial study of literacy in Americans' lives, Brandt makes two salient points about literacy sponsorship, the process by which "any agents, local or distant, concrete or abstract . . . support, teach, model, as well as recruit, regulate, suppress, or withhold literacy."[16] First, she explains, literacy sponsorship can actually lead to social stratification, rather than diminish it. Those who grow up with material conditions and opportunities conducive to incorporating reading and writing in their daily lives tend to rise socially and economically more than those who do not. But this social stratification is exactly what the Augusta Community Literacy Advocacy Project has the power to reduce, if not eliminate. The providers and supporters of the project are openly facing the fact that young parents, students, and adult nonreaders in their town have generally lacked affirmative, supportive sponsors of literacy, and the project has some power to provide such sponsorship. Second, Brandt asserts that the trope of "rising standards" for literacy that one hears in the media so regularly—those cries of "literacy crisis" that seem to emerge every five years or so—is actually just the opposite side of the literacy-sponsorship coin. We do not have literacy crises, Brandt would argue; instead, we have a gap, a lack of sufficient, appropriate, affirmative literacy sponsorship. Again, the Augusta Community Literacy Advocacy Project has the potential to make up at least part of this lack, this gap.

Above all else, as the Augusta Community Literacy Advocacy Project grows, its leaders must emphasize a veil of caution about the view that Harvey Graff in his eponymous 1979 book labeled "the literacy myth," the notion that literacy is somehow concomitant with moral uprightness, is a necessary and sufficient condition for social and economic advancement, and has, by nature, the power to "liberate" individuals.[17] Expanding on this work, Robert Arnove and Harvey Graff, in the introduction to their 1987 edited collection, *National Literacy Campaigns,* maintain that "in the twentieth century . . . pronouncements about literacy deem it a process of critical consciousness raising and human liberation. Just as frequently, such declarations refer to literacy not as an end in itself, but as a means to other goals—to the ends of national development and to a social order that elites, both national and international, define."[18] Arnove and Graff explain further: "Literacy is invested with a special significance, but seldom in and of itself. Learning to read, possibly to write, involves the acquisition or conferral of a new status—membership in a religious community, citizenship in a nation-state. Literacy often carries tremendous symbolic weight, quite apart from any power and new capabilities it may bring. The attainment of literacy per se operates as a badge, a sign of initiation into a select group and/or a larger community."[19]

In other words, Arnove and Graff argue, what gets occluded in campaigns to improve literacy are the individual goals and needs of the literacy learner. "Throughout history," they write, "the provision of literacy skills to reform either individuals or their societies rarely has been linked to notions of people using these skills to advance their own ends."[20] Everyone involved with the Augusta Community Literacy Advocacy Project, I believe, wants literacy learners to improve their reading and writing abilities so that the town and region can attract new businesses and industries, so that more high school students will go on to college (Arkansas now ranks fiftieth in the United States in the percentage of adults who hold a college degree), and so that adults can be more adequately prepared for a changing, literacy-demanding job market. But the people involved with the project, present company included, must recognize that the literacy learners' personal, individual goals—to read to their kids at home, to write their life stories, to read their Bibles and write for their church bulletins, and so on—must have the same priority as economic growth and civic revitalization. We all have our work cut out for us.

Notes

1. Jolliffe, "On Reading."
2. Toulmin, *Uses of Argument*. I am arguing that Toulmin's argument structure is essentially an enthymeme set on its side, with "data" representing the "minor premise" of the enthymeme, the "claim" representing its "conclusion," and the "warrants" representing the unspoken assumptions upon which the enthymeme is built.
3. Procter, *Civic Communion*, 5.
4. Ibid., 7.
5. Ibid., 8.
6. Ibid., 10.
7. Ibid., 14.
8. Long, *Community Literacy*, 15.
9. Ibid., 16.
10. Demographic data come from the U.S. Census Bureau (http://www.factfinder .census.gov) and from Sperling's Best Places Report (http://www.bestplaces.net/City/ Augusta-OVERVIEW-5052740000.aspx).
11. Augusta Recovery Initiative Meeting Notes, December 9, 2005.
12. Arnove and Graff, "National Literacy Campaigns," 604.
13. Procter, *Civic Communion,* 10.
14. Ibid., 14.
15. Street, "New Literacy," 430–31.
16. Brandt, "Sponsors of Literacy," 556.
17. Graff, *Literacy Myth*.
18. Arnove and Graff, "National Literacy Campaigns," 592.
19. Ibid., 596.
20. Ibid.

Works Cited

Arnove, Robert, and Harvey Graff. "National Literacy Campaigns." In *Literacy: A Critical Sourcebook*, edited by Ellen Cushman, Eugene R. Kintgen, Barry M. Kroll, and Mike Rose, 591–615. Boston: Bedford/St. Martin's, 2001.

Augusta, Arkansas. "Sperling's Best Places Report." http://www.bestplaces.net/City/ Augusta-OVERVIEW-5052740000.aspx (accessed August 31, 2008).

Brandt, Deborah. "Sponsors of Literacy." In *Literacy: A Critical Sourcebook*, edited by Ellen Cushman, Eugene R. Kintgen, Barry M. Kroll, and Mike Rose, 555–71. Boston: Bedford/St. Martin's, 2001.

Graff, Harvey. *The Literacy Myth: Literacy and Social Structure in the Nineteenth-Century City.* New York: Academic, 1979.

Jolliffe, David A. "On Reading and Writing Analytically: Theory, Method, Crisis Action Plan." In *Reading and Writing Analytically,* edited by David A. Jolliffe. New York: College Board, 2008.

Long, Eleanor. *Community Literacy and the Rhetoric of Local Publics.* West Lafayette, Ind.: Parlor Press, 2008.

Procter, David E. *Civic Communion: The Rhetoric of Community Building.* Lanham, Md.: Rowman and Littlefield, 2005.

Street, Brian. "The New Literacy Studies." In *Literacy: A Critical Sourcebook*, edited by Ellen Cushman, Eugene R. Kintgen, Barry M. Kroll, and Mike Rose, 430–42. Boston: Bedford/St. Martin's, 2001.

Toulmin, Stephen. *The Uses of Argument.* Cambridge: Cambridge University Press, 1958.

U.S. Census Bureau, "American Fact Finder." http://www.factfinder.census.gov (accessed August 31, 2008).

The Prospects for the Public Work of Rhetoric

A Coda on Codes

SUSAN C. JARRATT

The stimulating essays in this book display rhetorics for our times: publics variously concrete and elusive, interventions at times tentative, of mixed success, but full of energy. Even the most vividly present settings become publics differently according to the rhetorical order, tasks, and understanding brought to bear on them (Coogan). For guidance, the authors reach back into the eighteenth-century public as Habermas envisioned it—"a collaborative search for the common good"—but also look forward, beyond the hesitations of the Wingspread participants, into a newly realized array of millennial publics. The "public workers" of this volume find a *polis,* as Hannah Arendt predicted: in "the organization of the people as it arises out of acting and speaking together . . . its true space [lying] between people living together for this purpose, no matter where they happen to be."[1] A final word in response to these essays must work against finality in an effort to keep alive their activity, their fraught yet hopeful qualities: to the manifold and variegated qualities of the public works they record. Although there are oppositions and advocacies here, the dominant themes are qualification, principled hesitation, a stepping back from the reassuring rhetorics of pro, con, and happy compromise.

Like the participants in the Wingspread Conference of the 1960s, twenty-first-century public rhetoricians are made somewhat uneasy by the rhetorics of our times. Ackerman and Coogan identify this phenomenon as a problem of history: "What made Becker uneasy—what makes all of us uneasy—were publics that could not be contained by (or easily explained by) the rhetorical tradition, either in substance, style or medium." Traditions must be made anew, and new histories—"lost geographies"—are called forth by contemporary problems.[2] Urging readers to envision a postmodern *paideia,* the editors invite rhetoric's history in, not as an obligatory grounding or an answer to a dilemma but as a resource. Rather than clarifying through a general enlightenment, postmodern rhetorical history might resort to refraction: to gather diffuse sources from the present and angle them through the lens of the "prior" with the hope of sparking the imaginations of public rhetoric workers in the field, in the way that Coogan makes sophistic rhetoric over into a counter-public practice for Richmond teens. What are the rhetorical arts needful in this time, one in which "free-speech" and rational argument—or at least the ability to speak across ideological and political divides—seem to some to have lost force? Is there something other, or something more to be learned from pre-modern rhetorics? To shift the figure, might some newer historical narratives serve not as a stash but a font?

According to Bruner, "one way we can do the public work of rhetoric is by mapping the distance between history and memory, understanding how far those imaginaries are from historical fact, and with what consequence." Bruner refers to large-scale public memories of war, but we might apply his recommendation to rhetoric's histories and to ancient political history more generally. Changes in our own geopolitical realities may make it less and less possible to overlook (or to treat with a bland acceptance) the fact that the dominant ancient rhetorical cultures, even during the democracy and the republic, operated through the power of empire.

EMPIRE

"What word but 'empire,'" writes Michael Ignatieff in a *New York Times Magazine* article of January 2003, "describes the awesome thing that America is becoming?"—this on the eve of the invasion of Iraq.[3] With the fall of the Berlin Wall and the growth of multinational corporations, positive uses of this term begin to appear in middle-of-the-road political science journals and media outlets such as *Foreign Affairs, Harvard Review,* and the *Wall Street Journal.*[4] More pointed comparisons with *Pax Romana*, the Roman peace, can be found in political strategy statements produced by the Defense Department under George H. W. Bush and in the report of The Project for the New American Century, a nonprofit educational organization, used as a basis for Condoleezza Rice's 2001 National Security Strategy statement. The project's report, titled "Rebuilding America's Defenses," overtly argues that the United States, as the "world's most preeminent power," should resolve to "shape a new century favorable to American principles and interests." Despite the long-standing priorities of containment and deterrence, these documents openly employ a rhetoric of empire, referring to a global *Pax Americana* and "American peace" without irony[5]

In those years, we lived in a *Pax Americana* run by a government taking its cues from classical scholars in shaping its foreign policy. Daniel Mendelsohn, in his brilliant *New Yorker* reviews of new publications in ancient Greek history and literature, points out, for example, the "tendentious" angles of vision in a new history of the Peloponnesian war by Donald Kagan, coauthor of the strategy statement mentioned above, and in Victor Davis Hanson's works on Greek military strategy, recommended by Vice President Cheney to his staff during the 2001 war in Afghanistan.[6] These are the intellectuals who have guided the world's newest empire through the first, devastating decade of the new millennium. Some rhetors here are working very locally, in the geographies of community or neighborhood, but sometimes with a reach into the geographies of empire (for example, Cushman with the victims of nineteenth-century U.S. internal imperialism against American Indians; Grabill against the pressures driving international shipping). Many of the rhetors in this volume choose to work for and with disenfranchised groups, helping them to find and hone words that will give them power, working across class and professional space to put rhetorical expertise to work. The strength of the volume lies in its insistence on a dialogue among history (C. Miller), theory, analysis, and practical community work. Yet another direction we might take with a postmodern *paideia* would turn toward those in power, asking what are the networks of affiliation, the rhetorics of space, and rhetorical strategies that will enable us to move the emperors of our own era?[7]

This is not an easy task. What can be done rhetorically in our times, difficult times for rhetoric, when an Enlightenment dream of democracy is no longer recognizable, let alone sustainable (Cintron): a "twilight of democracy"?[8] What can be done rhetorically when the forces of "conspiracy" (Ackerman and Coogan) do not listen to reason? "Democracy is a beautiful thing," says George W. Bush in February 2003, as millions of protesters worldwide urged caution on the eve of the attack of Iraq.[9] The beauty lies in the freedom to demonstrate, but the obligation of those in power to listen, engage, and respond has fallen into disuse. The range of opinions reaching into and influencing the world's most powerful ruler has narrowed dramatically, and the multitude of ethics violations charged against legislators brings home the "inartistic" force brought to bear by corporations and heavily underwritten interest groups.[10] And yet as Ackerman and Coogan insist, scholars in *The Public Work of Rhetoric* "reject the idea that public life is dead, that it has been stripped of agitation, assembly, and deliberation." They create and call upon *poiêsis* for the production of thick publics (Bruner), recognize rhetorical agency as protean and promiscuous (Campbell), and in so doing, call forth a newly imagined rhetorical history to underwrite them. If Bush calls democracy "beautiful," rhetoricians have the option to take him at his word, returning to beauty, wonder, and fantasy as weapons, not of mass distraction, but of a new political imagination.

"LOST GEOGRAPHIES" OF PUBLIC LIFE

The editors of this volume, citing Neil Smith and Setha Low, cast the problem of publics into a wider space than any preexisting *agora* or *ekklesia*.[11] Histories of rhetoric are replete with lost geographies, and not only those pockets of populations excluded from public life whose words, in whatever forms they could take, are waiting to be retrieved. The culturally Greek intelligentsia from the eastern provinces of the Roman Empire inhabited one of those geographies. Until recently encased within a narrative of decline into "literariness," scholars have begun to reconsider this period in the last decade or so, arriving at a dramatic counterstatement to centuries-old historiography: that public rhetoric did not die out in the era of the Roman Empire. Opportunities for imagining, performing, and arguing for collective good for subjects of empire did not disappear but persisted—coded within an array of unfamiliar genres.[12]

The intersections of geography, language, and cultural practices for these "Greeks" differs decidedly from the famous autochthony of classical Athens. Tied neither to birthplace nor ancestry—that is, in the view of most critics, not to be understood as an "ethnicity"—Greek identity was a cultural acquisition on the part of a select group of elite men, often Roman citizens, closely identified with their provincial cities in the Near East. Overlooked or deemphasized in most treatments of these rhetors is a recognition that their performances enabled them to take on the responsibilities of the public intellectual on behalf of imperial subjects in extremely complex, multilayered speaking situations. Adopting the stance of Greek rhetor usually signaled an alienation from Roman power but not exactly subjection; it was a claim for prominence in a stratified and competitive social world as well as a position from which to act as critic and adviser to the indigenous power brokers of a province, as well as to the Roman governor and, on occasion, emperor. Among the remnants they mined resided the memory of discourses of democratic deliberation with its attendant critique of tyranny.

FREE SPEECH: PRACTICE, POLITICS, POSTURE?

To speak openly and truthfully to those in power or to cloak your ideas and opinions in artful allusions: these were the terms of a rhetorical debate during a period when arbitrary violence, in the city itself as well as in the provinces and even against members of the elite classes, was a constant possibility.[13] As Peter Brown puts it, "a tide of horror lapped close to the feet of all educated persons."[14] From the conquest of Philip of Macedon over Greece at the end of democracy, to the imperial sweep of Alexander, to the rise of Rome as a conquering power in the third and second centuries B.C.E., and finally to the declaration of empire by Augustus in 27 C.E., public exchange took place in "in the suspicious atmosphere of a court society, where people tend to assume a demeanour conformable to the pleasure of the ruler."[15] Yet the textual tradition in Greek from the very beginning records examples of characters risking violent retribution to break through the censorious barrier to speak uncomfortable truths. Parrhêsia originated in the classical period, and the recently published 1983 Berkeley lectures by Michel Foucault on its origins and history lay out its distinctive parameters as a rhetorical practice: the free-speaker "make[s] it manifestly clear and obvious that what he says is his *own* opinion . . . us[ing] the most direct words and forms of expression he can find."[16] Moreover, this "free-speaker" takes a risk, puts himself or herself in danger, by addressing someone in a position of power. The relationship to the interlocutor is a game, but with risk to only one party: it is a game but also a duty.

The "free-speaker"—*parrhêsiastes*—was assigned certain attributes in these discourses, a rhetorical posture that translated easily to republican Rome, with its legend and history of heroic challenge to tyranny, and became coded in a fusion of masculinity and national identity: "Rhetorical education was designed to instill in Roman boys habits that would make their masculinity literally visible to the world: along with constructing logical arguments, handling narration and interrogation, and creative ways to use words, they learned to stand up straight, look others straight in the eye, gesticulate with grace and authority."[17] As incomplete as a description of Roman rhetorical practice and unsustainable as this posture was, it nonetheless constituted one of the layers of (always multiply mediated) cultural assumption under which Greek rhetors in the provincial East had to work.

"Free speech" lies at the heart of a rhetoric invented in classical Athens—an ideology at least partially realized in practice—with its courts and deliberative assemblies. It is arguably the rhetoric that undergirds most contemporary educational rationales for courses in writing: the facility with language that enables public participation and assures the testing of ideas and policies in democratic forums. The persona most likely to deliver this speech is upright, honest, and straightforward, speaking earnestly in his or her own voice with nothing to hide. What Foucault suggests only briefly, but what Carolyn Miller discusses here for rhetoric more generally, and second sophistic rhetors exploited creatively is "free speech" as itself a figure, a stance, oscillating in relation to its other: "figured discourse." Cloaking one's criticism in metaphors, or, even better, lodging it within allusions to Greek history, myth, and literature, was not only a safer path for the Greek rhetor but sometimes more effective because more impressive and artful. Frederick Ahl points out, "Blunt speech gives way to oblique speech in situations where the speaker is (or feels) threatened or unsure of his audience. Many ancient poets, and all ancient rhetorical theorists, lived when overt criticism of the ruling powers was dangerous. They sensed the need for obliqueness. But they also sensed the greater persuasiveness of oblique suggestion." He goes on to observe that "rhetorical theorists wanted to train students not in how to achieve martyrdom, which requires no special education, but in how to deal successfully with the powerful and even shape and direct their power."[18] A successfully "figured" message gives the listener—a ruler, but also the others present—the pleasure of solving a mystery, of realizing the power of their common education: the *paideia* shared by Roman, Greek, and provincial elites alike. For Foucault, "the touchstone of the good ruler is his ability to play the *parrhêsiatic* game."[19]

Which "rulers"—power brokers—in our contemporary scene are willing to play such a game? In fact, the rhetorical, and thus political, success of George W. Bush in some part lay in his claim not to play the game of knowing, to be outside any *paideia*, to be the ignorant and thus innocent rustic operating through a kind of folk knowledge. A postmodern *paideia* demands the ability not only to take up stances on the part of public rhetors but to read the postures of those in power and, most important, to engage them, or to play their games, or to play some other game that is recognizable across lines of power. That would be the definition of a *paideia*—a common cultural language that can be taken up by many. When progressive (or "left") journalism and scholarship engages with the rhetorics of the powerful, the effect is most often a critique that marks difference. I have certainly engaged in such projects myself.[20] We create thereby a standoff of *parrhêsiastics,* or worse, isolate ourselves like philosophers during the period of the Roman Empire: hermetic social critics who are not involved in or dirtied by these rhetorical/power games. Practicing rhetoric across the boundary of university and community, say Ackerman and Coogan, requires "a shedding of academic adornments, a different professional disposition." The public works rhetorician of the twenty-first century sheds the beard, robes, hermetic habits, and isolationist disdain of the philosopher of the imperial era, most often moving down the ladder of public legitimacy and enfranchisement. Is it possible to imagine moving in the other direction? One scene that comes to mind from the collection here is Grabill's conversation with the mayor at a party. Just imagine—

DISPOSITIONS

A fanciful anecdote recorded by Philostratus in his third-century *Lives of the Sophists* imagines the emperor Trajan seating the Sophist Dio (called Chrysostom, or Golden-Mouthed) by his side on the golden chariot in which he rides in triumphal processions, turning to him and saying, "I don't understand what you say but I love you as I love myself."[21] This scene, no doubt apocryphal, dramatizes a relationship between rhetor and emperor organized around patronage and affiliation. Trajan, from a long-established Roman family that immigrated to Spain (a fully Romanized province) in his grandfather's time, came up through the army and was "adopted" by the emperor Nerva in 97 and chosen to succeed him without struggle in 98. Trajan stood as the first in a sequence of "good" emperors, following the violent and turbulent realms of Domitian and Nero before him.[22] He was a mild-tempered, generous, and judicious ruler who enacted a number of policies benefiting children and utilitarian building projects. He achieved more renown and popular goodwill, however, for his military conquest of Dacia and the elaborate gladiatorial games following thereon. He died in 117 returning from an attack on Parthians in Armenia, an attempt to extend the eastern reach of the empire.

Dio (40–110 or 120), a native of Prusa (now Bursa, on the Aegean coast of Turkey), chief city in the province of Bithynia, was born to wealthy parents who had been granted Roman citizenship. He was provided with a first-rate Greek education and, like many of the figures in this group, cultivated close relationships with powerful Romans, including the emperor Vespasian early in his career. Dio's free speaking, however, provoked the ire of Domitian, who exiled him from his native province and from Italy in 82. He was returned under Nerva in 96, and then formed a close relationship with Trajan, to whom he may have addressed his four discourses on kingship near the end of the century.[23]

Why, in this made-up story, does the emperor say he does not understand what the Sophist says?[24] On one interpretation, we can note the importance of the Sophist's proximity that may override any particular position or piece of advice he may be offering; "love" or *philia*—manly friendship, is what matters in the networks of power relations between rhetor and emperor.[25] On the level of rhetoric, the anecdote raises the question of how communication operated across cultural and power differences: not only what it was and was not possible to say, but how it was possible to be heard. In fact, local elites were essential to the management of the empire: "Everywhere it was the Roman policy to win over, and to enfranchise, the local leaders."[26] In the East, Roman rule maintained existing civic institutions and relied on the indigenous property-owners for crucial operations of the city.

So from the sophist's perspective, being heard *and* understood mattered a great deal, even though the historical distance and state of the archival record make linking any one sophistic discourse to a specific audience or outcome very difficult.[27] But, in an odd way, this circumstance provides a provocative mirror of the theoretical commitments in this volume in the adoption of a theory of "publics" over against "audience." Public rhetors are concerned with the circulation of discourse—its call, its constituents, and the climate it creates. These we can establish for the second sophistic, and they are, in many cases, powerfully oriented toward a vision of the polis as a sustaining form of human organization: the Greek concept and practice taken up—and blown up—by the Romans. Whether or not Trajan was influenced by Dio or by Pliny, a Roman of the same era who composed an extensive panegyric to the emperor, at points arguing for the exercise of good government, the emperor could not have imagined or enacted his benevolent policies in the absence of a discourse outlining and supporting such actions. This idea could also be understood in terms of legitimation. The Greek rhetors played a role, literally, in keeping alive the imagination and value of democratic rule, on the one hand, and the condemnation of tyrannical imperial behavior, on the other. What Peter W. Rose identifies as the ideological work of Cicero's oratorical arguments is perhaps even more true of the epideictic discourses of the Greek rhetors: "An oration does more than propose a specific course of action: its persuasive function is aimed at constructing a vision of the real. . . . This vision of the real is the oration's enabling fiction."[28]

FIGURED DISCOURSE

It is difficult to show figured discourse at work because the hidden message is embedded in culture and allusion—a matter of historically informed speculation at such a distance.[29] What is communicated through figured discourse is, most often, a stance, attitude, or posture, rather than a full-fledged argument (although there are examples of these from the imperial period). In the ceremonial contexts where Greek rhetors made their appearances, figured discourse runs against the grain of smooth, showy oratorical performance: it is the grain of sand in the oyster, the residue left echoing in the minds of the auditors— Roman, Greek, and all the others listening at such events—the uncomfortable or enlivening, depending on one's position, sense that all is not well in the political order.

The most characteristic examples are drawn from references to classical Greek mythology and literature. The prick comes when the educated listener, who brings a deep familiarity with conventional impressions of characters and stories from Homer, the tragedians, and Greek mythology more generally, hears a reference that subtly recasts the valences of the *paideia*. Consider the city encomium of Libanius (314–93), one of the imperial period's most prolific Greek rhetors: a native of Antioch, trained in Athens, called to serve in Constantinople by imperial command, and eventually allowed to return to his beloved city on the Orontes River as the official Sophist of the city.[30] The history of Libanius's relationship with imperial power is too complex to relate in detail here, but a few touch points will sketch a sense of the perilous balance between violence and coercion, on the one hand, and beneficence, on the other, within which Greek rhetors were held. When he was born in 314, Libanius's family was recovering from a disastrous punishment inflicted upon it a decade earlier "by the intemperate wrath" of the emperor Diocletian. When he returned to Antioch in 354, the entire city council, including Libanius's uncle, had been arrested by the Roman prefect whose policies had provoked riots. This excessive prefect was soon replaced by a friendly and effective one, and at the time of the composition of the "Antiochikos," Libanius was safe, respected, and soon to enjoy a brief period of stimulating exchange with the emperor Julian.[31] From these few details in a long and eventful life, the extreme vicissitudes of fortune, along with the actual impact, for good or ill, of public rhetoric at this time will become clearer.

What did empire mean to the Greek Sophists? Protection, employment, awe, threat, and the way things were. What was it possible for a Greek to say in the face of Roman imperial power? Libanius delivered this speech in 356 on the occasion of an Olympic games in the middle of a long career and at a hopeful moment in the course of his relations with emperors—on the eve of the accession of Julian to the highest office. Two-thirds of the way through a richly detailed description of the history and physical beauties of this thriving metropolis, Libanius mentions the existence of Rome almost as an aside. When the "will of heaven" decreed that post-Alexandrian rulers of Antioch were to be replaced and the world was "girt with the golden chain of Rome" (¶129), the transfer of power occurred with no violence or rancor, Libanius claims, and Romans simply added their customs to existing ones.[32] To a contemporary reader, Libanius sounds happily reconciled to the conditions of empire. If there are some constraints implied by the figure of a chain, material compensations, beauty, and technical artistry weigh against them, especially coming from a Greek intellectual who appeared to be faring reasonably well under imperial rule.[33] But educated listeners would hear more. The Greek expression "chain of gold" from the Homeric dialect is rare, used by Zeus in *Iliad*, Book 8, in a violent threat to the other Olympian gods. Any who violated Zeus's order would be snatched up, dangled by this golden cable, and then hurled "down to the murk of Tartarus" (l. 15). Zeus makes the threat to show "how far I tower over the gods, I tower over men" (ll. 20–31).[34] If the citizens of the lovely and prosperous Antioch were lulled through the first hundred paragraphs of Libanius's oration to feel that Rome was far away, they are wrenched back through this reference to a vision of a violent power struggle— one that only the *princeps*, the first among them, will win. With the ferocious power of the empire, he can drag even its most privileged members, "and the earth . . . and sea, all together," up with a golden cable and leave them dangling in midair.

Romans had a stake in appearing and acting in moderate ways. The ideology of benevolence at the center of Pax Romana cannot be sustained in complete contradiction, as the recent removal of the violent prefect demonstrated. The city Sophist's role required simultaneously speaking to his fellow Antiochenes and keeping the content of this ideology present to the mind and vision of the Roman rulers, both in its negative and positive aspects. Elsewhere in the speech, Libanius directly and eloquently defends practices of civic rhetorical deliberation (¶139–49), and thus we see the oscillation between *parrhêsia* and figured discourse. The council, Libanius asserts, has the wisdom and oratorical ability of a group of Sophists in their prime, and "this ability compels the governors to live up to their name, but not to go beyond it, and play the tyrant" (¶140). The mastery of deliberative oratory guarantees the independence of the council, providing it with a "magic" even greater than the governors' (¶141). Libanius gives precise instructions to the Roman governor about how to conciliate the local population and succeed: "any governor who wins a fair reputation thinks that he gained the crown of virtue, not because he has overcome insubordination, but because he has gained his praises among free and intelligent men" (¶143). Finally, the rhetor names the art of unconcealment specifically: "It is not a case that some may speak and others may not; there is a freedom of speech in which all share" (¶145).[35] And here we rotate back into the realm of the wished-for or projected state of affairs.

CODES

How might this very brief glimpse at postclassical Greek rhetoric give aid or inspiration to twenty-first-century public rhetors? In what ways would it prefigure their efforts, suggesting points of emphasis for future practice? First, the situation of the Greek rhetors might suggest the importance of spending more time and attention on ways of addressing those in power and mixed publics in mutually recognizable terms. As academics, many of us are more comfortable as polemicists or critics, or in many public settings, as enablers of the underdeveloped rhetorics of the disenfranchised. Perhaps it is time to cultivate the rhetorical arts of the polis-diplomate of the twenty-first century, seeking out the codes that travel across power and class differentials within whatever geographies are available.

Second, we find in the conjunction of postclassical and postmodern rhetorics a confirmation of "free speech" as a stance or posture rather than a revelation of the truth itself. Sophistic tactics combine *parrhêsia* with the arts of irony, allusion, and generic experimentation, tactics at present more at home in electronic media than print or face-to-face contexts both in and out of school.[36] Rhetoric and writing in twentieth-century U.S. schools have most commonly occupied the domains of the pragmatic and instrumental, the earnest and straightforward, the clear and self-present. We specialize in the arts of free speech: of rational argument, logic, clear thinking. No doubt these arts, in all their complexity and power, should remain a strong emphasis for rhetoric studies. Perhaps the twist in the postmodern *paideia* has to do with how we represent their status and effects, their place within the *poikilos* nature—the pied, multicolored, mottled, intricate, changeful, unstable, wily ways—of twenty-first-century communications. Reimagining pedagogical mixes of instrumental and literary is clearly not a call to set the aside logos, nor would it entail the wholesale adoption of an ancient curriculum.[37] In the work of public rhetoric of this volume, the logos is often embedded within other genres: the academic conference (Condit), the meeting (Grabill), and the online exchange (Cushman). As pedagogues, public works rhetors, like their predecessors, construct practice sessions: mock scenarios in which students with disabilities can invent terminologies for their conditions and experiment with and restructure their emotional stances (Flower). Coogan's literacy group works in expressive modes—producing stories in recognizably literary forms—to which publics responded powerfully.

The 2008 presidential campaign gives us a striking example of how far we have to go—we academics and we citizens—in mastering the codes of free speech and figured discourse. Barack Obama's success as a memoirist prior to his candidacy for the highest office made front-page news in an article titled "The Story of Obama, Written by Obama." Obama's self-presentation in *Dreams from my Father,* writes Janny Scott, "leaves *an impression* of candidness and authenticity that gives it much of its power." The article goes on to quote Stanford English professor Arnold Rampersad, author of a biography of Ralph Ellison: "The book is so literary. . . . It is so full of clever tricks—inventions for literary effect—that I was taken aback, even astonished. But make no mistake, these are simply the tricks that art trades in, and out of these tricks is supposed to come our realization of truth."[38] The journalist gets what the English professor finds "astonishing": that truth is realized though persuasive discourse.

Of the many truths realized by the public rhetors in this volume, I close by nominating as the most vividly hopeful the Richmond teens' "sanctuary" mural (see this book's dust jacket). A powerful fusion of word and image that becomes a public argument, this act of fabrication reminded me, in all of its colorful, courageous improbability, of the evocations of peace and harmony echoing through Greek rhetoric under empire.[39] Publics have always been constructed in the absence of and hope for an ideal. With their act of fabrication, the teens create a public space of appearance, asserting their "reality" in Arendt's sense, and their hope: "Power is actualized only where word and deed have not parted company, where words are not empty and deeds not brutal."[40]

NOTES

1. Arendt, *Human Condition,* 198.

2. See Royster, "Disciplinary Landscape," on traditions.

3. Ignatieff, "Burden," 22.

4. Foster, "Rediscovery," 2–3.

5. Kagan, Schmitt, and Donnelly, "Rebuilding," 1, iv. See also Hartnett and Stengrim, *Globalization,* 1–39.

6. Mendelsohn, "Theatres," 79–84.

7. Such a direction could also be understood as the historical equivalent of anthropology's turn toward "studying up." See Nader, "Up the Anthropologist," 284–311.

8. Hartnett and Stengrim, *Globalization,* 267–92.

9. *San Francisco Chronicle,* February 19, 2003. Bush made these informal remarks in reference to worldwide protests the day before in conversation with reporters after an unrelated event at the White House. Numerous national and international newspapers quoted the remarks on February 19, 2003.

10. Haussamen, "Editorial." For a longer history, see Wines, "Ethics Violations."

11. Smith and Low, Introduction, 1–16. See also Hauser, *Vernacular Voices,* 1–30.

12. See recent studies by Goldhill, *Erotic Edge,* 1–28; Pernot, *Rhetoric,* 128–201; and Whitmarsh, *Greek Literature,* 1–38, for general discussions of this group, including the problematic nature of the "Second Sophistic" label, and for an extensive bibliography. All subsequent dates will be in the Common Era unless specified.

13. Carolyn Miller's chapter in this volume provides an illuminating and carefully documented discussion of "concealment" as a transhistorical feature of rhetorical practice. The question here concerns the choice of tactics under specific historical and material circumstances.

14. Brown, *Power and Persuasion*, 51–52.

15. Konstan, *Emotions*, 31.

16. Foucault, *Fearless Speech*, 12.

17. Connolly, "Virile Tongues," 86.

18. Ahl, "Art of Safe Criticism," 184, 203.

19. Foucault, *Fearless Speech*, 22.

20. See, for example, Jarratt, "George W. Bush."

21. Philostratus, *Lives*, 21.

22. For accounts of the reigns of the two emperors who became the epitomes of violent misrule, see Suetonius, *Twelve Caesars*, 213–46, 299–314.

23. Dio Chrysostom, "Kingship Discourses."

24. On the literal level, the comment may be taken to refer to language differences, although translator Wilmer Cave Wright comments "that Trajan understood Greek is probable." Philostratus, *Lives*, 20–21 n.5. The best education was in Attic Greek, but Roman public life and legal actions were conducted in Latin, which not all of the Greek intelligentsia deigned to learn. It is assumed that were many vernacular languages spoken in the empire, although very few written records remain. Among them would have been demotic Greek, Celtic, Coptic, Punic, Aramaic, Syriac, and numerous others. On this topic, see Brunt, *Roman Imperial Themes*, 277–80, for an overview and bibliography.

25. See Whitmarsh, *Greek Literature*, 181–246.

26. Brunt, *Roman Imperial Themes*, 268.

27. See Whitmarsh, *Greek Literature*, 207, 246. Whitemarsh argues the unlikelihood that any of these orations were presented to Trajan. Within Whitmarsh's theoretical paradigm, searching for extratextual contexts and effects dooms the historian/critic to an "expressive-realist" methodology (see 20–38). His emphasis on the textuality of second sophistic rhetoric is accompanied by a severely diminished recognition of material circumstances. In my view, exile is more than a trope.

28. Rose, "Cicero," 367. See also Poulakos, *Speaking*, 4, on the political orientation of Isocrates' rhetoric in the classical era.

29. For a reading of figured discourse in Anna Comnena's Byzantine era history, *Alexiad*, see Quandahl and Jarratt, "'To Recall Him,'" 301–35.

30. Too late to fall under Philostratus's designation "Second Sophist," Libanius nonetheless belongs with them, as he carries on the rhetorical practices of the Greek revival in the Roman East. For background on Libanius, see Libanius, *Autobiography*; Norman, General Introduction, xi–xviii; Cribiore, *School of Libanius*, 13–41.

31. Norman, General Introduction, xi–xiii.

32. Libanius, "Oration 11," 31.

33. For Libanius's financial circumstances, see his own extensive *Autobiography* and Norman, General Introduction. On Libanius's school, see Cribiore, *School of Libanius*, 111–73.

34. Homer, *Iliad*, "Book 8," 231–50. (Fagles translates the key term as "cable.")

35. Libanius, "Oration 11," 34–36.

36. See Fishman et al., "Performing Writing," 224–52, on student performance within the academic sphere.

37. See Brady, "Review," 70–81, for a review of new books on composition and literature.

38. Scott, "Story of Obama," 22 (emphasis added).

39. See, for example, Aristides' encomium of Rome. Oliver, "Ruling Power," 901–3. See George, "From Analysis to Design," 11–39, on visual design as argument.

40. Arendt, *Human Condition*, 199–200.

WORKS CITED

Ahl, Frederick. "The Art of Safe Criticism in Greece and Rome." *American Journal of Philology* 105 (1984): 174–208.

Arendt, Hannah. *The Human Condition*. Chicago: University of Chicago Press, 1958.

Brady, Laura. "Review: Retelling the Composition-Literature Story." *College English* 71 (2008): 70–81.

Brown, Peter. *Power and Persuasion in Late Antiquity: Toward a Christian Empire*. Madison: University of Wisconsin Press, 1992.

Brunt, P. A. *Roman Imperial Themes*. Oxford: Clarendon Press, 1990.

Connolly, Jill. "Virile Tongues: Rhetoric and Masculinity." In *A Companion to Roman Rhetoric*, edited by William Dominik and Jon Hall, 83–97. Oxford: Blackwell, 2007.

Cribiore, Raffaella. *The School of Libanius in Late Antique Antioch*. Princeton, N.J.: Princeton University Press, 2007.

Dio Chrysostom. Vol. 1. Translated by J. W. Cohoon. Cambridge, Mass.: Harvard University Press, 1949.

Fishman, Jenn, et al. "Performing Writing, Performing Literacy." *College Composition and Communication* 52 (2005): 224–52.

Foster, John Bellamy. "The Rediscovery of Imperialism." *Monthly Review* 54, no. 6 (2002): 1–16.

Foucault, Michel. *Fearless Speech*. Edited by Joseph Pearson. Los Angeles: Semiotext(e), 2001.

George, Diana. "From Analysis to Design: Visual Communication in the Teaching of Writing." *College Composition and Communication* 54 (2002): 11–39.

Goldhill, Simon. "The Erotic Eye: Visual Stimulation and Cultural Conflict." In *Being Greek under Rome*, 154–94. Cambridge: Cambridge University Press, 2001.

Gusterson, Hugh. "Up Revisited." *Political and Legal Anthropology Review* 20 (1997): 114–19.

Hartnett, Stephen, and Laura Ann Stengrim. *Globalization and Empire: The U.S. Invasion of Iraq, Free Markets, and the Twilight of Democracy*. Tuscaloosa: University of Alabama Press, 2006.

Hauser, Gerard A. *Vernacular Voices: The Rhetoric of Publics and Public Spheres*. Columbia: University of South Carolina Press, 1999.

Haussmen, Heath. "Editorial: Ethics Violations Need Real Investigations." Citizens for Responsibility and Ethics in Washington. http://www.crewsmostcorrupt.org/node/413 (accessed September 12, 2008).

Homer. *The Iliad*. Translated by Robert Fagles. New York: Viking, 1990.

Ignatieff, Michael. "The Burden." *New York Times Magazine*, January 5, 2003, 22–27, 50, 53–54.

Jarratt, Susan C. "George W. Bush, 'Graduation Speech at West Point.'" *Voices of Democracy Project*. http://www.voicesofdemocracy.com/ (accessed June 1, 2002).

Kagan, Donald, Gary Schmitt, and Thomas Donnelly. "Rebuilding America's Defenses. Strategy, Forces and Resources for a New Century." Report of the Project for the New American Century, 2000. http://www.newamericancentury.org/RebuildingAmericas Defenses.pdf (accessed July 3, 2009).

Konstan, David. *The Emotions of the Ancient Greeks: Studies in Aristotle and Classical Literature*. Toronto: University of Toronto Press, 2006.

Libanius. *Autobiography (Oration 1) the Greek Text*. Translated by A. F. Norman. New York: Oxford University Press, 1965.

————. "Oration 11: The Antiochikos: In Praise of Antioch." Translated by A. F. Norman. In *Antioch as a Centre of Hellenic Culture as Observed by Libanius*, 3–65. Liverpool: Liverpool University Press, 2000.

Mendelsohn, Daniel. "Theatres of War." *New Yorker*, January 12, 2004, 79–84.

Nader, Laura. "Up the Anthropologist—Perspectives Gained from Studying Up." In *Reinventing Anthropology*, edited by Dell H. Hymes, 284–311. New York: Pantheon Books, 1972.

Norman, A. F. General Introduction. In *Antioch as a Centre of Hellenic Culture as Observed by Libanius*, xi–xxii. Liverpool: Liverpool University Press, 2000.

Obama, Barack. *Dreams from My Father: A Story of Race and Inheritance*. New York: Three Rivers Press, 2004.

Oliver, James H., trans. "The Ruling Power. A Study of the Roman Empire in the Second Century after Christ through the Roman Oration of Aelius Aristides." *Transactions of the American Philological Society* 43 (1953): 873–1003.

Pernot, Laurent. *Rhetoric in Antiquity*. Translated by W. E. Higgins. Washington, D.C.: Catholic University Press of America, 2005.

Philostratus. *Lives of the Sophists*. In *Philostratus and Eunapius*, 2–315. Translated by Wilmer Cave Wright. Cambridge, Mass.: Harvard University Press, 1921.

Plato. *The Republic of Plato*. Translated by Francis MacDonald Cornford. New York: Oxford University Press, 1941.

Poulakos, Takis. *Speaking for the Polis: Isocrates' Rhetorical Education*. Columbia: University of South Carolina Press, 1997.

Quandahl, Ellen, and Susan C. Jarratt. "'To Recall Him . . . Will Be a Subject of Lamentation': Anna Comnena as Rhetorical Historiographer." *Rhetorica* 26 (2008): 301–35.

Rose, Peter W. "Cicero and the Rhetoric of Imperialism: Putting the Politics Back into Political Rhetoric." *Rhetorica* 13 (1995): 359–99.

Royster, Jacqueline J. "Disciplinary Landscaping, or Contemporary Challenges in the History of Rhetoric." *Philosophy and Rhetoric* 2 (2003): 148–67.

Scott, Janny. "The Story of Obama, Written by Obama." *New York Times*, May 18, 2008.

Smith, Neil, and Setha Low. "Introduction: The Imperative of Public Space." In *The Politics of Public Space*, edited by Setha Low and Neil Smith, 1–16. New York: Routledge, 2006.

Suetonius. *The Twelve Caesars*. Translated by Robert Graves. London: Penguin Books, 1957.

Vitanza, Victor J. *Negation, Subjectivity, and the History of Rhetoric*. Albany: SUNY Press, 1997.

Wells, Susan. "Rogue Cops and Health Care: What Do We Want from Public Writing." *College Composition and Communication* 47 (1996): 325–41.

Westrup, J. A., and F. Ll. Harrison. *The New College Encyclopedia of Music*. New York: W. W. Norton, 1976.

Whitmarsh, Tim. *Greek Literature and the Roman Empire. The Politics of Imitation*. New York: Oxford University Press, 2004.

————. *The Second Sophistic*. New York: Oxford University Press, 2005.

Wines, Michael. "Ethics Violations in House Spur Call for Tougher Rules." *New York Times*, December 19, 1988.

Contributors

John M. Ackerman is an associate professor of communication at the University of Colorado at Boulder. He directs the Program for Writing and Rhetoric and holds the Ineva Baldwin Chair of Arts and Sciences. He codirects the 2011 Rhetoric Society of America Institute in Boulder and has chaired the Doctoral Consortium of Rhetoric and Composition. His research on disciplinarity, architecture, and everyday life has appeared in various journals and edited collections; an article with Louise Phelps on disciplinary visibility will appear in the sixty-year commemorative issue of *College Composition and Communication*.

M. Lane Bruner is currently professor of rhetoric and politics in the Department of Communication at Georgia State University in Atlanta, Georgia. He is the author of *Democracy's Debt* (2009) and *Strategies of Remembrance* (2002), and he is a coeditor of *Market Democracy in Post-Communist Russia* (2005). He has written numerous essays appearing in journals such as the *Quarterly Journal of Speech*, *Rhetoric and Public Affairs*, *Discourse and Society*, and *Text and Performance Quarterly*. His current research is on political psychoses, artful resistance, and the aesthetic state.

Ralph Cintron is an associate professor of English studies as well as Latin American and Latino studies at the University of Illinois at Chicago (UIC). He is the author of *Angelstown: Chero Ways, Gang Life, and Rhetorics of the Everyday*, which received honorable mention for the Victor Turner prize in ethnographic writing from the American Anthropological Association. He has also been a Rockefeller Foundation fellow; a Fulbright scholar at the University of Prishtina in Kosova, where he taught political science; and twice a Great Cities Institute scholar at the College of Urban Planning and Public Administration at UIC. He has been elected to the executive boards of the College Conference on Composition and Communication and the Rhetoric Society of America. He is currently working on a book tentatively titled "Democracy as Fetish: Rhetoric, Ethnography, and the Expansion of Life" and coediting with Robert Hariman *Power, Rhetoric, and Political Culture: The Texture of Political Action*.

Celeste M. Condit is a Distinguished Research Professor in the Department of Speech Communication at the University of Georgia. Her work on the social impacts of genetics has been supported by the National Institutes of Health's Ethical, Legal and Social Implications (ELSI) Program, and she has been a project PI in the CDC-funded Southern Center for Communication, Health, and Poverty at the University of Georgia. In addition to approximately a hundred scholarly essays, she has published five books, including *The Meanings of the Gene* (1999) and, with John Lucaites, *Crafting Equality: America's Anglo-African Word* (1994). She was elected to the National Communication Association's Distinguished Scholars in 2002.

David J. Coogan is an associate professor of English at Virginia Commonwealth University. His work on community literacy, rhetorical theory, and social change has appeared in the journals *College Composition and Communication*, *College English*, and Community

Literacy and in the book *Active Voices,* edited by Patty Malesh and Sharon Stetson. He is currently finishing a second book, *The Prison inside Me: Writing beyond the Bars,* the healing story of a writing workshop that began at the Richmond City Jail, followed twelve men into prison, and ended with their return to society.

Ellen Cushman is an associate professor of writing, rhetoric, and American cultures. She is currently finishing a book on the evolution of the Cherokee syllabary, based on four years of ethnohistorical research. She is a citizen of the Cherokee Nation and currently serves as a Sequoyah commissioner. In addition to *The Struggle and the Tools* (1998) and *Literacy: A Critical Sourcebook,* edited with Eugene Kintgen, Barry Kroll, and Mike Rose Bedford (2001), her research on literacy studies has included publications in *College English, College Composition and Communication, Research in the Teaching of English, Reflections,* and *Kairos* and is forthcoming in *Pedagogy* and *Ethnohistory.*

David Fleming is an associate professor of English and director of the Writing Program at the University of Massachusetts Amherst. He is the author of *City of Rhetoric: Revitalizing the Public Sphere in Metropolitan America* (2008) and *On the Hinge of History: Freshman Composition and the Long Sixties, 1958–1974* (forthcoming). He is currently at work on a book about rhetorical education: past, present, and future.

Linda Flower is a professor of rhetoric at Carnegie Mellon University and has been co-director of the National Center for the Study of Writing and Literacy at Berkeley and Carnegie Mellon and of the Carnegie Mellon Center for Community Outreach. She is the author of *Construction of Negotiated Meaning: A Social Cognitive Theory of Writing* (1994) and *Community Literacy and the Rhetoric of Public Engagement,* which won the 2009 RSA book award.

Diana George is professor of rhetoric and writing at Virginia Tech, where she currently serves as director of composition and the Writing Center. Her work has appeared in a number of collections and journals including *College English, College Composition and Communication,* and *Reflections.* She is a past Braddock Award winner and co-author with John Trimbur of the textbook *Reading Culture.*

Jeffrey T. Grabill is a professor of rhetoric and professional writing and codirector of the Writing in Digital Environments (WIDE) Research Center at Michigan State University. He is the author of *Community Literacy Programs and the Politics of Change* (2001) and *Writing Community Change: Designing Technologies for Citizen Action* (2007). His essays have appeared in *College Composition and Communication, Technical Communication Quarterly, Computers and Composition,* and *English Education.*

Erik Green is currently a Ph.D. student in the Department of Education at University of California, Santa Cruz, with a concentration on language, literacy, and culture, and a recipient of the Chancellor's Fellowship. A graduate from Michigan State University, he received a B.A. in English and an M.A. in critical studies in literacy and pedagogy. His research interests include the use of personal narrative in developing identity, queer literacies, and the sponsorship of nondominant discourses.

Gerard A. Hauser is a professor of communication and College Professor of Distinction at the University of Colorado at Boulder. He is editor of *Philosophy and Rhetoric.* His publications include *Introduction to Rhetorical Theory,* second edition (2002) and *Vernacular Voices: The Rhetoric of Publics and Public Spheres* (1999), recipient of the National Communication Association's Hochmuth-Nichols Book Award. He is past president of the Rhetoric Society of America and recipient of its George Yoos Distinguished Service

Award. He is an RSA Fellow and an NCA Distinguished Scholar. His current research focuses on vernacular rhetoric and rhetorics of resistance.

Susan C. Jarratt is professor of Comparative Literature at the University of California, Irvine and the past coordinator of the University of California, Irvine's Writing Program. Her research interests include public writing broadly construed, from ancient Greco-Roman rhetoric to contemporary writing, feminism, and critical pedagogy. She is the author of *Rereading the Sophists: Classical Rhetoric Refigured* and is currently working on a new manuscript, "Chain of Gold," about the Second Sophists.

David A. Jolliffe is professor of English and curriculum and instruction at the University of Arkansas at Fayetteville, where he holds the Brown Chair in English Literacy. He is the co-author, with William Covino, of *Rhetoric: Concepts, Definitions, Boundaries.* His most recent book, with Hephzibah Roskelly, is *Everyday Use: Rhetoric at Work in Reading and Writing.*

Erik Juergensmeyer is an assistant professor of composition and rhetoric at Fort Lewis College in Durango, Colorado. Beyond his work in action research, argumentation, and assessment, he has recently started a peace and conflict studies program and a community mediation center that seek to create increased opportunities for restorative justice. His past work appears in *Composition Studies, Rhetoric Review,* and *WPA Journal.*

Paula Mathieu is an associate professor of English and director of First-Year Writing at Boston College. Her writing, which focuses on public discourse, economics, homelessness, and university-community partnerships, includes a book, *Tactics of Hope: The Public Turn in English Composition,* and two coedited collections, *Beyond English, Inc.* with Claude Hurlbert and David Downing and *Writing Places* with Tim Lindgren, George Grattan and Staci Shultz, as well as articles in *CCCs, Rhetoric Review,* and *Works and Days.*

Carolyn R. Miller is SAS Institute Distinguished Professor of Rhetoric and Technical Communication at North Carolina State University. Her research interests are in digital rhetoric, rhetorical theory, rhetoric of science and technology, and genre studies. Her work has appeared in *Argumentation, Argumentation & Advocacy, College English, Configurations, Journal of Business and Technical Communication, Quarterly Journal of Speech, Rhetorica,* and *Rhetoric Society Quarterly,* as well as in many edited volumes. She has lectured and taught in North America, Europe, and South America, and she is a past president of the Rhetoric Society of America and current editor of *Rhetoric Society Quarterly.*

Thomas P. Miller teaches courses ranging from first-year composition to graduate seminars in the Rhetoric, Composition, and Teaching Program at the University of Arizona, where he is currently associate provost. He received the MLA's Mina Shaughnessy Award for the first volume of his history of college English, *The Formation of College English: Rhetoric and Belles Lettres in the British Cultural Provinces.* The second volume, *The Evolution of College English: Literacy Studies from the Puritans to the Postmoderns,* is forthcoming.

Candice Rai is an assistant professor at the University of Washington in Seattle. Her research interests center on the relationship between the rhetorical and the material, on public and everyday rhetorics, on urban and spatial theory, on ethnography as a method for studying rhetoric in action, and on community-based pedagogies. Her work has been published in the *Michigan Journal of Community Service, Reflections,* and the *Community Literacy Journal* and will soon appear in *Ethnography* and in *Texts of Consequence: Composing Rhetorics of Social Activism for the Writing Classroom.*

Index

CPSIA information can be obtained at www.ICGtesting.com
Printed in the USA
LVOW12s1042140713

342791LV00010B/883/P